Learning ArcGIS Pro 2
Second Edition

A beginner's guide to creating 2D and 3D maps and editing geospatial data with ArcGIS Pro

Tripp Corbin, GISP

BIRMINGHAM - MUMBAI

Learning ArcGIS Pro 2
Second Edition

Commissioning Editor: Kunal Chaudhari
Acquisition Editor: Denim Pinto
Content Development Editor: Rosal Colaco
Senior Editor: Rohit Singh
Technical Editor: Gaurav Gala
Copy Editor: Safis Editing
Project Coordinator: Deeksha Thakkar
Proofreader: Safis Editing
Indexer: Tejal Daruwale Soni
Production Designer: Aparna Bhagat

First published: December 2015

Second edition: July 2020

Production reference: 1240720

Published by Packt Publishing Ltd.
Livery Place
35 Livery Street
Birmingham
B3 2PB, UK.

ISBN 978-1-83921-022-8

www.packt.com

This book is dedicated to my mother, Fay Corbin. You taught me to have the strength to pursue my dreams both big and small. You are missed but not forgotten. This book is also dedicated to my wife, Polly Corbin, for once again putting up with all the craziness required to write a book.

– Tripp Corbin

Packt.com

Subscribe to our online digital library for full access to over 7,000 books and videos, as well as industry leading tools to help you plan your personal development and advance your career. For more information, please visit our website.

Why subscribe?

- Spend less time learning and more time coding with practical eBooks and Videos from over 4,000 industry professionals

- Improve your learning with Skill Plans built especially for you

- Get a free eBook or video every month

- Fully searchable for easy access to vital information

- Copy and paste, print, and bookmark content

Did you know that Packt offers eBook versions of every book published, with PDF and ePub files available? You can upgrade to the eBook version at www.packt.com and as a print book customer, you are entitled to a discount on the eBook copy. Get in touch with us at customercare@packtpub.com for more details.

At www.packt.com, you can also read a collection of free technical articles, sign up for a range of free newsletters, and receive exclusive discounts and offers on Packt books and eBooks.

Contributors

About the author

Tripp Corbin, GISP, has over 25 years of experience in the geospatial industry and is recognized as an industry expert in a variety of geospatial software platforms, including Esri, Autodesk, and Trimble products. He has assisted numerous organizations in implementing GIS to help solve problems and improve operations. He holds multiple certifications, including as a certified GIS professional, Esri-certified enterprise system design associate, and Esri-certified desktop professional. He is also the former president of URISA and the local Georgia Chapter. In recognition of his contributions to the GIS community, he has received several awards, including the URISA Exemplary Leadership award and the Barbara Hirsch Special Service award.

About the reviewer

Prasanth Ramachandran is currently working as an ArcGIS Enterprise Solution Engineer for a utility company. He provides solutions on ArcGIS deployments, ArcGIS upgrades, spatial geodatabases, and developing Python scripts using ArcPy and ArcGIS API for ArcGIS.

He also provides maintenance strategies on ArcGIS Portal and ArcGIS Server Manager tools. Over the years, he has worked on many products in the ArcGIS suite, including some of the major programming languages, tools, and APIs such as Python, .NET and C#, PL/SQL, Portal for ArcGIS, ArcGIS Server, Datastore, ArcGIS Online, ArcGIS Desktop (ArcMap and ArcCatalog), ArcGIS Pro, Web AppBuilder for ArcGIS, ArcPy, ArcGIS API for Python, and ArcGIS REST API.

Packt is searching for authors like you

If you're interested in becoming an author for Packt, please visit authors.packtpub.com and apply today. We have worked with thousands of developers and tech professionals, just like you, to help them share their insight with the global tech community. You can make a general application, apply for a specific hot topic that we are recruiting an author for, or submit your own idea.

Table of Contents

Section 2: Visualizing, Maintaining, and Analyzing Data

Preface

Learning ArcGIS Pro explains how to successfully use this new powerful desktop **Geographic Information System (GIS)** application to create maps, perform spatial analysis, and maintain data. Filled with hands-on exercises based on real-world use cases, this book will show you how to use ArcGIS Pro to visualize, analyze, and maintain GIS data.

Armed with powerful tools, ArcGIS Pro 2 is Esri's newest desktop GIS application that uses the modern ribbon interface and a 64-bit processor to make using GIS faster and more efficient. This second edition of *Learning ArcGIS Pro* will show you how you can use this powerful desktop GIS application to create maps, perform spatial analysis, and maintain data.

The book begins by showing you how to install ArcGIS and lists the software and hardware prerequisites. You'll then be introduced to the concept of named user licensing and learn how to navigate the new ribbon interface to leverage the power of ArcGIS Pro to manage geospatial data. Once you've got to grips with the new interface, you'll build your first GIS project and learn how to use the different project resources.

The book shows you how to create 2D and 3D maps by adding layers and setting and managing the symbology and labeling. You'll also discover how to use the analysis tool to visualize geospatial data. In later chapters, you'll be introduced to Arcade, the new lightweight expression language for ArcGIS, and then advance to creating complex labels using Arcade expressions.

You'll learn how to navigate the user interface to create maps, perform analysis, and manage data. You'll be able to display data based on discrete attribute values or ranges of values and label features on a GIS map based on one or more attributes using Arcade.

You'll also learn how to create map books using the map series functionality and be able to share ArcGIS Pro maps, projects, and data with other GIS community members. This book also explores the most widely used geoprocessing tools for performing spatial analysis and explains how to create tasks based on common workflows to standardize processes. You will also learn how to automate processes using ModelBuilder and Python scripts.

By the end of this ArcGIS Pro book, you'll have developed the core skills required to use ArcGIS Pro 2.x competently.

Who this book is for

If you want to learn how to use ArcGIS Pro to create maps and edit and analyze geospatial data, this book is for you. No knowledge of GIS fundamentals or experience with any GIS tool or ArcGIS software suite is required. Basic Windows skills, such as navigating and file management, are all you need.

What this book covers

Chapter 1, *Introducing ArcGIS Pro*, introduces ArcGIS Pro and explains some of its capabilities in relation to other ArcGIS Products. It also provides a general overview of its capabilities and discusses the installation and licensing requirements.

Chapter 2, *Navigating the Ribbon Interface*, introduces ArcGIS Pro's ribbon-based interface and commonly used interface panes or windows. It explains how to use it to access data, maps, and tools within an ArcGIS Pro project.

Chapter 3, *Creating 2D Maps*, shows you how to create 2D maps within the ArcGIS Pro project framework. You will learn how to add and manage layers, control symbology, label features, and configure other properties.

Chapter 4, *Creating 3D Scenes*, shows you how users can create 3D maps within their projects. You will learn how to add layers, extrude layers to show height, and apply 3D symbology.

Chapter 5, *Creating and Working with Projects*, introduces the concept of using projects to manage GIS content. You will learn how to create and organize a project. You will also learn how to create a template project.

Chapter 6, *Creating a Layout*, shows you how to create effective layouts using ArcGIS Pro.

Chapter 7, *Creating Map Books Using Map Series*, explains the process required to enable and configure the Map Series functionality so you can generate your own map books. Large maps are unwieldy and become difficult to use. Smaller maps just do not allow you to show the level of detail required when out in the field. A common practice is to create a map book or series for the area. ArcGIS Pro has built-in functionality for creating these map books, and this chapter will show you how.

Chapter 8, *Learning to Edit Spatial Data*, provides you with a basic understanding of the editing workflow in ArcGIS Pro and explains how to use many of the most commonly used tools to maintain and update your GIS data.

Chapter 9, *Learning about Editing Tabular Data*, explains how to edit and maintain the attribute data for the features in your GIS.

Chapter 10, *Performing Analysis with Geoprocessing Tools*, introduces many of the most commonly used tools, explains where they can be accessed, and covers what will determine the tools that are available to you within ArcGIS Pro.

Chapter 11, *Creating and Using Tasks*, shows how to create tasks for common workflows within your office to improve efficiency and standardization.

Chapter 12, *Automating Processes with ModelBuilder and Python*, introduces the basic concepts and skills needed to create simple models and Python scripts for ArcGIS Pro.

Chapter 13, *Sharing Your Work with Others*, illustrates different methods within ArcGIS Pro to share maps, data, and processes with others.

Chapter 14, *Using Arcade Expressions for Labeling and Symbology*, introduces the basic uses and syntax for Arcade. Arcade is a new lightweight expression language for ArcGIS. It allows you to create expressions that can generate text labels or control symbology.

GIS glossary, provides definitions and descriptions with examples relating to important GIS terminologies.

To get the most out of this book

You will need the following for this book:

- **ArcGIS Pro 2.6 or later version**—Basic or higher license level
- Internet connection
- Exercise data from GitHub

The following table explains the **operating system (OS)** requirements:

Software covered in the book	OS requirements
ArcGIS Pro 2.6	**Windows 8.1** or **Windows 10** (64 bit)
ArcGIS Online	N/A

This book will take you through the installation process for ArcGIS Pro as well as how to determine whether your computer is capable of running the application.

Download the example code files

You can download the example code files for this book from your account at www.packt.com. If you purchased this book elsewhere, you can visit www.packtpub.com/support and register to have the files emailed directly to you.

You can download the code files by following these steps:

1. Log in or register at www.packt.com.
2. Select the **Support** tab.
3. Click on **Code Downloads**.
4. Enter the name of the book in the **Search** box and follow the onscreen instructions.

Once the file is downloaded, please make sure that you unzip or extract the folder using the latest version of:

- WinRAR/7-Zip for Windows
- Zipeg/iZip/UnRarX for Mac
- 7-Zip/PeaZip for Linux

The code bundle for the book is also hosted on GitHub at https://github.com/PacktPublishing/Learning-ArcGIS-Pro-2-Second-Edition. In case there's an update to the code, it will be updated on the existing GitHub repository.

We also have other code bundles from our rich catalog of books and videos available at https://github.com/PacktPublishing/. Check them out!

Download the color images

We also provide a PDF file that has color images of the screenshots/diagrams used in this book. You can download it here: https://static.packt-cdn.com/downloads/9781839210228_ColorImages.pdf.

Conventions used

There are a number of text conventions used throughout this book.

`CodeInText`: Indicates code words in text, database table names, folder names, filenames, file extensions, pathnames, dummy URLs, user input, and Twitter handles. Here is an example: "The next line after the commented description is an `import` command that loads the `arcpy` model so that the script can access ArcGIS functionality."

A block of code is set as follows:

```
#Specifies the input variables for the script tools
#If the data is moved or in a different database then these paths will need
to be updated
Parcels =
"C:\\Student\\IntroArcPro\\Databases\\Trippville_GIS.gdb\\Base\\Parcels"
Parcels_Web = "C:\\Student\\IntroArcPro\\Chapter11\\Ex11.gdb\\Parcels_Web"
```

Bold: Indicates a new term, an important word, or words that you see onscreen. For example, words in menus or dialog boxes appear in the text like this. Here is an example: "Click on the **Tools** button in the **Insert** group on the **ModelBuilder** tab in the ribbon."

Warnings or important notes appear like this.

Tips and tricks appear like this.

Get in touch

Feedback from our readers is always welcome.

General feedback: If you have questions about any aspect of this book, mention the book title in the subject of your message and email us at `customercare@packtpub.com`.

Errata: Although we have taken every care to ensure the accuracy of our content, mistakes do happen. If you have found a mistake in this book, we would be grateful if you would report this to us. Please visit `www.packtpub.com/support/errata`, selecting your book, clicking on the Errata Submission Form link, and entering the details.

Piracy: If you come across any illegal copies of our works in any form on the Internet, we would be grateful if you would provide us with the location address or website name. Please contact us at `copyright@packt.com` with a link to the material.

If you are interested in becoming an author: If there is a topic that you have expertise in and you are interested in either writing or contributing to a book, please visit `authors.packtpub.com`.

Reviews

Please leave a review. Once you have read and used this book, why not leave a review on the site that you purchased it from? Potential readers can then see and use your unbiased opinion to make purchase decisions, we at Packt can understand what you think about our products, and our authors can see your feedback on their book. Thank you!

For more information about Packt, please visit `packt.com`.

1
Section 1: Introducing and Navigating ArcGIS Pro

This section will introduce you to the ArcGIS Pro application and explain some of its capabilities in relation to other ArcGIS products. It will also provide a general overview of its capabilities and we will discuss installation and licensing requirements.

You will be introduced to ArcGIS Pro's ribbon-based interface and the commonly used interface panes or windows. You will also learn how to use the ribbon to access data, maps, and tools within an ArcGIS Pro project.

In this section, we will cover the following chapters:

- Chapter 1, *Introducing ArcGIS Pro*
- Chapter 2, *Navigating the Ribbon Interface*

Introducing ArcGIS Pro 1

Esri's ArcGIS platform has become well-entrenched as the primary solution for GIS professionals seeking to implement a scalable integrated solution, which can start with a single user and grow to support multiple users across various platforms. With **ArcGIS Desktop**, **ArcGIS Enterprise**, **ArcGIS Online**, and **ArcGIS Apps**, **Geographic Information System (GIS)** professionals can design and implement a robust GIS solution that provides a wide range of functionality to meet the needs of a growing enterprise, which includes users of various skill levels, requirements, differing platforms, and data formats. However, Esri has not been content to rest on their laurels. They continue to push the GIS envelope.

In 2015, Esri released a new desktop GIS application named ArcGIS Pro. ArcGIS Pro has replaced ArcMap and ArcCatalog as the flagship desktop GIS application in Esri's solution stack. Those are not the only applications ArcGIS Pro has replaced. It has also replaced the ArcScene and ArcGlobe applications for 3D data viewing and analysis.

ArcGIS Pro is a completely new application from Esri. It is not just an update to their venerable ArcGIS Desktop platform. ArcGIS Pro has a modern ribbon interface that has become common in most current desktop applications. It is also designed from the ground up to take full advantage of modern hyperthreaded 64-bit architecture. This greatly improves its performance compared to the older applications it is replacing. In this chapter, we will begin to take a look at this new robust and smart interface.

ArcGIS Pro also introduces a new licensing model to Esri users. While it still supports the traditional Single Use and **Concurrent Use** license models of previous applications, at least for now, it defaults to the use of a subscription-based named user license model. This new license model requires you to manage your licenses through ArcGIS Online or ArcGIS Enterprise Portal. You will learn more about this later in the chapter.

ArcGIS Pro allows you to combine 2D and 3D content within a single application. In the past, you would need to utilize multiple applications, such as **ArcMap**, **ArcScene**, and **ArcGlobe**, to view 2D and 3D content. In this chapter, you will examine how you can view both 2D and 3D data within a single ArcGIS Pro project.

Here, the following topics will be covered:

- Checking requirements for installing ArcGIS Pro
- Downloading and installing ArcGIS Pro
- Managing and assigning ArcGIS Pro licenses

Once you have completed this chapter, you will be able to successfully install ArcGIS Pro on your computer, know whether your computer is capable of running the application, assign yourself and other users licenses to use ArcGIS Pro, and open an ArcGIS Pro project.

Technical requirements

To successfully complete this chapter, you will require the following:

- Internet access
- **ArcGIS Pro 2.6—Basic** or a higher license
- Sample data downloaded and installed for this book

Checking requirements for installing ArcGIS Pro

In order to use ArcGIS Pro, you must first install it. To install ArcGIS Pro, you will need to verify that your system meets or exceeds the minimum requirements. You will then need to download or have access to the installed files, and finally, have the rights to install the software on the computer you are using. We will look at each of these steps next.

It is possible to install and run ArcGIS Pro on a computer that already has ArcGIS Desktop (ArcMap and ArcCatalog) installed even if ArcGIS Desktop is an older version. The two applications may exist side by side or on separate computers. These are completely separate, independent installations.

In the following sections, you will learn the ArcGIS Pro system requirements, how to download the installation files, and how to install ArcGIS Pro on your computer.

Understanding ArcGIS Pro minimum system requirements

As mentioned earlier, ArcGIS Pro is a 64-bit application that supports hyperthreaded processing. This allows ArcGIS Pro to take full advantage of modern processors, such as the **Intel Core i7** or **AMD Ryzen** and **Random Access Memory (RAM)** larger than 4 GB. The ability of ArcGIS Pro to make use of this increased computing capability means it typically completes tasks much faster than the older applications it is replacing.

However, this ability to use modern computer hardware does come at a price. Compared with the older ArcGIS Desktop, ArcGIS Pro has much higher minimum computer specifications. This includes increased hardware and OS requirements as well as supporting application requirements. This means that just because your current computer is able to run applications such as ArcMap, it will not necessarily be able to successfully run ArcGIS Pro. It is important to verify that your computer meets or exceeds the recommended minimum specification if you want your experience using ArcGIS Pro to be positive and not frustrating.

At the following link, you will find the minimum requirements for the current version of ArcGIS Pro, **2.6**. These do change with new releases, so make sure to verify them based on the release you will be using. You can find the most current system requirements here: `https://pro.arcgis.com/en/pro-app/get-started/arcgis-pro-system-requirements.htm`

Learning about OS requirements

ArcGIS Pro requires a 64-bit **operating system (OS)**. It will not run on a 32-bit OS. ArcGIS Pro currently supports the following operating systems:

- **Windows 10 Home**, **Pro**, and **Enterprise**
- **Windows 8.1 Pro** and **Enterprise**
- **Windows Server 2019 Standard** and **Datacenter**
- **Windows Server 2016 Standard** and **Datacenter**
- **Windows Server 2012 R2 Standard** and **Datacenter**
- **Windows Server 2012 Standard** and **Datacenter**

Esri dropped support for **Windows 7** and **Server 2008 R2** after January 2020. They made this move because Microsoft ended their support for those operating systems. This means it might still be possible to run ArcGIS Pro on these operating systems, but neither Esri nor Microsoft will provide you with support if you encounter any problems. It also means that neither company will be providing patches or updates to fix security vulnerabilities or bugs in either of those operating systems. Consequently, it is recommended that you upgrade to a newer OS if you are still running on one of the unsupported ones.

ArcGIS Pro is currently not supported on **Linux** or **iOS** natively. Given Esri's current support for Linux with their ArcGIS Enterprise solution, it is possible ArcGIS Pro may be adapted to run on that platform sometime in the distant future. However, Esri has indicated that ArcGIS Pro will not be ported to run on the iOS platform. This seems to be due to their user base.

A large majority of ArcGIS users work in government, which typically runs Windows-based computers, and to get an Apple computer requires special procurement processes. As a result, ArcGIS Pro will not be supported on iOS. It is possible to run ArcGIS Pro on a Linux or iOS computer if you create a virtual Windows machine, set up a dual Windows boot, or run a Windows emulator.

I have actually heard some users claim that ArcGIS Pro actually runs better on an Apple computer that boots into Windows than on a traditional Windows-based computer. I have not tested that claim so I cannot verify, but I do know I have seen many Esri employees using Apple computers, so there might be some truth to the claim.

Understanding the hardware requirements

ArcGIS Pro has some hefty hardware requirements. It requires modern processors and large amounts of RAM. It also requires a graphics card powerful enough to display 2D and 3D data. To ensure that ArcGIS Pro runs smoothly, you need to make sure that your computer meets or exceeds the requirements shown here:

- A **hyperthreaded dual-core**. A 4 core processor is recommended with a 10 core or more processor being optional, such as the **Intel Core i9-10900** or **AMD Ryzen 9 3900**.
- A minimum of 4 GB of RAM with 8 GB of RAM is recommended. 16 GB is considered optimal by Esri.

- A minimum of 32 GB of hard disk space to install the software. A solid-state drive is recommended.
- A graphics card that supports **DirectX 11** and **OpenGL 4.3** with 4 GB of video RAM minimum. Esri recommends a graphics card that supports DirectX 11 and OpenGL 4.5 with 4 GB or more of dedicated video RAM.

Unlike ArcGIS Desktop, which has limits on the amount of RAM and processor resources it can use, ArcGIS Pro will use all the resources you can throw at it. So, the more processing power and memory your computer has, the better ArcGIS Pro will perform.

If you are not able to get a dedicated video card and are forced to use integrated video, then it is highly recommended that you increase the amount of RAM and level of your processor to compensate for the shared usage of both to run both the display and the software.

Ultimately I strongly recommend getting the dedicated graphics card. While this is not cheap, you will experience fewer issues and crashes if you have one. This, in turn, means you will be more productive, less frustrated and have less chance of your data getting corrupted. Over time, the dedicated graphics card will pay for itself as a result of the improved performance.

Other supporting software requirements

ArcGIS Pro is dependent on other applications that must be installed prior to installation. They provide supporting services that ArcGIS Pro relies on to function. These supporting applications include the following:

- **Microsoft .NET Framework 4.8** or later
- **Microsoft Internet Explorer 11** or above
- ArcGIS Online organizational account or ArcGIS Enterprise Portal – this is required if using Named User licensing

Although these are required for ArcGIS Pro to run successfully, the actual ArcGIS Pro install routine does not verify or check for these. It will install without them and indicate that the installation was successful. However, when you run the application, you will begin to experience problems. This might include the application not starting, the inability to access a license, frequent crashes, and more.

ArcGIS Pro does not require ArcGIS Desktop in order to be installed on a computer. They are two separate applications that are completely independent of one another. This means they can co-exist on the same computer or be installed individually.

Author system recommendations

I have been working with ArcGIS Pro since it was first released in beta. This has provided the opportunity to run it on various computers as it has moved through multiple beta versions to the release of version 2.6. This firsthand experience, along with my experience running ArcGIS Desktop since it was first released, has led me to several recommendations when it comes to selecting a system to run ArcGIS Pro.

Based on my experience, I recommend the following specifications when purchasing a computer to run ArcGIS Pro:

- Make sure that you have a separate graphics card. This will include a dedicated **Graphics Processing Unit (GPU)** and **Dedicated Video RAM (VRAM)**. ArcGIS Pro is a graphics-intensive program. Every time you pan, zoom, or add a new layer, you will be taxing the graphics capability of your computer. A video card will allow your computer to handle this load by processing graphics rendering requests without burdening your computer's CPU and system RAM. If your computer uses integrated video, then the computer's CPU and system RAM are used to handle all processing requests, including graphics rendering.

ArcGIS Pro is both a processor and graphics-intensive application due to the 2D and 3D maps it creates and the analysis it performs. This can put a tremendous load on your computer's resources. Having the dedicated GPU to handle the graphics rendering load on your computer will greatly improve the performance of ArcGIS Pro and your user experience.

I recommend getting a video card that has at least 6 GB of VRAM. I have had good success using video cards with **NVIDIA** GPUs. Currently, I am running a **GeForce RTX 2070 Super**. It has performed very well and is not too expensive, being around $550 at the time of writing this book. AMD video cards have been a bit lackluster until the recent release of their new **Radeon RX 5700 series**. This new card from AMD has been matching or beating NVIDIA's performance in most benchmarks, so this might be worth trying as well, especially since it is a little less expensive for the same (or better) overall performance.

- Use a solid-state drive. Solid-state drives are incredibly fast at accessing and storing data. They are almost as fast as RAM and are much faster than even the fastest hard disk drives. ArcGIS Pro will run at lightning speeds when installed on a solid-state drive. This is even truer if you can get a **Non-Volatile Memory Express (NVMe) M.2 PCIe drive**. These are small drives that look more like a memory stick than a hard drive, but have much greater performance than even traditional **Serial Advanced Technology Attachment (SATA)** solid-state drives. This is what I am using in my current workstation.
- There is no such thing as too much RAM. The more RAM your computer has, the better ArcGIS Pro will perform, especially if you don't have a solid-state drive. For anyone doing any heavy lifting with ArcGIS Pro, I would not consider running any less than 16 GB of RAM. I am currently running 32 GB of fast **DDR 4 3000 RAM** on my GIS workstation computer.

It performs well for most operations I perform on what I consider small to mid-sized datasets. If you are going to be working with **Light Detection and Ranging (LiDAR)**, **Raster**, or 3D data, I would encourage having more than 16 GB of RAM. However, if you are working primarily with vector data in mostly a 2D environment, 16 GB of RAM appears to be the optimum spot between performance and cost.

- If you are forced to use standard mechanical hard drives, then make sure they are 7,200 RPM or faster, and not 5,400 RPM drives. The seek times on the slower drives are just too slow to efficiently support effective GIS operations.
- If you are going to be doing a lot of analysis or editing and cannot get a solid-state drive, try using a **Redundant Array of Independent Disks (RAID)** system to improve performance. RAID systems utilize multiple hard drives to store data. They can be configured in multiple ways. A strip set-based RAID, such as **RAID 0**, **RAID 3**, or **RAID 5**, provides the best performance.

By storing the data across multiple drives, the computer can access the requested data from each one at the same time. This creates a multilane highway for your data to travel along. A RAID system will require at least two hard drives and often a separate controller card. Multiple solid-state drives can also be put into a RAID for increased performance if desired. However, for all but the largest datasets, I would say that would be overkill in most cases.

- Run two or more monitors. ArcGIS Pro, like ArcGIS Desktop, has multiple windows. Being able to display multiple windows at one time will increase your production. It can also allow you to have multiple applications open at one time. While I have not attempted to measure the increased production with ArcGIS Pro, I do know that it increased the production of my team using ArcGIS Desktop by 10–15%.

All these recommendations can also be applied to other applications as well, such as ArcGIS Desktop, **AutoCAD**, **MicroStation**, **Photoshop**, and other graphics-intensive applications. I have run all these applications and can say that based on those experiences, any of these recommendations will help them run better.

You might want to watch the YouTube video I have made on these recommendations: `https://youtu.be/tH7JemkC7SM`. You can also see the build for my current GIS computer, `https://youtu.be/GPXRqpqzHaQ`, so you can see the system I use to run ArcGIS Pro.

Testing to see whether your computer can run ArcGIS Pro

Before you attempt to install ArcGIS Pro, it is a good idea to test your system first to see whether it meets or exceeds the minimum requirements for installing the application. Luckily, Esri has a tool that can test your system. Let's run that tool now to check your computer:

1. You will start by opening your web browser, such as **Chrome**, **Firefox**, **Internet Explorer**, or **Safari**.
2. In your web browser, go to `http://pro.arcgis.com`. This site from Esri allows you to access various ArcGIS Pro resources. When it opens, you should see the following:

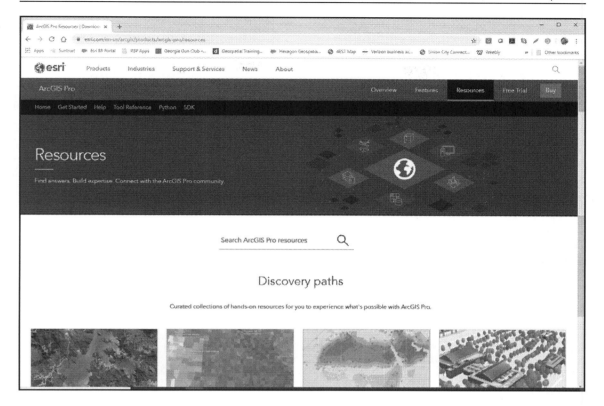

3. Next, click on the **Get Started** tab located just below the banner.

4. Click on **Set up** located in the left panel of the web page. This will expand the menu options located under **Set up**.

5. Click on **System Requirements** located under **Set up**. This will take you to the **System Requirements** page.

In the main body of the web page, you should see a link entitled **Check your computer's ability to run ArcGIS Pro 2.6**. This directs you to an application that will check your computer to verify whether it meets or exceeds the requirements needed to successfully run ArcGIS Pro.

6. Click on the **Check your computer's ability to run ArcGIS Pro 2.6** link. This will take you to the web page illustrated in the following screenshot, which allows you to download and install the utility needed to verify your system specifications:

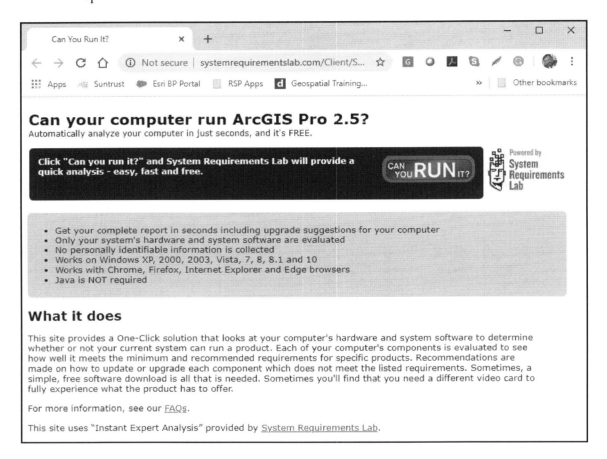

The version number will change as new versions of ArcGIS Pro are released by Esri. So do not be surprised if the version number is different when you go to run this tool. ArcGIS Pro 2.6 is the most current version at the time of writing this book.

 Please note that the preceding screenshot shows 2.5. As ArcGIS Pro 2.6 was just released, Esri had not updated this testing application at the time of writing this chapter.

7. Click on the **CAN YOU RUN IT?** button located on the far right in the black banner area. This will download a file called `Detection.exe`. That file is the utility you will need to run to check your computer's specifications.

8. Once the `Detection.exe` file downloads, click it to run the utility. You should be able to do this by clicking on the file shown at the bottom of your browser window. If you do not see it, open **Windows File Explorer**, which is typically shown as a file folder icon on your system tray. Then, click on **Downloads** in the left panel below **Quick Access**. You should see the `Detection.exe` file located there.

 You will need to make sure you have administrative privileges on your computer to run this utility. If you do not, you will need to coordinate with your IT staff to run it.

When you run the detection utility, your browser window should indicate that it is detecting your computer hardware as shown:

Once the utility has reviewed your computer specifications and compared them to the minimum and recommended specification from Esri for ArcGIS Pro, it will generate a report showing the results as illustrated in the following sample:

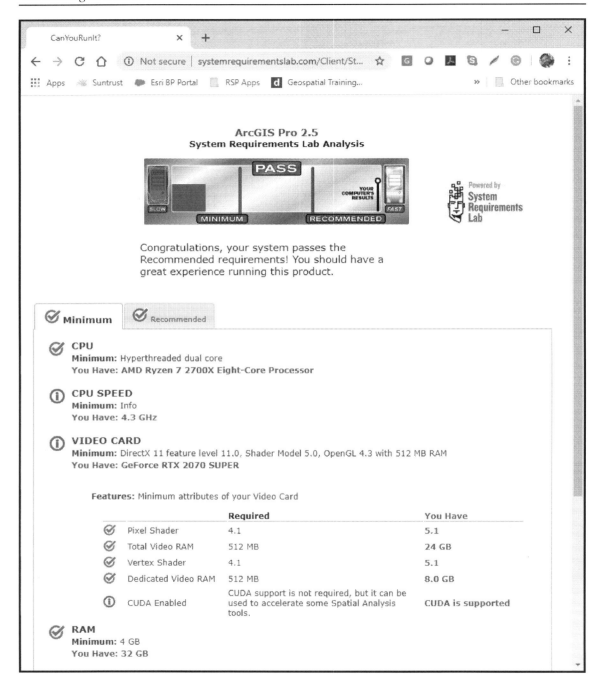

This will tell you whether your computer has the required horsepower to run ArcGIS Pro. If your system fails to meet any of the minimum requirements, you will be able to see where your system falls short.

You now have the knowledge in terms of minimum system and hardware requirements for ArcGIS Pro. We will now move on to the next section regarding the downloading and installation of ArcGIS Pro.

Downloading and installing ArcGIS Pro

Now that you know your computer can run ArcGIS Pro, it is time to install it. First, you will need to download the install files from Esri. Then, you will need to run the install on your computer so that you can run the application.

In order to complete both these steps, you will need to ensure that a couple of conditions are met. First, you must have the rights to download software from the **My Esri** web portal. Second, you must have install or administrative privileges on your computer. These aspects will be covered in the following sections.

How to download the installation files

In order to install ArcGIS Pro, follow these steps:

1. You will need to download the install files from the My Esri website at `https://my.esri.com/`.
2. Once there, you will need to log in using your Esri global account. You will need to make sure that your global account is linked to your organization's Esri customer account in order to do this. Lastly, you need to ensure that your user account has download permissions, as mentioned previously.

3. Once you are logged in to **My Esri**, you will need to click on the **My Organizations** tab and select the **Downloads** option, as shown in the following screenshot:

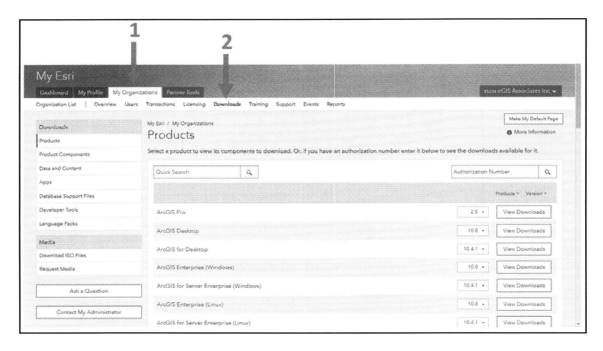

4. If you are not the administrator for your organization's Esri account or do not have download permissions, you might not see the **Downloads** tab. If this is the case, you will need to request permission from Esri to view the **Downloads** tab. To do this, you need to go to **My Organizations** and then the **Overview** tab.

   Then, you need to click on **Request Permissions**. From there, you will need to click on the **Continue** button in the **Request Permissions to your Organization** box. Lastly, fill out the online form, as shown in the following screenshot, and click **Send Request**:

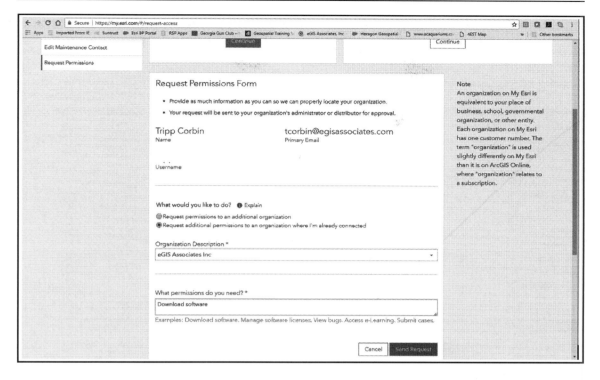

It can take up to 24 hours or more for Esri to update your permissions, so you will not have access immediately.

If you do not have download permissions and cannot wait, you can request a free trial license of ArcGIS through the Esri website. You can do this by going to `https://www.esri.com/en-us/arcgis/products/arcgis-pro/trial` and completing the sign-up form. You will then receive an email with a link to download the software. These are the same install files you would have downloaded from the **My Esri** web portal.

5. Once you are able to access the **Downloads** page, you will need to locate ArcGIS Pro and click on **View Downloads**. This will take you to the page that allows you to download several files, which you will use to install ArcGIS Pro and supporting applications. You can also check **System Requirements**, see additional **Products**, and select **Language Packs**:

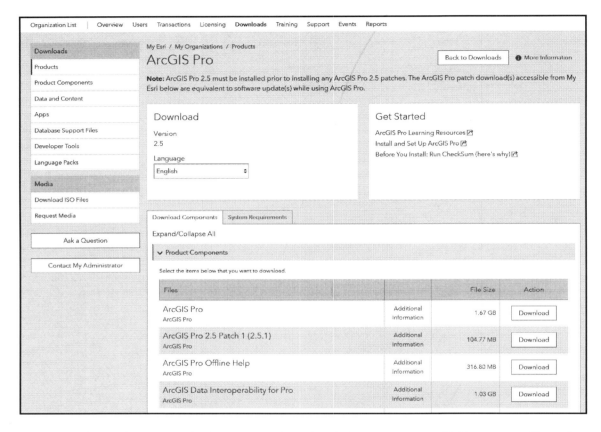

If you do not see the buttons to download the various install files, you will need to expand the **Product Components**. The ArcGIS Pro download is the primary install file for the main ArcGIS Pro application. You must download this file if you wish to install ArcGIS Pro. The other files are optional, but recommended.

The **ArcGIS Pro Offline Help** option will install help files on your local machine, so you can access them without having an internet connection. By default, ArcGIS Pro accesses help information located on the ArcGIS Pro website, `http://pro.arcgis.com`. This means that you will always see the most current help documentation for the version you are using.

You will need to download and install this file if you will be using ArcGIS Pro in a disconnected environment and think you might need to access **Help** documentation. Now that you have downloaded the install files, you are ready to begin installing ArcGIS Pro.

Installing ArcGIS Pro

First, you will need to make sure that you have sufficient rights to install new software on your computer. This typically requires you to have administrative privileges on your computer. If you do not have the required permissions, you will need to contact your IT department to see whether they can provide assistance in installing ArcGIS Pro. Then, you or the IT staff will need to perform the following steps:

1. To install ArcGIS Pro, click on the ArcGIS Pro installation file you downloaded. This will unzip the install files.
2. You will be asked where you want to unzip or extract the installation files. The default location is `C:\Users\your username\Documents\ArcGIS Pro 2.6`, as shown in the following screenshot. You can accept the default location by clicking **Next >**:

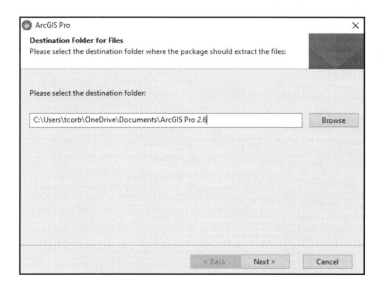

If you wish to unzip to another location, such as a network drive, click the **Browse** button and navigate to the desired location. Also, newer versions will unzip to a default folder that is based on the version you have downloaded.

3. Once unzipped, you will be asked to close the extraction process. There is a checkbox located at the bottom of the window. If it is checked, it will automatically launch the installation process as shown:

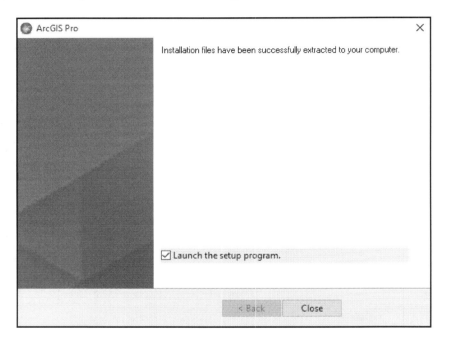

4. Once the install begins, you will first see the welcome screen. This recommends that you close all other applications to ensure they do not conflict with the installation. Because ArcGIS Pro does rely on other applications such as Internet Explorer, it is strongly encouraged that you follow the advice shown here and close any other applications you might have open or running. Once you have closed all other applications, click the **Next** button.

5. Next, you will be asked to review and accept the license agreement from Esri. If you wish to install the software, you must accept the license agreement. So, click the circle next to **I accept the master agreement** and click **Next** to accept. This will continue the installation process.

6. Now, you will have to choose who will have access to the application, all users or just the current user. If you want to install such that all users can use ArcGIS Pro, you will need to select **Anyone who uses this computer (all users)**. If you only want yourself to be able to run ArcGIS Pro, then select **Only for me** (your username). Select the appropriate option and then click **Next**.

7. Then, you will choose the install location. By default, ArcGIS Pro will be installed in C:\Program Files\ArcGIS\Pro\. To accept the default install location, just click the **Next** button. If you want to change the install location, click on the **Change** button and browse to your desired install location on your local computer.

It is generally recommended that you use the default location to avoid issues that could cause problems when running ArcGIS Pro after installation. This will also make it easier if you need support for software issues because the support person will be able to quickly find the installed files.

8. Finally, you will be asked whether you wish to take part in the **Esri User Experience Improvement** (**EUEI**) program. This will send Esri information about system crashes and other user information automatically if you choose to participate. Either leave the box checked to participate or click on the box to not participate and click **Install** to start copying the application files to your computer.

9. Once you have run the ArcGIS Pro installation and it is complete, you will see the install window saying it was successful. At the bottom of the window, you will see an option to start ArcGIS Pro once the installation is finished. This option is enabled by default. If your user account has been assigned an ArcGIS Pro license and you wish to start the application, click **Finish**. If you do not wish to run ArcGIS Pro at this time, click on the checkbox to disable the option and click **Finish**.

You have now successfully installed ArcGIS Pro. If you have a license assigned to you, you can now open and use the application. We will show you how to assign licenses later in this chapter.

Installing ArcGIS Pro offline help files

By default, ArcGIS Pro uses online help documentation. This ensures that users have access to the most current help and how-to information for the multitude of functions and tools found in ArcGIS Pro. However, there may be times when you find yourself working in a situation where you do not have access to the web.

You might be working in the field where no cellular connection is available or maybe working during an emergency where communications are down. In these types of situations, you will not be able to access the online help. You will need to have the help files installed locally on your computer. To do this, perform the following steps:

1. Open your web browser and go to `https://my.esri.com`.
2. Log in to the **My Esri** web portal using your Esri Global Account.
3. Follow the same steps you took to download the ArcGIS Pro application install files. The only difference is that you select the ArcGIS Pro Offline Help file as illustrated in the following screenshot:

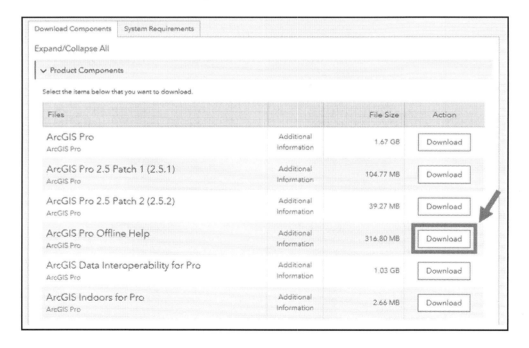

4. As you did with the application install file that was downloaded, click on the `ArcGIS ProHelp_26_build number.exe` file to extract the files.

5. Select the destination folder. The default is `C:\Users\your username\Documents\ArcGIS Pro 2.6`. If you wish to change the location from the default, click on the **Browse** button. If you wish to use the default or after you have selected the destination folder, click **Next**.

6. Once the install files for the local help have been extracted, click the **Close** button. By default, the setup program will launch.

7. Like the application install, you will first see the welcome screen. Click **Next** to proceed with the install of the local help files.

8. You should then see the **Ready to Install the Program** window. You may click **Back** if you wish to change any previous settings or **Cancel** to stop the install. If you want to continue with the installation of the local help files, click **Install**.

9. Once the setup program has finished copying the files to your computer, you will see that the installation has been successfully completed. Click **Finish** to complete the installation.

You have now successfully installed the local help files to your computer or device. However, there is still one more step you will need to complete before ArcGIS Pro actually makes use of the local help files. You will need to configure the ArcGIS Pro option. We will cover how to do that in the next chapter.

Managing and assigning ArcGIS Pro licenses

Unlike ArcGIS Desktop, ArcGIS Pro is not just limited to traditional Single Use licenses or Concurrent Use licenses. ArcGIS Pro supports those in addition to Named User licensing. This allows you to pick the licensing method that best meets the needs of your organization. *So what are the differences between these types of licensing methods?*

In this section, you will learn about ArcGIS Pro licenses, and how to download and assign them. We will also begin with opening our first ArcGIS Pro project.

Single Use licenses are the traditional software licenses, where you are allowed to install and run the application on a single computer. This was the most common form of license or use authorization for software until recently.

Concurrent Use licensing is often referred to as a network license. This type of license requires a license server to be set up and configured. It acts as a librarian for your software licenses. When a user starts the application, it first checks with the license server or manager to see whether one is available. If there is an available license, one is checked out to the user, and the application starts. If all licenses are in use, the user gets an error indicating all licenses are in use and the application will not start.

Question: *What types of licensing methods may be used with ArcGIS Pro?*

Concurrent licenses allow you to install the software on as many computers as you wish, but only the number of users equal to the number of licenses your organization has are able to be running the application at any given time. Esri is slowly eliminating this licensing method in favor of Single Use and Named User methods. If you or your organization is using Concurrent Use licensing, it is recommended you start looking into migrating to one of the other two as you implement ArcGIS Pro.

ArcGIS Pro uses the **Named User licensing method** by default. This is similar to the licensing used by **Adobe Creative Cloud** and **Microsoft Office 365**. You manage these licenses through ArcGIS Online or Portal for ArcGIS. This method assigns an ArcGIS Pro license to individual user logins that are part of your ArcGIS Online organizational account or Portal for ArcGIS. Because this is the default licensing method for ArcGIS Pro, we will show you how to assign licenses to your users in ArcGIS Online. The same basic method will also work if you are using Portal for ArcGIS.

Understanding the number and level of ArcGIS Pro licenses

If your organization has been using ArcGIS Desktop and has been paying the annual software maintenance fees, you will get an equal number of levels of ArcGIS Pro licenses. So, if you have 2 licenses for ArcGIS Desktop **Advanced**, 4 licenses for ArcGIS Desktop **Standard**, and 10 Licenses for ArcGIS Desktop **Basic**, you will have the same number and level of ArcGIS Pro licenses, which you can assign to users.

Question: *What is the default licensing method used by ArcGIS Pro?*

For completely new users, the number of licenses and levels will be dependent on what you purchase from Esri or one of their authorized business partners. Esri does offer discounts for multiple licenses as well as for non-profit and educational institutions.

ArcGIS Pro has three license levels, namely, Basic, Standard, and Advanced. The license level you have or purchase will determine the functionality of the software. Basic will have the least functionality, while advanced will have the most. The following are a few of the functionality differences between the three license levels:

Parameters	Basic	Standard	Advanced
Visualize spatial and tabular data	Yes	Yes	Yes
Edit shapefiles	Yes	Yes	Yes
Edit personal or file geodatabase	Yes	Yes	Yes
Edit workgroup or enterprise geodatabase	No	Yes	Yes
Perform spatial and attribute queries	Yes	Yes	Yes
Create and use geodatabase topology	No	Yes	Yes
Create and use geometric networks	No	Yes	Yes
Create, manage, and update relationship classes	No	Yes	Yes
Perform overlay analysis	Limited to union and intersect	Limited to union and intersect	Yes
Perform proximity analysis	Limited to buffer and multi-ring buffer	Limited to buffer and multi-ring buffer	Yes

To see the complete functionality comparison, go to Esri's product web page at `http://pro.arcgis.com/en/pro-app/get-started/license-levels.htm`.

 Question: *What are the three licensing levels for ArcGIS Pro?*

ArcGIS Pro also has extensions that provide increased functionality to the core application. The extensions are separate purchases and licenses, but do require a matching ArcGIS Pro license to run on. If you are migrating from the older ArcGIS Desktop platform, then the licenses for these extensions are also matched with the extensions for ArcGIS Desktop. So, if you have 1 license of Spatial Analyst extension, you will also have one Spatial Analyst for ArcGIS Pro extension license, assuming the annual maintenance for the extension is current.

Assigning ArcGIS Pro licenses

As we mentioned earlier, ArcGIS Pro supports multiple licensing models. The default model is Named User licenses, which are managed through ArcGIS Online or Portal for ArcGIS. To assign or manage licenses for ArcGIS Pro, you must be designated as an administrator. If you are, you can assign ArcGIS Pro and extension licenses to named users.

To manage or assign licenses, you must perform the following steps:

1. Log in to ArcGIS Online (www.argis.com) or Portal for ArcGIS.
2. Once logged in, you will need to click on **Licenses**, as shown in the following screenshot. This will require you to be an administrator for your organization:

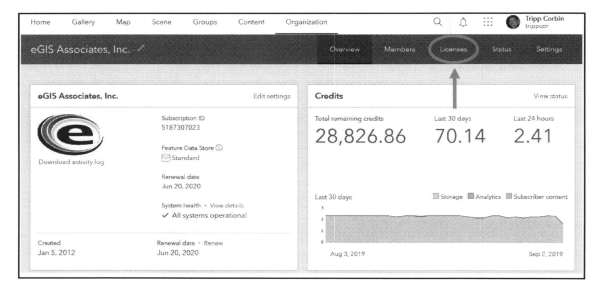

3. From the **Licenses** page, you can then assign ArcGIS Pro and extension licenses to named users within your organization's ArcGIS Online account or Portal for ArcGIS by clicking on the **Manage** link located under the license level you wish to assign to the user:

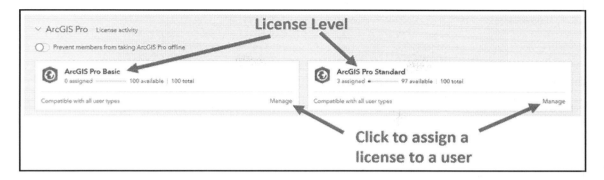

You will only see the license levels available to your organization. As shown in the preceding screenshot, my organization only has access to Basic and Advanced licenses. Your organization may only have a single level, or it might have two or even all three.

4. Once you are on the **Manage** page, simply click the toggle switch located to the right of the user you wish to assign the license to, illustrated as follows:

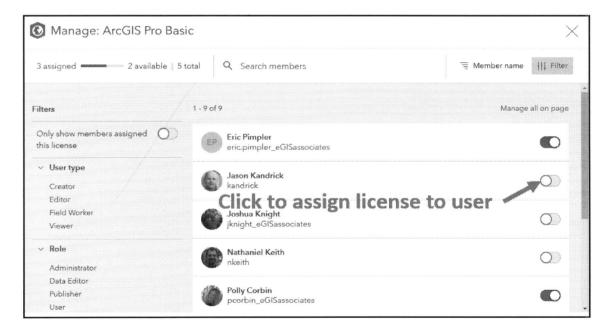

As you can see in the previous screenshot, **Eric Pimpler** and **Polly Corbin** have both been assigned ArcGIS Pro Basic licenses, while **Jason Kandrick**, **Joshua Knight**, and **Nathaniel Keith** have not. As an administrator, you can change the ArcGIS Pro licenses and extensions assigned to users as needed. You can assign licenses as new users are added or revoke licenses as older users are deactivated or removed.

 To assign a license to a user, they must be a Creator or Professional user type. ArcGIS Online and Portal for ArcGIS have at least five different user types, including viewer, editor, field worker, creator, and professional. If you want to know more about these user types and how to assign licenses, you might be interested in this video: https://youtu.be/Lny22sjzg9o

If ArcGIS Desktop is installed on the user's computer, the ArcGIS Pro license level does not have to match the ArcGIS for Desktop license level the user may be running. These are independent of one another.

Downloading and installing the exercise data

Before you can proceed further in the book and complete the exercises, you will need to download and install the exercise data. To do this, follow these steps:

1. Download the exercise data from Packt Publishing by going to https://www.packtpub.com/ and click on **Support** from the ribbon menu at the top of the page.
2. Then, click on **Code Downloads** and, in the search title box, type Learning ArcGIS Pro 2 - Second Edition. Click on the book title, which should appear under the search box.
3. If needed, click on the register link to create your user account. Then, follow the links to download exercise data.
4. Once the exercise data has downloaded, open Windows File Explorer, which is typically accessible by clicking on an icon located on your taskbar that looks like a small file folder in a holder.
5. Navigate to the location you downloaded the exercise data to. If you downloaded the data to the standard Windows default location, you should be able to click on the **Downloads** option under **Favorites** in the tree located in the left-hand side of the File Explorer interface.
6. Double-click on the LearningArcGISPro.zip file.

7. Right-click on the `IntroArcGISPro` folder located inside the zip folder you downloaded. Then, select **Copy**.

8. In File Explorer, navigate to your `C:\` drive (often named, Local Disk or OS). The `C:\` drive may be found under **This PC** in the tree on the left-hand side of the File Explorer interface, as shown in the following screenshot:

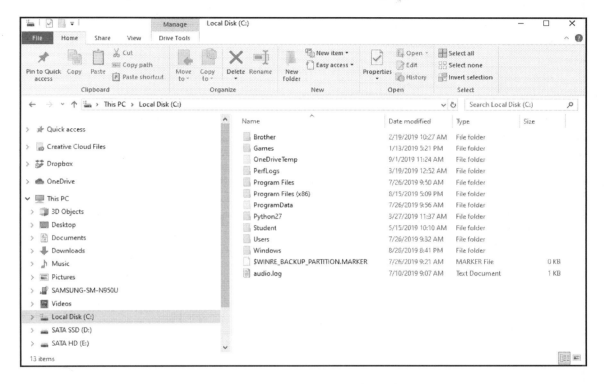

9. Right-click on the `C:\` drive and select **New** | **Folder**.

10. Name the new folder `Student`.

11. Right-click on the `Student` folder you just created and select **Paste**. This will copy the `IntroArcGISPro` folder to the `Student` folder you just created.

12. Close File Explorer once the copy is complete.

You have now copied the exercise data that will be required to complete the book to your local computer.

Launching ArcGIS Pro

Now that you have installed ArcGIS Pro and have a license, it is time to launch ArcGIS Pro for the first time. You need to ensure that you are connected to the internet because when you launch ArcGIS Pro, it will need to connect to ArcGIS Online or Portal for ArcGIS to make sure that you have a valid license.

Let's now open ArcGIS Pro:

1. Open ArcGIS Pro. How you do this will depend on your OS and whether you have added shortcuts to your desktop or taskbar. In most cases, the first time you launch ArcGIS Pro, you will need to go to the **Start** button located on the lower-left corner of your monitor. It looks like the Windows icon.
2. Once you click on the **Start** button, scroll through the list of installed programs until you see the ArcGIS folder or group and click on it. This will expand the list of installed ArcGIS programs installed on your computer.
3. Select **ArcGIS Pro** from the list of programs to start the application.

 If you want to add a shortcut for ArcGIS Pro to your taskbar, simply right-click on the application name in the **Start** menu. Then, select **More** and **Pin to Taskbar**. Once you have done that, all you need to do is click on the ArcGIS Pro icon in your taskbar to start the application.

4. Once you start ArcGIS Pro, you will need to sign in to your ArcGIS Online or Portal account. This allows ArcGIS Pro to verify your license. You do have the option to allow ArcGIS Pro to remember your login credentials for ArcGIS Online, so you will not have to log in every time you launch ArcGIS Pro:

After ArcGIS Pro verifies your login and license, it will take you to the window that allows you to start a new project or open an existing project. You will now open an existing project, but before you do that, you will need to make sure you have downloaded and installed the exercise data.

Opening an ArcGIS Pro Project

ArcGIS Pro makes use of projects that can contain maps, data connections, toolboxes, and more. You will now open an existing project and begin your first journey into ArcGIS Pro to help verify the successful installation of ArcGIS Pro and your exercise data. You will get an opportunity to explore 2D and 3D maps, a layout, and other project items as follows:

1. If you closed ArcGIS Pro from the previous section, open ArcGIS Pro and log in if required.

2. In the ArcGIS Pro start page, click on **Open another project**, as shown in the following screenshot:

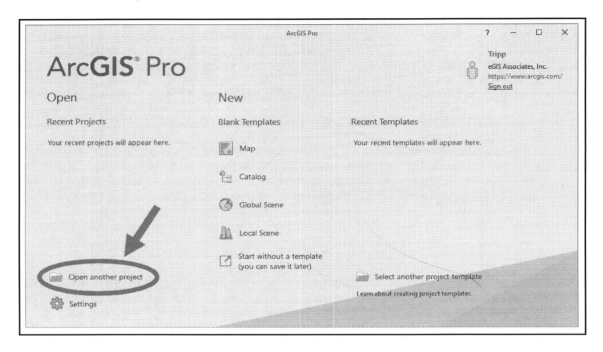

Take a moment to review the **Start** page. It is divided into three columns. The first is for opening existing projects like the one you are about to open. At the top of the first column is a list of recently opened projects. If this is your first time opening a project with ArcGIS Pro, this area will be blank, as shown in the previous screenshot.

If this is not the first time, you will see a list of one or more projects that you have opened. As you move through the book, you will see projects added to this section. The second column area is to create new projects. It contains a list of project templates included with ArcGIS Pro. You will learn how to create your own projects later in this book. The last column area is a list of project templates you have used recently to generate new projects as well as the option at the bottom to select a different template.

3. The last step should have opened the **Open Project** window. Click on **Computer** in the left panel of the window. This should be below **Portal**.

4. In the right panel of the window, double-click on (c:) to access your local drive.

These steps assume that you installed the exercise data in the default location called for in the section on downloading and installing the exercise data. If you installed it in a different location, navigate to that location instead.

5. Continue navigating to
   `C:\Student\IntroArcPro\Chapter1\IntroArcPro_Chapter1` or the location where you installed the exercise data and select `IntroArcPro_Chapter1.aprx`. Then, click **OK** (or double-click the file) to open the project:

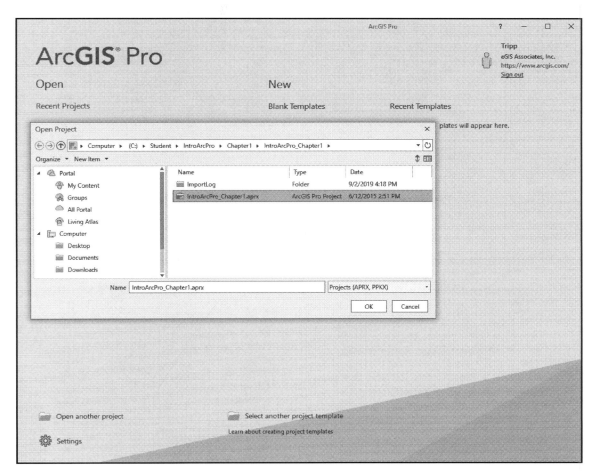

If the project opens successfully, you will see two map views located side by side showing a granite quarry, as shown in the following screenshot. One is a traditional 2D map, and the other is a 3D map. These two views have been linked together, so when you zoom or pan in one, the other updates to match:

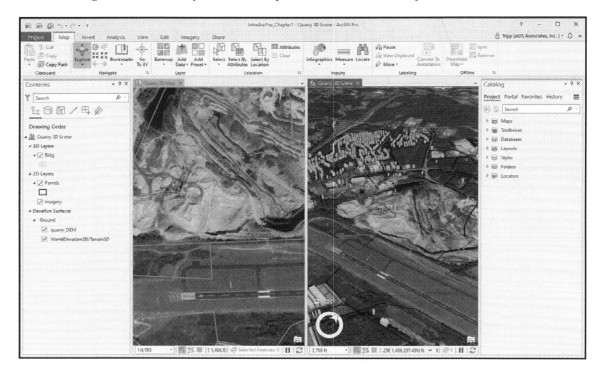

You will now explore this project and the two maps you see so you can better understand the relationship between the tool and examine some basic tools found in ArcGIS Pro. You will start by using the **Explore** tool. This is a very versatile tool that allows you to move within a map and retrieve information about the features you see.

6. At the top of the ArcGIS Pro interface, make sure the **Map** tab is active. If it is not, click on it.

7. Click on the **Explore** tool on the **Map** tab. This tool uses a blue and white spherical icon surrounded by small arrowheads, as shown in the following screenshot:

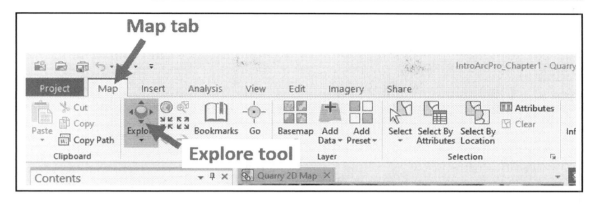

8. Move your mouse pointer to one of the two map views and click your left mouse button and drag it to pan within the view. As you pan in one view, watch what happens in the other view.

> Question: *What happens when you use the Explore tool within the two views in the project to pan or zoom?*

9. Using the **Explore** tool once again, click on a parcel in either view.

> Question: *What happens when you click on a feature in a map such as a parcel when using the Explore tool?*

10. Feel free to continue exploring the use of the **Explore** tool. Once you are done, close ArcGIS Pro without saving the project.

You have learned about ArcGIS Pro licenses and their levels, and you have also opened your first ArcGIS Pro project and begun navigating in a map. Congratulations on your first step toward leveraging the power of ArcGIS Pro to visualize and query information!

Summary

You have now successfully installed and started to use ArcGIS Pro. So you now have the skills to install and get working with ArcGIS Pro. This new 64-bit hyperthreaded application from Esri provides an effective tool to visualize a range of data, including 2D and 3D. This increased capability does require a greater amount of system resources to run effectively compared with the earlier ArcGIS applications.

In this chapter, you discovered that ArcGIS Pro makes use of a new licensing model, Named Users, in addition to a traditional Single Use or concurrent license. You also learned that ArcGIS Pro Named User licenses are managed through your organization's ArcGIS Online account or Portal for ArcGIS. It was also pointed out that only users in your organization that are creators or professional user types may be assigned an ArcGIS Pro license.

From there, you opened your first ArcGIS Pro project. This provided you with the skills to deal with projects that may contain multiple items, including 2D and 3D maps, but that is just the beginning, as you will learn in later chapters. Once you opened the project, you used the Explore tool to navigate within a map and retrieve information about the features you see.

In the next chapter, you will take a closer look at the ArcGIS Pro user interface. You will examine commonly used tools and where to find them.

Further reading

You may want to check out these additional resources for more information associated with the topics covered in this chapter.

- *ArcGIS Pro 2.x Cookbook,* by Tripp Corbin, GISP: https://www.packtpub.com/application-development/arcgis-pro-2x-cookbook
- *Comparing ArcGIS Desktop and ArcGIS Pro (Video)*: https://youtu.be/4_OOOQbLZDU
- *ArcGIS Pro 2.x: Does your computer have enough horsepower (Video)*: https://youtu.be/tH7JemkC7SM
- *Assigning ArcGIS Pro licenses via ArcGIS Online (Video)*: https://youtu.be/Lny22sjzg9o

Navigating the Ribbon Interface 2

Now that you have successfully installed ArcGIS Pro, it is time to begin examining the user interface and how it works. ArcGIS Pro is the first Esri desktop product to make use of a ribbon interface, and this has become commonplace in many current desktop applications, including **Microsoft Office**, **Adobe Creative Suite**, and **Autodesk**'s **AutoCAD**. The new ribbon makes accessing tools and functionality quicker and easier than the drop-down menu and toolbar interface used by the older ArcMap and ArcCatalog applications that ArcGIS Pro is replacing.

In this chapter, you will learn how to navigate this new ribbon interface used by ArcGIS Pro. We will also cover the following topics:

- Understanding the new interface terminology
- Using the interface
- Learning terminology associated with ArcGIS Pro ribbon menus
- Learning how to move between maps, scenes, and layouts
- Learning how to customize the ArcGIS Pro interface

Once you have completed this chapter, you will be much more comfortable working within ArcGIS Pro, as well as being more confident about where many of the tools you will use on a regular basis are located.

Technical requirements

To complete the exercises in this chapter, you will need the following:

- ArcGIS Pro **Basic** or higher license
- ArcGIS Pro 2.6 or higher installed on your computer
- An internet connection

Understanding the new interface terminology

Anyone who has worked in GIS will know that it has its own language. You will hear fellow GIS users using terms such as **topology**, **shapefiles**, **networks**, **geodatabase**, **feature class**, and more. As your experience with **Geographic Information Systems** (**GIS**) grows, this new language will become second nature. You will find yourself using those words in conversations without realizing you are doing it. While you may completely understand what you are saying, non-GIS users may not. Consequently, the new ArcGIS Pro ribbon interface will require you to expand your GIS dictionary.

In this section, you will begin to learn many of the new words and terms associated with the ribbon. This will allow you to navigate more easily within the interface and follow the instructions in the exercises. Understanding this will also help you better communicate with other users and Esri tech support should the need ever arise.

ArcGIS Pro interface terminology

The new interface used by ArcGIS Pro has a whole new set of words and phrases associated with it. To successfully use, navigate, and understand this interface, you need to make sure you know what some of these are and what they mean. Let's take a look at this in the following table:

ArcGIS Pro term	Definition
Ribbon	The rectangular menu area across the top of ArcGIS Pro. The ribbon is divided into tabs with group-related tools and functions. Some tabs are consistent while others are contextual, meaning they will change depending on tasks being performed.
Tab	A collection of related tools and functions accessed via the ribbon. Similar to Toolbars in ArcMap, tabs can be core or contextual. Core tabs are those that stay constant on the ribbon, such as **Project** and **Share**. Contextual tabs will change and appear depending on the tasks users are currently performing. Examples of Contextual tabs include **Map**, **Layout**, **Appearance**, and **Labeling**.
Pane	A dockable window that allows users to access information or tools. Similar to the dockable windows in **ArcMap**, such as **Catalog**, **Search**, **ArcToolbox**, and **Table** windows. Like those windows, panes can be opened and closed, pinned in place, or set to auto-hide.

Group (on a Tab in the ribbon)	A subset of related tools located within a tab. An example of a Group on a tab is **Layer**, which is located on the **Map** tab and contains multiple tools for adding layers to a map.
Quick Access Toolbar	A collection of shortcuts to commonly used tools and commands. The Quick Access Toolbar is typically located in the top left-hand corner of the ArcGIS Pro interface, although the position can be changed. This is similar to the Task Bar in Windows.
View	A window that allows you to view data and performs tasks. A view might be a 2D Map or a 3D Scene or a Layout, or some other visualization of your data. This is similar to the **Data** and **Layout** views in ArcMap. However, in ArcGIS Pro, you can have multiple views and see them displayed at the same time.

These are some of the key terms you will need to understand as you begin to use ArcGIS Pro and navigate through its interface. As you start to use the interface, and if you used the older ArcMap application, I believe you will find it much more intuitive than the one used by ArcMap, which hides much of its functionality through a myriad of toolbars and menus.

Introducing the user interface

Now that you understand the key terminology associated with the new interface, it is time to see where these items actually are within ArcGIS Pro. You may ask yourself how the new ribbon-style interface makes accessing tools and functionality quicker. The answer to this question is two-fold:

- First, the new interface is smart. It will present you with the tools and information relevant to your current operation. For example, when working in a layout, tools associated with creating and printing a layout are presented. If you switch your focus by selecting a layer in a map, then a new series of options will be presented automatically that allows you to control and configure various layer properties, such as symbology and labeling.
- Second, the new ribbon interface is similar to that found in many commonly used applications, such as those mentioned in the first paragraph. This greatly reduces the learning curve and make users feel much more comfortable when working with ArcGIS Pro.

This automatic behavior in the ribbon is referred to as **Contextual Menus** or **Tabs**. The smart ribbon presents you with the tools when you need them. As you move on to other items or tasks, the ribbon automatically updates accordingly.

This not only puts the tools you need at your fingertips, but it also removes the need to have a large number of toolbars and windows open at the same time, thereby reducing screen clutter and opening up screen real-estate for other uses.

Let's take a quick look at the interface and see where some of these components and functions are located:

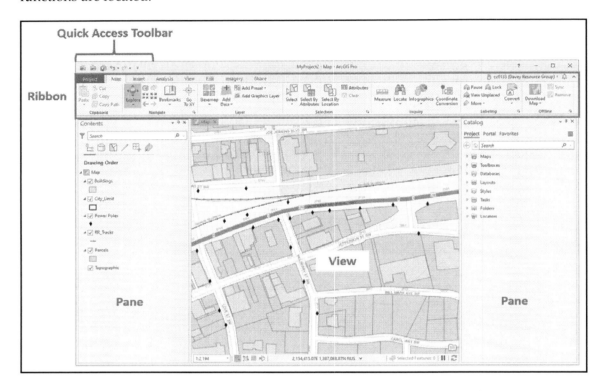

The preceding screenshot shows the location of several key components of the ArcGIS Pro interface. Starting at the top left-hand side, you will find the **Quick Access Toolbar**. This contains buttons that allow you to open an existing project, create a new project, save your project, undo, and redo. Located below that is the ribbon. This is where you access much of the ArcGIS Pro functionality through the various tabs. Below that you will find different panes and views. These will change depending on what your project contains and what you have open. The first time you open ArcGIS Pro, you will see the **Contents** pane on the left-hand side, the main view in the middle and the **Catalog** pane on the right-hand side.

As you progress through the book, you will see that you can dock and undock the various views and panes to best support your workflows and system. This provides great flexibility and increased efficiency when working in ArcGIS Pro.

Using the interface

It is time to start working with the ArcGIS Pro interface now that you know where several of the key components are located and the terms associated with the interface. You will start by using some of the tools in the core tabs on the ribbon. Then, you will work with different views and the contextual tabs associated with them. Lastly, you will investigate some of the panes.

Navigating the ribbon

Ribbon style interfaces are not new. They have become common for the majority of applications, including **Microsoft Word, Excel**, and **PowerPoint**, along with **AutoCAD** and **Photoshop**, as we have mentioned before. As a result, users have grown comfortable with the look of these ribbon interfaces and how they perform. However, Esri has been slow to adopt this type of interface in its desktop GIS applications until ArcGIS Pro.

ArcGIS Pro is Esri's first desktop application designed to fully embrace the ribbon interface. This new interface is much more user-friendly than the older toolbar-style interface found in their older ArcMap and ArcCatalog applications. As you will see, it is smart. It will make tools available based on what you have selected, and it will keep them active within the application. This means that you do not need to search to find the functionality you are looking for.

Now you will begin to investigate this interface more fully. We will start specifically with the ribbon, which is the rectangular area located at the top of ArcGIS Pro. It includes tabs, groups, and tools, as shown in the following screenshot:

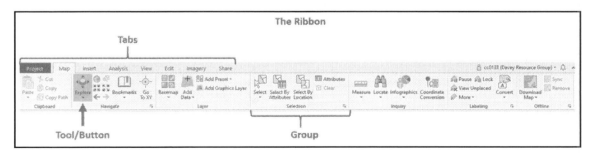

When you first open a new project, you will typically see the **Project**, **Map**, **Insert**, **Analysis**, **View**, **Edit**, and **Share** tabs on the ribbon. Each tab contains tools associated with the name of the tab. For example, the **Map** tab includes tools for navigating within the map, adding layers, selecting features, and accessing information about the features in the map.

Let's now begin taking a closer look at a couple of the most frequently used tabs and some of the key tools located within that tab. You will look at others as you move through this book. You will start with the Project tab.

Project tab

The **Project** tab provides tools needed to manage the project and configure options. This tab allows you to create new projects, open existing projects, save your current project, and make a copy of your current project. You can also connect to different ArcGIS Online accounts or portals from this tab. You can see many of these settings, as shown in the following screenshot:

Let us look at the function of these tabs in more detail:

- **New**: This will create a new project using a selected template. The template controls what is automatically included in the newly created project. ArcGIS Pro includes several project templates out of the box. These are **Catalog, Map, Global Scene**, and **Local Scene**.

- **Save**: This saves the current project you have open. This will include any changes you have made to maps, layer properties, and layouts. This does not save edits you have made to features in the map or their attributes.

- **Save As**: This creates a copy of the current project file with a new name in the location you select. It does not create copies of referenced databases, folders, files, tables, or other project items found in the original project. The newly saved project will reference the same locations as the original.

- **Portal**: This allows you to manage which portals you are connected to. This can include a connection to ArcGIS Online or **ArcGIS Enterprise Portal**. The **Primary Portal** is used by ArcGIS Pro to determine whether you have a valid license and what level as well as what extensions you have the ability to use. Other portals can be used to access data, services, and base maps, which can be used to create maps and perform analysis within ArcGIS Pro, thereby supplementing your own standard datasets.

- **Licensing**: This allows you to see what ArcGIS Pro license level and extensions you have been granted. Once you know what license level and extensions are available, you can then determine what functions you will be able to perform in ArcGIS Pro.

  After your initial login to use ArcGIS Pro, you do have the option to use your license offline, if your organization's administrator allows it. This checks out the license to the computer you are currently using and no longer requires you to be logged in to ArcGIS Online or ArcGIS Enterprise Portal to use ArcGIS Pro. Be careful when using this option. If the computer is lost or fails while the license is checked out for offline use, there is no easy way to get it back. You will need to contact **Esri Support** and have them resolve the issue.

- **Options**: This allows you to set various ArcGIS Pro user options, giving you the ability to customize it. You can set different options for the specific project you are working in, such as the units or for the application in general, such as a default base map for all new maps or scenes added to a project. As you explore each option, you can click on **Learn more about the link**, located at the bottom of the window for more information about the settings associated with that option.

- **Python**: This allows you to add additional Python modules for use in scripts to expand or automate ArcGIS Pro capabilities.
- **Add-in Manager**: This allows you to add custom extensions you or others may have created to enhance ArcGIS Pro's functionality. These add-ins must be created using **.NET**.

Map tab

The **Map** tab on the ribbon provides access to tools used to work with both 2D and 3D maps. From this tab, you can add new layers to your map, select features, change your base map, and more. For those who have used the older ArcMap application in the past, this tab combines functionality that was found on the **Standard** and **Tools** toolbars:

As you can see in the preceding screenshot, the **Map** tab contains seven groups:

- **Clipboard**
- **Navigate**
- **Layer**
- **Selection**
- **Inquiry**
- **Labeling**
- **Offline**

Each group then contains tools associated with the name of the group. For example, the **Selection** group tab includes several tools that allow you to select features in the map using various methods. You can select features directly from the map or based on specific attribute values or based on the spatial relationships between features in one or more layers. We will now take a closer look at a few of the most commonly used tools.

Navigate group

The **Navigate** group contains tools that allow you to navigate to locations within the map:

It includes tools that allow you to zoom in to areas, so you can see more detail, or to zoom out, so you can see a greater area. It also has tools that allow you to return to specific areas within the map. These are called **bookmarks**. Let's look at these tools in more detail:

- **Explore**: The **Explore** tool is a multifunction tool that allows you to zoom and pan within the map. It also allows you to click on features within the map and retrieve attributes linked to the feature. This tool combines the functions of the **Zoom In**, **Zoom Out**, **Pan**, and **Identify** tools into a single tool that is very similar to how your mouse works when using **Google Maps**.

You use this tool to navigate within your map using your mouse. The following list describes the function of the various mouse buttons for navigating the ArcGIS Pro interface:

  - **Left-click on a feature**: Opens the **Identify** pop-up window, showing attributes linked to the feature.
  - **Left or Right Drag**: Clicking and holding your left mouse button down and then dragging your pointer to the left and right pans your map view in that direction.
  - **Moving Scroll Wheel**: Zooms in and out on the map. Scrolling the wheel away from you causes the map to zoom in. Scrolling the wheel toward you causes the map to zoom out.
  - **Right-Click and Drag**: Continuously zooms the map in or out depending on the movement of the mouse.
  - **Single Right-Click**: Opens a menu. The menu that appears will vary depending on where you right-click.
  - **Hold Down Scroll Wheel and Drag (3D Map/Scene Only)**: Rotates and tilts the map view along the 3D axis.

This tool works best with a mouse that has a scroll wheel in between the right and left buttons. Other types of pointing devices can be used, but the functionality may be different depending on your hardware. Some of the buttons associated with this tool can be altered under the **Options** tool located on the **Project** tab. For example, you can change the zoom direction of the scroll wheel.

- **Bookmarks**: The **Bookmarks** tool allows you to zoom to saved spatial locations within your active map. This allows you to quickly return to important locations such as project areas, special event locations, key parcels, and more. Each map or scene within your project will have its own set of unique bookmarks.

  The drop-down arrow below the primary tool will allow you to access the bookmarks that have been saved with the active map or scene. It also provides access to tools for creating new bookmarks and managing existing ones. There is no limit to the number of bookmarks each map or scene can have.

We will now move on to the Layer group.

Layer group

The **Layer** group contains tools for adding new layers or data to your map:

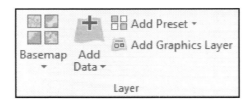

Some tools work with both 2D and 3D data. Others work best with one or the other. There are also tools for adding non-spatial data to your map. These tools use either coordinate values or addresses to show the location of points. Again, let's explore these tools:

- **Add Data**: This tool allows you to add new 2D or 3D layers to your maps. Added layers can reference various types of data and can come from different locations. It also allows you to add tabular data.

  If you look, you will notice a small arrow located below the icon for this tool. Clicking on the arrow or the text will display a list of methods for adding data to a map or scene. The methods you can select from include the following:

Data	This option adds spatial or tabular data to a map. It can be used to add layers that reference shapefiles, geodatabase feature classes, and ArcGIS Server web services. Standalone tables can be added to a map from various sources, as well as **dBase** files, `.csv` files, database tables, and Excel spreadsheets.

Add Data from Path	This option allows you to add data using a **Uniform Resource Locator (URL)** for a service, **Universal Naming Convention (UNC)** for a local data source, or a catalog path for a connected data source.
X,Y Point Data	This option allows you to add points to a map based on coordinates stored in a standalone table, `.csv` file, text file, or spreadsheet. Each point will also be linked to the additional attributes or information associated with that record or row.
Route Events	This option shows the location of the route between points of interest along a linear network.
Query Layer	This option creates a query layer from an enterprise database based on a **Structured Query Language (SQL)** `select` statement. This does not work with a file geodatabase, shapefile, or coverage.
Address Layer	This option geocodes a table of addresses using a specified address locator, creating a new geodatabase feature class or shapefile.
Add Multidimensional Raster Layer	This option allows you to add **Network Common Data Form (NetCDF)**, **GRIdded Binary (GRIB)**, or **Hierarchical Data Format (HDF)** raster formats to your map or scene. These are multidimensional raster formats commonly used with atmospheric, oceanographic, or earth science.
Elevation Source	This option allows you to add an elevation surface to a map or a scene. This can be a **Digital Elevation Model (DEM)**, **Triangulated Irregular Network (TIN)**, or web terrain service, among others. The elevation source might represent the ground elevation for an area or some other specific elevation, such as the maximum permitted building height.
Extract Locations	This option allows you to extract point locations from documents. The locations may take the form of an X and Y coordinate or an address. This requires the **LocateXT** extension for ArcGIS Pro.

As you can see, there are many ways to add data to a map or scene in ArcGIS Pro. The method you should use will depend on the type of data you wish to add. As you work through this book, you will get the opportunity to use several of the aforementioned methods.

- **Add Preset**: This tool is used to add new 3D layers to a scene with a predefined set of symbology settings. Predefined properties are determined from a gallery of defined symbology. ArcGIS Pro comes with galleries for **Realistic Trees**, **Thematic Trees, Realistic Buildings, Ground (Terrain), Icon Points**, and **Thematic Shapes**. Using this tool to add layers makes visualizing data in a 3D environment easier, especially for those who may be new to working with 3D data.
- **Add Graphics Layer**: This is a new tool which was added with ArcGIS Pro 2.6. It allows you to add graphics to a map such as a text box or an arrow or other shape. These graphics are not connected to any layer or feature within a map.

We will examine the Selection group next.

Selection group

The **Selection** group contains various tools used to select data, including **Select, Select By Attributes, Select By Location**, and **Clear**:

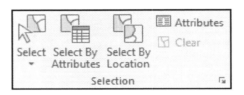

The selection tool you should use will depend on what you are trying to accomplish and how you need to select your data to complete your task. Let's look into these:

- **Select**: The **Select** tool allows you to select features from within a map or scene by clicking on a feature or drawing an area. The drop-down arrow located at the bottom of the tool lets you select what type of area you want to draw. You have options to draw a rectangle, polygon, freehand lasso, circle, or line, or to trace existing features in the map.
- **Select By Attributes**: The **Select By Attributes** tool allows you to select features based on specified attribute values. For example, you might want to select all parcels owned by Tripp Corbin or all sewer pipes made of ductile iron. This tool will allow you to do that.

  In the tool window, you will create a SQL `where` clause, which tells the application which specific values you are searching for. Do not be concerned if you do not know how to write a SQL clause. ArcGIS Pro builds the query based on a series of easy selections and inputs you are prompted to provide.

- **Select By Location**: This tool allows you to select features in one or more layers based on a spatial relationship. For example, you might select all parcels located within 100 feet of a road you know is going to have work done on it, so you can get a list of all those who live along the road. Or you might select all the roads that intersect or cross a floodplain, so you know not to include those in an emergency evacuation plan.

In earlier versions of ArcGIS Pro, the **Select by Attribute** and **Select by Location** tools opened in the **Geoprocessing** pane. In ArcGIS Pro 2.6, these now open in their own floating window. Next, we will explore the **Inquiry** group.

Inquiry group

The **Inquiry** group contains tools that allow you to retrieve some basic information about your map. You can measure lengths and areas in different units, retrieve some basic demographic data, or even find a point of interest using the tools in this group:

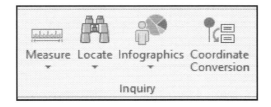

The details of these tools are as follows:

- **Infographics**: This tool allows you to retrieve basic demographic data for the area you select in the map. It will retrieve information and graphs showing average household income or population ethnicity makeup.

   This tool accesses Esri's GeoEnrichment service, which is connected through your ArcGIS Online login. So, this tool will require you to have an internet connection, be connected to ArcGIS Online, and have available ArcGIS Online credits to work. Using this tool will cost ArcGIS Online credits, and you should always keep that in mind when using this tool. The credit usage for this tool is small – only about one one-hundredth of a credit each time you use it.

- **Measure**: This tool allows users to measure length and area by simply clicking on locations within a map. If you are working within a 3D scene, you also have the option to measure vertical distances.

You can change the units used by this tool, so they are different from the units assigned to your map. This way, even if your map is in meters, you can have the **Measure** tool provide distances in feet, miles, or kilometres. Area units can also be set. Unlike ArcMap, you can still measure areas when your map is in a geographic coordinate system.

- **Locate**: This tool allows you to locate a place using an address or common name. By default, this tool uses the **Esri World Geocoder service** from ArcGIS Online. This service requires you to have an active connection to ArcGIS Online to work. However, unlike the **Infographics** tool, it does not use credits. You can add and use your own address locators to your project and they will then be available for use with this tool.
- **Coordinate Conversion**: This is another new tool that was added to ArcGIS Pro 2.6. It allows you to convert coordinates from one coordinate system to another. Currently this tool requires the input coordinates to be in the WGS84 geographic coordinate system. The output can be a shapefile, geodatabase feature class, KMZ or CSV file

You have now been introduced to the tools located on the **Map** tab in the ArcGIS Pro ribbon. These tools are some of the ones you will use most often while working in the application. We will now move on to an exercise concerned with working with the **Map** tab.

Exercise 2A – Working with the Map tab

You will now get to take some of the tools we have discussed for a test drive. You will see how they work within the ArcGIS Pro ribbon interface and some of the options associated with those tools first hand. We will start by opening an existing project and using the **Navigation** tools.

Step 1 – Opening a project

In this step, you will open a project that has already been created. This project includes a single 2D map with several layers for the imaginary City of Trippville:

1. Start ArcGIS Pro either by clicking on the Windows **Start** button and going to the ArcGIS program group, or by clicking on a shortcut located on your taskbar or desktop.

Remember, you will need to make sure you are connected to the internet so that your license can be validated. ArcGIS Pro should remember your user login from `Chapter 1`, *Introducing ArcGIS Pro*. If not, log in to ArcGIS Online when asked to.

2. In the **ArcGIS Pro** start page, click on the **Open another project** option located below **Recent Project**, as indicated in the following screenshot:

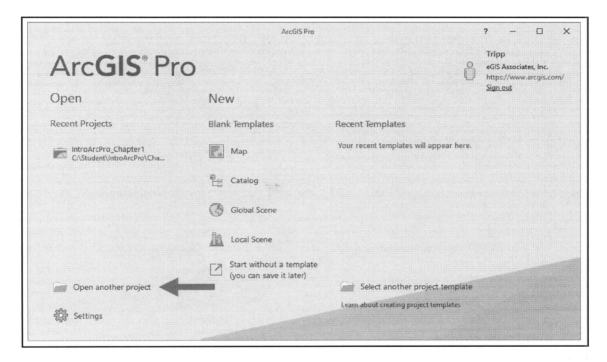

3. Click on **Computer** in the left panel of the **Open Project** window.
4. In the right panel, double click on your `C:` drive.

 Remember, if you installed the exercise data to a location other than the default, you will need to navigate to that drive and location. These steps assume that the data has been installed to the default location.

5. Navigate to `C:\Student\IntroArcPro\Chapter2` or to the location in which you installed your exercise data.
6. Select the `Ex 2A.aprx` file and click **OK**.

The project you selected should open in ArcGIS Pro and look similar to the following screenshot:

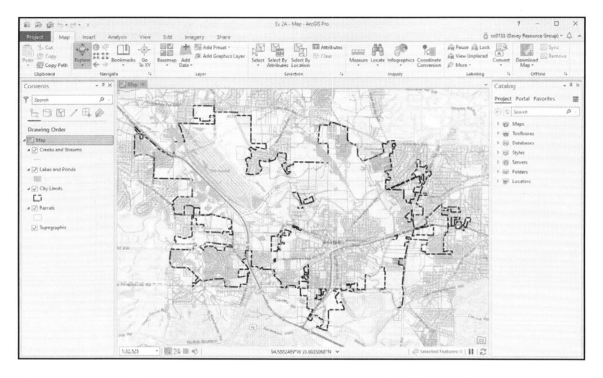

There are several things that might cause your project to look different. The size of the ArcGIS Pro application on your monitor will impact how it displays. The resolution you have your computer set to will also impact how the project looks. In addition to this, the panes, windows, and customizations you have open will also change how the project looks on your screen. So, do not be too concerned if the project you see does not look exactly like the screenshot. It should just be similar.

Step 2 – Navigating the map

With a project open, you will now begin to explore the map you see. You will use navigation tools located on the **Map** tab in the ribbon to zoom and access data:

1. Activate the **Map** tab in the ribbon. Then, click on the **Bookmarks** tool in the **Navigate** group and select the **Washington Park** bookmark. This will zoom you to the location of Washington Park automatically.

2. Click on the **Explore** tool in the **Navigate** group on the **Map** tab to make it the active tool.

3. Left-click on the parcel for **Washington Park**. Continue to hold the mouse button down and drag your mouse toward the lower left-hand corner of the map view until **Washington Park** is in the lower left-hand corner. Now, release your mouse button.

   You have just used the **Explore** tool to pan the map view. As you learned earlier in this chapter, the **Explore** tool has many uses. Now you will explore some of the other functions of this tool.

4. With the **Explore** tool still active, click on any parcel within the map view.

 Question: *What happens when you click on a parcel using the Explore tool?*

5. Close the pop-up window that has appeared by clicking on the small **X** in the upper-right corner of the window.

6. Click on the small drop-down arrow located below the **Explore** tool and select **Visible Layers**, as shown in the following screenshot:

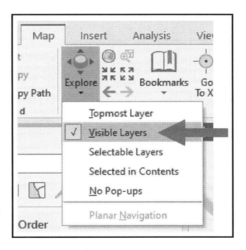

7. Click on the same parcel as you did in *step 4*.

8. Look at the bottom of the information pop-up window. You should see **1 of 2** located in the lower left-hand corner. Also in the upper panel of the window, you should see two items listed. If you do not, this part of the window is too small to show all the information at one time:

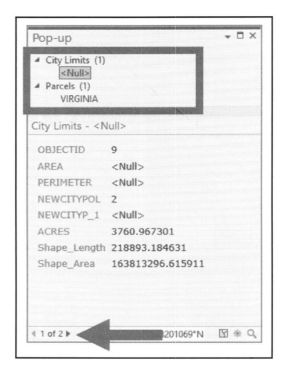

You can use the scroll bar on the right side to move up and down.

The information you see may be different depending on where you clicked on the map. Do not be concerned if that is the case. You just clicked on a different parcel or area of the map.

9. Click on the small arrow located to the right of **1 of 2**. This will toggle you to information about the other feature you clicked on. Also, watch what happens in the top panel of the window while you click on the small arrow.

10. In the top panel, you should also see two items. They are grouped by the layer they are in. Click on the value below **City Limits** and see what happens. Then, click on the value below **Parcels** and watch the information in the lower panel.

As you have now seen, you can click either on the small arrows at the bottom of the pop-up window or on the individual values in the top panel to access information about the features you clicked on while using the **Explore** tool. This is a quick way to retrieve basic information about the features you see on the map.

The pop-up window can also be resized and moved if needed. You can even move to another monitor or display by clicking on the title area at the top of the window and dragging it where you want it. You can also dock it within the ArcGIS Pro interface so it will always appear in the same location, making it easier to find. Let's see how that works.

11. Click on the title area of the pop-up window and continue to hold down your left mouse button. When you do this, you should see tan and white docking icons appear in the ArcGIS Pro interface, as illustrated in the following screenshot:

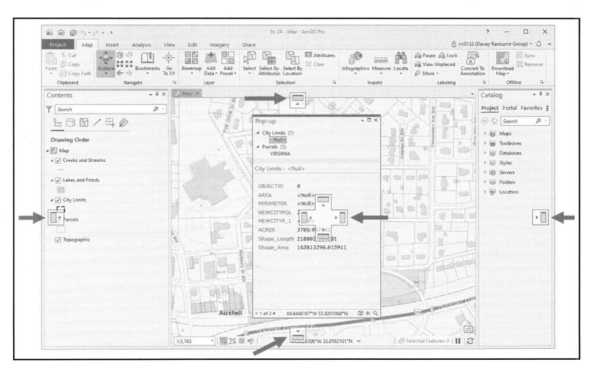

12. With your left mouse button still pressed, drag your mouse pointer to one of those docking icons. You can choose anyone you want. Once your pointer is hovering over one of the docking icons, release your mouse button.

Once you release your mouse button, the pop-up window should dock itself in that location within ArcGIS Pro. The window will then continue to appear in that location whenever you use this function of the Explore tool, even if you close the window.

13. Close the pop-up window by clicking on the small **X** located in the upper-right corner.

 It is generally recommended that you close any window or pane you are not actively using. This will free up more space on your monitor and keep the application performing better.

You have now explored some of the basic functions associated with the Explore tool. You will continue to use this tool throughout the book, allowing you to learn even more about it. But now it is time to move on to another tool.

Step 3 – Using the Infographics tool (optional)

Now, let's take a quick look at the **Infographics** tool. As mentioned earlier, this tool allows you to retrieve demographic information using **Esri's GeoEnrichment Service** from ArcGIS Online. This tool does use ArcGIS Online credits, which are the currency for ArcGIS Online. However, the amount used for this step will be minimal. You should use less than one credit by the time you complete this step.

If you are concerned about using ArcGIS Online credits, or you have been restricted by your administrator, you can skip this step:

1. In the **Contents** pane typically located on the left side of the ArcGIS Pro interface, right-click on the **City Limits** layer. Then, select **Zoom to Layer** from the menu that appears. The map should zoom to an area that displays the entire city limits for Trippville.

2. On the **Map** tab in the ribbon, click on the **Infographics** tool in the **Inquiry** group.
3. Click somewhere in the northern part of the city of Trippville within the city limits boundary and north of the railroad line that runs through the center of the city, as illustrated in the following screenshot:

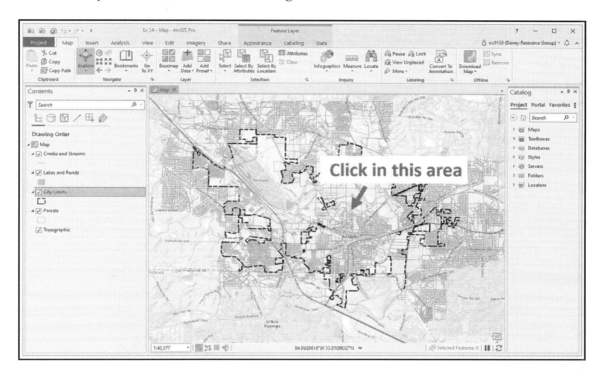

The **Infographics** window will open, displaying demographic information for the area. The window should look similar to the following screenshot. Esri is constantly updating and improving this tool, so what you see may look a bit different. Do not worry if it does, as long as you see something:

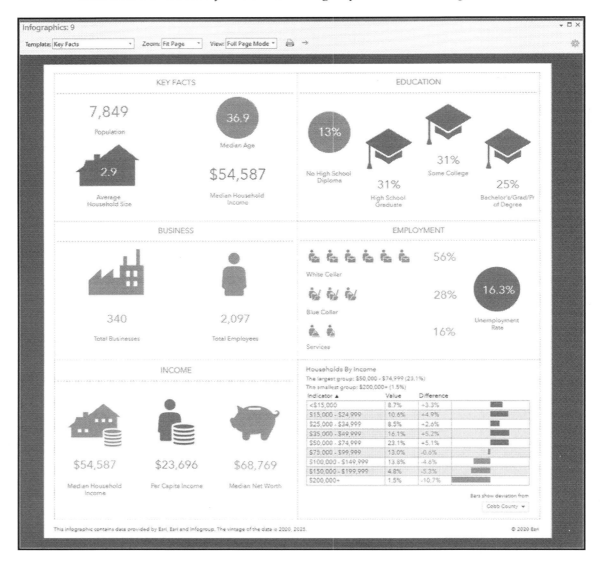

If this is the first time you have used this tool, you start with the **KEY FACTS** screen. This provides basic demographic information about the area you clicked on.

If you get an error, this is typically caused by two things. First, you are not logged in to your ArcGIS Online user account. You can check this by looking in the upper-right side of ArcGIS Pro to verify that your user name is logged in. The second common cause of an error is either you have run out of ArcGIS Online credits, or do not have permission to use credits.

4. In the **Infographics** window, click on one of the items you see. This will display more detailed information about the item you clicked on.
5. Continue exploring the **Infographics** tool. Try changing the **Template** option located at the top of the window. Explore some of the template options.
6. Once you are done exploring the **Infographics** tool, close the window.
7. Now, click on the **Project** tab in the ribbon.
8. Select **Save As** from the menu choices on the left side.
9. In the **Save Project As** window, navigate to `C:\Student\IntroArcPro\My Projects`. Name your project `your name_Ex2A` (that is, `Tripp_Ex2A`) and click **Save**.
10. Once you have saved your project, close ArcGIS Pro.

As discussed in `Chapter 1`, *Introducing ArcGIS Pro*, ArcGIS Pro requires a lot of computer resources to run successfully. The more you do in the application and the longer it runs, the more resources it will consume. So it is recommended that, at the start of each day, you begin with a fresh boot on your computer, either by turning it on or performing a restart. This will ensure that the maximum amount of computer resources are available. Then, when you break for a meal such as lunch, you close ArcGIS Pro and reopen it when you return. This, too, will release unnecessary resources and make the computer, as well as ArcGIS Pro, run better.

You have now successfully opened an ArcGIS Pro project, retrieved information about features you saw on the map, and navigated to different locations on the map. These are very common tasks that you will use a lot. Now it is time to move on to the concept of **contextual tabs**.

Now that you have had a chance to gain some experience of using ArcGIS Pro and the ribbon, you hopefully have begun to understand the concepts of tabs. It is time to move on to a more advanced but related concept, contextual tabs.

Learning about contextual tabs

Contextual tabs are smart tabs that appear when you select an item within ArcGIS Pro. This could be a layer, a map, a layout, a table and so on. When you select one of these items, a tab or tabs will appear on the ribbon that contains tools specific to working with that item.

These are often grouped into a contextual tab set. For example, if you select a layer from the **Contents** pane, the **Feature Layer** contextual tab set will appear, which contains three contextual tabs, namely, **Appearance**, **Labeling**, and **Data**. You will examine the **Feature Layer** contextual tab set and the tabs it contains next. You will explore other contextual tabs throughout other chapters in the book.

Understanding the Feature Layer contextual tab set

The **Feature Layer** contextual tab set appears when you select a layer within the **Contents** pane. It includes three contextual tabs, namely, **Appearance**, **Labeling**, and **Data** tabs. Each of these allows you to access various properties associated with the layer you have selected. The following screenshot illustrates this contextual tab set and its included contextual tabs:

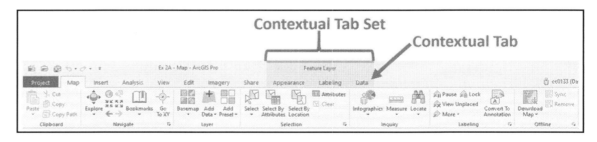

We will now examine each of these contextual tabs in greater detail, starting with the Appearance tab.

Learning about the Appearance tab

The **Appearance** tab contains tools that control the display of the selected layer. Here, you can change the symbology, set visibility scales, apply transparency, and more:

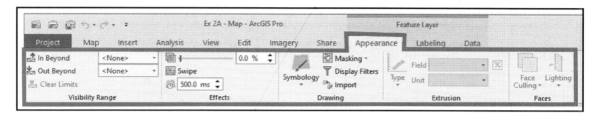

You can see that there are five groups within the **Appearance** tab. These are **Visibility Range**, **Effects**, **Drawing**, **Extrusion**, and **Faces**. We will learn about these groups in the upcoming sections.

The **Visibility Range**, **Effects**, and **Drawing** groups will be available for all layers.

Visibility Range group

Visibility Range allows you to set scales at which the layer will be visible or not. This allows you to control the level of detail displayed in a map based on how close you are zoomed in or out:

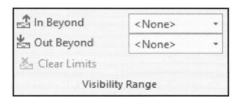

This reduces clutter, improves readability, and increases the redraw performance of the map. You would want to apply a visible scale range to a layer if it contains a lot of detailed information that may overlap or start to merge together if you zoom out. This is also good to apply to any map you intend to publish as a web service via ArcGIS Online or ArcGIS Enterprise.

Effects group

The **Effects** group, shown as follows, contains several interesting and useful tools if you have a map that contains overlapping layers that may hide one another:

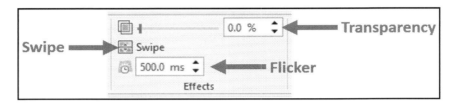

The following is a description of the functions of the various tools you will find in the **Effects** group:

- **Transparency**: The **Transparency** tool includes the slider bar, which is used to apply transparency to the selected layer. By making a layer more transparent, you can see other layers that may be beneath it in the map.
- **Swipe**: Below the **Transparency** setting is the **Swipe** tool. This tool does exactly what the name implies. It allows you to swipe the selected layer out of the way with your mouse. You can swipe left to right, right to left, top to bottom, or bottom to top. This allows you to temporarily turn a portion of a layer on or off as you swipe. This tool is good for performing comparisons between two or more layers.
- **Flicker**: Below the **Effects** tool is the **Flicker** tool. This tool will cause a layer to automatically flick on and off based on the specified interval.

We will examine the Drawing group next.

Drawing group

The **Drawing** group controls various display properties for the selected layer, such as what symbology is used, using one layer to hide or mask another, and applying display filters so that only specific features within the selected layer appear at specified scales. The following screenshot shows you the various tools you will find in this group:

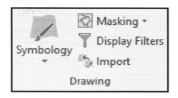

The following is a description of the function of the tools included in this group:

- **Symbology**: The **Symbology** tool allows you to control which type of symbology you wish to apply to the layer. This can be a single symbol, unique symbols, graduated color symbols, and more. You will learn more about the different types of symbol methods in `Chapter 3`, *Creating 2D Maps*.
- **Masking**: This tool allows you to mask or hide features in one layer based on features in another layer. This can reduce clutter in the map and make it easier to read.
- **Display Filters**: This tool allows you to control when specific groups of features within the layer become visible at specified scales. The groups are created based on a query or expression you create.
- **Import**: This tool allows you to import the symbology settings for a layer based on another existing layer or a layer file.

We will examine the Extrusion and Faces groups next.

Extrusion and Faces groups

Extrusion and **Faces** groups will only be available when working with a 3D scene. Extrusion allows you to extend 2D features above a 3D surface, such as building footprints or light poles. The following is a screenshot of these two groups:

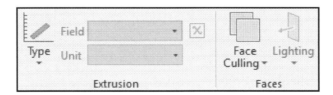

The **Extrusion** layer must be in the **3D Layers** category in the **Contents** pane. The **Faces** group contains tools to control transparency and lighting in a 3D scene. **Face Culling** allows you to see through parts of a 3D feature. **Lighting** allows you to create and control shadows. You will learn more about some of these tools and settings in `Chapter 5`, *Creating and Working with Projects*.

We will learn about the Labelling tab in the next section.

Learning about the Labeling tab

Labels are one method of adding text to a map or scene. They provide useful information about features shown in a map, such as a road name, parcel owner, or asset inventory number. Labels are dynamic. This means several things.

First, they are linked to values stored in the layer's attribute table. Second, the computer will place the labels based on the settings you configure. The labels will shift and change position as you pan or zoom within the map.

The following screenshot shows you the visual for the **Labeling** tab:

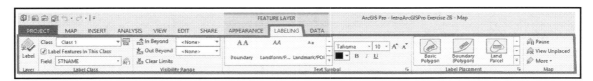

The **Labeling** tab contains six groups. These are as follows:

- **Layer**
- **Label Class**
- **Visibility Range**
- **Text Symbol**
- **Label Placement**
- **Map**

The contextual tab allows you to access tools for adding and configuring text labels to the features within the selected layer. The tools presented on this table will vary depending on what type of layer you have selected. Points, lines, and polygons will have different options.

For example, when labeling a line layer, you can place the label above, below, or on the line and oriented parallel, perpendicular or curved along the line, whereas with a polygon layer, you can choose to place the label within the polygon only or you can allow them outside the polygon. You can also select whether the label will be horizontal only or allowed along a diagonal in the polygon. This is called *straight* in ArcGIS Pro.

We will look at the aforementioned six groups in the upcoming sections.

Layer group

This group contains a single tool – **Label**. The **Label** tool turns labeling on or off for the selected layer. This is just one of several ways in which labels for a layer can be turned on or off.

Label Class group

The **Label Class** group contains tools that allow you to determine what features you wish to label and what field or fields from the attribute table you wish to label them with. The following screenshot shows the tools you will find in this group:

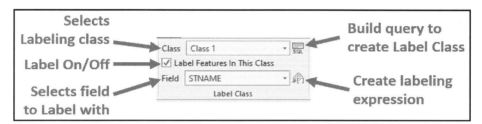

The following list provides descriptions of the tool functions in this group:

- **Class drop-down selection**: This allows you to select which label class you want to make setting changes to. Each label class can have its own unique label settings. For example, you could create a label class based on the type for each road so that highways could be labeled using a different setting than a local city road. This can greatly expand the flexibility of labels. A layer will have at least one label class, called **Class 1**. Unless you create a **Label Class** query, this default class will include all features in the layer.
- **Label Class Query**: This tool allows you to create a query, which, in turn, creates a new label class. The new class will contain features that meet the conditions called for by the query you build. For example, you might want to label all commercial properties differently to residential properties. So, you would want to create a label class for the commercial properties using a query that filters just those properties.
- **Label Features In This Class**: This turns the labels on or off for the class that is displayed in the **Class** drop-down selection. If the layer has only a single label class, this will turn the labels on or off for the entire layer.

- **Field drop-down selection**: This drop-down option allows you to select the field from the layer's attribute table that you want to label the features of on the map. This dropdown will automatically populate with the fields found in the selected layers attribute table.
- **Label Expression**: This tool will open the **Label Class** pane and allow you to build a custom labeling expression. Labeling expressions allow you to label using multiple fields, add more information to the label, split a label across multiple lines, and more. You can create expressions using the **VBScript**, **JScript**, **Python**, or **Arcade** languages.

Text Symbol group

The **Text Symbol** group tab contains tools and settings that control how a label is visualized:

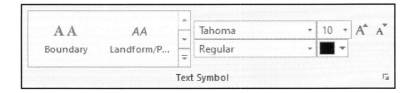

Here, you can change the font, size, and color. You can also choose to make the label bold, italicized or underlined. ArcGIS Pro also includes several predefined label styles that you can also choose to use from this group tab.

Label Placement group

The **Label Placement** group tab controls the general placement of the label in relation to the feature being labeled:

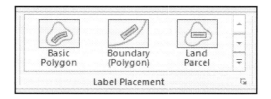

The options here will vary depending on whether you are working with points, lines, or polygons. For example, for a line layer, you will have the options to place the label above, below, or on the line. The options for a point or a polygon layer will be different.

Map group

The last group tab is **Map**. The tools located here control the drawing of the labels within the map:

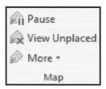

Let's look at these options in more detail:

- **Pause**: Pauses the redraw of labels on the map for faster performance.
- **View Unplaced**: Displays the location of labels that have not been placed on the map because of a conflict with other features or labels based on your configuration settings.
- **More**: This provides a drop-down menu to other options or settings, as shown in the following screenshot:

The tools located under the **More** menu provide more advanced settings for your labels and how they interact with other labels and features. You can also select what label engine you wish to use in your map. By default, ArcGIS Pro uses the **Maplex Label Engine**. This is one of two engines you can use. The other is the **Esri Standard Label Engine**. Maplex is the more advanced of the two and provides greater configuration options for your labels.

Learning about the Data tab

The **Data** tab contains tools that interact with the attribute table for the selected layer. It contains eight groups:

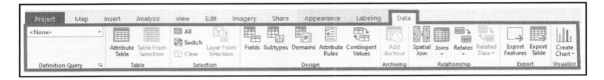

Those groups are as follows:

- **Definition Query**
- **Table**
- **Selection**
- **Design**
- **Archiving**
- **Relationship**
- **Export**
- **Visualize**

We will only explore some of the most commonly used groups and tools found on this tab.

Definition Query group

This group only contains a single drop-down list option. The dropdown will populate with any definition queries you have created for the selected layer and apply the query you select. Definition queries allow you to apply a filter to the features displayed in a layer so you only see those features that meet the criteria called for by the query. This helps reduce clutter in the map and improve performance.

Table group

This group contains two tools that will open the attribute table for the selected layer. One opens the entire table and the other only opens the table to show selected features. Let's explore these:

- **Attribute Table**: This option opens the attribute table for the selected layer. The attribute table contains additional information about the features displayed on the map.

- **Table from Selection**: This option opens the attribute table for the selected layer, but only displays records in the table for the features that have been selected. If no features are selected, then this icon will be grayed out.

Selection group

This group contains tools that allow you to select or deselect records from within the table. Records are the rows you see in the table. If you are looking at an attribute table, each record in the table corresponds to a feature within the layer on the map. Hence, selecting a record in the table will also select a feature on the map. Let's look at these in more depth:

- **All**: This tool selects all records within the active table.
- **Switch**: This tool reverses your selection. All records that were not selected originally become selected, and all those that were selected are deselected.
- **Clear**: This tool clears your selection. This means it deselects all selected records, leaving you with nothing selected.
- **Layer from Selection**: This tool creates a new layer that contains the features that were selected. This new layer will reference the same data source, but will only display the features that were selected originally.

Export group

This group contains tools that allow you to export features or records to a new data source. This can be a new feature class or standalone table, depending on what tool you choose.

- **Export Features**: This tool will export features in the selected layer to a new shapefile or geodatabase feature class, creating a copy of the layer at the time of export.
- **Export Table**: This tool will export the records from the selected layers attribute table to a new standalone table. The new table can be saved to a geodatabase or a `.dbf` file.

 With both of these tools, if any features or records are selected when the tool is run, only the selected features or records will be exported. If nothing is selected, then the entire layer or table will be exported.

The remaining groups on this tab will not be covered as they are too advanced for the level of this book. Some are discussed in the *ArcGIS Pro 2.x Cookbook* by Packt if you want to learn more about them. Now it is time for you to put some of this new-found knowledge to the test.

We will now move on to the next section about working with 2D and 3D layers as we are now familiar with contextual tabs and all of their components.

Exercise 2B – Working with 2D and 3D layers

It is now time to see how the tools contained in the Feature Layer contextual tab set work. In this exercise, you will use tools on the contextual tabs found in the tab set to make changes to layers within an existing project. You will change a layer's symbology, labels, and more.

Step 1 – Opening the project and adding layers

In this step, you will open a project that has already been created. You will then add some additional layers to a map:

1. Using the skills you have already learned, start ArcGIS Pro and open the **Ex 2B** project. This project is located in `C:\Student\IntroArcPro\Chapter2` or the location where you installed the course data.
2. Activate the **Map** tab and then click on the **Add Data** tool located in the **Layer** group.

Make sure to click on the button icon and not the arrow or text located below the icon. If you do click on the arrow or text and a menu appears, select **Data** from the menu.

3. Expand the **Project** folder in the panel located on the right-hand side of the **Add Data** window by clicking on the small arrowhead. Then, select the **Databases** folder so you see two geodatabases, `IntroArcGISPro Exercise 2A` and `Trippville_GIS`.
4. Double-click on the `IntroArcGISPro Exercise 2A` geodatabase so that you can see its contents.
5. While holding down your *Ctrl* key, click on the **bldg._footprints**, **RR_Tracks**, and **Street_Centerlines** feature classes to select them, as shown in the following screenshot. Then, click the **OK** button to add the selected feature classes to your map:

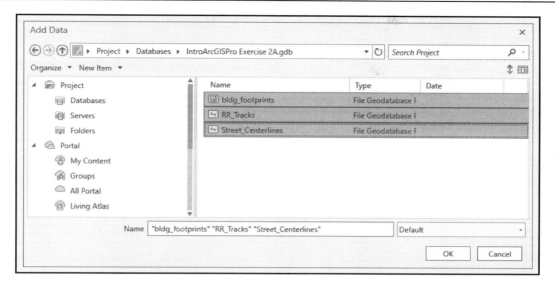

You have now added three new layers to a map from a geodatabase. They should appear in your map once you press the **OK** button. Take a moment to notice where the new layers were placed in the **Contents** pane within the layer list. The **bldg_footprints** layer should appear below the other two layers you added because it is a polygon layer. **Street_Centerlines** and **RR_Tracks** are added to the top of the list because they are line layers.

 Always remember when working with ArcGIS Pro that a project never stores the actual data being displayed. Each layer references an external data source, such as a geodatabase feature class.

Now that you have added the new layers, you need to configure some of their properties, such as symbology.

Step 2 – Changing symbology

You have just added three new layers to the map. Now you need to adjust the symbology for the layers you added. You will change the railroad layer you added to use a common railroad symbol. You will similarly change the building footprints. Lastly, you will adjust the road centerlines so that they are symbolized based on their condition:

1. Right-click on the **bldg_footprints** layer in the **Contents** pane and select **Properties** from the menu that appears. The layer may also be named **Buildings**.

2. Click on **General** located in the pane on the left side of the **Properties** window.

3. Change the name to Building Footprints and click **OK**. Notice what happens to the layer in the **Contents** pane.

   When you right-clicked on the **bldg_footprints** *layer, did you notice what happened to the ribbon?* The **Feature Layer** context tab automatically appeared, providing access to the tools it contains. You will now use those tools to make adjustments to the **Building** layer you just renamed.

4. Ensure that you still have the **Building Footprints** layer selected in the **Contents** pane. Then, select the **Appearance** contextual tab in the **Feature Layer** contextual tab set.

5. Click on the **Symbology** tool to open the **Symbology** pane on the right side of the ArcGIS Pro interface. The **Symbology** pane allows you to make changes to the symbology settings for a layer.

6. In the **Symbology** pane, verify that **Primary Symbology** is set to Single Symbol, as shown in the following screenshot. If it is not, use the drop-down arrow to set it to Single Symbol, like so:

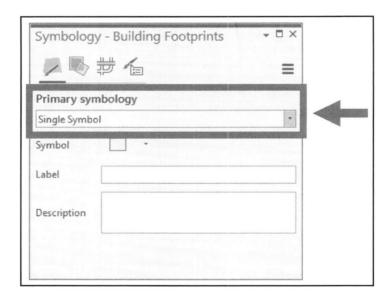

The color for your current symbol may differ from what is shown in the preceding example. ArcGIS Pro randomly assigns colors to new layers as they are added to a map.

7. Click on the small sample symbol located to the right of the word **Symbol**. This will open the **Symbology** pane to the Symbol **Gallery**, as shown in the following screenshot:

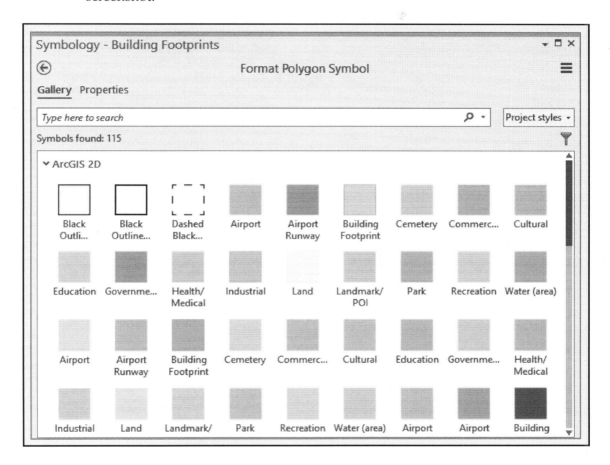

8. In the search box located near the top of the **Symbology** pane, type `Building Footprint` to filter the gallery to only symbology associated with building footprints.

   You have just changed the symbology for the building footprints layer. Symbology is important because it allows you to differentiate between different layers so that you can identify features in one layer from those in another.

9. Select any of the symbology samples that you see in the gallery that are associated with building footprints.

 Question: *What happens when you select the new symbol?*

10. Now, select the **RR_Tracks** layer in the **Contents** pane and watch what happens in the **Symbology** pane.
11. Click on the sample symbol located to the right of the word **Symbol** to once again open the gallery.
12. Using the same process from before, change the symbology to the **Railroad** symbol in **Gallery**, shown in the **Symbology** pane, as shown in the following screenshot:

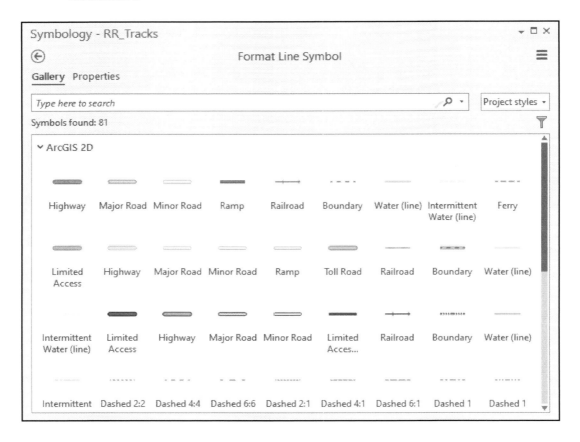

13. In the search box located at the top of the **Symbology** pane, type `Railroad` to filter the gallery to symbology for railroads.

14. Select any of the presented sample symbols you prefer. Close the **Symbology** pane when you are done by clicking on the small **X** in the upper-right corner.

It is generally recommended to close any panes or windows in ArcGIS Pro when you are done using them. This will reduce screen clutter and any drains on your system resources.

15. In the **Contents** pane, right-click on the **RR_Tracks** layer and select **Properties** from the menu that appears.

16. On the **General** tab in the **Layer Properties** window, change the name of the layer to `Railroad` and click **OK**.

17. Click on the **Project** tab and select **Save As**.

18. Navigate to `C:\Student\IntroArcPro\My Projects` and name your project `<your name> Ex2B`.

Unlike many other programs, ArcGIS Pro does not have an autosave function for your project. Therefore, it is always a good idea to save your project often when you are adding layers, changing symbology, adding new maps, and so on in order to ensure that these changes are saved and you do not lose what you have done.

Now you will change the symbology for the road centerlines to reflect their condition. This will be a bit more challenging than changing a single symbol.

19. Using the skills you have already learned, rename the `Street_Centerline` layer to `Streets`.

20. Ensure that the **Streets** layer is still selected in the **Contents** pane. Then, click on the **Appearance** tab in the ribbon.

21. Next, click on the small arrow located below the **Symbology** tool. Choose **Unique Values** from the drop-down options, as illustrated in the following screenshot:

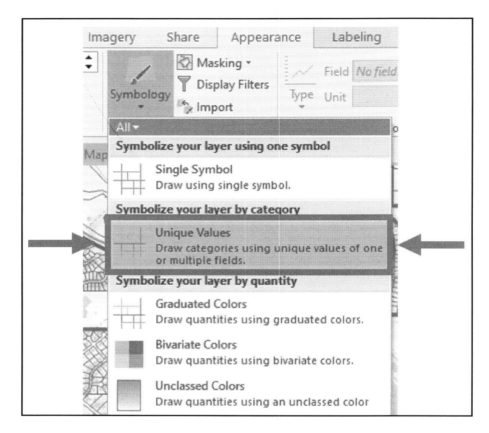

The **Symbology** pane will once again be opened on the right side of ArcGIS Pro. It will look different than what it did when you were working with **Single Symbol**. It contains many more options and settings. These allow you to configure your symbology based on the attributes found in one or more fields.

22. In the drop-down box located next to **Field 1**, select **Condition** as shown in the following screenshot. Notice that ArcGIS Pro automatically adds all values found in this field and assigns them a symbol:

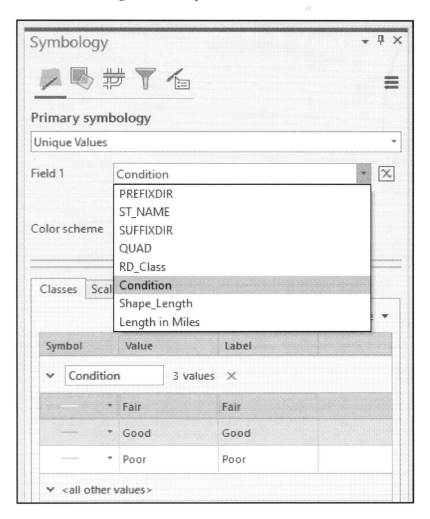

23. Click on the symbol located next to **Fair** in the grid located in the middle of the **Symbology** pane to open the symbol gallery.

24. Click on the **Properties** tab located at the top of the pane, as indicated in the following screenshot:

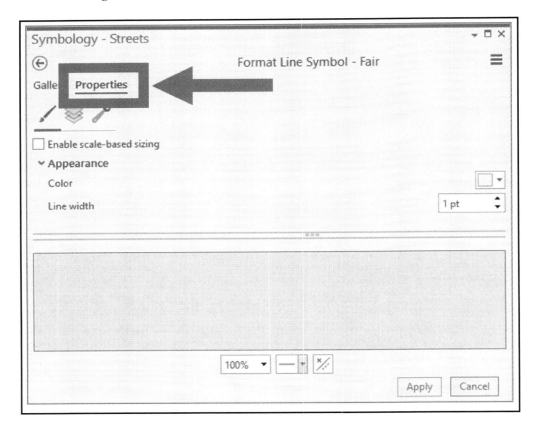

25. From the **Color** drop-down selection, set the color to an orange tone or another you prefer and set the width to 1 pt. Then, click **Apply**.
26. Click on the return arrow located at the top of the **Symbology** pane to return to the symbology settings for the entire **Streets** layer.
27. Using the same method from before, make the following adjustments shown in the following list to the symbols for **Good** and **Poor** values:
    - **Good**: A bright green color and **width** of 1.5 pt.
    - **Poor**: A bright red color and **width** of 3 pt.

When you are done, your map should look similar to this:

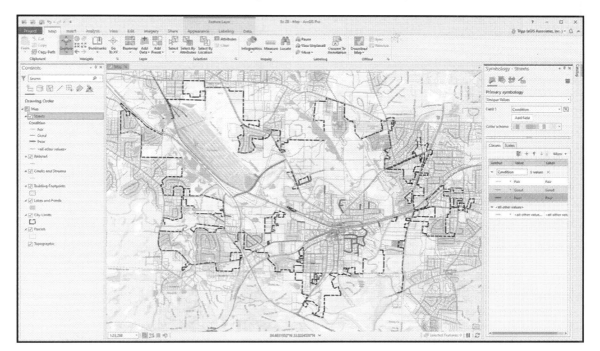

28. Close the **Symbology** pane when you are done changing the symbology. Feel free to make changes to other layers in the map.

29. Save your project by clicking on the **Save** button located on the **Quick Access Toolbar** located at the very top left-hand side of the ArcGIS Pro interface.

You have just adjusted symbology using the Feature Layer contextual tab. Initially, you simply changed the symbol for all the features in a layer. Then you changed the symbology for the Streets layer so that you could see the condition of each street within that layer. That ability makes your maps more informative and useful. It also shows the power of GIS, where spatial data is linked to attribute information. Now, let's add some labels to the maps.

Step 3 – Labeling

In this step, you will use the **Labeling** tab in the Feature Layer contextual tab set to add street names to the map. You will configure the labeling for the Streets layer to accomplish this task:

1. Select the **Streets** layer in the **Contents** pane.
2. Click on the **Labeling** tab in the **Feature Layer** contextual tab set.
3. Click on the **Label** button located on the far left of the ribbon in the **Layer** group, as shown in the following screenshot, to turn on labels for the **Streets** layer. You should see labels appear in the map once you click on the tool:

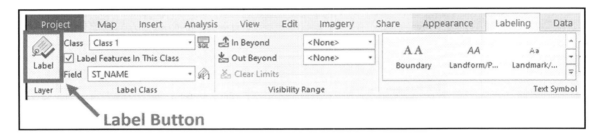

4. Within the **Label Placement** group on the **Labeling** tab, select the **North American Streets** option, as illustrated in the following screenshot. ArcGIS Pro will then use the placement properties defined by this placement style, including the road name appearing above the centerline and being curved to follow the road:

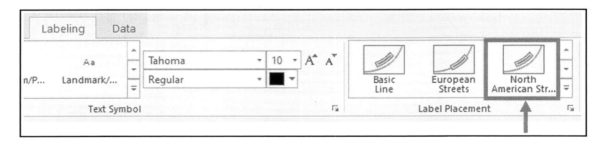

When you enabled labeling for the **Streets** layer, the **Label Class** pane also opened in the right side of ArcGIS Pro in the same place as the symbology pane. This pane allows you to refine various label settings.

5. Right-click on the **Streets** layer in the **Contents** pane. Select **Labeling Properties** from the menu that appears to open the **Label Class** pane.

6. Click on the **Position** tab located at the top of the **Label Class** pane, as illustrated in the following screenshot:

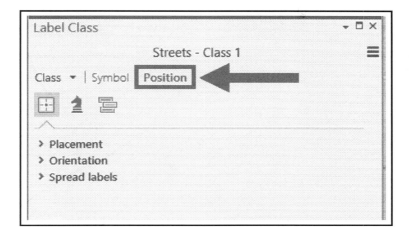

7. In the **Label Class** pane, click on the **Fitting Strategy** button. This is the one that looks like a *knight piece* in chess, as illustrated in the following screenshot:

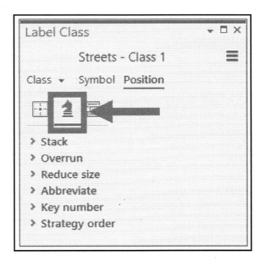

8. Click on the small arrow next to **Reduce size** to expand the options for that strategy.

9. Click on the checkbox next to the **Reduce font size** to enable this fitting strategy.
10. Set the **Lower Limit** to 5.0 pts and the **Step interval** to 1.0 pt.

This will allow ArcGIS Pro to automatically adjust the font size in order to get a road name to fit on the map. This will allow more road names to be displayed.

11. Zoom in and out to see how well your labels appear. Turn off the **Reduce font size** option and then zoom in and out again to see the impact that this option has.
12. Save your project and close the **Label Class** pane.

You have now added text to your map showing the street names. An automatic label was added to this text. Labels are dynamic text that is tied back to an attribute of the feature. As you have now seen, you can configure some options, but ultimately, the software decides what features are labeled and where the label will appear.

So far, you have worked solely on a 2D map. Now it is time to dip your toe into 3D with the next step.

Step 4 – Working with a 3D layer

One of the things that sets ArcGIS Pro apart from other GIS software is the ability to work and visualize data in 3D without needing additional software or extensions such as **3D Analyst**. The ability to view, edit, and query data in 3D is part of the core functionality found in ArcGIS Pro.

In this step, you will add a layer containing building footprints to a 3D scene and then extrude that layer so that you can see the heights of the building. Working with 3D data will tax your computer more than 2D data. So, do not be surprised if this step performs slower. If your computer barely meets the minimum requirements for running ArcGIS Pro, then you may encounter issues and crashes trying to complete this step:

1. In the **Catalog** pane normally located on the right side of the interface, click on the little arrow next to **Maps** located at the top of the pane to expand its contents.

If you don't see the **Catalog** pane, you may have accidentally closed it when you closed the other panes. You can reopen it by clicking on the **View Tab** and then the **Project** button.

2. Once you expand the **Maps** folder, you should see two maps, namely, **Map** and **Scene**. Right-click on **Scene** and select **Open Local View**, as shown in the following screenshot. This opens the 3D scene:

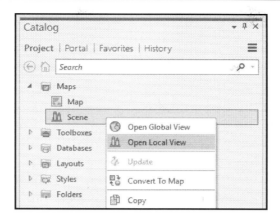

3. Activate the **Map** tab in the ribbon and select the **Explore** tool.

4. Press the scroll wheel on your mouse down and push your mouse away from you slightly to rotate the map view on the 3D plane until it looks similar to the following screenshot. It does not need to be exact, just close to the example:

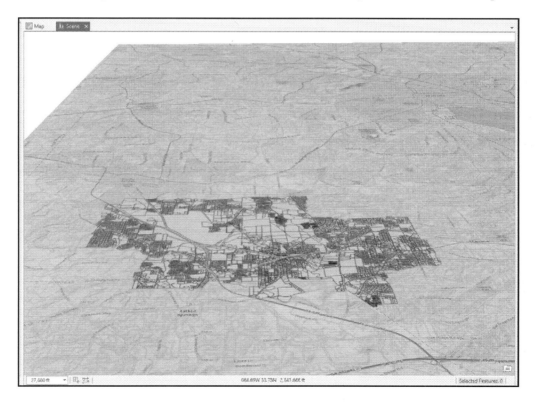

5. Place your mouse pointer near the center of the parcels layer and roll your wheel away from you to zoom in. Continue to work with the scroll wheel until you get comfortable with how it allows you to navigate within a 3D scene.

6. Click on the **Add Data** tool and navigate to `IntroArcGISPro Exercise 2A.gdb` located under **Projects** and the **Databases** folder. Click on the **bldg_footprints** feature class and click **Select**.

7. Rename the **bldg_footprints** layer to `Building Footprints` using the same process you learned in previous steps.

8. Select the **Building Footprints** layer in the **Contents** pane and drag it up to **3D Layers**, as depicted in the following screenshot. This will allow you to apply 3D symbology to this layer:

If you are unable to move the **Building Footprints** layer to **3D Layers**, you may need to ensure that you are looking at the **List by Drawing Order** option in the **Contents** pane. This is the first button located at the top of the pane.

9. Save your project.

10. If needed, activate the **Map** tab in the ribbon. Then, click on the **Bookmarks** tool and select **Buildings bookmark**. This will zoom the scene, meaning you can see the building as they overlay the ground elevation.

11. Select the **Buildings** layer once again and click on the **Appearance** tab. Notice it looks quite a bit different from what you saw when working with a 2D map.

12. In the **Extrusion** group, click on the small arrowhead below **Type** and select **Base Height**. This will allow you to extrude the building based on their estimated height, meaning you can see the differing heights of each building in a 3D view.

13. In the **Field** drop-down option next to **Type**, select **Estimated Height** from the list that appears, as shown in the following screenshot. This is the estimated height of each building:

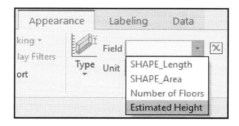

Your map should now look similar to the following screenshot. The colors of your buildings may be different, but that is to be expected. Remember that ArcGIS Pro assigns colors randomly to layers as they are added to a map or scene:

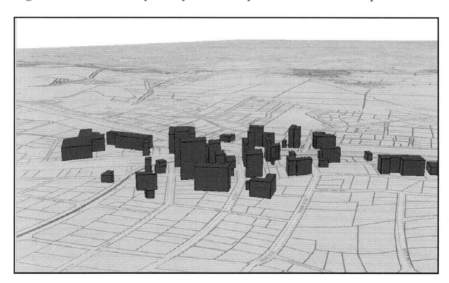

You have just added and symbolized a 3D layer in ArcGIS Pro. You can now see the 3D relationships between the different buildings within the city. The ability to visualize data in 3D opens up a whole new way to look at data. It can allow you to see relationships between features in one or more layers that you might not see in a 2D view. Any layer can be visualized in 3D. This capability is not limited to just layers dealing with infrastructure. You will learn more about creating 3D scenes in `Chapter 4`, *Creating 3D Scenes*.

Challenge

Using the knowledge you have gained in this exercise, try to change the symbols for the buildings in the scene to one of the gray building footprint symbols found in the symbol gallery you saw in the previous step. Changing symbology for a 3D layer is very similar to the method you used to change the symbology for the railroad and building footprints layers in the 2D map.

Summary

In this chapter, you have learned how to use the ArcGIS Pro ribbon interface and the terminology associated with it. As you have seen, the ribbon provides easy and quick access to tools. The contextual tabs make specific tools associated with tasks and items available to you with minimal clicking or searching.

Many of the tools in the ribbon work in conjunction with panes that appear to the right side of the interface. These panes provide access to the settings and inputs used by the selected tool to refine its function.

Putting these tools to use, you were able to work with both 2D and 3D data, as well as labeling features and changing their symbology. You also learned how the Explore tool has a wide variety of functions, from navigating in the map to retrieving data.

In the next chapter, you will explore how to create a new 2D map in a project. This will include various methods for adding a new map, importing a map from external sources, and making copies of existing maps. You will also look at different ways in which you can add new layers to a map.

2
Section 2: Visualizing, Maintaining, and Analyzing Data

In this section, you will learn how to visualize, maintain, and analyze GIS data.

To visualize your data, you will learn how to create 2D maps and 3D scenes. This will include how to add, manage, and configure layers. Then you will learn the basic skills needed to maintain your GIS data, both spatial and tabular. Lastly, you will examine how to perform simple analyses using the tools found in ArcGIS Pro.

In this section, we will cover the following chapters:

- Chapter 3, *Creating 2D Maps*
- Chapter 4, *Creating 3D Scenes*
- Chapter 5, *Creating and Working with Projects*
- Chapter 6, *Creating a Layout*
- Chapter 7, *Creating Map Books using Map Series*
- Chapter 8, *Learning to Edit Spatial Data*
- Chapter 9, *Learning about Editing Tabular Data*
- Chapter 10, *Performing Analysis with Geoprocessing Tools*

3
Creating 2D Maps

One of the key functions of a **Geographic Information System (GIS)** is to visualize data. In a GIS, we use maps as our primary method for visualizing data. Maps allow us to see and analyze the spatial relationships between features in one or more layers. We create maps for many different reasons. Often, we are trying to show the location of specific assets or to highlight attributes associated with features, such as a parcel's zoning classification or a pipe size. Sometimes we wish to show the results of the analysis we have performed.

So, each map we create in ArcGIS Pro has a reason for existing. This purpose will help to dictate what layers we include in the map and how they are visualized. There is no limit to the number of layers a map can contain. However, it is possible to have so many layers in a map that it distracts from the purpose. As the author of the map, you must strike a balance between the amount of information you include in a map and its overall purpose.

Each layer in a map has a set of properties. This includes things such as the source, symbology, visibility ranges, coordinate system and more. When you create a map and add layers, you must configure many of these settings manually to ensure your map is legible and supports its intended purpose.

As you have already experienced, ArcGIS Pro allows you to create both 2D and 3D maps within a project. In this chapter, you will focus on creating a 2D map. These have been the mainstay of GIS since it was first developed over 50 years ago. In this chapter, you will learn how to do the following:

- Creating and configuring 2D maps
- Creating a new map
- Skill challenge

Technical requirements

In order to complete this chapter, you will need the following:

- **ArcGIS Pro 2.6—Basic** or higher license
- An internet connection
- Exercise data

It is also recommended that you complete all previous chapters before starting this one unless you have experience of using ArcGIS Pro.

Creating and configuring 2D maps

ArcGIS Pro provides several methods for creating new 2D maps within a project. As you will learn later, creating a new project using a template can automatically create a new map that you can build on. Of course, you can also add new maps to existing projects as needed. ArcGIS Pro supports several methods for creating or adding maps to existing projects. Which method is best will depend on several factors, including personal preference. It also depends on whether the map already exists in another project or the current one, or if it is a map document file from the old ArcMap application ArcGIS Pro is replacing.

Another thing to remember is that an ArcGIS Pro project can contain multiple maps. It is not uncommon for a single ArcGIS Pro project to contain multiple maps required to support daily operations. For example, if you are the GIS manager for a city, you might have most maps in a single project, such as zoning, land use, voting districts, police zones, tax districts, and more. That might make it easier to manage your GIS files and maps.

A map only provides a canvas for displaying your data to support its purpose. You must add and configure the content. This normally means adding layers that represent the features you wish to display within your map. Just as there are multiple methods for creating new maps, there is also more than one way to add new layers to a map.

You will now investigate different methods for creating new maps and adding layers.

Creating a new map

Maps are the primary way we visualize data in a GIS. As already mentioned, you may need to have multiple maps in your projects to support the various needs of your organization or clients. Each map you create should have a specific purpose. The purpose will help you determine what layers you will need, and which need to be the primary focus.

One thing to always be mindful of is map readability. You can put too much information into a single map. So to keep from making a single map too cluttered, you might actually need to create multiple maps that focus on one to two primary layers.

So how do you create new maps within ArcGIS Pro? There are many ways, as follows:

- One way is using the **Insert** tab on the ribbon. From there, you can choose the **New Map** button, as shown in the following screenshot:

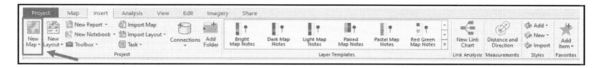

- Another way is to right-click on **Maps** within the **Project** pane and select **New Map** as shown here:

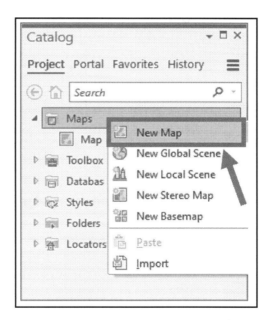

- Another way is to import an existing map. ArcGIS Pro allows you to import maps in multiple formats including map documents, map packages, and map files. Each of these has a unique file extension. The following table provides more detail on this:

Item	File extension	Software used to create it
Map Document	`.mxd`	**ArcMap**
Map Package	`.mpk`	**ArcMap** or **ArcCatalog**
	`.mpkx`	ArcGIS Pro
Map File	`.mapx`	ArcGIS Pro
ArcScene Document (3D)	`.sxd`	**ArcScene**
ArcGlobe Document (3D)	`.3dd`	**ArcGlobe**

As you can see in the preceding table, when you import an existing map from one of these files, the new map it creates in your project will contain the layers along with all of their settings such as the symbology and labels that were in the map you imported. This provides a way to help quickly populate a new project with items so you can get to work faster. This is especially true for those who are migrating to ArcGIS Pro from ArcGIS Desktop.

It should be noted that the last two file types listed are actually 3D maps. When you import those into ArcGIS Pro, they will create new 3D scenes in the project. You will learn more about those in the next chapter.

Now that you know some of the different methods for creating new maps in your project, it is time to put that knowledge to use in the following exercises. You will start by adding new layers to an existing map and configuring them. Then you will add a completely new map to a project and add layers to it.

Exercise 3A – Adding and configuring layers in a map

You have been asked by the Community and Economic Development Director for the City of Trippville to prepare several maps for a business that wishes to open a location in the city. He needs a map that shows the locations of all commercial property in the city. Then he wants another that shows all commercial parcels over 1 acre, but less than 3 acres in size.

In this exercise, you will create a new project using the Map template. You will create the first map requested by the director. This will require you to add and configure several layers using various methods. You will add the second map to the project in another exercise.

Step 1 – Creating the project

In this step, you will create the project that will be used to develop the maps requested by the Community and Economic Development Director:

1. Open ArcGIS Pro.
2. In the ArcGIS Pro start window, select **Map** under **New** and **Blank Templates**, as shown in the following screenshot:

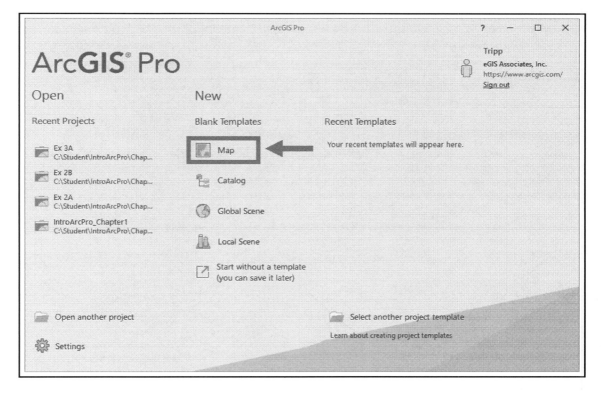

3. In the **Name** box, type `Your Name_Ex3A` (that is, in this case, `Tripp_Ex3A`).

In general, it is always best to avoid using spaces and special characters when naming anything in ArcGIS Pro. Sometimes ArcGIS Pro will allow them and other times not. This can also change from one version to the next. So, I recommend just not using them to avoid problems. Underscores are acceptable, as you can see in this exercise.

4. For the location, click on the **Browse** button located at the end of the box or cell. It looks like a small open file folder with a blue arrow. This will open the **Select a folder to store the project** window.

5. In the left panel of the **Select a folder to store project** window, click on **Computer**, located below **Project**.

6. In the right panel of the window, double-click on **(C:)** or the drive in which you installed the exercise data.

7. Then double-click on the Student | IntroArcGISPro folder.

8. Select the My Projects folder and click **OK**. Your **Create a New Project** window should now look like the following screenshot; of course, the project name will include your name and not mine:

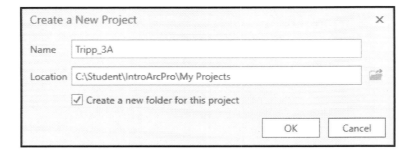

You have just created a new ArcGIS Pro project using the included Map project template. The new project you just created should open with a single empty map.

If you mistakenly double-click on the My Projects folder, you can click on the small *up* arrow located to the left of the displayed path at the top of the **Select a folder to store the project** window to take you back to the previous folder.

Eventually, you will add and configure new layers on this map. You will learn more about how to create new projects in Chapter 5, *Creating and Working with Projects*.

Step 2 – Connecting data sources

Creating a new project is just the first step. Now you need to connect to the folders and databases you need to use for this project. You will connect to the `Trippville_GIS` geodatabase and the folders that contain other files you need:

1. In the **Catalog** pane, expand the `Databases` folder by clicking on the small arrowhead located to the left. This will allow you to see the list of all currently connected databases.

 Questions: *What databases are currently connected to this project? Which geodatabase is the default geodatabase?*

You should only see a single database connection. This is the project database that was created with the new project. Typically, most organizations already have an existing GIS database. For this exercise, the city of Trippville is no different. It already has a GIS database. You just need to connect to it to use the existing GIS data.

2. Right-click on the `Databases` folder in the **Catalog** pane and select **Add Database**, as illustrated in the following screenshot:

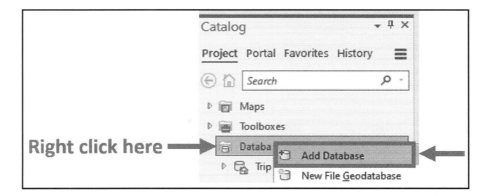

3. In the **Select Existing Geodatabase** window, navigate to
   C:\Student\IntroArcPro\Databases and select Trippville_GIS.gdb by
   clicking on **Computer** in the left panel. Then double-click on the C: | Student |
   IntroArcGISPro | Databases folder. Lastly, select the Trippville_GIS.gdb
   geodatabase and click **OK**.

   The Trippville_GIS.gdb database should now appear under the Databases
   folder in the **Catalog** pane. This means you have successfully connected to the
   database and will be able to use the data contained in that database.

   Now you will also need to connect to a folder that contains files you will also
   need to complete this project.

4. Right-click on the Folders folder in the **Catalog** pane, then select **Add Folder
   Connection**.

5. In the **Add Folder Connection** window, navigate to
   C:\Student\IntroArcPro\ and select Chapter3 using the same method you
   did to navigate and connect to the **Trippville_GIS** geodatabase. Click **OK** once
   you have selected the Chapter3 folder.

   You have now connected to all the resources you will need to complete this
   project. Your **Catalog** pane should look like this if you have connected to all the
   project items as directed:

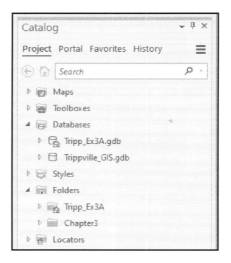

6. Save your project.

Establishing these connections may seem to be a hassle and something you do not do in other applications. This is true to an extent. However, in GIS we often work with large datasets that can be gigabytes to terabytes in size. This is why a project or map does not actually store the data we use but instead connects and references it. That allows us to work with large datasets without crashing the computer.

The good thing is you only need to establish these connections once in a project. After you save the project those connections are remembered and will be there every time you open the project.

Step 3 – Adding layers

Now that you have created your project and established connections to your data, it is time to begin on the maps requested by the Community and Economic Development Director. You will start with the first one he requested, showing the location of all the commercially zoned property within the city.

You will use the map created when you generated your new project using the project template as your starting point. You will add and configure a few layers using various methods.

The first layer you want to add is the city limits so everyone will know which areas are in the city and those that are out:

1. In the **Catalog** pane, expand the Databases folder and then the Trippville_GIS.gdb geodatabase. Once expanded, you should see that it contains many feature classes. This represents the entire GIS data for the city.
2. Expand the **Base** feature dataset so you can see its contents. Feature datasets are indicated by a unique icon that looks like three overlapping squares.
3. Select the **City_Limit** feature class. Holding your mouse button down, drag the **City_Limits** feature class into the map view. Once your mouse pointer is over the map view, release your mouse button.

   The city limits have now been added to your map using a drag and drop method. This is one of the methods you can use to add a new layer from resources connected in the **Catalog** pane. Also, notice that the map scale and zoom location changed.

You were automatically zoomed into the extents of the **City_Limit** layer you just added, as shown in the following screenshot. Remember, your colors may differ:

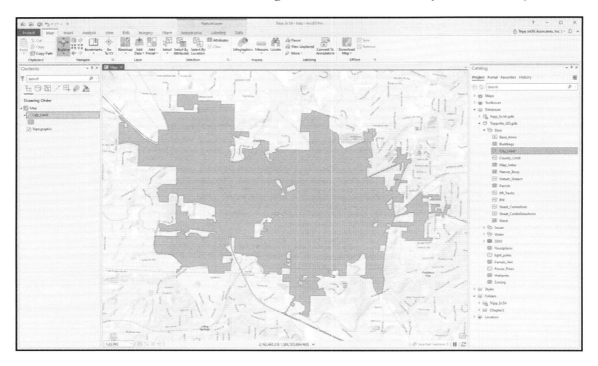

In a new map, the first layer you add is special. First, it sets the coordinate system used by the map. All future layers will be projected to match the coordinate system of the first layer added, if they use different coordinate systems. This is called *projecting on the fly*. Second, your map will automatically zoom to the extent of the data contained in that first layer, as you have now seen. It will only do this for the first layer added at the time it is added.

Now you will need to change the symbology for the **City_Limit** layer. As you can see, the **City_Limit** layer currently has a solid fill that is hiding the information underneath. You will change the symbology for this layer so you can see through the layer but still see the boundary.

4. Double-click on **City_Limit** in the **Contents** pane to open the **Layer Properties** window. In the **General** page, type City Limits in the name box to give the layer a new, more descriptive name and click **OK**.

5. Click on the symbol located below the **City_Limit** layer name in the **Contents** pane to open the **Symbology** pane on the right side of the interface.

6. The **Symbology** pane should open to the **Gallery** view. Select the **Black Outline (2 Points)**, which should be the second sample symbol in the top row, as indicated in the following screenshot:

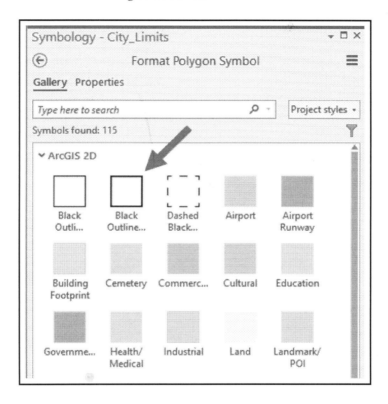

If you do not see the **Black Outline (2 Points)** sample symbol, use the search box at the top of the **Symbology** pane to search for it. You may also need to change the search option from **Project Styles** to **All Styles** as well.

7. Next, click on the **Properties** tab located at the top of the **Symbology** pane next to the **Gallery** tab.

8. Set the **Outline Width** from **2 pt** to **3 pt**. This will thicken the line representing the city limits boundary, so it stands out more. Click the **Apply** button located at the bottom of the **Symbology** pane.

9. Click on the **Map** tab on the ribbon. Then click on the **Add Data** button to add a few more layers.

10. Click on the `Databases` folder in the left panel of the **Add Data** window. Then double-click on the `Trippville_GIS.gdb` geodatabase in the right panel of the window to display the contents of the database.

11. Double-click on the **Base feature** dataset in the right panel of the window.

12. Holding down your Ctrl key, select the **County_Limit**, **Natwtr_Body**, **Natwtr_Stream**, and **RR_Tracks** feature classes.

13. Click **OK** to add these new layers to your map. Your map should now look similar to the following screenshot, but as always, remember that your colors may be different:

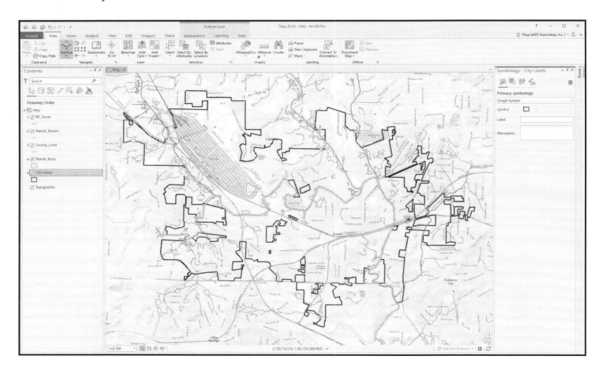

As you can see from the preceding screenshot, you have added five new layers to your map. For the first, you used the drag and drop method from the **Catalog** pane. The last four layers you added using the **Add Data** button on the **Map** tab. Now you know two different ways to add new layers to a map.

Next, you need to configure the symbology for the four new layers you just added.

14. Make the following changes to the layers you just added using the skills you have learned so far:
    - For the **RR_Tracks** layer, make sure of the following:
        - Set the **Name** field to `Railroad`.
        - In the **Symbol** field, type `Railroad` (Hint: Look in the Gallery).
    - For the **Natwtr_Stream** layer, make sure to do the following:
        - In the **Name** field, type `Streams & Creeks`.
        - In the **Symbol** field, type `Water (line)`.
        - Set the **Line Width** field to 1 pt.
    - For the **County_Limit** layer, make sure to do the following:
        - In the **Name** field, type `County Limit`.
        - Set the **Color** field to **Gray 60%**.
        - Set the **Line Width** field to 2 pt.
    - For the **Natwtr_Body** layer, make sure to do the following:
        - In the **Name** field, type `Lakes & Ponds`.
        - Set the **Color** field to **Yogo Blue**.
        - Set the **Outline Color** field to **Cretan Blue**.
        - Set the **Outline Width** field to 1 pt.

15. Close the **Symbology** pane when done.
16. In the **Contents** pane, ensure you are looking at the **List by Drawing Order**. That is the first button, the icon for which looks like a folder tree.
17. In the **Contents** pane, select the **County Limit** layer and drag it below **City Limits**.
18. Move the **Lakes & Ponds** layer above the **Streams & Creeks** layer in the **Contents** pane.

Your map should look like the following screenshot once you are done:

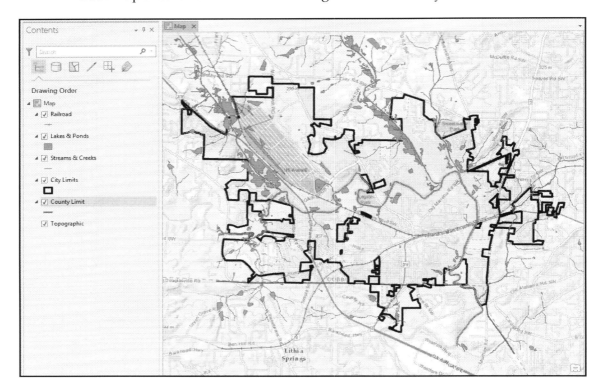

19. Once you have verified you have configured your layers successfully, save your project.

You have now added the layers needed to put what will be the primary layers into context. Some refer to the layers you have added as basemap layers. However, over time, Esri has developed a specific type of map called a basemap, which you can also create. A true ArcGIS basemap can be added to any map and all the layers it includes are automatically added. Esri publishes several basemaps via ArcGIS Online that anyone can use.

You can see one of those in the graphic showing the results of the exercise to this point. It is at the bottom of the layer list and is called **Topographic**. True basemaps have improved drawing performance, meaning they will redraw faster than normal layers. The drawback to using a true basemap is that your ability to do anything other than viewing the data is limited.

The last layer you need to add to this map to meet the request from the director is a layer that shows all parcels zoned as commercial. Luckily, another user has created a Zoning layer file. As you saw earlier, layer files can be used to set the symbology for a layer you already have on your map.

It can also be used to add a new layer that is already symbolized. You will use this layer file to add a Zoning layer to the map and then limit it to only show those parcels with a commercial zoning classification. The zoning classes that delineate commercial zoning include **GC (General Commercial)**, **GC-S (General Commercial with special stipulations)**, and **CBD (Central Business District)**.

20. Expand the `Folders` folder in the **Catalog** pane.

Question: *What folders are available in this project?*

21. Expand the `Chapter3` folder and right-click on the `Trippville Zoning.lyr` file. Select **Add to Current Map**, as illustrated in the following screenshot:

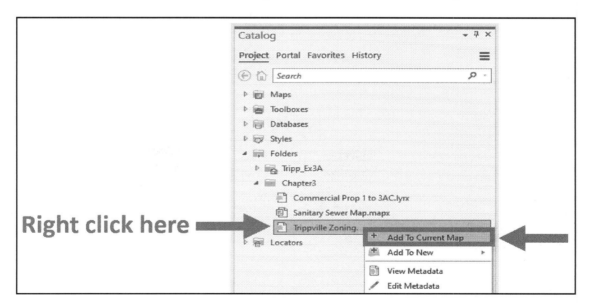

A layer file stores all the layer property settings including symbology, labeling, definition queries, field visibility, zoom scales, and more. This makes it easier to add the layer to other maps with the same settings. Layer files can help standardize how specific layers look across multiple maps and projects, as well as reducing the time needed to create new maps.

You have added a layer that shows the zoning of all parcels in the city. Now it is time to limit the layer to only the commercial zoning classes.

22. If needed, expand the symbology for the Zoning layer in the **Contents** pane by clicking on the small arrow located to the left of the Zoning layer so you can see all the zoning classifications and their associated symbology.

23. With the Zoning layer selected in the **Contents** pane, select the **Appearance** context tab in the ribbon.

24. Click on the **Symbology** drop-down menu and select **Unique Values** to open the **Symbology** pane on the right side of the interface, as illustrated in the following screenshot:

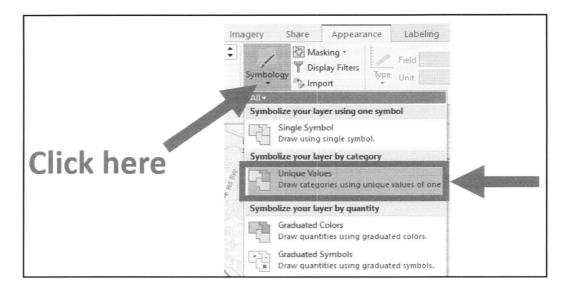

25. In the **Symbology** pane, select the row for the **PUD** symbol settings in the grid that shows the list of zoning classifications and their assigned symbols. You can click anywhere in the first three columns on the row for **PUD** in that grid to select the row, as shown in the following screenshot:

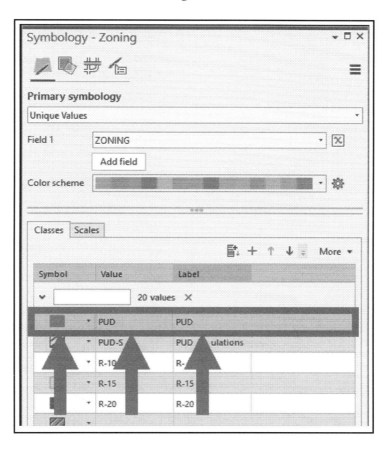

26. Holding down your *Shift* key, click on the row containing the value with **Mobile Home Park** to select all values from **PUD** to **Mobile Home Park**. If you are successful, your symbology pane should look like the following:

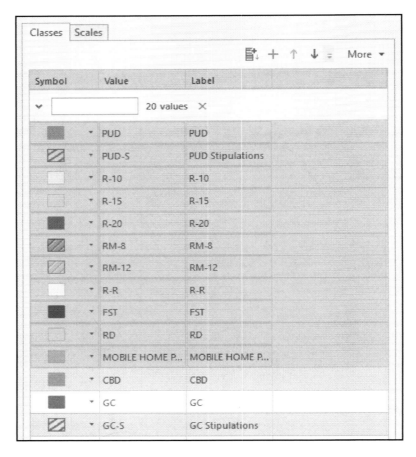

27. Right-click on one of the selected rows and select **Remove**.

You have just removed those selected symbology values from the layer legend that are not considered commercial zoning classifications. This removes those features that were assigned those values so they are no longer shown on the map. Remember, you are trying to create a map that only displays parcels with commercial zoning.

The layer is still displaying some parcels that are not commercially zoned. You will need to remove those classifications as well.

Removing classifications from the legend for the layer does not actually remove them from the source data the layer references. It just hides them from the display.

28. In the **Symbology** pane, select the row containing the **Government Land** value. It is located just below **GC-S**.
29. Holding your *Shift* key down, select the last row containing the OS value so you have all values from **Government Land** to **OS** selected.
30. Right-click on one of the selected rows and click on **Remove** from the menu that appears.

You have now isolated the commercially zoned parcels within the city, as requested by your director. Your map should now look like this:

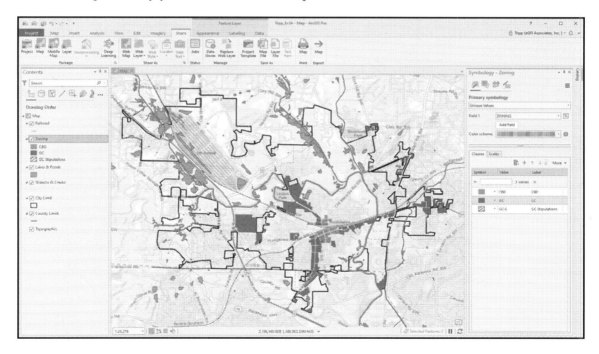

31. Once you have verified your map is correct, close the **Symbology** pane.

Step 4 – Saving a layer file

As you have now experienced, it took some effort to get the Zoning layer configured so it only displayed commercially zoned properties. So, to ensure you can easily retrieve these settings in the future, you will now create a layer file:

1. Select the Zoning layer in the **Contents** pane if needed.
2. Click on the **Share** tab in the ribbon.
3. In the **Save As** group, click the **Layer File** tool. This will open the **Save Layers As LYRX File** window.
4. In the left panel of the window, expand the **Computer** option so you can see all available choices.
5. Select **(C:)** from the list of resources. If you installed the exercise data on a different drive or location, select the appropriate drive.
6. Scroll down and double-click on the `Student` folder in the panel on the right side of the window.
7. Continue navigating to the `IntroArcGISPro | My Projects` folder.
8. Once you are in the `My Projects` folder, name the new layer file `Commercial_Only_ Zoning`, as illustrated in the following screenshot:

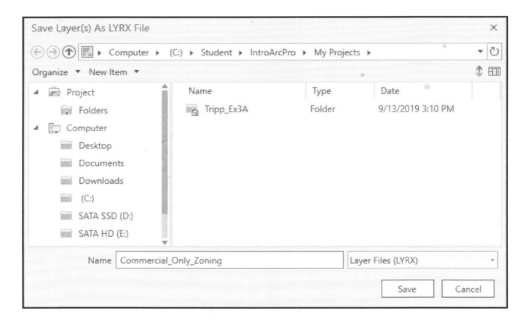

9. Once you have verified your file location and name, click the **Save** button to create your new layer file.

You have now created a new layer file. This will allow you to quickly add this same layer to other maps with these same exact settings. You experienced this at the beginning of the previous step when you added the Zoning layer to your map using a layer file. When you added the layer file, the Zoning layer was added to the map with the various Zoning classifications already symbolized.

Step 5 – Renaming your map

When you first created this project, the template you used automatically created a single map within the project that you have been working with. This single map was named **Map** automatically. Since a project can contain an unlimited number of maps, it is recommended that you provide each one with a unique name so users can easily identify which one they might need within the project:

1. In the **Catalog** pane, expand the **Maps** folder by clicking on the small arrowhead so you can see its contents.
2. Right-click on **Map** and select **Rename** from the menu that appears, as illustrated in the following screenshot:

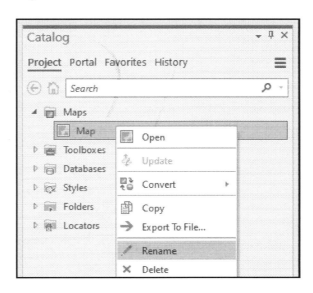

An edit box should appear around the name. This will allow you to type in a new name for the selected map.

3. In the edit box that appears around the name, type `Commercial Zoned Prop`. Press your *Enter* key when done.

4. In the **Content** pane, look at the name of the map located at the top of the layer list. It should reflect the new name you just entered.

 The **Catalog** pane is just one location that allows you to change the name of a map. You can also right-click on the map name in the **Contents** pane and select **Properties**. Then open the **General** tab in the **Map Properties** window and type in a new name. Double-clicking on the map name in the **Contents** pane will also open the **Map Properties** window.

5. If you are not continuing to the next exercise, save and close your project. If you are continuing, just save your project and continue.

Congratulations! You just created a new map that shows all the parcels in the city that are zoned for commercial use. This required you to add a layer using a layer file. Then you had to filter out all the non-commercial zoned parcels by removing those symbology values.

Exercise 3B – Adding a new map to a project

In the last exercise, you created the first map asked for by the Community and Economic Development Director. Now you need to create the second map. This map needs to show those commercial properties over 1 acre in size, but less than 3 acres. You will use the map you created in the last exercise as a starting point by copying it.

Step 1 – Creating the new map in a project

In this step, you will create a new map in your project by copying the map you created in the last exercise:

1. If you closed ArcGIS Pro at the end of the last exercise, start the application and select the project you created in the previous exercise from the list of recently opened projects. It should be named `Your Name_Ex3AB` in the `C:\Student\IntroArcPro\My Projects\` folder.

2. In the **Catalog** pane, expand the **Maps** folder and right-click on the **Commercial Zoned Prop** map you created in the previous exercise. Then select **Copy** from the menu that appears.

3. Again, in the **Catalog** pane, right-click on the **Maps** folder and select **Paste**, as shown in the following screenshot:

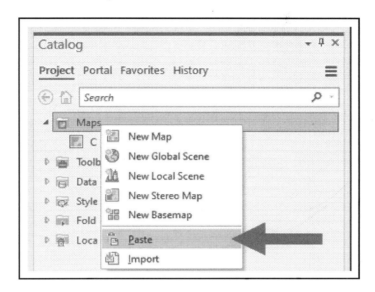

As you can see in the preceding screenshot, a **New Map** should appear in the **Maps** folder, named **Commercial Zoned Prop 1**. This new map is an exact copy of the map you created in the previous exercise. Starting with this copy will reduce the amount of effort needed to create the second map the Community and Economic Development Director has requested, which should only show commercially zoned properties greater than 1 acre but less than 3 acres in size. Next, you need to rename the new map you just created so it is not confused with the original.

4. Right-click on the new map you just created in the **Catalog** pane and select **Rename** from the menu that appears.
5. In the edit box that appears around the map name, rename the map as `Commercial Between 1 to 3 acres` and press *Enter* when you are done typing.
6. In the **Catalog** pane, right-click on the map you just renamed and select **Open**. The map should now appear in the view area of the ArcGIS Pro interface.
7. Save your project to ensure you do not lose any of the work you have done so far.

Step 2 – Filtering a layer with a definition query

Now that you have created the new map in your project, you need to filter the Zoning layer so it only shows those commercially zoned properties larger than 1 acre and less than 3 acres:

1. Right-click on the Zoning layer in the **Contents** pane and select **Properties**.
2. Select **Definition Query** in the right panel in the **Layer Properties** window.
3. Click on the **New Definition query** button located in the center of the right panel, as illustrated in the following screenshot:

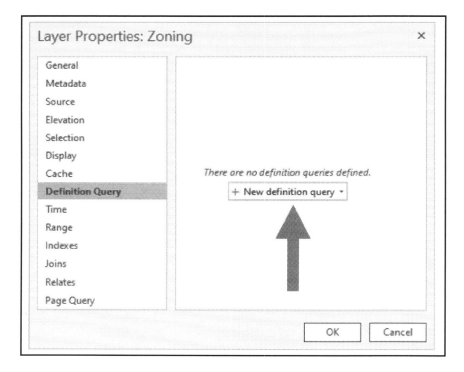

4. In the drop-down box located to the right-side of **Where**, select **ACRE_DEEDE**.
5. In the next drop-down box, set the operator to **is greater than**.
6. Type 1 in the next box in the query builder.

7. Verify your query looks like the following screenshot:

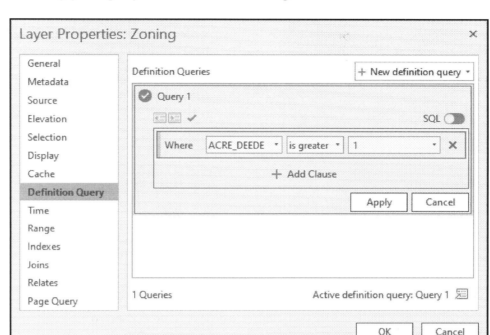

You have just built a query that will filter the Zoning layer so only those properties with a deeded acreage greater than 1 acre will be displayed. This is one part of what the director wanted to see. You now need to expand this query so it also filters out any properties greater than 3 acres.

8. Once you have verified the query, click the **Add Clause** option located below the query you have already built. Another line should appear below the clause you have already built.

9. Using that same process adds another clause that states **ACRE_DEEDE, is less than**, and **3**. It should look like the following screenshot:

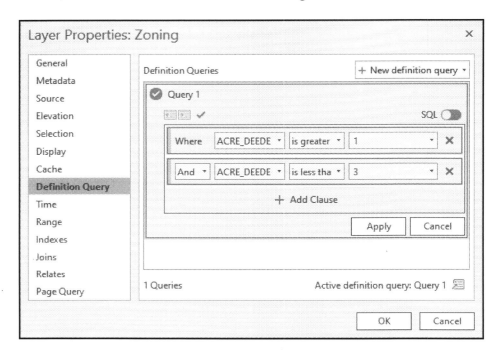

10. Once you have verified your query has been built correctly, click **Apply** and then **OK** to apply the definition query.

You have just added a filter to the Zoning layer so only those commercially zoned parcels that are over 1 acre and less than 3 acres in size are shown on the map. However, you need to add some more layers to place the zoning information into context. Let's do that now.

11. Save your project.
12. Expand the **Databases** folder in the **Catalog** pane.
13. Expand the **Trippville_GIS** database and the **Base** feature dataset so you can see their contents.

14. Right-click on the **Parcels** feature class and select **Add to Current map** from the menu that appears, as shown in the following screenshot:

As you can see in the preceding screenshot, the new **Parcels** layer should appear on your map. It will be added above the Zoning layer because it is a new polygon layer. You may notice that the **Parcels** layer is hiding the Zoning layer. So you now need to move the **Parcels** layer below the Zoning layer in the layer list.

15. In the **Contents** pane, drag the newly added **Parcels** layer below the **County Limit** layer. You can now see the commercially zoned parcels that are between 1 and 3 acres in size and how they relate to the rest of the parcels in and around the city.

16. Since ArcGIS Pro assigns a random color to new layers, you may need to adjust the symbology for the parcels layer so that the commercial zoning stands out more. Using the skills you have learned so far, adjust the symbology for the parcels so that it does not overpower the other layers, specifically the Zoning layer.

17. To also help the Zoning layer stand out more, you need to change your basemap. Click on the **Basemap** button on the **Map** tab. Select the **Light Gray Canvas**.

18. Click on the name for the Zoning layer so the edit box appears around it. Rename the layer to `Commercial Properties 1 to 3 AC`.

19. Right-click on the **City_Limit** layer and select **Zoom to Layer**.

20. In the **Scale** box located on the bottom left side of the map view, type `24000`.

Your map should look similar to the map shown in the following screenshot, although the color of the parcels may be different depending on what you chose:

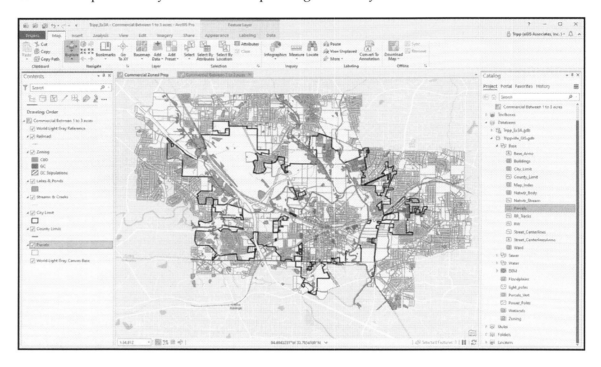

21. After you have verified that your map looks similar, save your project.

Step 3 – Adding annotations to the map

You have now successfully created the map the director asked for. However, after reviewing it with you, he has decided he wants to see road names and points of interest added to the map as well.

Luckily, you already have an annotation feature class in the **Trippville_GIS** database that contains these. You will now need to add that annotation geodatabase to your map:

1. Expand the **Databases** folder in the **Catalog** pane and then expand the **Trippville_GIS** geodatabase so you can see its contents.

2. In the **Trippville_GIS** geodatabase, expand the **Base** feature dataset so you can see the feature classes it contains.

3. Click on **Base_Anno** and drag it into the map view to add it to your map.

4. In the **Contents** pane, right-click on the **City_Limit** layer and select **Zoom to Layer** from the menu that appears.

5. In the ribbon, click on the **Map** tab. Next, click on the **Bookmarks** button and select **New bookmark**.

6. In the **Create Bookmark** window, name your new bookmark as Entire City. Then add This bookmark will zoom the map to the extents of the City_Limit layer as the description. Lastly, click **OK** to create the new bookmark.

Bookmarks allow you to return to a specific location and scale within a map. They are very useful to ensure you can print a map at a specific scale or review specific locations during a meeting.

7. In the **Map** tab in the ribbon, select the **Explore** tool.

8. Zoom into your map until you are able to clearly see the annotation layer you just added.

9. Click on **Bookmark** again. This time, select the entire city to return your map to the original view.

10. Save your project.

You have now successfully created the two maps requested by the director. You created the first map, which showed all the commercially zoned parcels within the city. You then created a new map that limited the commercially zoned parcels shown to only those between 1 and 3 acres in size.

Exercise 3C – Using map and layer files

The director has decided he wants an additional map added to this project. He needs to know the location of the city's sewer system in relation to the commercial properties that are between 1 and 3 acres in size. This is because the new business wants to be able to connect to the city's sewer system.

Luckily, you have a map file of the city's sewer system that was created for another project. This will serve as a great starting point for this new map you need to add to your project. Map files allow you to share previously created maps so they can be used in other projects without having to start over from scratch.

Once you import the map file, you will then need to add the commercial properties that are between 1 and 3 acres. To make that easier, you will create a layer file from the map you just created and then use that file to add the layer to the sewer map.

Step 1 – Adding a new map using a map file

In this step, you will add a map of the city of Trippville's sanitary sewer system using an existing map file. This will add a new pre-configured map to your project. You will now add items to the map:

1. If you closed **ArcGIS Pro** after the last exercise, launch the application and open the project %Your Name%Ex3A.
2. Right-click on the **Maps** folder in the **Catalog** pane and select **Import** from the bottom of the menu that appears.
3. In the **Import** window, select **Folders** located under **Project** in the left panel of the window. If you do not see **Folders**, you may need to expand the **Project** tree by clicking on the small arrowhead located to the left.
4. Double-click on the Chapter3 folder in the right panel of the **Import** window.
5. Select the Sanitary Sewer Map.mapx file and click **OK**.

Your project should now have a new map that shows the location of the Trippville sewer system, as in the following screenshot:

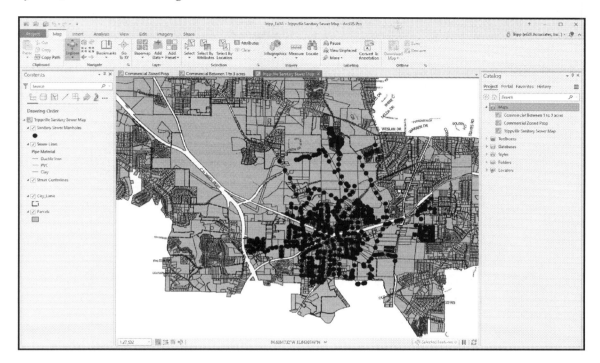

Let's move on to the next step to learn about creating a layer file and using it.

Step 2 – Creating and using a layer file

Now you need to add a layer showing the location of the commercial properties that are between 1 and 3 acres in size. You will create a layer file from the previous map you created and then use this layer file to add the new layer to the sewer map:

1. Select the tab for the **Commercial Between 1 to 3 acres** map located at the top of the view area of the interface.

If you closed this map after the previous exercises, you will need to open it. To do that, expand the `Maps` folder in the **Catalog** pane and right-click on the **Commercial Between 1 to 3 acres** map. Then select **Open** from the menu.

2. Right-click on the **Commercial Properties 1 to 3 AC** layer in the **Contents** pane. Go to the **Share** option and choose **Save as Layer File**. The **Save Layer(s) As LYRX File** window will open.

If you do not see the **Save as Layer File** button as being available, you most likely have the name of the map selected and not the layer. Go back to the **Contents** pane and verify that you have the layer selected and not the map. Once you have the layer selected the **Save as Layer File** button should be available to use.

3. Select **Folders** in the left panel under **Project**. Double-click on the Chapter3 folder in the right panel of the window.

4. Name the new layer file as Commercial Prop 1 to 3AC and click **Save**. If asked whether you wish to overwrite an existing file, click **Yes**.

5. Click back on the **Trippville Sanitary Sewer Map** tab at the top of the view area to activate it.

6. Click on the **Add Data** button located in the **Map** tab on the ribbon.

7. Select the Folders | Chapter3 folder.

8. Select the Commercial Prop 1 to 3AC.lyrx file you created and click on the **OK** button.

You have just added to your map a layer showing the commercial properties that are between 1 and 3 acres in size that are located in the city. Now, the director will be able to see which of those parcels is near the sewer system and thus be able to connect to the city's sewer service. Using the layer file made adding this new layer much easier and ensured that the symbology is consistent with the other maps within the project.

Step 3 – Labeling the pipe sizes

Now, the director wants you to label the pipe sizes for the sewer system so he can ensure there is enough capacity to handle the load the new business may add to the system. You need to turn on and configure labeling for the sewer line layer:

1. Select the **Sewer Lines** layer in the **Contents** pane.

2. Now you need to determine which field contains the size of the sewer pipes. Right-click on the **Sewer Lines** layer and select **Attribute Table**. This will open the attribute table in a pane located below the main map view.

3. Scroll through the available attribute fields to determine which field contains the pipe size.

Question: *What is the field name or alias that contains the size of the sewer pipes?*

4. Close the attribute table for the **Sewer Lines** layer.
5. Ensure the **Sewer Lines** layer is still selected in the **Contents** pane. Then, click on the **Labeling** tab in the ribbon.
6. Click on the **Label** button to turn on the labels for the **Sewer Line** layer.
7. Set the **Field** to the one you identified in the previous question.
8. At the current full view of the map, it is hard to read the pipe sizes. So, you will set a scale visibility range for the labels that will allow them to become visible at a scale that makes them easier to read. In the drop-down list located next to **Out Beyond** on the **Labeling** tab, in the **Visibility Range**, select **1:10,000**. The size labels should disappear.
9. Zoom in until the size labels appear.
10. To make the pipe size labels stand out a bit more, make them bold and adjust the color on the **Labeling** tab in the **Text Symbol** group tab.
11. The placement of the labels is not optimum, so you need to adjust the placement. Click on the small arrow with the line above it in the **Label Placement** group tab. You should see several placement options listed that were not shown before.
12. Select the **Water (Line) placement** option.

We will now move on to the next step.

Step 4 – Configuring label conflict and placement options

You have successfully added the pipe size labels to your map. However, there are some additional configuration options that might improve how they look and perform. You will now make some adjustments to these:

1. Right-click on the **Sewer Lines** layer and select **Label Properties**. This will open the **Label Class** pane on the right side of the interface. This pane allows you to make further adjustments to the labeling configuration settings to refine their appearance.

2. Click on the **Position** tab located near the top of the pane. Then select the **Conflict Resolution** icon, which looks like three textboxes stacked on top of one another.

3. Expand **Remove duplicate labels** in the **Label Class** pane.

4. In the drop-down menu that appears underneath, select **Remove within a fixed distance**.

5. Set the **Search radius** to **500** and the units to **Map units**. It should look like this:

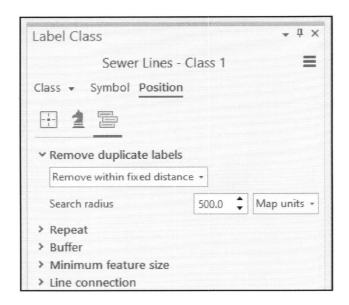

That makes the labels appear a little less cluttered. However, you are not done yet. There are still some adjustments that will improve the labels further.

6. Expand the **Minimum feature size** option in the **Label Class** pane.

7. Set the **Minimum for labeling size** to **100** and the units to **Map units**. This will further reduce the clutter in the map.

8. Save your project and close ArcGIS Pro unless you wish to attempt the following skill challenge or try applying other labeling option settings on your own.

Continue to try other labeling options to see how they impact the placement of the labels and the overall appearance of the map. Pan and zoom to other places on the map to see whether your settings still work well in different locations.

Skill challenge

The Community and Economic Development Director was very impressed with the maps you created – so much so that he has another project that he would like your help with. A company would like to open a new manufacturing center within the city, so they are looking for a parcel that has a zoning classification of "light or heavy industrial" that is situated near the railroad, and can easily be provided with both water and sewer services. The parcels need to be 5 to 10 acres in size.

Using the skills you have learned, create a new project that contains the following maps for this scenario:

1. A map showing the location of all heavy and light industrial properties within the city (zoning codes HI and LI).
2. A map showing the location of all industrial-zoned parcels between 5 and 10 acres in size.
3. A map showing the location of industrial-zoned parcels between 5 and 10 acres along with the sewer system. Symbolize and label the sewer system the same way you did in *Exercise 3C*.
4. A map showing the location of the industrial-zoned parcels between 5 and 10 acres, along with the water lines and fire hydrants. Symbolize the water lines based on their size. The symbology for the fire hydrants is up to you.

Summary

In this chapter, you learned how to create a new project and add multiple 2D maps to it. You were introduced to several methods to add new maps to your project including using a project template, adding a blank map, and using a pre-configured map file. Once you created the maps, you then used various methods to add new layers.

These skills form the foundation needed to be a successful user of ArcGIS Pro. Without maps, you are not able to make use of some of the more advanced capabilities of ArcGIS Pro such as performing data edits, analyzing data, and sharing your data with others either via printed maps or digital formats. All of these capabilities start with a map.

In the next chapter, you will continue to build on these skills. You will learn how to create 3D maps that allow you to view data in a more realistic-looking environment. The ability to view data in 3D is an enhancement ArcGIS Pro provides over Esri's older desktop software, which did not allow users to view data in 3D natively.

Further reading

If you would like to explore the concepts covered in this chapter in greater detail, the following resources are recommended:

- *Mapping with ArcGIS Pro*, by Amy Rock and Ryan Malhoski
- *Adding Symbology Styles to ArcGIS Pro*, a video from eGIS Associates, available at `https://www.youtube.com/watch?v=iBfmcbsZg2Alist=PLKPzofPslSJ_xlzX35oBwE0PPJc0SB41eindex=13t=12s`
- *ArcMap vs ArcGIS Pro - Comparing these two GIS applications from Esri*, a video from eGIS Associates, available at `https://www.youtube.com/watch?v=4_OOOQbLZDUlist=PLKPzofPslSJ_xlzX35oBwE0PPJc0SB41eindex=12t=234s`

Creating 3D Scenes

4

As the world becomes a more crowded place, the need to view data in a 3D environment grows. With the infrastructure of modern urban areas expanding both up and down as well as outward, the importance of seeing what is above and below the ground is becoming critical to planning new projects, responding to emergencies, and managing the infrastructure.

ArcGIS Pro allows users to create 3D maps or Scenes natively. In the past, this required users to have extensions such as **3D Analyst** for ArcGIS. The ability to create 3D Scenes natively in ArcGIS Pro opens up a whole new world and way to view your data quite literally.

This chapter will provide you with the skills to extrude data from above or below the ground to see things such as verifying whether there is an existing natural gas line that interferes with a new sewer line that is being planned, or whether the new office building that is being constructed will obstruct the mayor's view of the park. In short, ArcGIS Pro allows you to visualize your data in the same way as it exists in the real world.

The following topics will be covered in this chapter:

- Understanding 3D Scenes
- Learning about elevations and how to use them

Technical requirements

Rendering 3D Scenes requires more computer resources than traditional 2D maps. In order to successfully complete this chapter, you will need a computer that meets or exceeds the requirements detailed in the *Author system recommendations* section outlined in Chapter 1, *Introducing ArcGIS Pro*.

If your computer only meets the minimum system specifications as listed by the **Environmental Systems Research Institute** (**Esri**), then you will have difficulty completing the exercises in this chapter.

Understanding 3D Scenes

ArcGIS Pro allows you to easily add 3D maps to your projects. 3D maps are referred to as **Scenes** in ArcGIS Pro. When you add a new Scene to a project, you select which type or view mode you wish to use. ArcGIS Pro supports two modes—namely, **Global** and **Local**.

A **Global Scene** is designed to support large areas where the curvature of the earth has a noticeable impact. This might be used to show the track of a hurricane or the path of a gas pipeline that crosses many states or countries, as illustrated in the following screenshot:

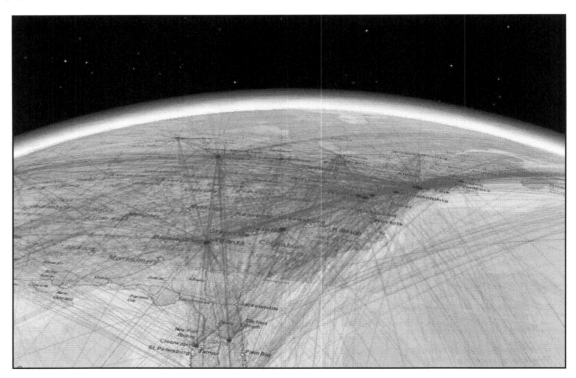

The previous screenshot is an example of a Global Scene that shows airline flight paths over the east coast of the United States. The curvature of the earth certainly has an impact on these over long distances. Because of the extent of the area covered by a Global Scene, these typically use a geographic coordinate system.

A **Local Scene** is designed for smaller areas where the curvature of the earth has less impact, and most often uses a projected coordinate system. A Local Scene might be used by a city to show its downtown area, by engineers planning a new road extension with a bridge, or by a cell phone company to site a new cell tower within a community.

The following screenshot shows an example of a Local Scene that depicts the buildings in a specific project area. They have been extruded vertically based on their height to create a 3D view, showing how each building is related to those surrounding it, both horizontally and vertically:

Scenes do not have to be limited to displaying infrastructure. Any data can be visualized in 3D. In the following screenshot, you can see a map showing the number of **Geographic Information Systems Certified Professional (GISP)** in each state in the continental United States:

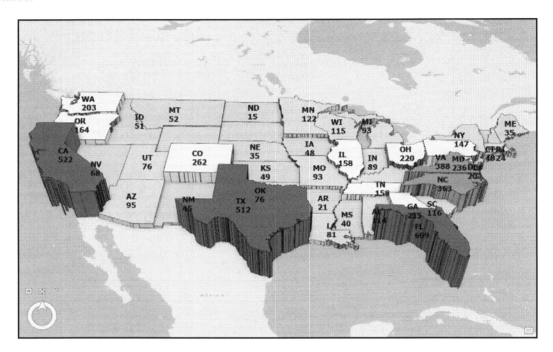

From the previous screenshot, the information could have been displayed in a traditional 2D map using graduated colors. But as you can see, extruding each state vertically based on the number of GIS-certified professionals in each adds a new level to the map, which makes it very easy to see which states have the most GIS-certified professionals and which have the least.

This same type of visualization technique could be used to view the total population of an area, average rainfall amounts, median age, number of crimes, and so on with an even greater impact than when using traditional 2D maps. Scenes can be an effective way of communicating the results of your analysis or highlighting differences, in addition to displaying features in real-world views.

You will have an opportunity to put the knowledge you have just gained into practice with a hands-on exercise. The exercise that follows will have you create a simple Scene in ArcGIS Pro.

Exercise 4A – Creating a simple 3D Scene

In this exercise, you will create a simple 3D Scene using an **Esri project template**. You will add and extrude a layer so that it has a height above the ground level. To accomplish this, you will start by creating a new project that will contain a new Scene. You will then add both 2D and 3D layers to the Scene. Once you have done that, you will extrude the 3D layers so that they appear to rise above the ground.

Step 1 – Creating a project and 3D Scene

In this step, you will create a new project using one of the templates included with ArcGIS Pro. This template will include a Local 3D Scene automatically. To create the project and the 3D Scene, we will use the following steps:

1. Open ArcGIS Pro.
2. In the **ArcGIS Pro Start** window, select the **Local Scene** template located in the **New** column, as illustrated in the following screenshot. This will create a new project that contains a single Local 3D Scene:

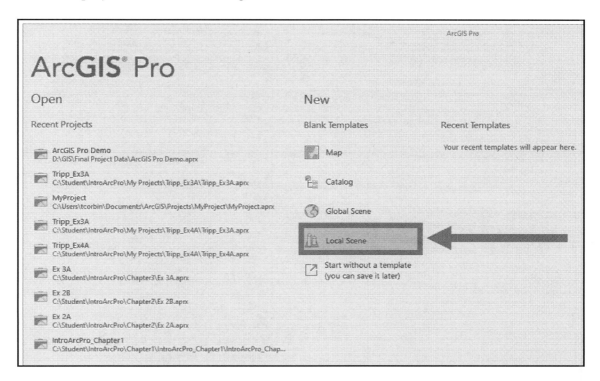

3. Name your new project %your name%Ex4A (for example, TrippEx4A) and set the location to C:\Student\IntroArcPro\My Projects, then click **OK**.

Your new project should open with a Scene already created. The Scene will be empty, with the exception of a basemap. In your **Contents** pane, you should see two categories—that is, **2D Layers** and **3D Layers**. 2D layers are draped across your ground elevation surface. 3D layers may be extruded above—or possibly below—the ground surface.

In the next step, you will add a layer and make it 3D.

Step 2 – Adding a layer

In this step, you will add several layers to your map. Some layers will remain 2D layers and will serve as a general backdrop. You will make the Building layer 3D and extrude it to show the height of the buildings by following these steps:

1. Make the **Map** tab active in the ribbon and select **Add Data**.
2. In the tree located in the left panel of the **Add Data** window, expand **Computer**.
3. Then, select the C: drive in that same pane, as illustrated in the following screenshot:

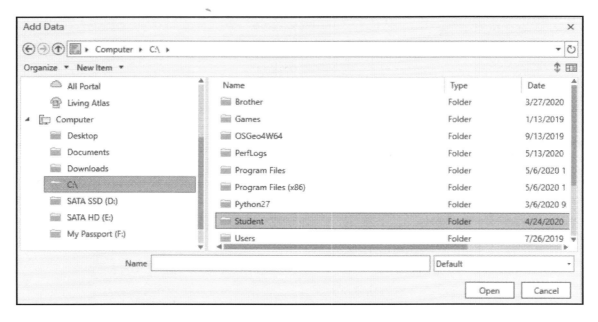

4. After that, double-click on **Student** | **IntroArcPro** | **Databases**.

5. Then, double-click on the **UnionCity** geodatabase.

6. While holding your *Ctrl* key down, select the following feature classes:
   - **Census_Blocks**
   - **CityLimits**
   - **Railroad**
   - **StreetRW**

7. Click on the **OK** button once you are done. The new layers are added to your Scene, and ArcGIS Pro automatically zooms you to the extent of the new layers that you have added.

8. Adjust the draw order of your layers in the **Contents** pane by dragging them into the following order:
   - **City Limits**
   - **Railroad**
   - **Street Rights-of-Way**
   - **Census Blocks**

 If you have trouble getting the layer order to change, make sure that you are on **List by Draworder** in the **Contents** pane. This is the only list which allows you to change the layer's draw order in a map or scene.

When complete, your **Contents** pane should look like the following screenshot:

9. Using the skills that you have learned so far, set the symbology for the layers (that you can see on your screen) you just added to the following settings:
    - For the **City Limits** layer, proceed as follows:
        - Select **No Color** for the **Color** property.
        - Select **Black** for the **Outline Color** property.
        - Set 3 pt for the **Outline Width** property.
    - For the **Railroad** layer, proceed as follows:
        - Select the Railroad symbol from the Gallery.
    - For the **Street Rights-of-Way** layer, proceed as follows:
        - Select **Black** for the **Color** property.
        - Set 1 pt for the **Line Width** property.
    - For the **Census Blocks** layer, there is no change for now.

Your Scene should now look very similar to the following screenshot:

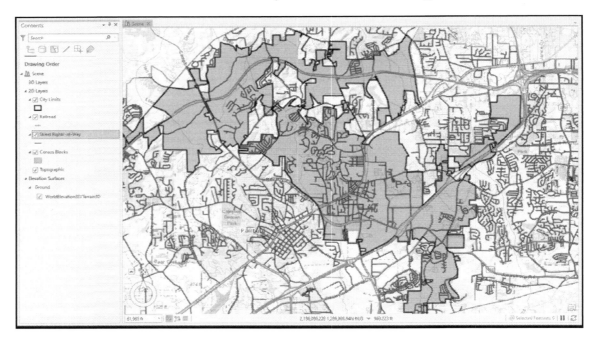

10. Finally, save your project.

When working in ArcGIS Pro, it is always a good idea to save your project regularly. This is certainly true when working in a Scene. Scenes take a lot of computer resources to render. This makes them more prone to issues, especially if your computer is on the lower end of hardware requirement specifications. Saving often means you will have to do less repetitive work if the application crashes.

You have added several layers to your Scene, but so far, they are all 2D. In the next step, you will take one of the 2D layers and make it a 3D one.

Step 3 – Making a 3D layer

In this step, you will turn the **Census Blocks** layer from a 2D layer into a 3D layer. You will extrude the height of each block polygon based on an attribute field, to show the total population in each. You will do this by following the next steps:

1. In the **Contents** pane, select the **Census Blocks** layer. Then, drag and drop it from the **2D Layers** category to the **3D Layers** category.

   When you do this, you may notice that parts of the Census Block outlines disappear. This is because some of the features contained in the 3D layer are now below the elevation surface.

2. Make sure you still have the **Census Blocks** layer selected, then click on the **Appearance** tab on the **Feature Layer** contextual tab.

3. In the **Extrusion** group tab, click on the small drop-down arrow below **Type** and select **Base Height**, as illustrated in the following screenshot:

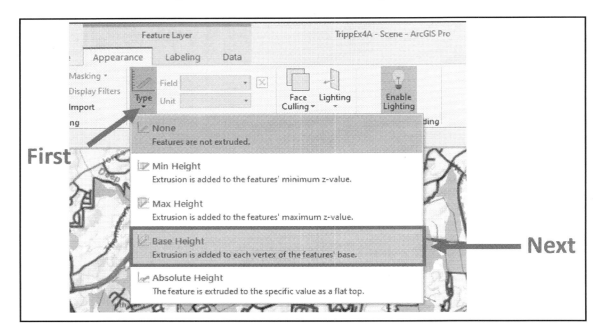

From the previous screenshot, you can see that extruding a layer allows it to be displayed in 3D. It sets the method that ArcGIS Pro will use to determine the height of features and how to display the height. The **Base Height** option will add the value of a specified field to each vertex of a feather to create the 3D view. There are four types of extrusion you can choose from in ArcGIS Pro. You will learn more about those later.

4. In the **Field** cell, click on the small drop-down arrow and select **Total Population** from the list of fields populated from the attribute table associated with the **Census Blocks** layer.

5. Then, set the Units to **Feet**. This means that it will extrude each polygon to a height equal to the total population values in feet.

The **Census Blocks** layer should now appear to have some depth because it now has the height displayed for each feature. You will now verify that this is the case.

6. After that, right-click on the **Census Blocks** layer and select **Zoom to Layer** from the menu that appears, as shown in the following screenshot:

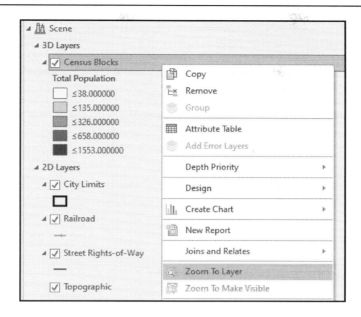

7. If necessary, activate the **Map** tab in the ribbon, then select the **Explore** tool so that you can navigate in the Scene.

8. Move your mouse pointer near the center of the **Census Blocks** layer.

9. Then, hold your scroll wheel down, and then move your mouse toward the top of the Scene to make it rotate along the z axis. This allows you to see the extruded census blocks, with their total population values displayed as a height. Continue to rotate the map until you can clearly see the census blocks' height.

Your Scene should now look similar to the following screenshot:

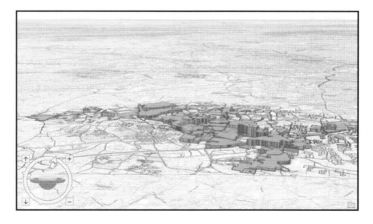

Remember that the color for the census blocks might be different because ArcGIS Pro assigns a random color to newly added layers.

10. Continue to use your mouse to zoom, rotate, and pan within your new Scene. Experiment with how the navigation works in a 3D environment.

 You can also use the compass arrow in the lower-left corner of the map to pan and zoom in the map. The + and – icons zoom the map scale in and out. The up and down arrows pan up and down along the z axis. The ring in the center with the arrow can be used to rotate the view. If you expand the compass, you will see an additional ring around the center of a sphere, which you can use to rotate the view along the z axis as well.

11. Lastly, save your project.

Congratulations! You have just created your first 3D Scene in ArcGIS Pro. For many of you, this may be the first Scene that you have ever created. In the next section, you will see how you can combine 3D extrusions with traditional 2D style symbology to create a really impactful map.

Step 4 – Combining types of symbology

In addition to extruding a layer so that it appears in 3D, you can also apply traditional symbology methods such as those you learned about in Chapter 3, *Creating 2D Maps*. This makes Scenes even more powerful when visualizing data, by making them more informative.

In this step, you will apply traditional graduated color symbology to the **Census Blocks** layer to make the Scene even more informative and easy to interpret. You will symbolize each census block, using a color that represents the population range it falls into. You can do this by following these steps:

1. In the **Contents** pane, select the **Census Blocks** layer.
2. In the ribbon, click on the **Appearance** tab.
3. Click on the small arrowhead located below the **Symbology** button, then select **Graduated Colors**, as shown in the following screenshot:

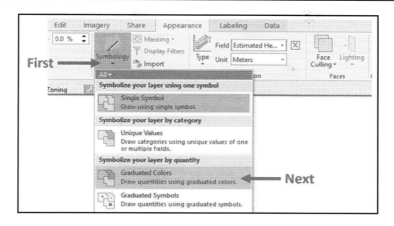

4. The **Symbology** pane should now be open. Then, set the **Field** value to **Total Population**, using the drop-down arrow.

5. Next, select a color scheme you think best displays the total population values. Usually, you want the lower values to be represented with a less intense color than for higher values.

6. Save your project once you are happy with the color scheme that you have selected, then close the **Symbology** pane.

When you have completed the preceding steps, your map should look similar to the example given in the following screenshot (of course, your colors may be different depending on the scheme you selected):

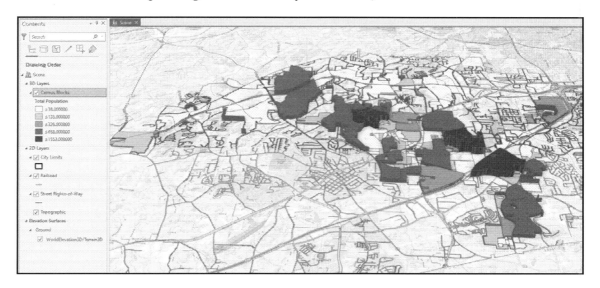

Now, not only can you quickly identify which blocks have the highest total population based on their height, but you can also see the population range each block falls into. This makes the Scene a very powerful tool for disseminating information.

7. Lastly, close ArcGIS Pro. If asked to save your project, please do so.

You have now created your first 3D Scene in ArcGIS Pro. An important component of any Scene is the use of elevations. This defines the ground surface as well as the location of features in space.

In the next section, you will learn about the importance of elevations in creating Scenes, what you can use as elevation sources, and how to control them within your Scene.

Learning about elevations and how to use them

When you create a 3D Scene within ArcGIS Pro, there are several elevations you need to be concerned about. You first need to define a ground elevation. The ground elevation provides a baseline for your Scene and is the canvas many other layers are applied to within your map.

Once you have established your ground elevation, you then need to determine the elevations of your 3D features. You will often find two elevations used for your 3D features, the first being the starting or base elevation, and the second being the height or depth of the features. These may be directly related to the ground or at an absolute elevation.

We will now take a closer look at these different elevations that you need to set in your Scene. We will start with a discussion on how to set the ground elevation and which data formats you can use to establish the ground elevation for your Scene. Then, we will examine methods you can use to set the base and height or depth elevations for your features.

Establishing ground elevations

The ground elevation is used by ArcGIS Pro to represent the surface of the earth within the 3D Scene you are creating. Each Scene should have a ground surface specified. By default, ArcGIS Pro uses the Esri World Elevation surface, which is published through **ArcGIS Online**. Don't worry though, as using this surface from ArcGIS Online does not use any of your ArcGIS Online credits. This surface, as with the **ArcGIS Online Basemaps** surface, is completely free to use.

You are not required to only use the Esri World Elevation surface—you can choose to use your own elevation surface if desired. Your own local surface is often much more accurate, so it will provide better results.

The extents of a Scene are limited to the extents for the data sources used as ground elevations. This means that your Scene extents will be clipped to the total combined area covered by your ground elevation sources. To ensure your Scene displays the amount of area you need, it is possible to use more than one data source as a ground elevation. This is especially useful when trying to show large areas or when needing to stitch together multiple datasets.

When using multiple data sources as ground surfaces, you need to make sure they align well with one another. The following screenshot shows you an example of two surfaces being used as ground elevations that do not align properly. You can easily see how this distorts the Scene along the common seam:

If there are significant differences between the elevation sources, as illustrated in the previous screenshot, this will warp your Scene along those seams and will negatively impact any analysis you might perform.

There are several types of data that you can use as a ground surface. This includes a **Digital Elevation Model (DEM)**, a **Triangulated Irregular Network (TIN)**, and web elevation surfaces.

Understanding DEMs

A DEM is a raster dataset that represents elevations over a defined extent. Raster data is made up of a series of equal-sized cells, with each cell containing a numeric value. What the value represents will depend on the purpose of the raster.

In the case of a DEM, the raster cell values represent the average elevation for the area covered by the cell. The following screenshot is an example of a DEM:

As you can see in the previous screenshot, if you were to zoom in on this DEM at some point, you would start to see individual squares that are the cells making up the raster data. The squares you see are now commonly referred to as a pixel, even though that is not correct. Each cell is assigned the value of the averaged elevation it covers. The cell might be 1 foot x 1 foot, or 2 meters x 2 meters. It is the size of the cells that determines the resolution and plays a part in its accuracy.

Pixels actually refer to the display resolution. They are equal to a combination of the resolution of the image itself and the capabilities of your computer to display the image.

How does the DEM know the average elevation for the areas covered by its cells? As with all GIS data, it can be derived using many different methods. It might be created based on elevation information acquired by a land surveyor. It might have been compiled by a **photogrammetrist** using stereo photography methods. It may have been interpolated using contour lines, or some combination of all these methods.

Common raster formats include `.jpg`, `.jpeg`, `.jp2`, `.tiff`, `.png`, **Seamless Image Database** (`.sid`), **Enhanced Compressed Wavelet** (`.ecw`), `.img`, `.bmp`, and **GRID** (Esri native raster format) formats.

Creating a DEM in ArcGIS Pro requires you to have the **Spatial Analyst** extension. However, if you already have access to one, you can create a 3D Scene and use the DEM as your ground surface without the extension.

Let's move on to TINs.

Understanding TINs

A TIN is a vector-based representation of a surface. It is constructed from a series of nodes and lines that form a network of adjacent triangles. The triangles form facets of a 3D surface that include areas of the same elevation.

The following screenshot shows you an example of a TIN as it is being drawn—you can see the triangles that make up the TIN:

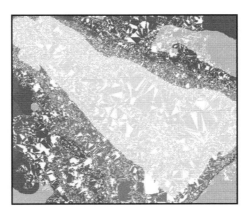

Once all the triangles are drawn, you are presented with what appears to be a solid surface. It is easy to see the elevation changes within the TIN, as shown in the following screenshot:

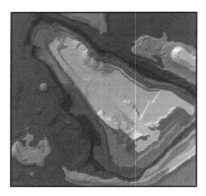

Because TINs are formed of vector-based data, they tend to be smaller in total file size to an equivalent DEM. However, due to their complexity, they can take much longer to draw or process when used in the analysis. It is strongly recommended that you ensure your computer has a dedicated graphics card if you will be working with TINs when using ArcGIS Pro.

Being vector-based, TINs can be created from a range of input data such as streams, ridgelines, roads, and so on. When the TIN is generated, these input features will remain in the same location and be matched with nodes or edges within the TIN. This can allow the TIN to achieve a high degree of accuracy and detail that is not normally possible with a DEM.

Creating a TIN does require you to have the 3D Analyst extension. However, if a TIN already exists, you may use it in ArcGIS Pro without an extension as a ground surface or a layer.

You now have a much better understanding of what elevations are and how they work in ArcGIS Pro. *But what about the features within your GIS layers? How do you display them in 3D with the proper height?* In the next section, we will explore how to do that.

Understanding extruding features

Extruding features is how you turn them from flat 2D shapes into 3D objects, providing them with height. For example, you can extrude power poles or trees so that you can see how tall they are.

Both of these are normally stored as point features. When you extrude them so that they have height, they become vertical lines. In the following screenshot, you can see an example of buildings and power poles that have been extruded to create 3D features:

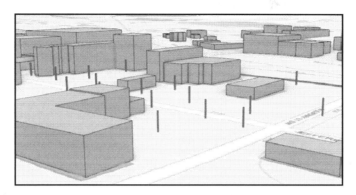

From the previous screenshot, you can see that the buildings in this Scene started as a 2D polygon layer, which just shows the footprint of the buildings on the ground. By extruding them, you can now see their height above ground, gaining a greater appreciation of the spatial relationships between them and other features. The power poles were a 2D point layer that was extruded to show their height. Now, you can visualize the relationship between the buildings and the power poles.

ArcGIS Pro provides four methods for extruding features. The one that you use will depend on which information you have for your features, as detailed in the following table:

Extrusion type	Description	Requirements	Data Types
Minimum Height	This adds the extrusion height to the minimum **z** value, producing a flat-top feature.	It requires an attribute field that contains an elevation value for the lowest point of the feature along the ground surface.	Lines or polygons
Maximum Height	This adds the extrusion height to the maximum **z** value, producing a flat-top feature.	It requires an attribute field that contains the elevation for a feature at its highest point along the ground surface.	Lines or polygons
Base Height	This adds the extrusion to the base elevation of each feature vertex. The result may not be a flat top, depending on the base height of feature vertices.	No attribute fields are required. However, the extrusion can be based on a field such as measured height, if available.	Points, lines, and polygons
Absolute Height	Features are extruded to a specified height regardless of base elevations or other z values.	It requires an attribute field that contains the top elevation of each feature.	Points, lines, and polygons

Extrusion is one of many ways in which we can display GIS data in 3D. In the next section, you will explore some other methods that you can use. The one that works best for you will depend on your data—for example, whether it actually stores a z coordinate or has elevational or height information stored within its attributes.

Other methods to display 3D data

Extrusion is not the only method to display data in 3D. ArcGIS Pro includes many 3D symbol styles that can add a level of realism to your Scenes. 3D symbols are designed to display features using commonly expected textures, materials, and details. For example, they can provide a building with a brick appearance or show a fire hydrant with a real-looking hydrant that you would expect to see when driving down the road. Often, these symbols have built-in 3D settings that do not require the features to be extruded.

You can also use **CityEngine** symbology rules to apply even more realistic Scenes if you have the 3D Analyst extension. CityEngine is another application for Esri that allows users to create advanced 3D renderings of their data.

The following screenshot shows you an example of what can be accomplished using 3D symbology styles in ArcGIS Pro. Here, you can see a realistic-looking streetscape that includes buildings, light poles, fire hydrants, and power poles:

Let's move on to an exercise to better understand advanced 3D renderings. This will provide you with some hands-on experience, using some of the methods you just learned about.

Exercise 4B – Creating a Local Scene

The scenario for the exercise is as follows: A **community and economic development director** is working on a presentation that they will be presenting to a group of concerned citizens. They have asked you to create a 3D Scene of the central downtown business district that they can use in the presentation.

In this exercise, you will create a Local Scene to fulfill the director's request. This Scene will use a locally developed DEM that is more accurate than the Esri World Elevation model. You will then add and symbolize layers using 3D symbology to create a more realistic Scene.

Step 1 – Opening a project and adding a Local Scene

In this step, you will open the last project you created and add a new Local Scene. To do this, we follow these steps:

1. Start ArcGIS Pro.
2. Open the project you created in the *Exercise 4A* section. This should be in your list of recently opened projects.
3. In the **Catalog** pane, right-click on the **Maps** folder and select **New Local Scene**.

4. Once the new Scene is generated, right-click on it and select **Rename** from the menu that appears, as illustrated in the following screenshot:

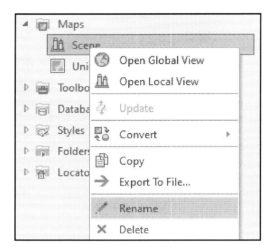

5. Type **Local Scene** as the new name, and press your *Enter* key.

You have just created a new Local Scene in the project that you created in the last exercise. Remember—a single project can contain multiple maps and Scenes. This makes it easier to manage and access.

Step 2 – Setting the ground surface

In this step, you will assign the DEM that the city engineer has provided as the ground surface. This DEM was created by the city engineer based on survey data that they had collected from a professional surveyor. We use the following steps to assign the DEM:

1. In the ribbon, click on the **Map** tab.
2. Click on the small drop-down arrow located below the **Add Data** button to expose the menu.
3. Select **Elevation Source** from the menu. This is located near the bottom of the menu, as illustrated in the following screenshot:

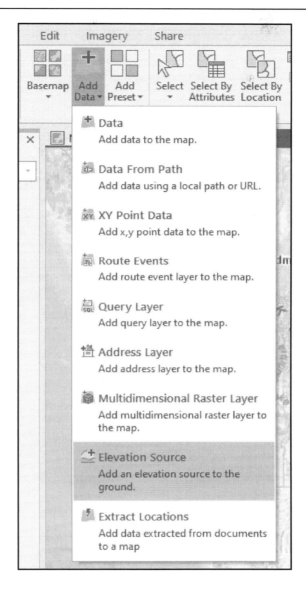

4. Then, in the left panel of the **Add Elevation Source** window, select **Databases**, located under **Project**.
5. After that, in the right panel of the window, double-click on the **Trippville_GIS.gdb** geodatabase.
6. Then, select **DEM** from the right panel of the window and click **OK**.

The DEM should now appear in the **Contents** pane under the **Elevation Surfaces** category. As you can see in the following screenshot, your Scene now has two **Ground** surfaces—the **DEM** surface you just added and the **WorldElevation3D/Terrain3D** surface from ArcGIS Online:

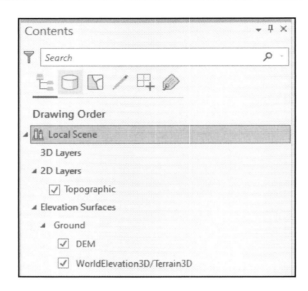

Now, you will remove the **WorldElevation3D/Terrain3D** surface from your Scene. You do not need to use this surface provided by Esri since you have your own, which covers the entire area of the city you are working with.

7. Then, right-click on the **WorldElevation3D/Terrain3D** surface and select **Remove** from the menu, as illustrated in the following screenshot:

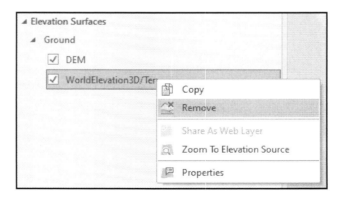

You have just set the ground surface for your Scene to the DEM provided by the city engineer. Don't be concerned if your Scene currently appears to be blank. This will be fixed as you add more layers to the Scene.

Step 3 – Adding layers and setting symbology

Now that you have the ground surface defined, it is time to start adding the layers requested by the director, by following these steps:

1. Using the skills that you have learned, add the following layers to your Scene from the `Trippville_GIS.gdb` geodatabase:
   - **Buildings**: This is located in the `Base Feature` dataset.
   - **Fire_hyd**: This is located in the `Water Feature` dataset.
   - **Light_Poles**: This is located in the root of the geodatabase.

2. Then, drag the **Buildings** layer to the **3D Group** layer.

3. Click on the symbol patch located below the layer name to open the **Symbology** pane on the right side of the interface, as illustrated in the following screenshot:

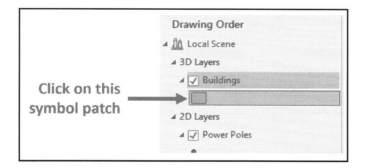

4. Ensure that the **Gallery** tab is selected at the top of the **Symbology** pane. Then, in the search area, type `Building`, and then set the search to **All styles** in the drop-down box located to the right of the search cell.

5. Select **International Building** under **Procedural Symbols**, then right-click on the **Buildings** layer and select **Zoom to Layer**. Then, make sure that the **Explore** tool is selected on the **Map** tab in the ribbon.

6. Place your mouse pointer near the center of one of the buildings and depress the scroll wheel on your mouse. While holding your scroll wheel down, move your mouse pointer toward the top of your Scene to rotate your Scene so that you can view the height of the **Buildings** layer, which is now using the 3D symbology style you just applied.

Once you have rotated your Scene, zoom in to get a closer look. Your Scene should look similar to the following screenshot. You will notice your buildings now have a much more realistic appearance than they had when you just extruded them in the last exercise:

 Your Scene will not look exactly like the previous screenshot as your scale, rotation, and location will most likely be different. However, the general appearance of your buildings should be similar.

7. Now, drag the **Light Poles** layer to the **3D** category.
8. Then, click on the point symbol located below the layer name.
9. In the **Symbol** pane, first, ensure the **Gallery** tab is active, and then, in the search area, type Light. You may also need to ensure the **All styles** option is still set as the search option.
10. Then, select the **Light On Post - Light Off** symbol from the 3D street Scene as this most closely matches with the ones used by the city of Trippville (you can choose a different one if you wish).
11. After that, right-click on the **Light Poles** layer and select **Properties**, then click on the **Display** option in the left-side pane.

12. Then, check the box that says **Display 3D symbols in real-world units**, and click **OK**.

This will allow you to set the correct height on the light poles. The standard height of the light poles used in the city is 18 feet. Before you can set the height for the light poles, you will need to make one more change to the project settings. By default, 3D symbols use **meters** as the unit for specifying height. You need to change this in project options to feet.

13. Click on the **Project** tab in the ribbon and select **Options**, then click on **Units** under **Project**.

14. Expand **3D Symbol Display Units**, and then click on the radio button located at the end of the row for **Foot_US** in the grid, as shown in the following screenshot:

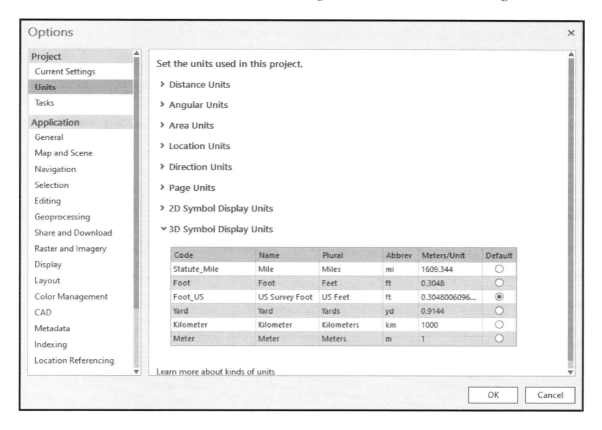

15. Once you have verified the setting, click **OK**.

16. Click the back arrow located on the upper left-hand side of the **Project** window to return to your Scene.

17. Then, save your project.

18. After that, click on the symbol patch located below the **Light Poles** layer name.

19. Then, click on the **Properties** option in the **Symbology** tab, ensuring that the **Light Poles** layer is still selected.

20. After that, set the **Size** option to 18 ft, and then click **Apply**.

21. Repeat this process for the **Fire_Hyd** layer and use the following settings:
    - Select **Fire Hydrant** for the **Symbol** field.
    - Set 3 pt for the **Height** field.

Your Scene should now look similar to this, depending on your rotation and zoom scale, if you have correctly applied all the settings:

You are almost done. Now, you need to apply a basemap that adds a more realistic backdrop and applies the sky to the Scene.

22. Click on the **Basemap** button on the **Map** tab in the ribbon.

23. Select the **Imagery** basemap. This will allow you to use aerial photography as a basemap, which will add a touch of realism to the Scene.

24. Now, to add the sky, you will need to apply a fill to the entire Scene. Right-click on **Local Scene** in the **Contents** pane, and select **Properties**.

25. Then, select the **General** option in the left-side pane of the **Map Properties** window.

26. Set the **Background color** option to **Sodalite Blue**, using the drop-down arrow to display a color palette (you can choose a different color if you think another will work better), and click **OK**.

27. Lastly, save your project. Take some time to pan, rotate, and zoom within the Scene that you just created. It has a very realistic appearance, which is exactly what the director was hoping to accomplish.

Your final Scene should look similar to this (yours may be slightly different depending on your rotation and scale):

Congratulations! You have created a realistic-looking 3D visualization of a downtown area. Now, make sure to save your project so that you don't lose all the hard work you have completed.

Summary

Now, you have seen that ArcGIS Pro supports some very powerful tools for visualizing data in 3D. This opens new levels of understanding, using your GIS data. You have learned how you can create different Scenes to support different spatial extents.

You have also learned how you can use different methods to turn 2D data into 3D features, using extrusion or 3D symbol styles. When using extrusion, you can illustrate the true height of features using one of four methods supported in ArcGIS Pro. Now, you can use 3D symbols to add a level of visual realism to your Scenes.

The key element to creating a 3D Scene is to define a ground surface. You learned that you can use the default Esri-provided World Elevation surface or one of your own. You are now able to use one of your own surfaces—this can be a DEM or a TIN. Using your own ground surface can increase the accuracy of the elevation data within your Scene and the relationships between features along the z axis.

In the next chapter, you will learn more about how projects work within ArcGIS Pro. So far, you have been working largely on projects that were already created. Next, you will explore the parts that make up an ArcGIS Pro project and how you can create new ones yourself.

Further reading

If you would like to explore these concepts in more detail, you may want to check out the following:

- *ArcGIS Pro 2.X Cookbook, Chapter 10, 3D Maps and 3D Analysis*

5

Creating and Working with Projects

ArcGIS Pro has reintroduced the concept of projects to Esri users. Esri first introduced the concept of managing your **Geographic Information System (GIS)** using project files with their **ArcView GIS** application. ArcView GIS used projects to manage map layouts, views, tables, data connections, and more all within a single `.apr` file. This allowed us to access everything associated with a project from a single location.

When Esri released ArcGIS in 1999, the previously described method was dropped. In its place, Esri decided to use separate files called **map documents** (`.mxd` files) for **ArcMap**. A map document contains a single map with one or more data frames. So, for each map you need, you will have to create a separate map document. If you also had to create 3D maps, you would need another separate file called a scene (`.sxd`). All of this means you often have tens to hundreds of files to manage and keep track of, which makes management much harder.

ArcGIS Pro projects greatly simplify GIS management. Now, projects allow you to consolidate all of the resources needed to complete a project in a single place. So, this chapter will help you learn that you no longer need to search for the correct map document. You just need to open the ArcGIS Pro project file for the project that you are interested in and all the maps, data connections, layouts, tools, and more will appear there. This chapter will also help you to locate services much faster. Also, after completing this chapter, you will be able to create your own project and templates.

In this chapter, you will learn how to work with projects. This will include the following topics:

- Working with an ArcGIS Pro project
- Creating a new project and project templates
- Creating custom project templates

Technical requirements

To complete the exercises in this chapter, you will need access to **ArcGIS Pro 2.6** or higher. Any license level for the software will suffice.

Working with an ArcGIS Pro project

ArcGIS Pro utilizes project files in place of map documents and scenes to access GIS data, make maps, perform analysis, and share work. Project files have a `.aprx` file extension and include all the GIS resources that are needed for a given project. Projects can be created and shared on your local network so that others in the project team can quickly access the resources that they need to complete their assigned tasks.

This section will help you learn how to create a new project with Esri templates by working through a hands-on exercise.

Each project will have components and resources that are associated with each specific project. Some of these components and resources will be common to multiple projects, while others will be unique to individual projects. So, just because a component or resource is linked to one project, does not mean it cannot be used in another project.

Projects also have their own terminology associated with them. It will be important to understand this terminology when working with projects. We will now begin by exploring the terminology associated with projects and some of the components or resources that can be included in a project.

Understanding project terminology

Like the ArcGIS Pro application, projects in ArcGIS Pro have a vocabulary associated specifically with them. We will quickly define some of these terms so that you can begin to understand what they mean as you will come across them throughout this book, hear about them at conferences, see them in Esri publications, and so on:

- **Project item**: A project item is any item, component, or resource stored within an ArcGIS Pro project. Project items include maps, scenes, folder connections, database connections, ArcGIS Server connections, **Web Map Service** (**WMS**) connections, toolboxes, locators, and more. These items are accessed within ArcGIS Pro from the **Catalog** pane or the catalog view.

- **Portal**: A portal in ArcGIS Pro refers to a connection to either **ArcGIS Online** or **Portal for ArcGIS**. ArcGIS Online is Esri's cloud solution for storing and accessing GIS resources, including maps, data, and applications. Portal for ArcGIS provides the same functionality as ArcGIS Online but is installed and hosted on your organization's local infrastructure. Portal for ArcGIS is also part of **ArcGIS Enterprise**, formerly called **ArcGIS Server**.
- **Portal item**: A portal item is any item that is accessed via a designated portal. Portal items might include web maps, feature layers, tile layers, layer packages, map packages, and project packages.
- **Project package**: A project package is similar to a layer or map package. It bundles or zips all items associated with a project into one consolidated file. A project package can be used to share projects with others that may not be connected to your network or to archive a project. The project package will have a .ppkx file extension and can be stored in a local folder or uploaded to your portal.
- **The** Home **folder**: The Home folder refers to the folder where the project file is stored. The Home folder is where ArcGIS Pro creates project-specific content unless the user specifies a different location. The Home folder can only be changed by saving a project to a different folder. The default home folder for new projects is C:\Users\%user name%\Documents\ArcGIS\Projects.
- **Default geodatabase**: The default geodatabase is used by the geoprocessing tools as the automatic default workspace for the resulting output items of the tools. This means new feature classes resulting from the use of analysis, conversion, and other tools will automatically be saved to the default geodatabase unless you specify a different location. Any geodatabase can be used as the default geodatabase. When a new project is created, ArcGIS Pro will automatically create a new geodatabase file for the project in the Home folder.

Now that you understand some of the terms associated with a project, it is time to look at how to manage one. As you will see, a single ArcGIS Pro project can contain a large number of items. In the next section, you will learn how to use the **Catalog** pane to manage and access these items.

Using the Catalog pane

When you open a project or create a new project in ArcGIS Pro, the **Catalog** pane will be one of the first things you see. By default, it will be located on the right-hand side of the ArcGIS Pro interface, opposite the **Contents** pane.

The **Catalog** pane consists of the following:

- The **Project** tab
- The **Portal** tab
- The **Favorites** tab

We will look at these elements in the following sections.

The Project tab

The **Catalog** pane provides access to the **Project** items. From there, you can access maps, scenes, folder connections, layouts, database connections, and other elements that are associated with the project, as shown in the following screenshot:

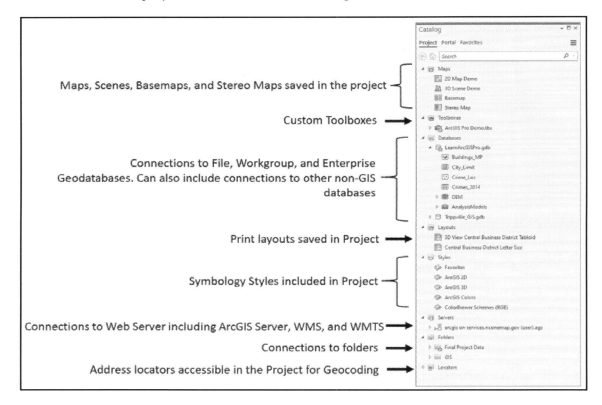

The **Catalog** pane, shown in the previous screenshot, contains three tabs at the top—**Project**, **Portal**, and **Favorites**. The **Project** tab allows you to access project items that are either stored within the project, such as maps or layouts, or that you have established a connection to for the project, such as a folder, database, or web connection. It should be mentioned that ArcGIS Pro does not support personal geodatabases. However, files, workgroups, and enterprise geodatabases are supported.

We will now move on to the **Portal** tab section.

The Portal tab

The **Portal** tab provides access to connections that you have established to either ArcGIS Online or Portal for ArcGIS. From this tab, you will be able to access content that has been published and content that you have permission to use. This can include web maps, feature layers, and web apps. The **Portal** tab has four buttons located on it:

- **My Content**: The first button is **My Content**. This allows you to access content that was created by you in ArcGIS Online or Portal for ArcGIS. This might include web maps, web scenes, the dashboard, layer packages, and more:

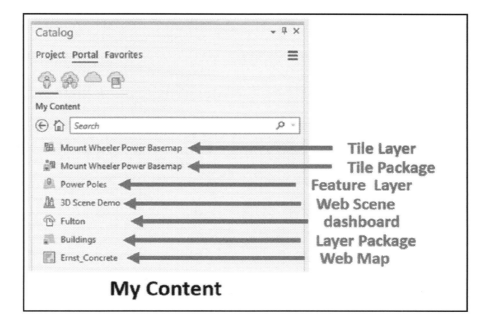

- **Groups**: The second button is **Groups**. This button allows you to see the various groups that you are a member of and the content shared to these groups:

- **All Portal**: The next button is **All Portal**. This allows you to see content shared with you in all the portals that you have connected other than your primary portal. If you are connected to ArcGIS Online, this includes any data that has been published in ArcGIS Online and shared with everyone. Because of the amount of data that can be available, when you click on this button, the content area will appear blank. So, you must search for content for it to appear. The following screenshot shows the **All Portal** tab:

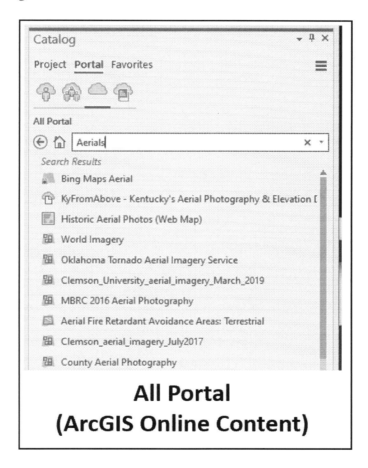

- **Living Atlas**: The last button is **Living Atlas**. Esri's **Living Atlas** feature provides data that you can access that can only be posted from authoritative sources:

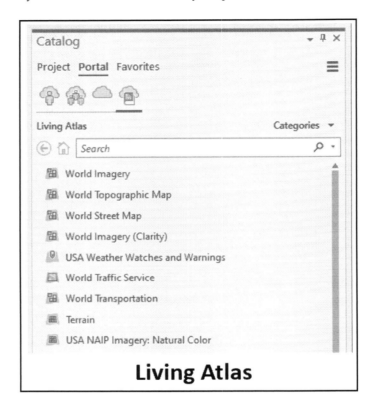

Living Atlas

General ArcGIS Online content can be published by anyone with an account, but only vetted contributors are allowed to publish data to **Living Atlas**. This makes it a great starting point if you are looking for data that you can have some level of trust in.

We will now move on to the **Favorites** tab section.

The Favorites tab

The **Favorites** tab in the **Catalog** pane allows you to store connections to databases, folders, and servers that you use on a regular basis across multiple projects. This provides easy access to these resources from ArcGIS Pro and the ability to quickly add them to your current active project.

For example, if your organization has a primary GIS database that it uses for all its projects, then you might want to add it as a favorite so that you can easily add it to new projects as you start them. The following screenshot shows some examples of favorite connections:

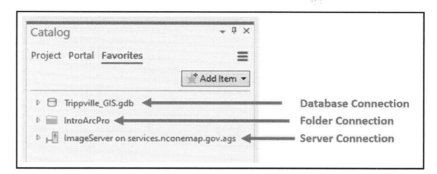

As you can see from the preceding screenshot, favorites are stored as part of your user profile, just like your `Documents` folder in **Windows**. If your organization uses roaming profiles, then your ArcGIS favorites will follow you from one computer to another within your network.

If your organization only uses local profiles, which is fairly common, then your favorites will only be available on the computer that you are using when you add the resource to your favorites. As of ArcGIS Pro 2.5 and earlier, there is no way to share favorites with others or through an entire organization.

Once an item has been added to your favorites, you can also choose to have that item automatically added to any new project that you create. This means that it will automatically appear in the **Catalog** pane and the **Project** tab for each new project that you create.

Now that you have learned some of the terms associated with a project and have been introduced to the **Catalog** pane, it is time for you to see it in action.

Exercise 5A – Using the Catalog pane

In this exercise, you will work to create a map that shows the floodplains and drainage basins for Union City. You will need to use the **Catalog** pane to establish several connections, including a geodatabase and server to access additional information that is needed to create the map. You will start with an existing project that is included with the data that you downloaded, which already contains a basic map.

Step 1 – Opening and saving a project

In this step, you will open an existing project and then save it. This will be the project you will continue to work with during this exercise:

1. Start **ArcGIS Pro**. Again, remember that you will need an internet connection and access to ArcGIS Online.

2. Using the skills you have learned in past chapters, open the ArcGIS Pro `Exercise 5A` project located in `C:\Student\IntroArcPro\Chapter5`.

3. Then, save the project as `%your name% Ex5A` (for example, `Tripp Ex5A.aprx`). Save the project in the same location as the one you opened in the previous step.

If you have successfully opened the correct project and saved it, you should see the following visual:

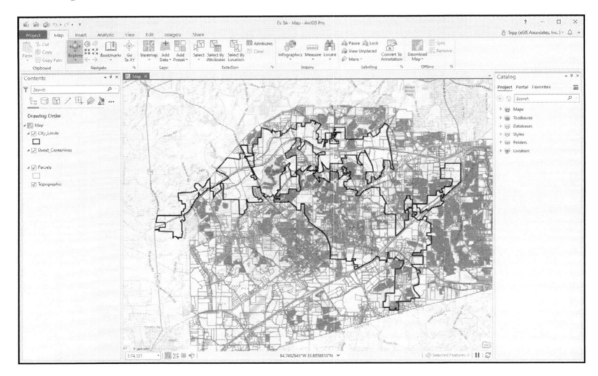

Now, let's continue with the exercise and move on to the next step, where you will use the **Catalog** pane to explore the project you just opened.

Step 2 – Navigating the Catalog pane

Now that you have opened the project, you should see the **Catalog** pane located on the right-hand side of the ArcGIS Pro interface. In this step, you will see what content is already available in the **Catalog** pane:

1. In the **Catalog** pane, click on the small arrowhead located on the left-hand side of **Maps** to expand that section.

Question: *What do you see listed under* **Maps***?*

2. Expand the **Databases** section under the same pane.

Question: *What do you see listed under the* **Databases** *section?*

3. Expand the ArcGIS Pro `Exercise 5A` geodatabase to see which feature classes it contains.
4. Compare the layers in the map to the feature classes in the geodatabase for the project.

Question: *Does the map contain all the layers that reference all the feature classes in the geodatabase? Does the project geodatabase contain feature classes that represent the floodplains or drainage basins?*

5. Expand the remaining sections within the **Catalog** pane to see the rest of the project items you currently have access to.

Question: *What other items are currently available in this project?*

6. Click on the **Portal** tab in the **Catalog** pane. By default, you start on the **My Content** list.

7. Explore the portal items that are available to you in **My Content** list by moving your pointer over some of them.

 It is possible that you may see nothing if you have never published any content to ArcGIS Online or Portal for ArcGIS. Later in this book, you will publish a map and project to ArcGIS Online. These items will then show up in your portal and the **My Content** list.

8. Click on the **Groups** button located on the **Portal** tab to see what groups you are a member of or have access to.

 Question: *What groups do you see?*

Again, you may see nothing here if you have not created groups for your organization in ArcGIS Online or Portal for ArcGIS before. As your organization makes more use of these technologies, expect the list of groups to grow.

Step 3 – Adding a database connection

In this step, you will add a connection to another geodatabase that contains additional data you need for this project:

1. Click back on the **Project** tab in the **Catalog** pane.
2. Right-click on **Databases** and click on **Add Database**, as in the following screenshot:

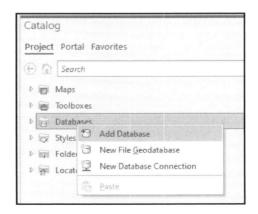

3. In the **Select Existing Geodatabase** window, navigate to
   `C:\Student\IntroArcPro\Databases`. Select `UnionCity.gdb` and click
   Open. You should now see the `UnionCity` geodatabase in the **Catalog** pane
   located below **ArcGIS Pro Exercise 5A project geodatabase**. The `UnionCity`
   geodatabase contains additional layers that you will need to add to your map.

4. Expand the **UnionCity** geodatabase so that you can see what feature classes it
   contains. Select the **Floodplains** feature class.

5. Holding down your *Ctrl* key, select the **Watersheds** feature class.

6. Right-click on one of the two selected feature classes and choose the **Add to
   Current Map** option.

Your map should look similar to the map shown in the following screenshot:

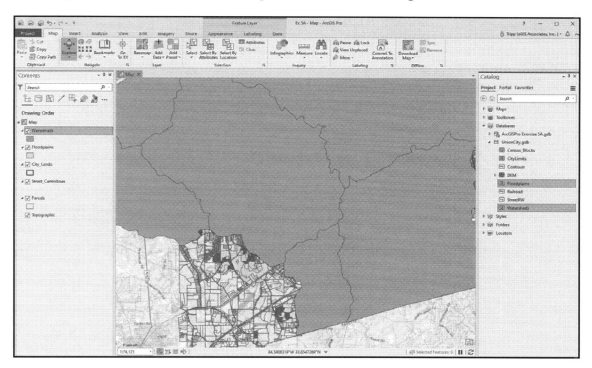

You have just added two layers from a different geodatabase to your map after you made
the connection to it.

Your colors may be different, depending on what colors ArcGIS Pro assigned to the new layers you added. Remember that ArcGIS Pro assigns a random color to new layers added to the map.

Although the layers are now visible on the map, you will need to make some adjustments to the layers to improve the readability of the map.

Step 4 – Adjusting the layers

In this step, you will make changes to the symbology and layer orders so that the map is easier to read. First, you will make changes to the layer draw order:

1. Select the **Watersheds** layer in the **Contents** pane located on the left-hand side of the ArcGIS Pro interface.
2. While holding your left mouse button down, drag the **Watersheds** layer so that it is below the **Parcels** layer in your layer list.
3. Now, drag the **Floodplains** layer so that it is below the **Parcels** layer but above the **Watersheds** layer, as in the following screenshot:

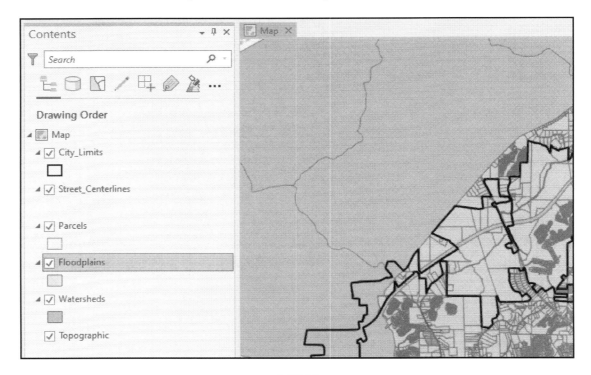

4. Right-click on the **Floodplains** layer and select **Zoom to Layer**.

Now that you have the layers of the drawing in the order you want them, it is time to work on the symbology for each. You will need to add a new style to your project first that contains the symbol for the floodplains.

5. In the **Catalog** pane, right-click on **Styles** and select **Add** | **Add Style**, as in the following screenshot:

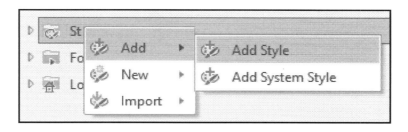

6. In the **Add a style file** window, click on the folders located under **Project** in the left panel.
7. Double-click on the **Chaper5A** folder in the right-hand side panel of the window.
8. Choose **ESRI.stylx** and click **OK**. If you are asked to upgrade the style, click **Yes**.

This style originally came from Esri's older **ArcMap** product. ArcGIS Pro is able to make use of styles that were created to use with ArcMap using this method.

You have just added this new style to your project, which will allow you to use the symbols it contains for the layers in your map. Styles store symbols, colors, north arrows, scale bars, and other map elements that are used to create maps and layouts.

9. Click on the symbology patch located below the **Parcels** layer to open the **Symbology** pane.
10. Click on the **Properties** tab and set the **Color** to **No Color** using the drop-down arrow.
11. Make sure **Outline color** is set to **black** and click **Apply**.
12. Select the **Floodplains** layer in the **Contents** pane.
13. Select the **Appearance** group tab from the ribbon.

14. Click on the symbology drop-down arrow and select **Unique Values**. This will open the **Symbology** pane on the right-hand side of the ArcGIS Pro interface.

    The contents of the **Symbology** pane should change. You should now see options to select a field to use to control the symbology, as well as a **Color Scheme** option, a **Classes** tab, and a **Scales** tab. We will configure some of these options next to symbolize the **Floodplains** layer based on values stored in the attribute table associated with this layer.

15. For **Field 1**, select **SFHA**, as in the following screenshot. This field is used to specify whether an area is in or out of the **Special Flood Hazard Area** (**SFHA**), which is also commonly referred to as the 100-year flood zone. You want to symbolize the areas that are in the SHFA:

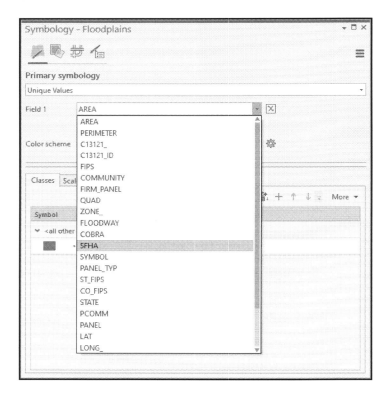

16. Click on the symbol patch located next to **IN** in the grid.
17. Make sure the **Gallery** tab is selected in the **Symbology** pane.

18. At the top of the **Symbology** pane in the search bar, type `Flood` and press the *Enter* key.

19. Select the symbol named **100 Year Flood Overlay**. Note that this is in the Esri style you added to the project. It is only available for you to use because you added it.

20. Click on the back arrow located in the top-left corner of the **Symbology** pane to return to the setting for the **Floodplain** layer.

21. Click on the symbol patch next to **OUT** and set it to **Hollow**. Use the search function again if needed.

22. Click on the back arrow to return to the **Unique Values** settings.

23. In the **Symbol** grid, select where it says **SFHA** and type `100 Year Floodplain` to replace it, as in the following screenshot:

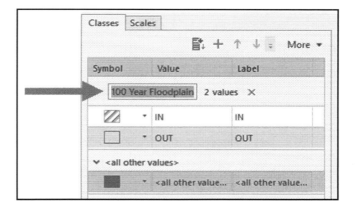

24. Click on **More**, located on the right-hand side just above the **Symbol** grid, and deselect or untick **Show all other values**, as in the following screenshot. This removes the values from appearing in the **Contents** pane and the legend:

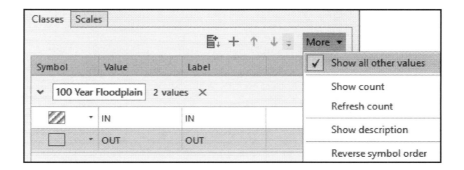

So, you have now added a new style to your project and used a symbol contained in that style to update the symbology for the **Floodplains** layer. You have one last layer to adjust, the **Watershed** layer. We will now apply symbology to this layer using an existing layer file.

25. Select the **Watersheds** layer in the **Contents** pane.
26. Select the **Appearance** tab in the ribbon.
27. Click on the **Import** tool. This will open the **Geoprocessing** pane on the right-hand side of the interface.
28. Click on the browse button, located next to the **Symbology** layer.
29. Click on the **Folders** option, located under **Project** in the left panel.
30. Select the **Watersheds.lyrx** file and click **OK**.
31. Make sure the **Type** field is set to **Value_Field**, **Source Field** is set to **WATERSHED**, and **Target Field** is set to **WATERSHED** under **Symbology Fields** in the **Geoprocessing** pane, as in the following screenshot:

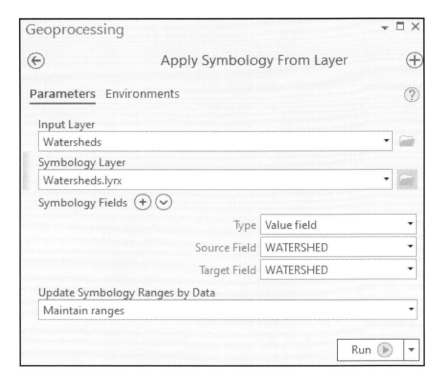

32. Once you have verified the **Symbology Fields** options, click the **Run** button located at the bottom of the **Geoprocessing** pane.

Your map should now look similar to the one in the following screenshot:

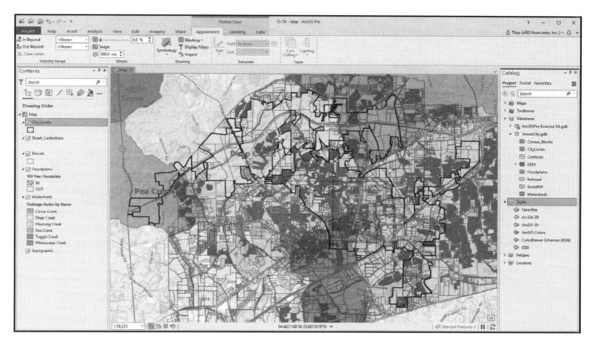

You just used a layer file to adjust the appearance of the **Watershed** layer. Layer files can not only be used to apply symbology settings but also to other layer properties, such as **labeling**. You can also see that each watershed is labeled with its name.

33. Save your project.

So, you have added multiple layers to your map and made several adjustments to the added layers. You adjusted the draw order in the **Contents** pane so that each layer is visible. Then, you changed the symbology that is used by these layers using different methods.

Step 5 – Accessing and adding a layer from a portal (optional)

We are almost done. Suppose that at the last minute, it has been decided that you need to add an aerial photograph to the map. You have been instructed to use aerials served by Fulton County to ArcGIS Online. We will use the following steps:

1. In the **Catalog** pane, select the **Portal** tab at the top.
2. Select the **All Portal** button so that you can access and search all the ArcGIS Online content.
3. In the search cell, type `Fulton County Pictometry Imagery` and press your *Enter* key.
4. Scroll down and locate the most current `Pictometry` tiled image service, as in the following screenshot:

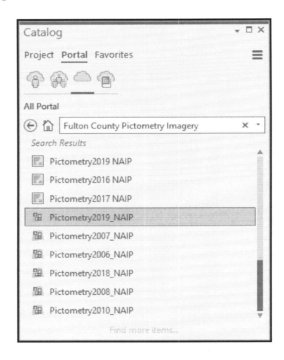

You should remember that a tiled image service will be indicated by a yellow trapezoid with several green-blue squares on top of it. Do not confuse a tiled image service with a map service.

5. Right-click on the most current image, such as the **Pictometry2019_NAIP** tiled service, and select **Add to Current Map**.
6. Save your project.

You have now added an aerial photography layer to your map from your **Portal** connection. Next, let's explore how to add a favorite in the **Catalog** pane.

Step 6 – Adding a folder connection as a favorite

As you know, all the data that you have been using throughout this book is stored in a single folder—IntroArcPro. So, you are going to add this folder to the **Favorites** tab in the **Catalog** pane for easy access when needed:

1. In the **Catalog** pane, click on the **Favorites** tab.
2. On the right-hand side, click on the **Add Item** button and select **Add Folder** from the menu that appears, as shown:

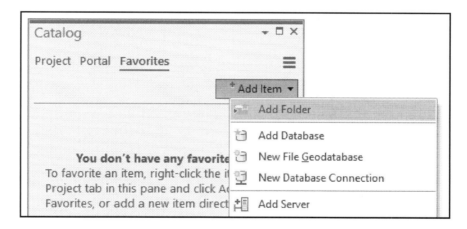

3. In the **Add Folder Connection** window, expand the **Computer** option in the left panel so that you can see its contents.
4. Click on the **C:** drive so that its contents appear in the right panel of the window.
5. Scroll down until you see the **Student** folder and double-click on it.
6. Select the **IntroArcPro** folder and click **OK**.

You should now see the IntroArcPro folder in your **Favorites** list in the **Catalog** pane. This folder will now always appear in this list on the computer that you are using until you decide to remove it. Next, we will add this favorite to your project.

Step 7 – Adding a favorite to a project

Now that you have added a favorite to your list, you will still need to add it to your current project as a connection. This is easy to do now that the folder connection is a favorite. In this step, you will see just how easy this is by adding it to your currently open project:

1. In the **Catalog** pane, click on the **Favorites** tab, then right-click on the **IntroArcPro** folder connection that you added in the previous step.
2. Select **Add to Project** from the menu that appears, as in the following screenshot:

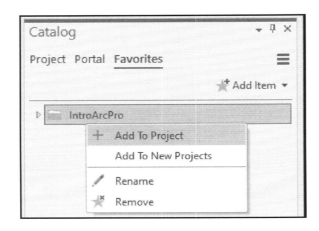

3. Now, click on the **Project** tab in the **Catalog** pane.
4. Expand the Folders folder so that you can see the folder connections available in this project.

   You should see two folder connections available—Chapter5 and IntroArcPro. The IntroArcPro connection is the one that you just added from your favorites. Now, all the data and other folders stored within the IntroArcPro folder are available for you to access and use in the project that you have been working in. You will also be able to just as quickly add the IntroArcPro connection to any other project you work on now or in the future.

5. Save your project and close ArcGIS Pro.

In this exercise, you learned how to navigate the **Catalog** pane and how to use it to add new layers to your map. You also learned how to access portal connections and create favorite connections that can then be easily added to projects. Next, you will explore how to create new projects from the beginning.

Creating a new project and project templates

As you have seen, projects are the very core of ArcGIS Pro. They contain all the things that a user needs to complete various GIS tasks. So far, the projects that you have used have already been created for you. They have included maps, three-dimensional scenes, and various connections. *So, how do you create a new project from scratch?*

In this section, you will learn how to create a new project using one of the Esri-provided templates. Then, you will learn how to create your own template that you can use to create new projects.

Creating a new project with Esri templates

When you open ArcGIS Pro, you have the option to open an existing project or create a new one. If you choose to create a new one, you first select a template. The template automatically generates content and connections within the new project that is created. The template can create maps, scenes, layouts, folder connections, database connections, and more.

In addition to what is created by the template, a new project-specific file geodatabase and toolbox are created in the Home folder. Remember that the Home folder is the folder that contains the new project that is created by us. Your new project will set these as the default geodatabase and toolbox used by the new project automatically.

Esri has already created some templates that you can use to begin creating new projects as soon as you install ArcGIS Pro. This includes four templates, each with a specific use in mind. They are as follows:

Esri Template Name	General Description
Map	Primarily for use with two-dimensional data. Automatically includes a two-dimensional map that includes your organization's default basemap layer.
Catalog	Creates a new completely empty project with no maps, scenes, or layouts. This was formerly called the Blank template in earlier versions of ArcGIS Pro.
Global Scene	Primarily for use with three-dimensional data that covers a large area. Automatically includes a three-dimensional global scene.
Local Scene	Primarily for use with three-dimensional data that covers a smaller area. Automatically includes a three-dimensional local scene.

To use one of the previously mentioned templates, you simply select it from the **New** panel on the opening screen of ArcGIS Pro, or from the **New** option located in the **Project** tab. Since **ArcGIS Pro 2.3**, you also have the option to start a project without a template. This is similar to using the `Catalog` template, but it does not automatically create the supporting project structure, which you will learn about soon.

You also have the option to select another project template if you do not want to use one of the four Esri-provided templates. You will learn how to select other templates later in this chapter. Let's now see how one of these Esri templates works.

Exercise 5B – Using an Esri template to create a new project

In this exercise, you will create a new project that will contain a local scene using some of the same data you used in the last exercise. You have been asked to create a three-dimensional scene for Union City showing the elevation change of the city and the locations of the basins.

Step 1 – Creating a new project using the Local Scene template

In this step, you will create and explore a new blank project created using the `Local Scene` template:

1. Open **ArcGIS Pro**.
2. On the right-hand side in the ArcGIS Pro start page, select the **Local Scene** template, located under the **New** column.

3. In the **Create a New Project** window, name your project %Your Name% Ex5B and set your location to C:\Student\IntroArcPro\My Projects. Your window should look similar to the one in the following screenshot:

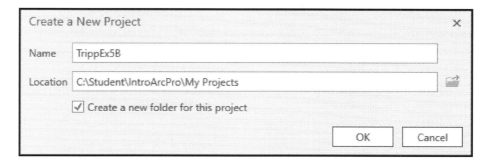

4. Click **OK** to open your new project.

Your new project should have opened with a new scene that only contains a two-dimensional **Topographic** basemap layer. We will now take a moment to explore what else was done automatically by using this Esri template. Explore the **Catalog** pane.

Question: *What is available or listed under* **Maps**? *What is available or listed under* **Toolboxes**? *What is available or listed under* **Databases**?

5. Continue to explore the remaining items in the **Catalog** pane until you have become completely familiar with the new project that you have created and what you currently have access to.

Now, we will take a look at the backend of what happened when you created your new project so that you can see what ArcGIS Pro does when a new project is created. You should look at your project using your operating system's File Explorer.

6. Open your File Explorer application. It uses an icon that resembles a file folder in a file organizer. You can normally find it on the taskbar or desktop.

7. Once you have opened the File Explorer, navigate to `C:\Student\IntroArcPro\My Projects`. You should see a folder inside the `My Projects` folder named `%Your Name% Ex5B`. This folder was automatically created by ArcGIS Pro when you created the new project. This is your project's home folder.

8. Open the home folder so that you can see its contents. The home folder should contain several folders and files, all of which were automatically generated by ArcGIS Pro when you created the new project, as shown:

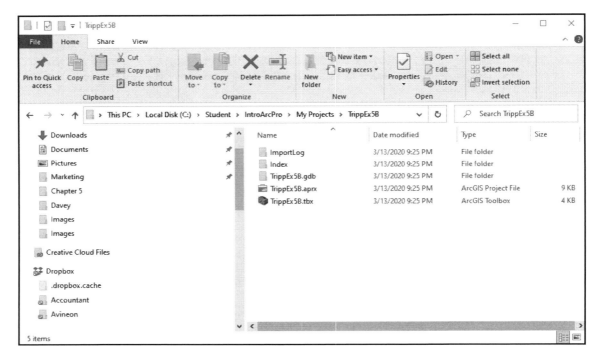

Different templates will create different files and folders. Remember, templates are created with specific purposes in mind, so each one will be different to some extent. Feel free to explore some of the folders in-depth, if desired.

9. Once you are done, close your File Explorer and return to ArcGIS Pro.

You have just created a new project using the Esri-provided `Local Scene` template. Now, let's move on to the next step.

Step 2 – Connecting to data sources and adding your surface

In this step, you will connect to the Union City geodatabase that you used in the last exercise. You will then set up your scene to use the **Digital Elevation Model (DEM)** in that geodatabase as the elevation surface. The elevation surface serves as the ground level or height that all the other layers are overlaid onto within the three-dimensional views provided in a scene:

1. Right-click on your scene in the **Contents** pane and select **Properties**.
2. Click on the **General** option in the left-hand side window and rename the scene Union City.
3. Click on the **Coordinate System** option in the left-side window, then click on the drop-down arrow located adjacent to the **Add Coordinate System** button. It looks like a wireframe globe with a green plus sign.
4. Select the **Import Coordinate System** option from the list of options that can be seen in the following screenshot:

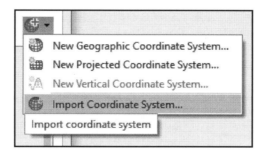

5. In the **Import Coordinate System** window, navigate to C:\Student\IntroArcPro\Databases\UnionCity.gdb. Then, select **DEM raster** and click the **OK** button. This sets your scene so that it will use the same coordinate system as the DEM and other layers that you will add to the scene during this exercise.
6. Click **OK** in the **Map Properties** window to apply your changes, and then close the window.
7. In the **Catalog** pane, right-click on the **Databases** folder and select **Add database** from the menu that appears.
8. Under **Computer**, navigate to C:\Student\IntroArcPro\Databases\ and select **UnionCity.gdb**. Click the **OK** button to add the database connection.

Before you add any layers to your scene, you need to define the elevation surface. By default, ArcGIS Pro uses Esri's World Elevation model from ArcGIS Online. However, you can use your own if you have one. In our case, we do have our own digital elevation model, and it is more accurate than Esri's model. So, should now configure your scene to make use of your local, more accurate DEM.

9. Select the **Map** tab from the ribbon.
10. Click on the **Add Data** text located below the **Add Data** button in the **Layer** group, then select the **Add Elevation Source** option from the list that appears.
11. Click on the **Databases** option, located under **Project** in the left panel.
12. Double-click on **UnionCity.gdb** in the right panel of the **Add Elevation Source** window.
13. Select the DEM that appears and click **OK**.

You should now see the Union City DEM above the default ArcGIS Pro ground elevation in the **Contents** pane. Since we are not concerned with areas outside the immediate Union City area, in this scene, you will remove the default ArcGIS Pro ground surface.

14. In the **Contents** pane, right-click on **World Elevation 3D/Terrain 3D surface** and select **Remove** from the menu that appears, as in the following screenshot:

15. Using the skills that you learned in previous exercises, add the **Floodplains** and **Watersheds** feature classes to the scene.

16. Using the same process you used in the last exercise, adjust the symbology so that they are symbolized in the same way that they were in *Exercise 5A*:

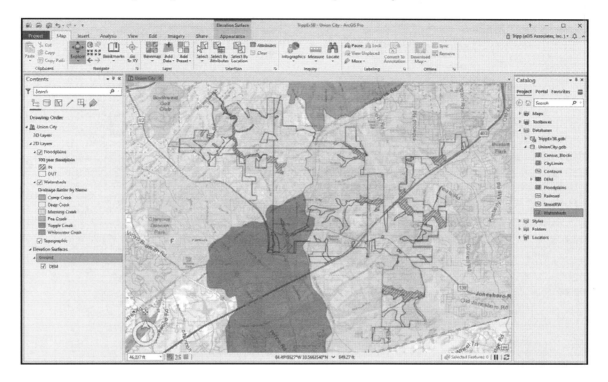

In order to complete this task, you may need to connect to the `Chapter5` folder and add the Esri style again.

17. Save your project.
18. Click on the **Map** group tab in the ribbon.
19. Click on the **Add Data** button and navigate to the `Chapter5` folder located in `C:\Student\IntroArcPro\`.

If you are connected to the `Chapter5` folder, all you need to do is click on **Folders | Chapter5** as a shortcut to quickly access the folder.

20. From the `Chapter5` folder, choose **3D Buildings.lyrx** and click **OK**.

You have just added a new layer to your scene using a layer file. As you can see, the layer was automatically assigned specific symbology. This was because you used a layer file to add the data instead of going directly to the geodatabase and adding the feature class. A layer file contains predefined settings for a layer, including symbology, labeling, transparency, the source, and more. It allows you to standardize layers for use in multiple maps.

21. Right-click on the **Buildings** layer you just added and select **Zoom to Layer**.

22. Using the **Explore** tool, along with the scroll wheel on your mouse, zoom into the area where the **Whitewater Creek**, **Morning Creek**, and **Deep Creek** watershed basins intersect. Zoom in until your map looks as in the following screenshot:

As you can see in the preceding screenshot, you can now see the buildings in 3D with a realistic facing applied. You can see what basin they are in, and if you pan around, you can also see which ones are in the 100-year floodplain.

23. Save your project and close ArcGIS Pro.

So, in this section, you have learned how to create a new project using Esri's `Local Scene` template and how to build out the scene with layers and a local elevation surface. *But how do you create your own project templates for use by ArcGIS Pro users in your organization?* We will investigate that next.

Creating custom project templates

In the last exercise, you saw how useful a template can be to start a new project. In this section, you will learn how to create a custom project template.

Templates can standardize all the projects that you or your organization create in ArcGIS Pro so that they access the correct databases, contain the appropriate styles, and have the proper layout elements. Project templates are really specialized versions of a project package that can be used to create new projects. They have a `.aptx` file extension.

Project templates can be saved to several locations. You can save them to your computer, a network share, ArcGIS Online, or Portal for ArcGIS. Where you save them will help determine who can use them.

Project templates saved to your computer generally can only be used by you. This can limit their value to an organization. However, since they are stored locally on your computer, they can be better suited for your personal use. This is because they can contain connections to local resources that exist on your computer, which others may not have access to. Also, if you include connections to secure data sources or files, you do not have to worry about whether other users will have permission to also access those locations.

Project templates you save to a network share—for example, a folder on your file server or to ArcGIS Online—can be used by others in your organization when creating new projects, assuming they have sufficient privileges to access the location. This allows you to standardize projects created by ArcGIS Pro users throughout your organization, which has several advantages:

- Templates can ensure you're using common map layouts, which include standard title blocks, north arrows, logos, and legal disclaimers.

- Templates can ensure everyone accesses the correct data sources, folders, styles, and toolboxes.
- Templates can ensure data and files are saved to the proper locations by standardizing a common project structure.
- Templates can ensure everyone uses the correct basemap when creating maps or scenes.

The preceding points are just a few of the advantages of using templates within an organization. If you are going to save your templates to ArcGIS Online, there is a security concern that you need to make sure to pay careful attention to, which is who you choose to share with.

If your organization has enabled sharing outside your organization, it is possible that others who are not in your organization will access your templates. When you create and save a template to ArcGIS Online, you are asked about who you wish to share the template with. If you select everyone, then you will be sharing your template with any users that have access to ArcGIS Online. That includes those who are not part of your organization. This means ArcGIS Pro users who are not affiliated with your company or group will be able to use your template. This also means they will be able to see everything you included in the template, such as database connections, logos, folder connections, layouts, and more. Access to your templates could represent a security breach waiting to happen if you are not careful. So, when you save a template to ArcGIS Online, make sure to pay attention to who you choose to share it with.

Let's work on another exercise next that helps us create a custom template.

Exercise 5C – Creating a custom project template

Now that you understand why you would want to create custom project templates, let's look at the how to do so. In this exercise, you will create a custom project template that you will save to your computer. This template will include a map, database connections, and more. Once you create the template, you will then create a new project that uses the template.

Step 1 – Creating a project

All templates start as a project. So, to create a new template, you must first have a project that contains all the standard settings you wish to include in the template. So, we will start this step by creating a new project using the `Catalog` template, which provides you with a blank slate upon which you can build your template:

1. Start **ArcGIS Pro**.
2. On the right-hand side in the ArcGIS Pro start page, select the **Catalog** project template.
3. In the **Create a New Project** window, name your project `%Your Name% Ex5C` and set your location to `C:\Student\IntroArcPro\My Projects`.
4. In the **Catalog** pane, right-click on **Database** and select **Add Database**.
5. In the **Select Existing Geodatabase** window, navigate to `C:\Student\IntroArcPro\Databases` and then select the `Trippville_GIS.gdb` file to add it as a connected database.
6. Using the skills you have learned, add the `ESRI.stylx` style to the project.
7. Save your project.

We will now move on to the next section, which describes the next step.

Step 2 – Setting up a default map in the template

Now that you have opened a new project and established some default connections to databases and styles, you will now create a default map that will be included in the template. You will configure a basemap and then set a default view extent:

1. In the **Contents** pane, right-click on **Project** and select **New Map**. This will add a new map to your project.
2. On the **Map** group tab in the ribbon, click on the small drop-down arrow under **Basemap** and select **Imagery**.
3. In the **Catalog** pane, expand the **Databases** folder and the **Trippville_GIS** geodatabase that are you connected to.

4. Expand the **Base** feature dataset and right-click on the **City_Limit** feature class, then select **Add to Current Map**.

Your map should zoom to the new **City Limits** layer you just added, so it should look similar to the following screenshot:

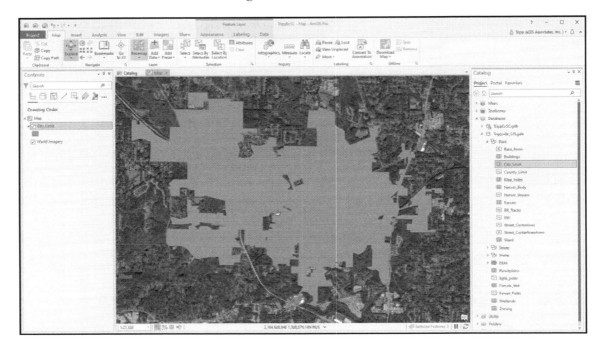

Remember that the color for the **City_Limit** layer may be different in your map because ArcGIS Pro assigns a random color to new layers unless you add the new layer using a layer file.

Adding the **City_Limit** layer also assigns the coordinate system you wish to use for the map and in your template. Just as with ArcMap, the first layer you add to a map in ArcGIS Pro assigns the coordinate system to the map. Now, you will set the view extents, which will be the default for this map in your project.

5. Right-click on **Map** in the **Contents** pane and select **Properties**.

6. In the **Map Properties** window, select **Extent** from the left-hand side pane.

7. Click on **Use a Custom extent** tab in the right-hand side panel.

8. Click on the **Current visible extent** option located under **Get extent from**. This will set your map so that when you select the **Zoom Full extent** button, it will take you to this zoom scale. Then, click **OK** to apply the setting.

9. Using the skills that you learned in `Chapter 2`, *Navigating the Ribbon Interface*, make the following changes to the **City_Limit** layer:

   - Set the symbology to a hollow fill.
   - Set the outline to **Mars Red**.
   - Set the outline width to `2` pt.
   - Rename the layer `City Limits`.

10. Save your project.

You have created a simple map that will be part of the template you are working to create. This means anyone that uses the template will start with this map in their project.

Step 3 – Adding a layout from an existing map document

There is one last thing to add to your project before you save it as a template. We want to add the layout that we have been using in the map documents we created with **ArcMap**, which is another Esri application. This will allow our maps to look the same, regardless of whether they are created in ArcGIS Pro or ArcMap:

1. Click on the **Insert** group tab in the ribbon.

2. Click on the small drop-down arrow located next to **New Layout** and select **Import layout file...**, located near the bottom of the window that appears, as shown:

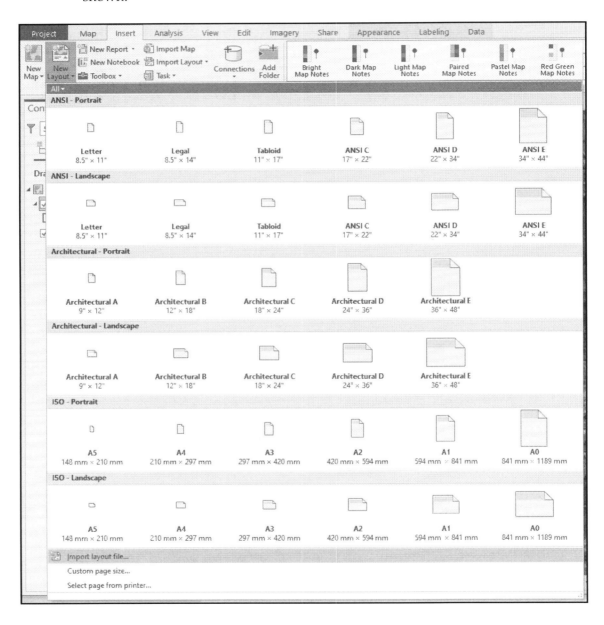

3. In the **Import** window, navigate to C:\Student\IntroArcPro\Chapter5. Choose the Sample Layout.mxd file and click **OK**.

You have just imported the map layout, which was in the map document. This layout was created with ArcMap and is used by your organization as a standard layout for all the maps you print. You will need to make some adjustments to this layout for it to work properly in ArcGIS Pro.

4. Right-click on **Map Frame** in the **Contents** pane and select **Properties** to open the **Format Map Frame** pane on the right-hand side of the interface.
5. Make sure the **Options** button is selected in the pane. It is the first one located under **Map Frame**.
6. You should see two options—**General** and **Map Frame**. In the **General** option, rename the frame Map Frame.
7. In the **Map Frame** option, click on the drop-down menu and select **Map**. When you do that, you should see the map you created in *step 2*; it should appear in the layout. It should look like this now:

8. Close the **Format Map Frame** pane.

9. You should save a bookmark for this layout so that you can easily return to this location and scale. Select the **Layout** tab on the ribbon.

10. Click on the small arrowhead located below the **Bookmarks** button in the **Map** group.

11. Then, choose **New Bookmark**. In the **Create Bookmark** window, name your bookmark `Print Layout`. For the **Description** type, this bookmark will return you to the correct location and scale to print the entire city limits area. Then, click **OK**.

12. Close the sample layout and save your project.

Let's look at the next step in the next section.

Step 4 – Saving a project as a template

Now that you have configured the project to have your standard style and folder connection, plus included a sample map and layout, which will be the common basis for new projects, you are ready to save your project as a template:

1. Click on the **Share** tab on the ribbon.

2. Select the **Project Template** button in the **Save As** group tab.

3. The **Create Project Template** pane is displayed on the right-hand side of the interface. Under the **Start Creating** section, select **Save the template to file**.

4. Click the **Browse** button, located under **Name and Location**, to specify the location you will save the template to and the name you will give it.

   The default location is located in your user profile and the `ProjectTemplates` folder. You will accept the default location so that the template appears on your list when you start ArcGIS Pro.

5. Name your template `%your name% 2D Project Template` (that is, `Tripp 2D Project Template`) and click **Save**.

6. You will now need to fill out the item description information for the template. The item description is a shortened form of metadata. Complete the following, as indicated:

- **Summary**: This serves as a template for two-dimensional ArcGIS Pro projects and includes a single two-dimensional map and a layout. It will automatically connect to the `Trippville_GIS` geodatabase and add the Esri symbol style.

- **Tags**: Tags are keywords used by the search function in ArcGIS Pro, such as `2D`, `Trippville`, `layout`, `map`, and `template`.

7. Click the **Analyze** button to make sure your template does not contain any issues that would prevent it from working properly. The **Analyze** button will automatically take you to the **Message** tab in the pane. You should not see any errors or warnings. If you do, correct them, as recommended by ArcGIS Pro.

8. Once you have no errors in the **Messages** tab, click on the **Create** button in the pane. If you are asked whether you want to save your project, click **Yes**.

   When ArcGIS Pro is done creating the template, you will see a message letting you know that it is complete.

9. Close ArcGIS Pro. You can choose to save the project if you desire, but it is not required.

We will now move on to the last step of the exercise.

Step 5 – Creating a new project using a custom template

Now that you have created a custom project template, you need to know how to use it when you create a new project. In this step, you will use the project template you just created to create a new ArcGIS Pro project:

1. Start ArcGIS Pro.

2. In the ArcGIS Pro start page, click on **Select another project template**, located on the lower-right-hand side, as shown:

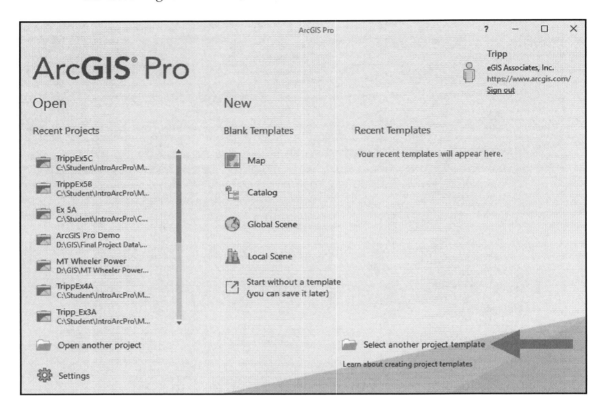

3. Select the template you created in the previous step. It should appear in the right panel of the **Create New Project From Template** window. Then, click **OK**.
4. Name your new project %your name% template test.
5. Set the save location to C:\Student\IntroArcPro\My Projects and click **OK**.

    Your new project should open with a map that looks very familiar. You should see the **City Limits** layer with the **Imagery** basemap.

6. Take some time to explore the **Catalog** pane. Look at what connections, maps, layouts, and styles are present.
7. When you are done exploring your new project, save it and close ArcGIS Pro.

You have just created a new project using your own custom template.

Word of warning

When creating custom templates using ArcGIS Pro, there is something you should know that happens if your template references data or folders that are located on mapped drives. A **mapped drive** is one that is referred to by a drive letter, such as the C: drive, which is normally the local drive on your computer, or the M: drive, which is located on a network file server.

While using ArcGIS Pro, it is preferred that you don't use mapped drives, especially when creating templates. It's preferred that you use a **Universal Naming Convention (UNC)** path. *So, what is a UNC path?* This is what IT people use to connect mapped drive letters to a folder on their server. A UNC path looks something like \\GIS_Server\GIS_Data_folder. GIS_Server is the name or IP address for the server on your network. GIS_Data_Folder is a share created by the server administrator on that server to allow others on the network to access the files contained within it.

ArcGIS Pro's preference for UNC paths makes sense for data that resides on a server because it is not uncommon for different people in an office to use different drive letters to reference the same location on a server. For example, I might have \\GIS_Server\GIS_Data_folder mapped to the M: drive because I think GIS is mapping, so I think it makes sense to map the GIS data to the M: drive. However, my colleague may map the same server location to the G: drive for GIS. However, if I used the UNC path instead, it would be the same location for both of us.

So, what happens if you create a template that references mapped drives? Well, when you create a new project based on the template, ArcGIS Pro will actually create copies of your data. It does this without any warning and unless you look closely at your layer sources, you will not notice that this has happened. To learn more about this, visit https://youtu.be/ tyu439Uownk.

It should be mentioned that if you are referencing an Enterprise/SDE database or web services, this duplication will not happen.

Summary

In this chapter, you learned how important projects are when using ArcGIS Pro. They are the very core of the application. You have seen how they contain all the items associated with a project, including database connections, maps, styles, toolboxes, layouts, server connections, and more. By having all of these in a project, it is much easier to access the resources that you will need to perform GIS work in ArcGIS Pro.

You now know how to create new projects using the Esri-provided templates, as well as custom ones that you can create. Once you create a project, you also know how to add new resources to the project so that you are able to perform the required GIS functions to complete tasks. As you have seen, a project is not limited to a single database, map, folder, or style. You can choose to make as many connections as you wish so that you are able to access whatever datasets, tools, and symbology that you need.

Because a single project can contain multiple connections and other items, it is important to manage all the items included in the project to ensure the project runs effectively and provides access to the most relevant data. The **Catalog** pane in ArcGIS Pro provides the tools and methods to access, add, view, or remove those resources. This will ensure the project performs efficiently.

Lastly, you learned how a project template can be used to make creating new projects more efficient by preconfiguring various project items. You have the option to use one of the predefined ArcGIS Pro templates, or you can create your own custom templates.

You now have the skills and understanding for creating maps, scenes, and projects. The next chapter will take you through how to create layouts so that you can present your work in a professional manner.

6
Creating a Layout

You have seen how you can create informative and interesting 2D and 3D maps using ArcGIS Pro. While these are impressive, they are not complete. The last step to producing any map is to put it in a frame with other information, which helps the viewer comprehend the information you are presenting. This frame is called a **layout**.

Each layout you create will include several elements, such as a north arrow, a scale, and a title, in addition to one or more map frames. The need to include various elements in your layout will depend on the story that you are trying to impart to the viewers. Before you create your layout, you need to take some time to figure out the following:

- *What is the purpose of this layout?*
- *How will it be used?*
- *Who will be using it?*

This chapter will help you answer these questions, which will impact how you design your layout. They will help you determine the size, scale, and details that you need to include. So, some thought should be given before you even start building the layout in ArcGIS Pro. This chapter will help you learn how to create a layout and a layout template of your own.

The one thing you always need to keep in mind is that the layout represents your final product. It will form the basis upon which all your efforts are judged. It will not matter how good your data or analysis happens to be if it is not presented in a clear and professional manner.

Designing a well-thought-out layout will lend credibility to all your hard work. It is also an opportunity to let your creative side show. The one thing I always tell those who are new to **Geographic Information Systems (GIS)** when they reach this point is to *make it pretty*. While that seems simple, there are plenty of examples of GIS maps that fail to meet that simple guideline.

In this chapter, you will learn about the following topics:

- Understanding the considerations of designing a layout
- Creating a layout in ArcGIS Pro
- How to add a new layout to a project
- How to design a layout that contains one or more map frames
- How to create and use a layout template

Technical requirements

This chapter has no special technical requirements other than access to an **ArcGIS Pro 2.5** or higher license. Any license level will work—**Basic**, **Standard**, or **Advanced**. You will also need to have completed *Exercise 3A* and *Exercise 3B* from `Chapter 3`, *Creating 2D Maps*.

Understanding the considerations of designing a layout

Creating an effective layout that communicates the results of your GIS efforts takes thought and planning. There is more to it than just printing your map or randomly adding some elements to a page. In general, there are three basic considerations that you need to address as you are creating a new layout:

- **Purpose**: Why does this map exist?
- **Audience**: Who will be using the map?
- **Situation**: How will it be used or presented?

All of the preceding three factors will impact how you design your layout. They will guide the size of the map, the orientation, the content, and more.

In this section, we will understand the purpose of a map, along with working out the audience for a map.

Understanding the purpose

Each map or poster exists for a reason. It has some purpose—it may be trying to show the location of the city hall, what parcels are in the flood zone, or how to get from one location to another. The purpose of a map or layout defines the overall theme of that map. It also helps determine what content needs to be included. Some common map purposes include the following:

- To show the location of features
- To highlight specific attributes associated with features, such as zoning classification, population size, pipe material, or road type
- To show spatial relationships between features in one or more layers
- To present the results of the analysis
- To meet legal requirements, such as the **official zoning map** for a city

It is now easy to see how the purpose will be a factor in determining the content of your layout. If you are creating a zoning map, you will certainly need a map frame that shows the zoning classification of each parcel. You will also need a legend that allows the map viewers to understand the different classifications. If this is the official zoning map for the city, you may also need to add places for city officials to sign the map and the date of adoption.

In the next section, we will understand how to determine the purpose of a map.

Practice exercise – Determining the purpose

Based on the five purposes listed previously, let's try to determine the purpose for each of the following maps:

- The following screenshot of **map 1** shows you a visual of the city of Trippville. *What is the purpose of this map?*

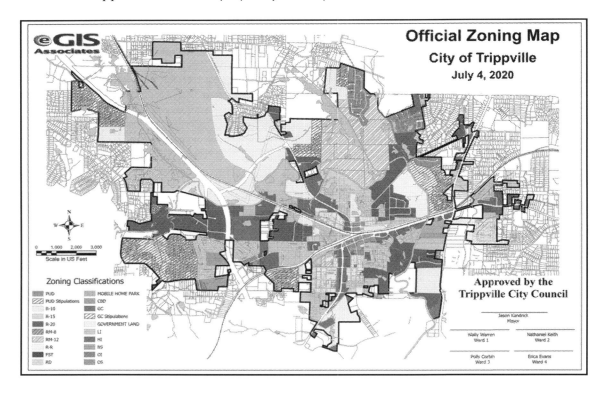

- The following screenshot of **map 2** shows you the underground sewer system for the city. *What is the purpose of this map?*

- The next screenshot of **map 3** shows you the parcels in relation to wetlands. *What is the purpose of this map?*

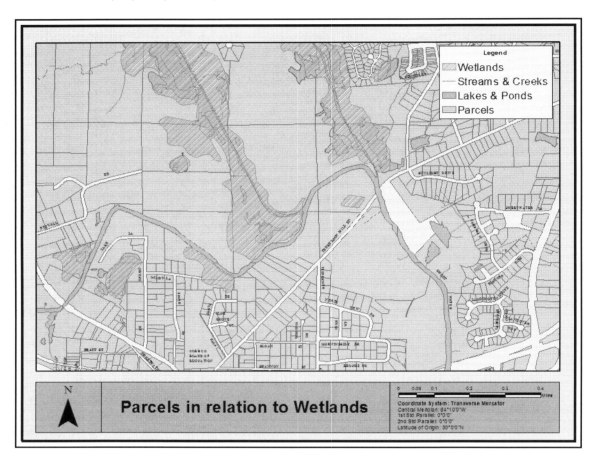

The preceding maps are just a few examples.

Think back to other maps you have seen or used and see whether you can remember their purpose. See whether you can think of any other purposes in addition to the ones mentioned here in this book. We will discuss the audience in the next section.

Understanding the audience for the map

Who will use your map will also have a great impact on how you design and present your map. This is your audience. There are several factors about your intended audience that you should consider, such as the following:

- **Age**
- **Education or knowledge level**
- **Physical abilities or disabilities**

We will look at each of the preceding factors in the upcoming sections.

Learning about the age factor

If you are preparing a map for an older audience, you may need to make the font bigger to make it easier to read. This may mean you cannot put too much detail into a single map to avoid over-cluttering it, which might also mean you need to create multiple maps for this audience. Age may also impact the choice of symbology styles you use. If you are making a map for a very young audience, you might want simple, brightly colored symbols, for example.

Age can also impact the methods you use to present the maps you create to ensure the greatest impact. Younger audiences tend to prefer digital media to printed maps, while older audiences tend to prefer printed maps to digital media.

Understanding the education and knowledge level

The education and knowledge level of your intended audience will also have an impact on your map and layout design. For example, if you are creating a map of your sewer system for a group of civil engineers, they are going to want a lot of detail. They will want to know the pipe sizes, flow direction, treatment capacities, and more.

However, if you are creating a sewer map for the general public, that level of detail will confuse many because they do not have engineering education or knowledge. The public will more likely just be interested in knowing whether they have sewer service or not.

Physical abilities or disabilities are something you should also consider:

- *Will the audience include a lot of people that wear glasses?*
- *Will some of them be color blind?*

These factors are to be considered as well when designing your layout and maps.

 Question: *If you know that your audience might include someone that is color blind, what can you do or change so that they can successfully use your map as well?*

We will now move on to the next section, which covers learning about the situation.

Learning about the situation

The situation is all about how your map will be presented and used:

- *Will it be presented in a digital format or will it be printed?*
- *Will it be hung on a wall, used during a presentation, or taken out into the field?*
- *Is it a legal document? If so, are there any defined requirements?*

All of the preceding points will impact your design.

You may wonder why you would design a map differently if you are going to print it versus publish it digitally. Well, the simple answer is that each has its own limitations. When printing a map, you are limited by the capabilities of your printer. *Is it color or just black and white? What sizes will it print? How much memory does it have?* It does little good to design a colored 36 inch by 48 inch map with aerial photography if all you have is a small desktop color printer that has only a couple megabytes of memory.

Your map will overwhelm a printer like this. Another thing you need to consider when printing maps is paper quality, especially if you're using an inkjet-style printer. The quality of the paper you use in an inkjet printer has a big impact on the quality of your final output and even what you can print. Low-grade, 20 lbs bond paper will not produce a high-quality map. It will also not do well with a map that has a large amount of fill or aerial photos. The paper just cannot absorb the amount of ink that is applied, so it will become wrinkled and rip very easily. It might even damage your printer.

There are several options that you have for publishing a map digitally. You can publish it in a .pdf file. This allows people without GIS software to view your creation on a wealth of devices and even add the map to a website without the need for special GIS web servers. .pdf files can also be secured, requiring a password to open them. Current versions of the **Portable Document Format (PDF)** format even support layers and attribute data. This allows you to create an interactive map, even for those without GIS software. When creating a PDF, you must consider the file size. The more you include in a map and the higher the resolution, the larger the PDF becomes.

You can also publish your maps to **ArcGIS Online** or **ArcGIS Enterprise**. These allow even greater levels of access and functionality. However, these are web-based technologies, so you must always be concerned about performance when you are designing a map that will be published in this manner. Simpler is always better. You will need to avoid complex symbology and labels wherever possible. Reducing the number of layers also helps.

Another popular way to present a map digitally is by using a projector. This is especially common when presenting the map at a meeting. Projectors tend to wash or fade colors, however, so you may need to choose a more intense color palette for your map if you intend to project it. Also, remember that projectors will impact the scale of your map. Even though you might set the map to one scale in ArcGIS Pro, the projected image will not always be on that same scale.

Those are just a few of the ways that the situation might impact your map design. Let's see what other things you can think of where a given situation might impact your design. Answer the following questions:

- You are preparing a map of your water system that will be given to the field crews to help them locate the system in the field. The maps will be stored in their trucks and used in all kinds of weather. *How might this impact your design?*
- You are preparing the official zoning map for a city. This will be the legal zoning map, as required by the city's zoning ordinance, and will hang in the city hall for city officials and citizens to use. *What factors should you consider that might impact your design?*

Now, you know what three things need to be considered when designing your layout and how you should plan to present it to your audience. You also learned about the purpose and audience of a map. It is time to begin building your layout.

Creating a layout in ArcGIS Pro

Now that you know what factors can impact the design of your layout, it is time to learn how to actually create a new layout in ArcGIS Pro. ArcGIS Pro supports several methods for creating new layouts. You can start from scratch, adding a new blank layout to your project, or you can import an existing map document file that was created using **ArcMap**, another Esri desktop GIS application. You can also copy an existing layout within your project, or you can use a map or import a layout file as a template.

We will now explore a couple of these methods using the project that we created in *Exercise 3B* and *Exercise 3C* in Chapter 3, *Creating 2D Maps*. The director has asked you to print a few of the maps you created in those exercises. So, you will create a layout for each map that the director wants to be printed.

However, before you get started on creating the requested layouts, in this section, you will explore the general workflow required to create a new layout. Once you have done that, you will jump into a hands-on exercise to create your own layout.

Understanding the general workflow to create a layout

As we have discussed, creating a new layout in ArcGIS Pro does take some time and thought. There are several steps that make up the general workflow required to generate a new layout within your projects, as illustrated in the following diagram:

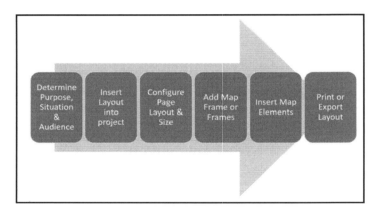

As you can see, you will first start with the three considerations discussed previously—the purpose, situation, and audience. Once you have determined those considerations, you will need to insert the new layout into your project. Once you have inserted the layout, you will need to configure the page size and layout.

This will be heavily influenced by the situation and audience considerations you have determined that will apply to this layout. With that complete, you will then insert the map frame or frames needed to support the purpose. Next, you will begin to insert map elements, such as a title, north arrow, scale, and legend, into the layout. Lastly, you will print your layout or export it to a file, such as a **PDF**.

Now, it is time for you to put this new knowledge to work with a hands-on exercise. In the following exercise, you will create a new layout based on a request from the director.

Exercise 6A – Creating a simple layout

The director wants you to print a copy of the map you created previously that identified commercial properties that were between 1 and 3 acres. He needs to use the map in a meeting that he will conduct with the executives of the company to search for a new office in the city.

Step 1 – Opening ArcGIS Pro and your project

The first step is to open the project in which you will be creating the layout:

1. Start **ArcGIS Pro**.
2. If you see the %your name% Ex3B project listed in the **Open a recent project** list, select it and proceed to next step. Otherwise, click on the **Open another project** option.
3. Click on **Computer**, located under **Open**.
4. Select the **Browse** button.
5. In the **Open Project** window, select your C: drive from the tree in the left-hand side pane.
6. Navigate to C:\Student\IntroArcPro\My Projects\Tripp Ex3A and click on %your name% Ex3B.aprx, then click on the **Select** button.

Your project should open to a familiar map. You should see up to three tabs across the top of the map view area for each of the three maps you created in the exercises from Chapter 3, *Creating 2D Maps*.

Step 2 – Adding a new blank layout

In this step, you will add a new blank layout to your project and then add a map frame that will display the map. This map shows the commercial properties that are between 1 and 3 acres in size.

Since this map will be used in a meeting with multiple people, you will create a large layout. This will allow you to create a map that is easy for a group to view and use in a meeting. For this meeting, the director only wants to focus on those parcels that are within the size limit specified. He does not need to see the entire city:

1. Activate the **Insert** tab in the ribbon menu.
2. Click on the **New Layout** button in the **Project** group tab.
3. From the list of available layout options, select **Architectural E 36" x 48"**, as in the following screenshot:

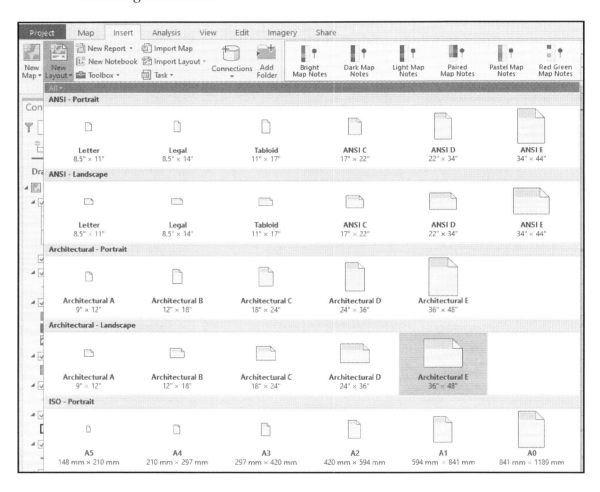

You should now see a new blank layout in your project. In addition, a new folder has been added to your **Project** pane, named **Layouts**.

4. Ensure you still have the **Insert** tab active in the ribbon.
5. Click on the small drop-down arrow located below the **Map Frame** button located in the **Map Frames** group of the **Insert** tab.
6. Select the **Entire City** option from the available options, as in the following screenshot:

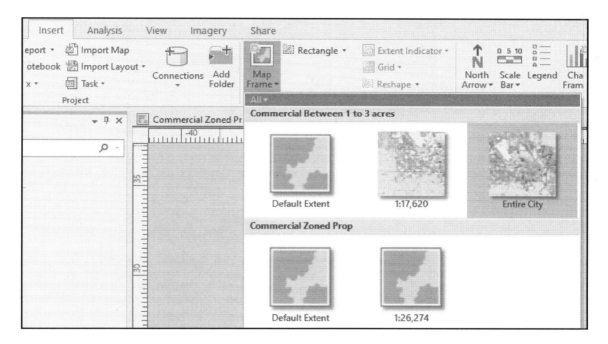

You may remember that **Entire City** is a bookmark. You created it in *Exercise 3B* in Chapter 3, *Creating 2D Maps*. You can either insert the default extent for a map, the current view extent, a scale, or any bookmarks that you have created as the map frame.

7. Using your mouse, double-click in the lower-left corner of the layout. Your layout should look as in the following screenshot:

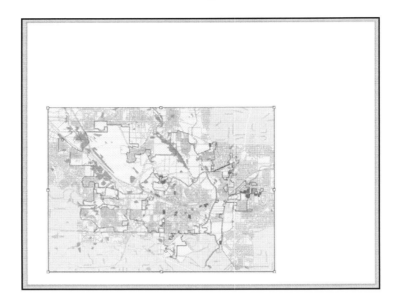

As you can see, the map frame only occupies the lower-left corner of your layout. You will now need to resize it.

8. With the map frame inserted, a new tab should have appeared in the ribbon—**Format**. Click on the **Format** tab to activate it.

9. In the **Size and Position** group on the **Format** tab, set **Width** to 45 and **Height** to 30. You will need to press your *Enter* key to apply the values after you type them in.

10. Set **X** to 1.5 and **Y** to 4.5, as in the following screenshot. This should shift the map frame so that you have room at the bottom for elements such as a title, a north arrow, and legend:

11. Save your project.

You have just added your map frame to the layout. This particularly simple layout will only contain a single map frame. The next step will be to ensure the map in the map frame shows the desired area at the required scale.

Step 3 – Displaying the desired area

Now that you have added the desired map to your layout and sized it appropriately, you need to focus on the area that contains the parcels of interest to the director for his meeting. You should notice that these parcels are concentrated on the east side of the city. So, you will need to zoom into that area:

1. From the **Layout** tab, select the **Activate** button, located in the **Map** group.

> Activating a map in a layout allows you to work on it similar to how you do when you have the map open. For those that have used ArcMap, this is the same as double-clicking on the data frame in a layout.

2. The **Map** tab should automatically appear with the **Explore** tool active. Using the **Explore** tool, click on a point that is located near the center of the commercial parcels, which are between 1 and 3 acres in size.
3. Using your scroll wheel and mouse, zoom in on your map until it looks similar to this:

This gets your map very close to where it needs to be, but the director wants the map printed at a scale where 1 inch equals an even number of feet, such as 400 feet or 500 feet. This will allow him to use a ruler to check the distances between features in the map easily.

4. Check the current scale of your map frame by looking at the scale window located in the lower left-hand corner of the map view.

Can you specify what your current scale is?

Your scale should be somewhere between 1:4600 and 1:5600, depending on the size of your monitor. This is very close to a scale that would make 1 inch equal 400 feet. 1:4800 scale is equal to 1 inch, equaling 400 feet if your map is set to use feet as its units.

5. Type `1:4800` into the scale cell located in the lower left corner of the view area as illustrated in the following screenshot:

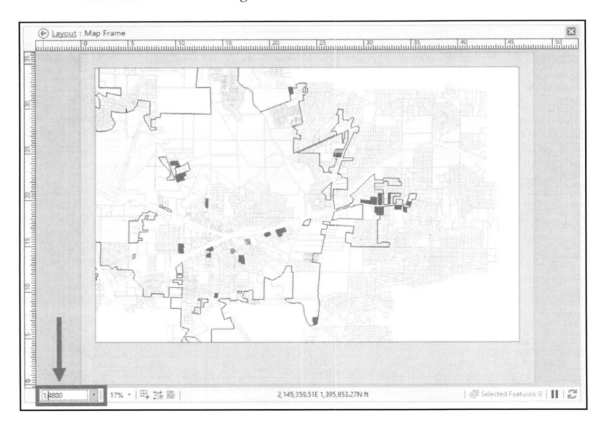

6. If required, use the **Explore** tool from the **Map** tab to pan your map some more until all the parcels in the **Commercial Properties from 1 to 3 AC** layer are visible.

This would also be a good time to create a bookmark for the map, which would allow you to easily return to this scale and location in case the map is somehow disturbed.

7. Once you have verified that all the parcels of interest are visible, click on the **Layout** tab in the ribbon, and then click on the **Close Activation** button.

In ArcGIS Pro 2.6 or later, you can also click on the **Layout** link located at the top of the layout view. This will also close the activation of the map frame.

8. Save your project.

Let's move on to the last step, which is adding the other elements.

Step 4 – Adding other elements

You are very close to completing your layout. You just need to add a few more elements to your layout, such as a title, north arrow, legend, and scale:

1. Click on the **Insert** tab in the ribbon. From here, you can insert various elements into your layout.
2. Using your scroll wheel, zoom into the lower center of your layout, which is blank. This is where you will place the title.

3. Click on the small drop-down arrow, located to the right of the **Dynamic Text** option, and select **Name of Map**. You should use the name of the map that you added to the layout:

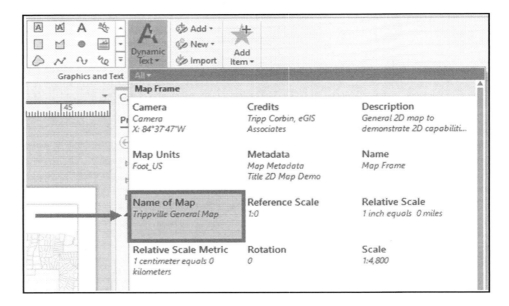

As you can see from the preceding screenshot, **Dynamic Text** is the text that references a specific property of the map frame, project, layout, or your computer system. Dynamic text will automatically update if the value for the specific property changes.

4. Click on a blank area in the layout to place the text. Once you click on a location, the name of the map referenced in **Map Frame** should appear. You will need to make some edits to its properties so that it appears correctly.

5. Click on the **Format** tab that appears in the ribbon. This should also cause the **Format Text** pane to open. If the pane does not open, right click on the **Text** item which appears in the **Contents** pane and select **Properties** from the menu that appears.

6. In the **Format Text** pane, expand the **General** option and rename this element `Title`, as in the following screenshot. If the **Format Text** pane does not appear, double-click on the text you just added to open it:

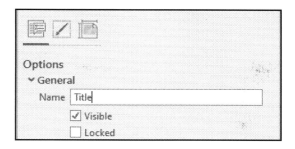

7. Expand the **Text** option, located below **General**. In the field located below **Text**, delete the text string **Name of Map:** from the window so that you can only see **mapName**. Then, click on another area of the pane—for example, click on the **Name** field to apply the change, as in the following screenshot:

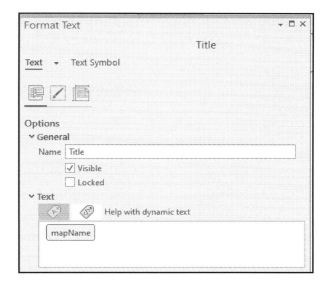

8. Go back to the **Format** tab in the ribbon. Make the following adjustments to the size and position of the text in order to center it at the bottom of the layout and make it large enough to adjust the font size:
    - Set **18.5 in** for the **Width** field.
    - Set **1.5 in** for the **Height** field.
    - Set **14.75 in** for the **X** field.
    - Set **3 in** for the **Y** field.

9. In the **Text Symbol** group, set your font size to **72 pt** so that it fills up most of the text box area.

10. Now, we want to center-justify the title. Go back to the **Format Text** pane and click on the **Text Symbol** tab, as in the following screenshot:

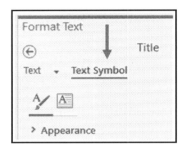

11. Click on the **General** button located below the **Text Symbol** tab. The icon for this button is the letter **A** with a small paint brush below it.

12. Expand the **Position** option by clicking on the small arrow so that you can see the options underneath.

13. For **Horizontal Alignment**, click on the **Center Justification** icon and click **Apply**.

14. Close the **Format Text** pane.

15. Save your project.

You have now configured the title for your map layout. As you have seen, this often serves as the main identifier for the purpose of the map.

16. Now, you need to insert a north arrow. Make sure the **Insert** tab is active and click on the drop-down arrow below **North Arrow**. Select a north arrow style you like, such as **ArcGIS North 1**. (I generally like to keep it simple since the north arrow is only a small element in a larger picture.)

17. Click anywhere to the left of the title you just added to place the north arrow.

18. Click on the **Format** tab in the ribbon. Make the following adjustments to the size and position:
    - Set **1.2 in** for the **Width** field.
    - Set **2.5 in** for the **Height** field.
    - Set **2.8 in** for the **X** field.
    - Set **2.75 in** for the **Y** field.

This will place a north arrow similar to **ArcGIS North 1** in the lower left-hand corner of the layout. If you chose a longer north arrow style, such as **ArcGIS North 4**, then you may need to make additional adjustments to the size and position to get the arrow to fit appropriately. Use your judgment as to what looks best. Remember that this is a chance for you to exercise some artistic flare.

19. Save your project.
20. Zoom in to the area between the north arrow and map title.
21. Activate the **Insert** tab in the ribbon and click on the words **Scale Bar** under the icon to make the different types of scale bars you can insert appear.
22. Select the **Double Alternating 4** scale bar in the **Imperial** group. It should be the last one in the group.
23. Click on a location between the north arrow and title where you want to place the scale bar.

    When it appears in the layout, it will be larger than you need and will overlap on the title. We will fix all that next.

24. Select the **Design** tab in the **Scale Bar** context tab. This tab allows you to control various design settings for the scale bar. Since the director wants the scale to be in inches, you need to make some adjustments to the scale bar.
25. A 1:4800 ratio is the same as 1 inch for 400 feet. So, you need to adjust your scale bar to show that. Change the resize behavior to **adjust the number of divisions**. This will keep the division spacing from changing, allowing you to set it so that the divisions are shown in inch increments.
26. Set the units to **US Feet** in the **Units** group on the **Design** tab.
27. Change **Division Value** to **400**. This sets the division increments so that they are 1 inch.
28. Next, click on the **Format** tab in the ribbon so that you can adjust the size and position of the scale bar:
    - Set **6.5 in** for the **Width** field.
    - Set **1.0 in** for the **Height** field.
    - Set **7.0 in** for the **X** field.
    - Set **2.5 in** for the **Y** field.
29. In the **Text Symbol** group in the **Format** tab, set the font size to **18 pt**.

30. Click on the **Layout** tab and click on the **Full Extent** button, located in the **Navigate** group.

    Your layout should now look similar to the following. Your north arrow and scale bar may look different, depending on which style you selected:

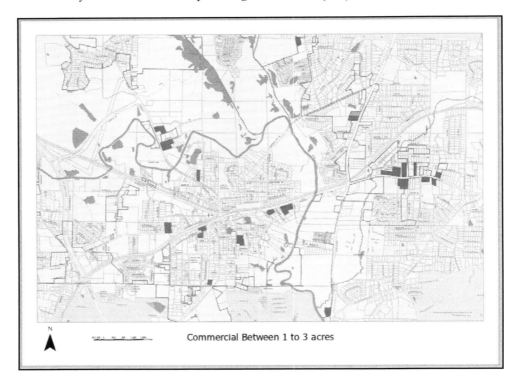

31. Save your project.

You have just created your first layout from start to finish. This is a very simple and clean layout. There are many more things that you could add, such as a legend, an organizational logo, a disclaimer, data source citation, and more. If you would like to try to add other items to your layout, try the *Challenge 1* section.

As you have seen, creating a layout takes many steps, even to create just a very simple one. You can create and use layout templates to help make this process shorter. You will learn about that in the next section.

Challenge 1

Using the skills you learned to insert a north arrow and scale bar, add a legend to your layout. Now, position the legend in the lower-right corner of the layout to help balance its overall appearance.

Exercise 6B – Creating and using a layout template

The director was very happy with the map you made for his meeting and now wants another one. He wants a map printed in the same size but that shows all the commercially zoned parcels in the city.

In this exercise, you will use the layout that you created in the last exercise to create a template file. You will then use that template to create a new layout.

Step 1 – Saving a template file

In this step, you will create a template layout based on the layout you created in the last exercise:

1. Ensure you still have the layout that you created in *Exercise 6A* open. If not, go to the **Catalog** pane, expand the `Layout` folder, right-click on **Layout**, and select **Open**.
2. Click on the **Sharing** tab on the ribbon.
3. Click on the **Layout File** button in the **Save As** group tab.
4. In the **Save Layout as PAGX File** window, select your `C:` drive and then navigate to `C:\Student\IntroArcPro\My Projects`.
5. Name the new layout file `Layout Template` and click **Save**.

You have just created a layout file that can be used as a template for other layouts. New layouts based on this template will contain all the same standardized elements.

Step 2 – Creating a new layout using the layout file

You will now use the file you created in the previous step to add a new layout to your project:

1. Click on the **Insert** tab in the ribbon.
2. Click on the small drop-down arrow located next to **New Layout**.
3. Select **Import a Layout File**, which is located near the bottom of the displayed window.
4. In the **Import** window, navigate to `C:\Student\IntroArcPro\My Projects` and select the `Layout Template.pagx` file you created in *Step 1*.

A new layout has been added to your project that looks exactly like the layout you created in the last exercise. Now, you will need to configure the layout to display the correct map and make adjustments to a few of the elements.

Step 3 – Configuring the new layout

In this step, you will configure the layout to display a map that shows all the commercially zoned parcels in the city:

1. Double-click on the **Select the Commercial Between 1 to 3 acres** map frame in the **Contents** pane to open the **Format Map Frame** pane so that you can adjust the properties.
2. Click on the **Options** button in the **Format Map Frame** pane.
3. Expand the **Map Frame** option if needed.
4. Click on the drop-down arrow for the **Map** option and select **Commercially Zoned Prop**. This assigns the correct map to display in the layout.
5. Change the element name to **Commercially Zoned Property** and press the *Enter* key.

   So that the title appears with the word property spelled out fully, you need to change the name of the map that is being displayed, since the title is in dynamic text.

6. Select the **Commercial Zoned Prop** tab at the top of the map view. This will make that map visible. If this map has been closed, you can open it from the **Catalog** pane by right-clicking on it and selecting **Open**.
7. In the **Contents** pane, right-click on **Commercial Zoned Prop** and select **Properties**.

8. In the **General** properties, rename the map `Commercially Zoned Property` and click **OK**.

9. Click back on the new layout that you have created. (Hint: it may be named `Layout1` or `Layout2`.)

The title should now be changed to reflect the new name of the map displayed in the map frame. Now, you need to adjust the scale of the map so that it displays all the commercially zoned properties, and the legend so that it shows your layers.

10. Using the skills that you learned in *Exercise 6A*, change your scale to `1:7200` so that you can see all the commercially zoned properties in the city, as requested by the director.

11. If you completed the challenge in the previous exercise, select the legend in the **Contents** pane.

12. If required, expand the contents of the legend so that you can see which layers are included in the legend.

13. Click on the **Layers** drop-down menu and turn on all the layers by clicking on the box located next to each layer name.

Once done, your layout should look like the one in the following screenshot. If you did not complete *Challenge 1* from the previous exercise, your layout will not contain a legend:

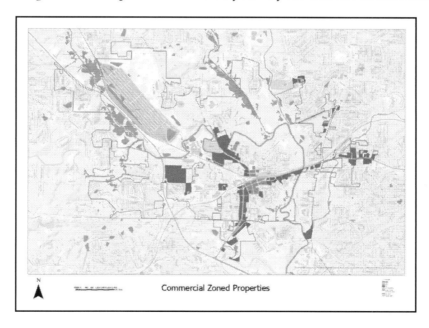

Commercial Zoned Properties

You have just created a new layout using a layout file as a template. It automatically included the same style north arrow and scale bar. All the layout elements were properly positioned. After making some simple adjustments, you quickly created a new layout that is ready for printing.

Challenge 2

You had to change the scale in the new layout that you created so that the scale bar no longer has divisions that are 1 inch in size. See whether you can adjust the scale bar so that the divisions are once again 1 inch in size. It just so happens that 1:7200 equals 1 inch = 600 feet.

Summary

As you have seen, layouts allow you to present your efforts in a professional manner, allowing others to appreciate them. In this chapter, you learned that there are three basic considerations that you need to take into account as you design your layout—the purpose, audience, and situation. You now know how these considerations can impact the design of your layout and how to respond to those impacts.

Once you design your layout, you will need to implement the design within ArcGIS Pro. This will include adding several elements, such as a north arrow, a scale, a title, and more. This chapter has provided you with the skills to insert and configure many of the commonly included elements found in a layout.

Lastly, you learned how to create a layout file that can be used as a template for future layouts you need to create. This allows you to standardize layout elements across projects within your organization, which will help brand your maps and speed up their production.

In the next chapter, you will expand on the skills you learned in this one and learn how to create map books or atlases using the **Map Series** functionality. Map books are helpful in many situations, such as for use in the field by repair or inspection crews or for the inclusion of maps within a report.

7
Creating Map Books Using Map Series

In the previous chapter, you learned how to create new layouts for presenting and printing your maps. This is one of the primary methods that we use to share our **Geographic Information System (GIS)** data with others.

However, in many cases, a single large or small map will not meet the needs of the user. This can be especially true for those who work out in the field. Large maps are unwieldy and become difficult to use. Smaller maps are often unable to clearly display the detailed level of data required when out in the field.

A common practice to resolve these issues is to create a map book or series for the area you need to display. ArcGIS Pro has built-in functionality for creating these map books called **Map Series**. For those who have used the older **ArcMap** application, **Map Series** provides the same basic functionality as **Data Driven Pages**.

This chapter will teach you the process required to enable and configure the Map Series functionality so that you can generate your own map books. In this chapter, you will learn the following topics and skills:

- What is a map series?
- Learning about indexes
- Enabling the Map Series functionality
- Printing a map series

Technical requirements

To complete the exercises in this chapter, you will need access to an **ArcGIS Pro 2.6** or higher license. Any of the three license levels will work, as **Map Series** is part of the core functionality of the software.

What is a map series?

In ArcGIS Pro, a map series refers to two things:

- The first is the automated functionality within the software that allows you to easily create a map book or atlas.
- The second is the result of that functionality.

So, a map book or atlas can also be called a **map series**. This is because it is a series of individual map pages that can be put together to form a larger map area.

In ArcGIS Pro, a single project can contain multiple map series, just like it can contain multiple maps, scenes, or layouts. As you will learn later, the Map Series functionality is linked to a layout. So, each layout, in theory, could be turned into a map series. We will look at steps to create a map series in this section.

Understanding and creating a map series

Just as creating a layout requires some forethought, so does creating a map series. You still need to consider the audience, purpose, and situation. Like a traditional layout, these three considerations will guide you to create your map series. They will help you determine which layers should be included, how much detail is needed, and what size you need to make the pages in the series, which will also impact the scale that you can use to display the data.

Once you have determined the requirements based on the audience, purpose, and situational considerations, you are ready to begin setting up your map series. This will generally consist of five steps, illustrated in the following diagram:

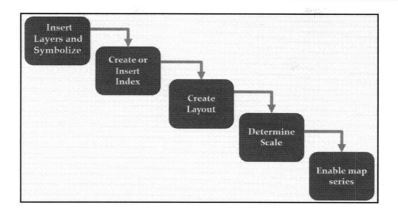

The preceding diagram illustrates the following steps to create a map series:

1. The first step is to add and symbolize the layers to the map that you will be using in your map series layout. These layers will support the purpose of the map series or provide contextual information.
2. The next step will be to determine what layer you want to use as the index for the map series. The index defines the location, number, and extent for each page that will be included in the series. We will discuss indexes in much greater detail later in this chapter.
3. Then, you will need to start creating your layout. This will follow the same basic process that you use to create a traditional single map layout, but with a few minor differences.

   The first difference is determining the page orientation and size. This determination will be based on several factors, such as whether the map series will end up being in a bound booklet or report. If so, *what side will the binding be located?*

   Secondly, *do you need to include a page or sheet number on each page in the series?* Then, *do you need to include a scale, north arrow, legend, or other map elements on each page that you need to make room for?* These are just a few examples of the things that can impact the overall design of your layout.

The following screenshot is an example of a map series layout:

As you are working to create your layout, and even when determining your index, you should also be considering the scale at which you want your map series to be displayed and printed. This can be a single scale for all pages in the series, or it can be variable based on your index.

4. If you want the series to use a variable scale based on each index feature, you will have two options. The first will be to scale each page so that the index feature defining that page fits in the map frame area of the layout. This is the easiest method, but it means that you will not know the exact scale of each page in the series.

   The second option is to use a field in the attribute table of the index layer that contains the specified scale values for each index feature. This provides you with exact scales that you know. The downside is that you must determine the scale for each individual index feature and page.

5. Lastly, you will need to enable and configure the map series in your project. This starts with opening the layout that you want to use for the series. Then, click on the **Layout** tab in the ribbon. Next, you will need to click on the **Map Series** button in the **Page Setup** group. This will open the **Layout Properties** window to the **Map Series** tab. From there, you can configure the various settings that are presented. We will cover those settings in a later exercise in this chapter.

Now that you know the basic steps required to enable and configure a map series, we will take a deeper dive into the types of indexes you can use to define a map series.

Learning about indexes

You cannot have a map series without having an index layer. In this section, you will learn about the types of indexes you can use and how to create them.

The index determines what pages will be included in the map series and the location that they will cover. There are four types of indexes that you can use; they are as follows:

- **Grid index**: A grid index consists of rectangular or square polygons. They are typically identified by the rows and columns that they occupy within the grid, similar to cells in a spreadsheet. In most cases, the polygons are the same size, but they do not have to be the same size. The following screenshot illustrates an example of a grid index:

	GT-256	GU-256	GV-256	GW-256	GX-256	GY-256	GZ-256	HA-256					
	GT-257	GU-257	GV-257	GW-257	GX-257	GY-257	GZ-257	HA-257					
GR-258	GT-258	GU-258	GV-258	GW-258	GX-258	GY-258	GZ-258	HA-258	HB-258				
GR-259 GS-259	GT-259	GU-259	GV-259	GW-259	GX-259	GY-259	GZ-259	HA-259	HB-259	HC-259	HD-259	HE-259	HF-259
GR-260 GS-260	GT-260	GU-260	GV-260	GW-260	GX-260	GY-260	GZ-260	HA-260	HB-260	HC-260	HD-260	HE-260	HF-260
GS-261	GT-261	GU-261	GV-261	GW-261	GX-261	GY-261	GZ-261	HA-261	HB-261	HC-261	HD-261	HE-261	HF-261
GS-262	GT-262	GU-262	GV-262	GW-262	GX-262	GY-262	GZ-262	HA-262	HB-262	HC-262	HD-262	HE-262	HF-262
GS-263	GT-263	GU-263	GV-263	GW-263	GX-263	GY-263	GZ-263	HA-263	HB-263	HC-263	HD-263	HE-263	HF-263	HG-263
GS-264	GT-264	GU-264	GV-264	GW-264	GX-264	GY-264	GZ-264	HA-264	HB-264	HC-264	HD-264	HE-264	HF-264	HG-264	HH-264
GS-265	GT-265	GU-265	GV-265	GW-265	GX-265	GY-265	GZ-265	HA-265	HB-265	HC-265	HD-265	HE-265	HF-265	HG-265	HH-265
GS-266	GT-266	GU-266	GV-266	GW-266	GX-266	GY-266	GZ-266	HA-266	HB-266	HC-266	HD-266	HE-266	HF-266	HG-266	HH-266
GS-267	GT-267	GU-267	GV-267	GW-267	GX-267	GY-267	GZ-267	HA-267	HB-267	HC-267	HD-267	HE-267	HF-267
GS-268	GT-268	GU-268	GV-268	GW-268	GX-268	GY-268	GZ-268	HA-268	HB-268	HC-268	HD-268	HE-268
	GT-269	GU-269	GV-269	GW-269	GX-269	GY-269	GZ-269	HA-269	HB-269	HC-269	HD-269	HE-269
				GW-270	GX-270	GY-270	GZ-270	HA-270	HB-270	HC-270	HD-270
					GX-271	GY-271	GZ-271	HA-271	HB-271	HC-271	HD-271
						GY-272	GZ-272	HA-272	HB-272

- **Strip index**: This follows linear features, such as road centerlines, power transmission lines, and so on. As you can see in the following screenshot, it will often have a rotation that is based on the feature that it is following. The following screenshot shows you an example of a strip index:

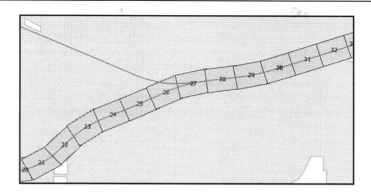

- **Irregular index**: The irregular index is an index based on an existing layer where every feature in the layer gets its own page in the map series. For example, in the following screenshot, we can see the census blocks within a city. If you use that as your index, then each census block becomes a page in the series. Any layer can be used as an index, regardless of its geometry type (point, line, or polygon):

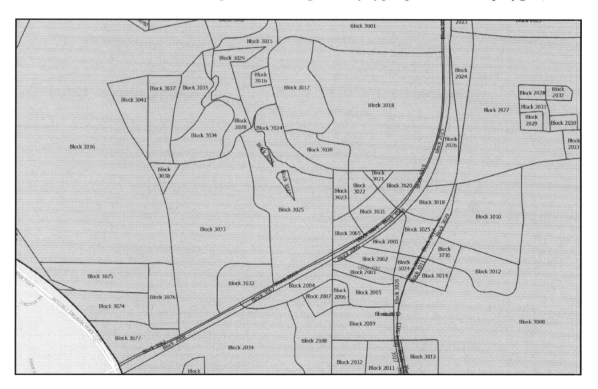

If you want to create a map book that, for example, shows the location of each monitoring well at a solid waste disposal site on its own page, you can do so by using the monitoring wells as an irregular index, even though the monitoring wells are point features.

- **Bookmark index**: The last type of index is one which references the bookmarks which have been saved in the map. You have worked with bookmarks in previous exercises within this book. Bookmarks are saved spatial locations which allow you to quickly return to that spot in the map. Not only do they return to the same location but also to the same visible extent and scale. A map can contain multiple bookmarks, as shown in the following screenshot:

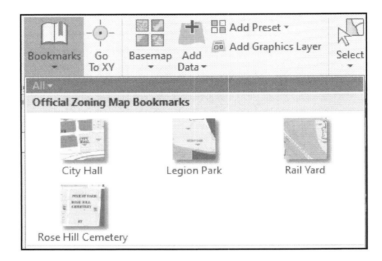

When used as an index each bookmark represents a page within the map book you are creating. This type of index was added in ArcGIS Pro 2.6. It is not available in the prior versions.

Which index works best? That will depend on the purpose of the map series. If you are attempting to highlight specific features located in a single layer, then an irregular index based on that single layer would most likely be the best option. If you are trying to create a map series for a project located along a road or utility transmission line, then a **strip index** would most likely be the best choice. If you are trying to create a map series that will cover the entirety of a city or utility system, then a **grid index** would typically be the best choice.

In the next section, you will learn about creating a grid and strip index. As mentioned, different situations will dictate which of these types of indexes is the best to use. So, it is important that you understand how to create both.

Creating grid and strip indexes

If you do not already have an index created, ArcGIS Pro does provide tools for creating grid and strip indexes. If you look in the **Cartographic** toolbox and the **Map Series** toolset, you will find those tools. We will explore two of these tools next—namely, **Grid Index Features** and **Strip Map Index Features**—in the following few sections.

Understanding the Grid Index Features tool

The **Grid Index Features** tool creates a polygon **feature class** or **shapefile** in a regular grid that can be used as an index to specify pages for a map series. You also have the option of creating a grid that only includes polygon features that intersect with another feature layer or layers. So, if you are creating a new grid index for your bus routes, the tool can be set to ignore any areas within your map that do not contain a bus route.

The following screenshot shows how there are several parameters that you can specify for this tool:

As you can see in the preceding screenshot, **Output Feature Class** is a mandatory parameter because the purpose of this tool is to create a new feature class that will serve as the index for a map series. If you only want index polygons created for areas where specific layers exist, then you will need to add those limiting layers to **Input Features**.

The parameters for **Polygon Width**, **Polygon Height**, **Number of Rows**, and **Number of Columns** are interrelated. These settings work to determine the size of the index polygons and their total number. If you set the width and height, ArcGIS Pro will automatically calculate the number of rows and columns.

If you set the number of rows and columns, ArcGIS Pro will automatically calculate the width and height. It calculates these values based on the full spatial extent needed to cover all the layers in the map you run the tool from, unless you specify **Input Features**.

Learning about the Strip Map Index Features tool

The **Strip Map Index Features** tool creates a polygon feature class or shapefile that follows linear features. Not only does this tool create the index polygons, but it also creates attributes that are automatically calculated. These attributes can be used to rotate and orient the map on the page with the linear feature that the index follows.

In addition, it will also generate attributes that indicate which index features are located around the various sides of the index feature. The following screenshot shows you the parameters of the **Strip Map Index Features** tool:

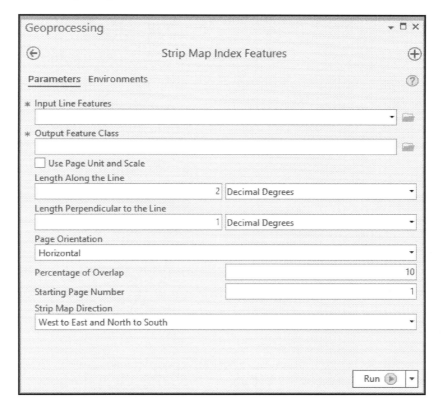

As you can see in the previous screenshot, the **Strip Map Index Features** tool requires you to specify both **Input Line Features** and **Output Feature Class**.

For **Input Line Features**, you designate a specific layer that must be a line or polyline layer or feature class. If you also select specific lines before running the tool, it will only generate index polygons along the selected lines. If you do not have any features selected in the **Input Line Features**-designated layer, it will create index polygons along all the lines contained in that layer.

Let's look at an exercise next for creating a grid index.

Exercise 7A – Creating a grid index

The field crews for the city of Trippville sanitary sewer system need map books to use in the field so that they know where the various components of the sewer system are located when they go out to repair or replace parts of the system. They would like you to print the pages at a scale of 1:1200, where 1 inch is equal to 100 feet. Before you can create the requested map books, you will need to create an index.

In this exercise, you will use the **Grid Index Features** tool to create the index you will need to create the requested map book. You will create the grid index so that it only contains index polygons for the areas within the city that contain components of the sewer system.

Step 1 – Opening ArcGIS Pro and your project

The first step is to open the project in which you will be creating the layout:

1. Start **ArcGIS Pro** as you have done in the previous exercises. Then, click on the **Open another project** option, located at the bottom of the **Recent Projects** column in the ArcGIS Pro start page.
2. In the **Open Projects** window in the left-hand panel, expand the **Computer** option and navigate to C:\Student\IntroArcPro\Chapter7.
3. Then, select the Ex7A.aprx file and click the **OK** button.

Your project should open with a map that contains several layers, including **Sewer Manholes**, **Sewer Pipes**, **City Limits**, **Railroads**, and **Parcels**. It may also contain a basemap, such as topographic, depending on your organization's settings.

Step 2 – Creating the grid index

Since the project is open, it is time to create the index using the **Grid Index Features** tool.

Given that a sewer system consists primarily of pipes, which are linear features, you might wonder why you will be creating a grid index instead of a strip index.

The answer is that the sewer system consists of many connected pipes that are often located close together and run in multiple directions. That would make creating a strip index that is oriented to match the linear features problematic at best.

As a result, a grid index is the better choice. If, on the other hand, there were only specific parts of the sewer system that needed to be covered for a limited project, then a strip index may be better.

Now, it is time to create the index. Follow these steps:

1. From the ribbon, click on the **Analysis** tab.
2. Now, click on the **Tools** button, located in the **Geoprocessing** group, to open the **Geoprocessing** pane.
3. Next, click on the **Toolboxes** tab, located at the top of the pane, so that you can see all the system toolboxes that are included in ArcGIS Pro.
4. Locate and expand the **Cartography Tools** toolbox so that you can see its contents.
5. Now, locate and expand the **Map Series** toolset.
6. Click on the **Grid Index Features** tool to open it.
7. Click on the **Browser** button to the right of the **Output Feature Class** cell. This will open the **Output Feature Class** window.
8. In the left-hand panel of the window that just opened, expand the **Project** option, which should contain databases and folders.
9. Select the **Databases** folder and then double-click on the **Ex7A** database.
10. In the **Name** cell at the bottom of the **Output Feature Class** window, type Sewer_Index and click **Save**.
11. Under the **Input Features** option, use the drop-down arrow to select **Sewer Manholes** from the list that appears. When you do this, another cell should automatically appear below the **Sewer Manholes** layer that you just selected.

12. In the new cell that appeared under **Input Features**, click on the drop-down arrow and select **Sewer Pipes**.

13. Ensure the **Generate Polygon Grid that intersects input feature layers or datasets** option is checked, as in the following screenshot:

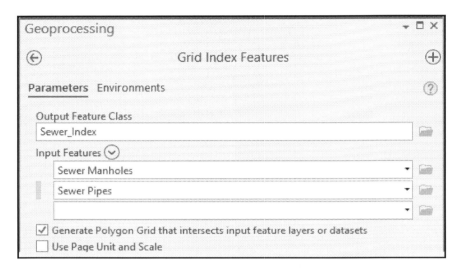

The next step is to either set the polygon height and width or the number of rows and columns. Luckily for you, our city has a standard layout that it likes to use for map books.

This is an 11 inch by 17 inch sheet that has a defined map view area of 10 inches by 15 inches, which is designed to allow binding along the left side. Knowing this and the scale that the field crews need will allow you to calculate the width and height of the new index polygons and define those values here in the tool.

14. Set **Polygon Width** to 1500 and change the units to **Feet**.

15. Set **Polygon Height** to 1000 and change the units to **Feet** if required. Notice how the **Polygon Grid Origin Coordinate**, **Number of Rows**, and **Number of Columns** values are automatically calculated based on the size of the polygons that you entered. It also uses the spatial extent of the two input layers that you defined.

16. Verify that your **Grid Index Features** tool settings look as in the following screenshot and click **Run**:

Once the tool runs successfully, the newly created **Sewer_Index** layer should appear in your map, as in the following screenshot:

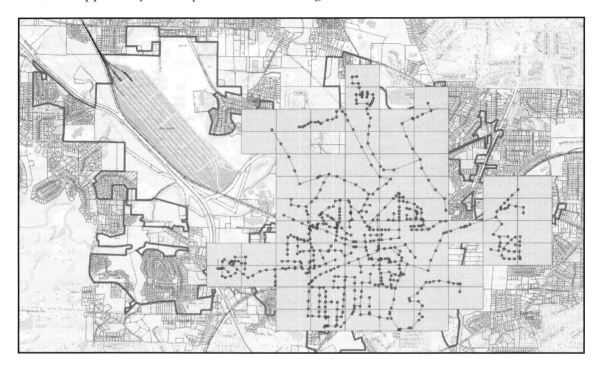

As you can see, the newly created polygons do not cover the entire city. They only cover the portions that contain features in both the **Sewer Manholes** and **Sewer Pipes** layers.

17. Once you have verified that the **Grid Index Features** tool ran successfully, close the **Geoprocessing** pane and save your project by clicking on the **Save** button on the **Quick Access** toolbar.
18. Close **ArcGIS Pro**.

You have now created your index, which you will use to define the pages that will be included in the map series, which you will enable in a later exercise. Each polygon you see in the **Sewer_Index** layer that you created will be a page in the map series. By creating this index, you know what parameters you must provide to generate this layer using the **Grid Index Features** tool.

Now that you know how to create an index, it is time to see how to enable the **Map Series** functionality within a project and layout in ArcGIS Pro.

Enabling the Map Series functionality

The next step is to enable the **Map Series** functionality. You need to do this from the layout that you plan to use for the series, through the **Layout** tab in the ribbon or via the layout properties.

Enabling a map series is not as easy as toggling a switch or radial button. While there is a toggle switch that must be enabled, there are several parameters or settings that must be configured, as you can see in the following screenshot:

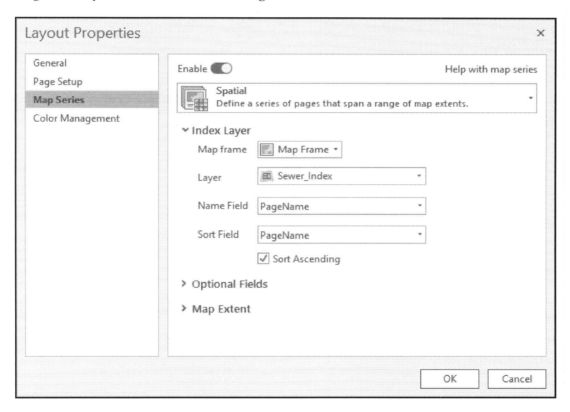

As you can see from the previous screenshot, these settings are grouped into three categories—**Index Layer, Optional Fields**, and **Map Extent**. Before you configure the settings in these three groups, you must first set the map series from **None** to **Spatial**.

To configure the **Index Layer** settings, follow these steps:

1. You will typically start by configuring the settings for **Index Layer**. First, you need to select which map frame will be the primary one for the map series. From that map frame, you then choose the layer that will be used as the index.

2. Next, you set which attribute field associated with the index layer to use for **Name Field**. This field will serve to identify the name for each page in the map series.

3. The last setting you need to configure for **Index Layer** is **Sort Field**. This field will be used to place the various pages in the series into the desired order. **Sort Field** can be set to the same field as **Name Field**, or to a completely different field.

4. Next, you can configure the **Optional Fields** settings if needed. None of these settings are required for the **Map Series** functionality to work, but may provide greater abilities or control for how the series will run. Some of the **Optional Fields** settings you can configure are shown in the following screenshot:

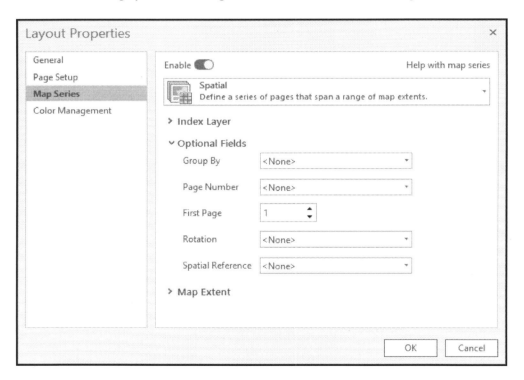

As you can see in the preceding screenshot, the **Optimal Fields** setting includes the following:

- **Group By**: This uses the values found in the specified field from **Index Layer** to group the pages in the series—for example, you may have a field that identifies delivery zones or voting districts.
- **Page Number**: This allows you to specify a field from **Index Layer** that contains page numbers. This can be the same field used by **Page Name** or **Page Sort**, or a completely different field.
- **First Page**: This allows you to set the starting page number for your series. This allows you to plan for other pages, such as the title page or table of contents, to be included in your map book.
- **Rotation**: This allows you to specify a field that contains a rotational value, which will be used to automatically rotate the map view in the layout. This is most often used with strip indexes.
- **Spatial Reference**: This allows you to use different coordinate systems for the various pages in the series based on a field in **Index Layer**. You might want to use this setting if the area you need to cover crosses different coordinate system zones, such as from **Universal Transverse Mercator (UTM)** 16 to UTM 17.

5. Lastly, you will need to configure your **Map Extent** settings. This determines the scale for the map frame that appears in your layout. The options here include the following:

  - **Best Fit**: This option will automatically scale the map frame for each page so that the index feature fits within the bounds of the map frame. This means the scale may vary from one page to another, especially when using an irregular index that contains features of different sizes. You can control the margin size and scale rounding under this extent option.
  - **Center and Maintain Scale**: These options will center the map view on the index feature and maintain whatever the current scale of the map frame happens to be; or, you can specify a scale to be used for all pages.

- **Use Scale from Field**: This option allows you to use a field in the attribute table for the index layer to control the scale of the map frame in the layout. This can be very useful if your index layer consists of features of various sizes and you want to ensure that they are displayed at specific scales instead of just being scaled so that they fit on the page.

Now, it is time for you to configure the map series for the Trippville sewer system using the index you created in *Exercise 7A*.

Exercise 7B – Enabling the map series

In the last exercise, you created an index for the Trippville sanitary sewer system so that you could produce a map book for the city's field crews. It is now time to put that index to use and enable the map series for the sewer system, which means you need to complete *Exercise 7A* before you can move to solve this one.

In this exercise, you will enable the map series using the city of Trippville standard 11 inches by 17 inches layout, which already exists in the project that you will use.

Step 1 – Opening the project and layout

In this step, you will open the project you used in *Exercise 7A* and the layout that you will use for the new map series that you are enabling:

1. Start **ArcGIS Pro** as you have done in the past. Then, click on the **Open another project** option located at the bottom of the **Recent Projects** column on the ArcGIS Pro start page.
2. In the **Open Projects** window in the left-hand panel, expand the **Computer** option and navigate to C:\Student\IntroArcPro\Chapter7.
3. Then, select the Ex7A.aprx file and click the **OK** button.
4. Once the project opens, expand the **Layouts** folder in the **Catalog** pane so that you can see its contents.
5. Right-click on the **Map Series** layout in the **Layouts** folder and select **Open** from the menu that appears.

The layout should look similar to the following:

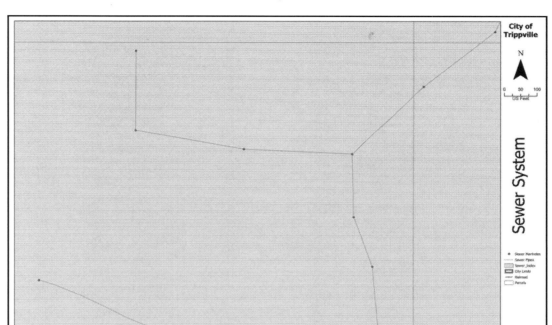

The layout should open in the primary view area.

 Your scale and extent may be different, as well as the fill color for your index layer.

Now that you have the layout open, it is time to enable the map series and configure its settings.

Step 2 – Enabling and configuring the map series

In this step, you will enable the **Map Series** functionality in ArcGIS Pro and configure the required settings:

1. Click on the **Layout** tab in the ribbon. Next, click on the **Map Series** button, located in the **Page Setup** group. This will open the **Layout Properties** window with the **Map Series** tab already selected.

2. In the right panel of the **Layout Properties** window, click where it says **None** to expose a drop-down list. Select **Spatial** from the list, as indicated in the following screenshot:

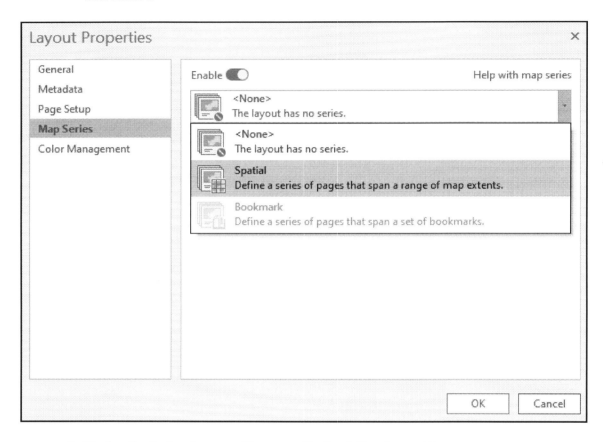

3. Under the **Index Layer** settings, verify the following settings:
   - For the **Map Frame** field, select the **Map Frame** option.
   - For the **Layer** field, select the **Sewer_Index** option.
   - For the **Name Field** field, select the **PageName** option.
   - For the **Sort Field** field, select the **PageName** option.
4. For this map series, you do not need to configure any of the **Optional Fields** settings since all your index grids are the same size, have the same rotation, and do not span multiple coordinate system zones. So, you can skip them. However, feel free to expand and review them if desired.
5. Click on **Map Extent**, located below **Optional Fields**, to expose those settings.

6. Select the **Center and Maintain Scale** option. Click in the **Scale box** and type `1:1200`. This will center each page on the index grid for that page and display it at the scale desired by the field crew.

7. Once you have finished configuring the settings for the map series, click **OK** to finish enabling the functionality.

8. Save your project.

When the map series is enabled, the **Contents** pane should automatically switch to **List Map Series Pages**. This displays a list of all the pages in your series. We will investigate how to use this list later in the exercise. Next, you need to make a small addition to your layout.

Step 3 – Adding a page name to your layout

With the map series enabled, it is time to add a page name to the layout so that as it updates to display each page in the series, the page name will update automatically. You will use **Dynamic Text** to do this:

1. Click on the **Insert** tab in the ribbon.

2. Click on **Dynamic Text**, located in the **Text** group of the **Insert** tab. This will cause a menu of options to appear.

3. Scroll down to the **Map Series** group in the menu. Then, select **Page Name**, as in the following screenshot:

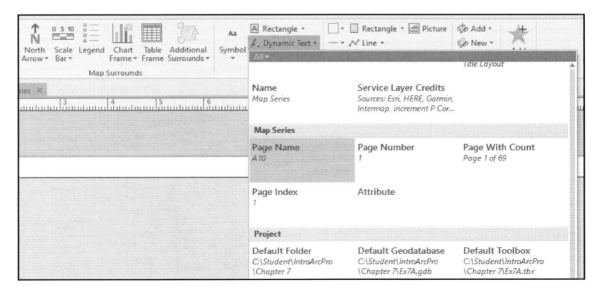

4. You will need to add the **Page Name** dynamic text to the lower-right side of the layout. So, move your mouse pointer to a point just below the lower-left side of the legend. Click and hold your mouse button down while dragging your pointer down and to the right, as shown in the following screenshot, and release it:

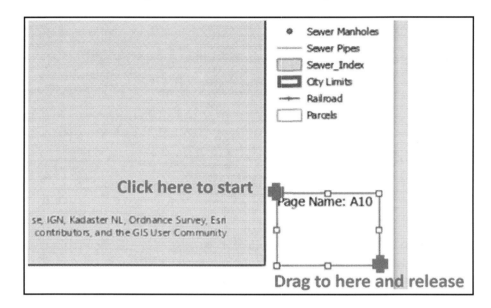

You have just inserted the **Page Name** dynamic text into the layout. This value will automatically update as you look at different pages in the series. You will get a chance to see that a bit later in this exercise. However, the text you inserted is a bit small, so next, you will need to change its size.

5. Click on the **Format** tab that just appeared in the ribbon.
6. Change the size of the text to 14 pt in the **Text Symbol** group of the **Format** tab. The font for the dynamic text that you just inserted should enlarge and should now be more readable.
7. Save your project.

You have now enabled and configured a map series in the ArcGIS Pro project you have been working on. *How do you know it worked? How do you view the individual pages in the series?* These are great questions. So let's learn the answers in the next section.

Step 4 – Viewing pages in a series

It is now time to verify whether the series is working. You will do this by viewing several of the pages in the series, using the **Contents** pane to navigate through them:

1. In the **Contents** pane, click on the **List by Drawing Order** button so that you can see the contents of your layout.
2. Expand **Map Frame** by clicking on the small arrowhead to the left of it.
3. Expand **Sewer System Map** by clicking on the small arrowhead to the left of it. You should now see the list of layers included in the map.
4. Turn off the **Sewer_Index** layer by clicking on the checkmark located to the left of it. You should now be able to see the other map layers.

   After you enable and configure the map series, you do not need to display the index layer for the map series to function. The layer must remain in the map being used, but it does not need to remain turned on.

5. In the **Contents** pane, click on the **List Map Series Pages** button to see the list of pages in the series.
6. Double-click on any page in the list of pages displayed in the **Contents** pane and watch what happens in the layout. Pay close attention to both the map view and the page name text.
7. Continue to double-click on several more pages in the **Contents** pane and watch what happens in the layout.
8. Save your project.

As you can see, when you double-click on a page in the **Contents** pane, the map view and the page name text automatically update to match that page. The map view zooms to the location of that grid polygon and the page name changes to match the value for that page.

Step 5 – Printing a map series

The last step when creating a map book is to print it. In this step, you will see how to print the map series you have created:

1. Click on the **Share** tab in the ribbon.
2. Next, click on the **Layout** button in the **Print** group of the **Share** tab. This will open the **Print Layout** pane.

Normally, you would select the desired printer and then configure the page. With this layout, that would mean setting the page size to **Ledger (11 x 17 in)** and setting the orientation to **Landscape**. You would then typically verify the **Output Quality** settings so that they match the type of printer and paper you are using.

For this exercise, however, we will assume these basic configuration steps have been done and skip straight down to the **Map Series** settings.

3. In the **Print Layout** pane, scroll down to **Map Series** and expand it.
4. Notice all the options for printing your map series. You can print **All**, **Current**, **Selected**, and **Page Range**.

If you wanted to actually print, you would select the desired option under the map series and then click the **Print** button. Since we do not know what printer you have, nor do we want to waste your paper or printing supplies, you will just close the **Print Layout** pane without printing. However, the following screenshot illustrates how a page in the series should look if you were to print it:

5. Close the **Print Layout** pane.
6. Save your project and close ArcGIS Pro.

Now that you have completed this exercise, you know how to properly enable and configure a map series in ArcGIS Pro, as well as how to print it.

Summary

In this chapter, you learned that the **Map Series** functionality allows you to create a map book quickly and easily using a single map and layout in a project. You now have the skills to create a map series, which can be very helpful in the field or for use in a report.

As you learned, there are three types of indexes—namely, grid, strip, and irregular. Which one you should use depends on the purpose of the map series that you are creating. ArcGIS Pro includes geoprocessing tools for creating grid and strip indexes. These are found in the **Cartography** toolbox and the **Map Series** toolset. You can now use an index that defines the location and area for the pages that will be included in the series that you create.

In the next chapter, you will learn the basic workflow required to edit your spatial data. You will examine common workflows and methods used to update the points, lines, and polygons referenced by the layers in your map.

Learning to Edit Spatial Data

8

One of the favorite questions I often hear from administrators, directors, and elected officials is *When will our GIS be done?* The honest answer is *never*. Much of the information that we store in a **Geographic Information System (GIS)** is constantly changing – new roads are built, parcels are split and sold, new sewer lines are installed, and more. All of these changes need to be incorporated into our GIS databases. To do this, you must be able to edit your GIS data.

ArcGIS Pro allows you to edit your GIS data, both spatial and tabular. You can add new features or modify existing ones. You can also edit the structure of your GIS database. With ArcGIS Pro, you can create new feature classes, add new attribute fields, create new tables, add domains, and more. It also supports the editing of both 2D and 3D data.

Since ArcGIS Pro was released in 2015, Esri has continually improved the editing capabilities of ArcGIS Pro. Most of the tools that were available in the older **ArcMap** application are now included in ArcGIS Pro. However, there are still a few data types, such as personal geodatabases and geometric networks, that cannot be edited with ArcGIS Pro. These most likely will never be supported in ArcGIS Pro. The old **ArcMap Parcel Fabric** is also not editable with ArcGIS Pro. Esri has developed a new version of Parcel Fabric for ArcGIS Pro.

It is now time for you to start exploring how to edit spatial data in ArcGIS Pro. In this chapter, you will learn the following topics:

- Understanding the editable data formats
- Editing data using ArcGIS Pro
- Learning what types of data can be edited

- Creating and managing feature templates
- Creating and updating spatial data
- Knowing which data types can be edited

The skills that you will learn while working through these topics will provide you with a basic understanding of the editing workflow in ArcGIS Pro and how to use many of the most commonly used tools to maintain and update your GIS data.

Technical requirements

Like the other chapters in this book, you will need to have **ArcGIS Pro 2.6** or newer installed. A basic license should be sufficient to complete the exercises contained in this chapter. You might find it helpful to have multiple monitors, although this is not mandatory.

Understanding the editable data formats

ArcGIS Pro allows users to access and use a lot of data formats to make maps, perform queries, and more. However, using and accessing is very different from being able to edit. It is important to know the limits of ArcGIS Pro with certain common data formats.

In this section, you will learn what data storage formats you can edit in ArcGIS Pro and how you can tell what format your data is stored in while working in ArcGIS Pro. This section will also provide you with a short introduction to the Esri geodatabase storage format, which is the preferred format for ArcGIS Pro.

Data formats – editable or not

The more you work in GIS, the greater the number of different data formats you will encounter. Esri's ArcGIS platform supports many of the most frequently used formats. However, as we said earlier, there is a big difference between being able to view and query data, and being able to edit it.

ArcGIS Pro has various data storage formats that you are likely to encounter on a regular basis. The following table outlines some of the limits that ArcGIS Pro has when using some of these various storage formats:

Data format	Display	Edit	Comments
Personal geodatabase	No	Yes	Esri has said they will never support this format in ArcGIS Pro.
File and Enterprise (also known as **Spatial Database Engine (SDE))** geodatabase	Yes	Yes	Enterprise geodatabases require a standard license or above. **Geometric Networks** and ArcMap Parcel Fabric editing are currently not supported, but **ArcGIS Pro Utility Network** and Parcel Fabric are supported.
Shapefiles	Yes	Yes	
CAD files (`.dwg`, `.dxf`, or `.dgn`)	Yes	No	ArcGIS Pro may have some issues displaying newer versions of **AutoCAD**'s `.dwg` format.
ArcGIS Feature Layer Service	Yes	Yes	Published with **ArcGIS Server**, **ArcGIS Enterprise**, or **ArcGIS Online**. It must have editing enabled on the service.
Web Map Service	Yes	No	ArcGIS Pro can access web map services, including ArcGIS Server/Enterprise, ArcGIS Online, **Warehouse Management System (WMS)**, and **Web Map Tile Service (WMTS)**.
Excel spreadsheet	Yes	No	
DBF file	Yes	Yes	
Text files (`.txt` or `.csv`)	Yes	No	

The preceding list is just those data types that are most frequently encountered with a focus on vector or tabular data. There are many other GIS data formats. **Shapefiles** and **geodatabases** are the primary spatial formats that ArcGIS Pro is designed to interact with in their entirety.

Understanding geodatabases

It is important to note that the **Personal geodatabase** format is not supported in ArcGIS Pro. Esri has been slowly reducing support for this type of geodatabase, which is built on top of **Microsoft Access Database technology**. This is largely due to the limitations of **Microsoft Access**, which is restricted to 2 gigabytes in size and whose performance slows down as the database gets larger. This is the reason why Esri developed the file geodatabase.

It is strongly recommended that if you are still using personal geodatabases, you migrate them to a file or enterprise geodatabase, especially if you wish to begin using **ArcGIS Pro** or **ArcGIS Online**. File and enterprise geodatabases offer much better performance and storage capacity. The following table is a general comparison between the three general types of geodatabases that can be created with the ArcGIS platform:

	Personal	File	Enterprise/SDE
Supporting database	Microsoft Access	Individual files designed by Esri	**SQL Server Express, SQL Server, Oracle, DB2, Informix, SAP HANA, SQLite, Teradata Data Warehouse**, and **PostgreSQL**
Storage limit	2 GB (performance degrades as size increases)	1 TB at the base of the database, plus 1 TB per feature dataset up to the maximum limit allowed by the hardware.	10 GB plus depending on the supporting database
Number of editors	1	1 per feature dataset (if the map references layers from multiple feature datasets, each dataset will be locked when editing)	10 or more depending on the supporting database

Now that you know that ArcGIS Pro allows you to work with multiple data storage formats, but that you can only edit a few, *how do you tell what format the data you are using is stored as?* That is a good question. The next section will help you answer this question.

Identifying your data format

Just as ArcGIS Pro allows you to visualize your data, it also provides visual clues about the data you are working with. Different icons are displayed next to various types of data to help you easily identify the type of data you are working with. The following screenshot illustrates some of the icons used by ArcGIS Pro to identify different types of data:

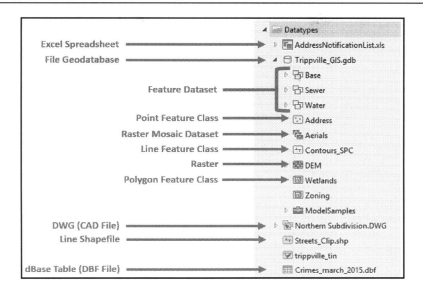

As you can see in the preceding screenshot, ArcGIS Pro uses different icons to indicate the data type. For example, shapefiles use green icons with a graphic to tell whether the shapefile contains points, lines, or polygons. **Computer Aided Designing (CAD)** files are identified with blue icons; `.dwg`, `.dxf`, and `.dgn` files all use the same blue icons. ArcGIS does not distinguish between files created with **AutoCAD**, **MicroStation**, or one of the other many drafting and design software packages used by engineers and surveyors.

Notice that some data formats support the storage of multiple data and feature types, while others only allow users to store a single data type. For example, the geodatabase allows you to store points, lines, polygons, raster, and more within a single database, whereas a shapefile will only allow you to store a single data type. A shapefile will be a point or a line or a polygon shapefile. It cannot contain more than one data type in a single shapefile.

It is important for you to know what data formats you are working with as this will determine what they store and what you are able to do with the data in ArcGIS Pro. As you have seen, some formats allow for the storage of multiple feature types while others only allow for one. With some formats, you can only display the data in ArcGIS Pro, and with others you can also edit the data.

Now that you are aware of some of the various data formats you might encounter while using ArcGIS Pro, it is time to start exploring how to edit your GIS data so that it stays up to date.

Editing data using ArcGIS Pro

The world is ever-changing, so your GIS needs to keep up with those changes. Whether it is splitting a parcel, adding a road, adding a new attribute field, or creating a new layer of data, it is important that your GIS data reflects the most current conditions of the real-world features it represents and meets the needs of your organization.

ArcGIS Pro contains tools that allow you to do all of this. You can add new features to an existing layer. You can modify existing features to show changes. You can create new layers and tables. In other words, ArcGIS Pro allows your GIS to grow, change, and flourish as reality changes.

In this section, we will learn the workflow required to edit data in ArcGIS Pro. You will examine the steps and some of the basic tools that are commonly used to maintain GIS data. We will start with the steps required to prepare ArcGIS Pro to edit data.

How to start editing features and attributes

To begin editing data in ArcGIS Pro is fairly easy. The first step is to open a project that contains layers that reference data that is stored in an editable format, such as a shapefile or geodatabase. From there, all you need to do is click on the **Edit** tab in the ribbon assuming you are using the default application editing option settings. It is that easy.

For those who have been using **ArcMap**, this may seem too easy. *What happened to start editing?* In ArcGIS Pro, you no longer need to start editing. You can immediately start editing once your project is open. This has changed somewhat with the release of ArcGIS Pro 2.6. With this release, Esri did introduce an option such that if enabled it does require you to start an editing session before you are able to make changes to your data. By default, this option is not enabled. ArcGIS Pro also does not limit you to editing data in one workspace at a time. If your map contains layers that point to data stored in a geodatabase and as shapefiles, you can edit them all at the same time. You no longer need to start and stop editing each time you need to switch between **workspaces**.

 What is a workspace? A workspace is a location in which your data is stored. It can be a database or a folder. Hence, a geodatabase is considered a single workspace. A folder that contains shapefiles or other data files would be another workspace.

Let's now move on to learn about preparing ArcGIS Pro for editing.

Preparing ArcGIS Pro to edit data

Before you start editing your data, you need to take some time to prepare both your data and ArcGIS Pro. Generally speaking, you should take the time to do the following before you start editing:

1. Ensure that all the spatial data that you plan to edit is in the same coordinate system. This avoids errors that can be the result of transformation issues.

2. Add and symbolize all layers that you wish to edit to your map. The simpler you can keep the symbology for each layer in the map, the faster it will redraw as you pan and zoom during editing. Also, save the complex symbology for printing. Since ArcGIS Pro supports multiple maps in a single project, you may want to have one map that you can use to edit data and another to include in a layout for printing.

3. Simplify your attribute fields so that only those you wish to edit, or that are needed to verify whether the proper features selected, and that you have, are visible. This will increase your efficiency and reduce the chance that you will mistakenly edit an attribute value that should not be changed.

4. Adjust the **Project Option** settings for editing from the **Project** tab:
   - Ensure that proper units are set for distance, angle, direction, and area.
   - Ensure that edit option settings are set as desired, such as, allow editing to be enabled or disabled from the **Edit** tab, or how and when to save your edits.

5. Set which layers you wish to edit in **List by Edits** within the **Contents** pane.

6. Set the snapping options.

Taking the time to go through the preceding steps before editing for the first time in a project will make editing easier and reduce the chance of errors.

After you have configured your editing options, the next step to edit data is to go to the **Edit** tab on the ribbon.

Learning about the Edit tab

In the **Edit** tab, you will find many of your most commonly used editing tools. These will allow you to modify existing features or help create new features. In addition to editing spatial data, you can also edit attribute values and standalone tables.

The following screenshot shows us the visual of the **Edit** tab:

As you can see in the preceding screenshot, the **Edit** tab contains nine group tabs:

- The **Clipboard** group tab
- The **Manage Edits** group tab
- The **Snapping** group tab
- The **Features** group tab
- The **Selection** group tab
- The **Tools** group tab
- The **Elevation** group tab
- The **Corrections** group tab
- The **Data Reviewer** group tab

Each of these groups contains tools related to their function. For example, the **Manage Edits** group contains tools that allow you to save, discard, or apply topology to your edits.

Let's now look more closely at some of these groups and the tools they contain.

Clipboard group

The **Clipboard** group contains tools that will copy or paste to and from your computer's clipboard. The following screenshot shows you the **Clipboard** group tab:

As you can see in the preceding screenshot, using these tools, you can copy features in one layer to another, or cut them from one layer and paste them into another. You can also use these tools to duplicate features in the same layer.

Manage Edits group

The **Manage Edits** group helps you control your edits. Here you can save your edits or discard them. If you discard edits, ArcGIS Pro will revert all your data back to the way it was prior to the last time you saved. The following screenshot shows you the **Manage Edits** group tab:

By default, ArcGIS Pro does not automatically save your data edits. If you want to have your data edits automatically saved, you must enable this option under your **Project Editing Options**. You can choose to automatically save at specific time intervals or after a number of operations. Setting up an automatic save can help ensure that you don't lose edits you have performed if your system or ArcGIS Pro were to crash.

Two things to remember when saving. First, you can only undo back to the point of your last save. Second saving data edits and saving changes to your project are two different things. To save data edits, you must either enable the **autosave** function or click the **Save** button on the **Edit** tab. To save changes to your project, such as the addition of a new layer or changes to symbology, you must click on the **Save** button in the **Quick Access** toolbar or from the **Project** tab.

From this group, you can also select any topology that you want to apply to your data when editing, and if it is a geodatabase topology, then you can also use the **Error Inspector** to locate topological errors in your data.

Topology is a model of how features in one or more layers of data are related to one another spatially. In ArcGIS Pro, there were two types of topology, namely, **Map** and **geodatabase**.

Geodatabase topologies allow you to assign rules to your data, such as the fact that parcels must not overlap, or a manhole must be connected to a utility line. This allows you to easily find and fix errors in your data.

A Map topology does not have rules, but does allow you to edit data so that any existing spatial relationships are maintained. If you want to learn more about topologies and how they work, you might want to look at *Chapter 5* of the *ArcGIS Pro 2.x Cookbook*.

Snapping group

The next group is **Snapping**. It includes a single button with a drop-down menu that controls snapping and snapping options. Snapping allows you to easily draw features so that they maintain connections to other features on the same or a different layer while editing. From the Snapping group, you can set where you want to snap to new features or sketches to existing features.

A **sketch** is something you create while editing. It can represent a new feature, such as a new street centerline or parcel polygon. Sketches can also be shapes you draw to modify or reshape existing features, such as a line drawn to split a polygon. Sketches are temporary and only exist in the memory of your computer.

If the sketch represents an update or change to one of your layers, it is not committed back to your GIS data until you save your edits. Once you save your sketch, it becomes a true feature. This is why you should save often.

With **Snapping** enabled, you can snap to the end, edge, midpoint, intersections, and vertex of other features, as shown in the following screenshot:

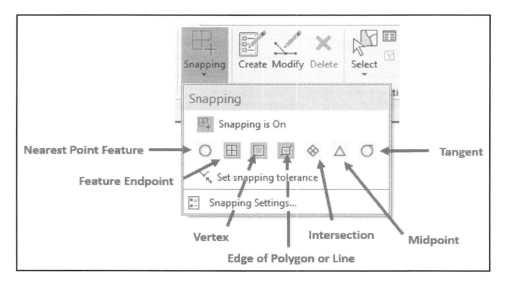

As you can see in the preceding screenshot, from the **Snapping** dropdown, you can also enable and disable snapping. Holding down your space bar will also temporarily disable snapping as long as it is held down.

Features group

The **Features** group contains tools for creating and editing features. You access the **Create** or **Modify** panes from here. You can also delete selected features or records using the **Delete** button, as shown in the following screenshot:

Clicking on the **Create** button opens the **Create Features** pane. The **Create Features** pane contains the feature templates used to create new features in your layers.

The **Modify** button opens the **Modify** pane, which includes tools for changing existing features, such as move, rotate, split, and more. Many of these same tools are also found in the **Tools** group. The **Tools** group just provides a quicker way to access them.

Selection group

The **Selection** group includes the tools for selecting features interactively within your map, viewing attributes, and clearing your selection. The **Select** tool includes five different shapes that can be drawn to select features for editing, as shown in the following screenshot:

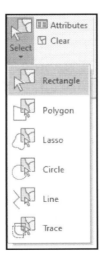

As you can see from the preceding screenshot, most of these are self-explanatory, with the exception of **Lasso**. The **Lasso** select tool allows you to draw a freeform polygon shape. The drawing follows the movement of your mouse pointer as long as you hold the left mouse button down. Releasing the mouse button completes the shape.

Now that you have learned all about the Edit tab and all its components, let's move on to the next section about creating new features as an editing task.

Creating new features

Creating a new feature is a very common editing task. It might be adding a new road, a new sewer manhole, or a new stormwater detention pond. As new things are built, we need to add them to our GIS. Creating new features requires a **feature template.**

Learning about feature templates

Feature templates define the properties required to create a new feature. This includes the target layer, default construction tool, default attribute values, and symbology, as you can see in the following screenshot:

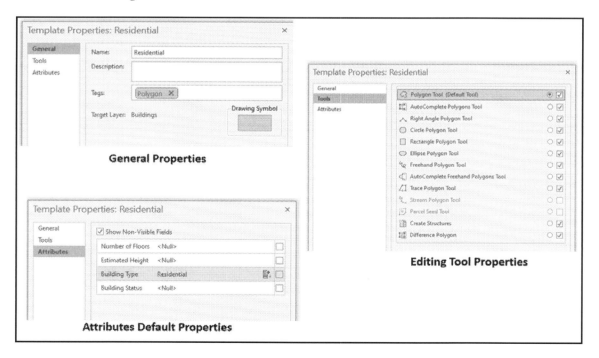

The **General Properties** associated with a feature template allows you to define metadata for the template and indicates where the layer's new features will be inserted. This is called the **target layer**.

As you can see in the preceding screenshot, the **Tools** tab in the template properties allows you to set properties associated with editing tools you can use to create new features using the template. Here, you can select which tools users are allowed to use to create new features and which tool will be the default tool that users will automatically start with when creating a new feature.

Lastly, the **Attributes** tab allows you to set default attribute properties for the fields contained in the attribute table for the target layer identified on the **General** tab. On this tab, you can input a default value for each field, which will automatically be populated into the indicated field, and which fields are required by the user to enter a value in when creating a new feature.

These templates are tied to your map's contents. So, for each layer in your map, you will have a matching feature template. If you symbolize a layer with unique values, graduated colors, or graduated symbols, you will have a feature template for each unique symbol associated with that layer.

For example, if you symbolize a parcel layer based on its zoning classification and there are three zoning classes, namely, **Residential**, **Commercial**, and **Industrial**, you will have three feature templates for that layer, as illustrated in the following screenshot:

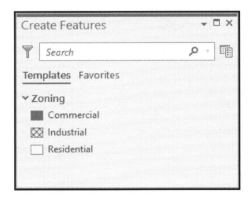

When you add a layer to your map or adjust the symbology, then your available feature templates are adjusted to match it. You can also manually create feature templates, adjust the properties of existing templates, and delete templates. This is all accomplished in the **Manage Templates** pane.

Now, let's move on to the exercise about creating new features.

Exercise 8A – Creating new features

In this exercise, you will update several layers based on a plat you have been given for a new subdivision that has been built in the city of Trippville. This is part of your normal duties as the city's GIS specialist. The plat is from a local surveyor and has been scanned.

Using the information shown in the plat, you will need to update the sewer system layers, road centerlines, and parcels.

Step 1 – Opening your project and preparing to edit

In this step, you will take some time to make sure everything is ready to begin editing. You will open your project to verify that the layers you need to update are editable. You will ensure there are not any warnings or messages that might cause problems while you update the data. You will also verify other editing option settings:

1. Open **ArcGIS Pro**.
2. Using the skills you have learned in previous chapters and exercises throughout the book, open Creating new features.aprx, located in C:\Student\IntroArcPro\Chapter8.

   When the project opens, you should see a single map that contains the layers you will be updating. It should look very similar to the following screenshot:

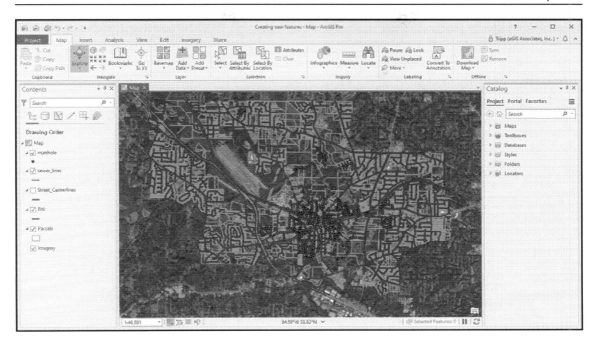

Now that your project is open, you need to verify a few settings.

3. Click on the **List by Source** button in the **Contents** pane to verify the location of the source data for the layers in your map.

 Question: *What geodatabase is being referenced by the layers and where is it located?*

4. Right-click on the **Parcels** layer and select **Properties**.
5. Select **Source** from the pane on the left side of the **Layer Properties** window.
6. Scroll down in the right-side pane until you see **Spatial Reference** and expand it by clicking on the open arrowhead located next to it. This will show you what coordinate system this layer is in.

 Question: *What coordinate system is the parcels layer in?*

7. Using that same method, check the remainder of the layers within the map. See that coordinate system they are in.

Question: *Are all your layers within the same coordinate system?*

Now it is time to set up the symbology for the layers you will be editing.

ArcGIS Pro will allow you to edit data that is in a different coordinate system. However, the recommended best practice is to have all data being edited within the same coordinate system. This helps avoid errors caused by using different transformations.

For the most part, the current symbology will work. However, the Public Works Director wants the new sewer lines entered with the correct size and material. To make that process more efficient, it would be good to have a feature template with those default values defined ahead of time. Since feature templates are linked to the layers in your **Contents** pane, you will change the symbology for the sewer lines to be based on the pipe's size and material.

Luckily there is already a layer file that has the symbology settings already defined. You will be able to import those settings from the layer file without having to configure the symbology for the **sewer_lines** layer from the outset.

8. Select the **sewer_lines** layer in the **Contents** pane.
9. Select the **Appearance** tab.
10. Click on the **Import** tool located in the **Drawing** group tab. This will open the **Geoprocessing** pane on the right side of the interface.
11. Click on the **Browse** button located at the end of **Symbology Layer**.
12. In the **Symbology Layer** window, click on **Folders**, located in the left pane of the window.
13. Double-click on the Chapter8 folder.

14. Click on the `Sewer Lines.lyrx` file and then the **OK** button.

Your **Geoprocessing** pane should now look like this:

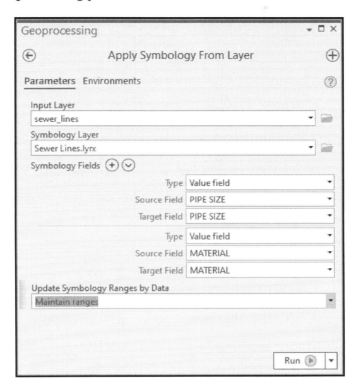

15. Once you have verified that everything is filled out correctly, click **Run**.
16. When the process has completed successfully, close the **Geoprocessing** pane.

You have just used a layer file to import predefined symbology for your sewer layer, which allows you to distinguish between each sewer pipe's size and material. If, for some reason, this did not work, you can right-click on the existing sewer layer and select **Remove**. Then, go to the **Catalog** pane and the **Folders** connection. In the `Chapter8` folder, you can right-click on the `Sewer Lines.lyrx` file and choose **Add to Current Map**.

You are almost ready to start editing. However, there are a couple of other settings you need to check beforehand:

17. Click on the **Project** tab in the ribbon and select **Options**.

18. Select **Units** and verify that the following settings are chosen. If they are not, then select the correct units:

- In the **Distance Units** field, select **Foot_US**.
- In the **Angular Units** field, select **Degrees Minutes Seconds**.
- In the **Area Units** field, select **Square_Foot_US**.
- In the **Location Units** field, select **Foot**.
- In the **Direction Units** field, select **Quadrant Bearing**.
- In all others fields, just accept assigned values.

19. Select **Editing** in the left side panel of the **Options** window, as illustrated in the following screenshot:

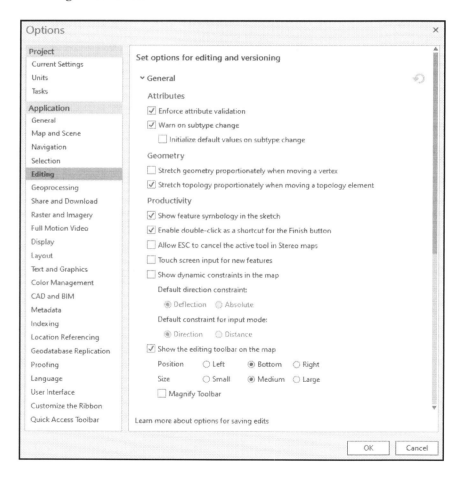

20. If needed, expand the **Session** section in the right-side pane.
21. Ensure the enable and disable editing from the **Edit** tab is not enabled.

> When this option is selected, users will need to enable editing from the **Edit** tab in the ribbon before they are allowed to make changes or updates to the data.
> For those that have used the older ArcMap application, this is similar to starting and stopping an edit session. If this option is not enabled, users are able to make changes to data at any time.

22. Ensure that **Automatically save edits** is not enabled. Since you are new to ArcGIS Pro, you don't want edits to be saved until you have verified them to be correct.
23. Also, make sure **Save edits when saving project** is not enabled.
24. Feel free to examine the other **Editing** options that are available. Once you are done exploring, click **OK**. Click on the back arrow located in the **Project** window to return to the main ArcGIS Pro interface.

You have one last thing to verify. You need to make sure **Snapping** is enabled and what will be snapped to. You also need to verify the snapping tolerance.

25. Click on the **Edit** tab in the ribbon.
26. Click on the small drop-down arrow located below **Snapping**.
27. Select **Snapping** options.
28. Set your x,y tolerance to **10 Map Units**.
29. Set your **Snap tip color** to **Mars Red** as shown in the following screenshot and click **OK**:

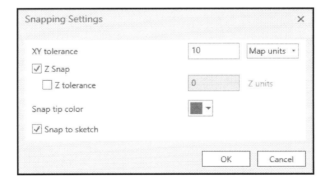

30. Click on the arrow below **Snapping** once more. Verify what snapping position options are enabled.

Question: *What snapping position options are enabled?*

You can change the snapping tolerance and snapping positions as required while you edit. As a new user, you will need to change those settings frequently as you try to find a happy medium that will work in most cases. Once you figure out what works best for you, you will not need to change the tolerance as often. The snapping positions will be changed much more frequently because they depend largely on what you are editing.

31. Set your snapping positions to endpoint and edge as illustrated in the following screenshot:

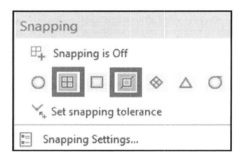

32. Save your project.

You are now ready to begin editing. You have taken the time to ensure that your editing environment has been set up properly.

Step 2 – Adding your source data

The surveyor has provided you with a paper copy of the plat for the new subdivision. The plat shows the layout of the parcels, streets, sewer, and water features in the new subdivision. Luckily, one of your other staff members scanned and georeferenced the scanned plat so that you can easily add it to your map:

1. Click on the **Map** tab in the ribbon, and then select **Bookmarks**.
2. Choose the **New Subdivision 1** bookmark to zoom you to the location of the new subdivision, as illustrated in the following screenshot:

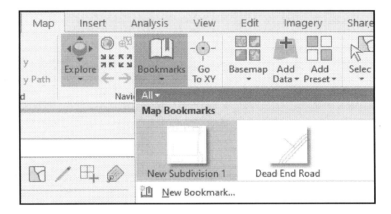

3. In the **Catalog** pane, expand **Folders** and the **Chapter8** connection.
4. Right-click on `Forrest Park Subdivision.jpg` and choose **Add to Current Map**. Depending on your computer, it might take a moment for the file to display on your map.

Your map should now look like this. Your zoom scale and display area may be slightly different depending on the size of your monitor and its resolution:

5. There is no need to have the **Imagery basemap** visible at this time. It will only slow you down as you pan and zoom during editing. So, turn off the **Imagery** layer by unchecking the box next to the layer.

You have just added the scanned plat as a layer to your map. This will allow you to use it as a guide for adding new features and updating your GIS database. This is just one example of a data source you can use. There are many other ways in which you may acquire new information to use in your GIS.

Step 3 – Drawing a new sewer line

Now that you have the plat added to your map to use as a guide, you will start drawing new features. You will start with simple lines and points that make up the sewer system:

1. Zoom into the north-east corner of the new subdivision so that you can see where the new sewer line connects to the existing sewer line.
2. Click on the **Edit** tab in the ribbon.

3. Click on the **Create** button to open the **Create Features** pane on the right side of the interface.

   Question: *What templates are available?*

You will now add a new sewer line and manhole by tracing the features shown in the plat. Before you do that though, you will examine a feature template.

4. Right-click on the **8 inch PVC** template in the **Create Features** pane and select **Properties**. This should open the **Template Properties** window for that template.

   Question: *What are some of the properties associated with the template?*

5. Under **Attributes**, look at the values next to **Pipe Size** and **Material**.

   Question: *What values are assigned to those fields for this template and where do you think they came from?*

6. Since you are adding new pipes that were recently constructed, you will set the value for the **Condition** field to **Good** for this template. Click in the cell next to the condition and select **Good** from the drop-down list.
7. Click **OK** to close the **Template Properties** window.

   The reason you were presented with a drop-down list for the condition field is that it had a **coded values domain** assigned to that field. A coded values domain is a list of predefined accepted values that can be entered into a field. When editing, you can only select a value that is included in the domain. This helps increase editing efficiency and reduce errors.

Now that you have configured your feature template for the sewer lines, you are ready to begin drawing new features.

8. Select the **8 inch PVC** template in the **Create Features** pane. You know to use this template because your development ordinance requires this size and pipe material for all new residential subdivisions.

9. Click on the end of the existing 8-inch ductile iron pipe near the intersection of the existing **GA HWY 50** and the new **Oak Place**.

10. Move your mouse to the manhole located to the west at the intersection of the new **Oak Place** and **Pine Drive**, as illustrated in the following screenshot, and double-click on it:

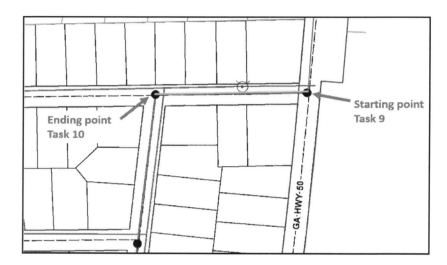

As you can see in the preceding screenshot, you have just drawn one of the new sewer lines that were constructed for the new subdivision.

If you forget to double-click or move your mouse away too fast and only single-click, you can press your *F2* button to finish the sketch.

Drawing the new features is only part of creating a new feature. Next, you need to update the attributes associated with the feature. The power of GIS comes from the combination of both spatial and attribute data, which allows you and others to ask your map questions and get answers. Those answers are only as good as the data. So it is just as important to keep your features attributes up to date as it is to draw them correctly.

Step 4 – Updating attributes

Now you will update the attributes for the new feature you just created. Attributes are the information about that feature. They will vary from one feature to another, and from one layer to another:

1. Click on the **Attribute** button located on the **Edit** tab in the ribbon. This will open the **Attributes** pane in the right side of the interface.
2. Notice that the values for **Pipe Size**, **Material**, and **Condition** have already been assigned by the template you used to draw the line.
3. Click in the cell to the right of **LINEID** and type 1200. This field is used to identify each sewer line in the system, which can then be linked to a work order management system to track the maintenance history of each sewer line segment.
4. In the **Edit** tab, click on the **Save** button to save the data edits you have made.

Challenge

Using the skills you have just learned, draw the remaining sewer lines shown on the plat for the new subdivision. Assign sequential **LINEID** numbers to the new pipes you draw. You will need to create individual pipe segments between each of the manholes shown on the source plat you are using to digitize the locations of the sewer lines.

Step 5 – Drawing the manholes

Now that you have drawn the sewer lines, you need to add the new manholes as well. A manhole is generally located at the end of each pipe segment:

1. Select the **Create Features** pane using the tab at the bottom of the right-hand side pane in the ArcGIS Pro interface.
2. Click on the manhole template and ensure that the **Point** tool is selected underneath the template name.
3. Click on the west end of the first pipe that you drew in *step 3* to add a new manhole.
4. Click on the **Attributes** tab located next to the **Create Features** tab.

   You should now see all the attribute fields associated with the manhole layer. You do not have all the information to fill out all of these as of yet. However, you can update a couple of them.

5. Click in the cell next to **Condition** and select **Good** from the drop-down list.

6. If you completed the *Challenge* section, continue to add the other manholes shown on the plat using the same process, setting the **Condition** for each new manhole to **Good**.

7. Once you are done adding new manholes, turn off the **Forrest Park Subdivision** plat in the **Contents** pane to view your handy work.

If you completed the challenge and added all the new manholes, your map should now look like this:

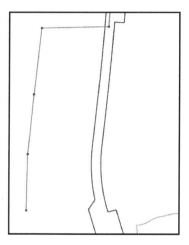

8. If you are happy with the new sewer features you have added, click on the **Edit** tab and the **Save** button in the **Manage Edits** group. This will save your edits back to the **Trippville_GIS** geodatabase.

Remember when editing that your edits are only shown on your computer and stored in the computer's memory. They are not committed to the source for the layer so others can see them until you save your edits. Up until the point when they are saved, all edits are considered a sketch.

This also means that if your computer crashes or ArcGIS Pro fails for any reason before you save, all your edits will be lost and unrecoverable. So, if you do not have the autosave function enabled, make sure to save often.

Step 6 – Adding the street centerlines

Now that you have learned how to add simple new features, it is time to do something a bit more challenging. You will add the road centerlines and rights-of-way. The first step will be to digitize the street centerlines and then use those to construct the rights-of-way:

1. Turn the **Forrest Park Subdivision** plat back on so that it is visible once again.
2. Turn off the **manhole** and **sewer_lines** layers.
3. Turn on the **Street_Centerlines** layer.
4. Zoom into the north-east corner of the new subdivision where you first started drawing the new sewer lines in the last step.
5. Click on the **Create Features** tab in the pane on the right side of the interface.
6. Select the **Street_Centerlines** template and ensure that the line tool underneath is active, as shown in the following screenshot:

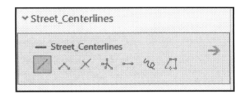

7. To draw your first centerline segment, start at the point where the plat shows **Oak Place** intersecting **GA HWY 50**. Click at that intersection to start drawing your first street segment.
8. Move your mouse pointer in a westerly direction toward **Pine Drive**, as shown on the plat. Then, right-click and select **Direction/Distance** from the menu that appears.
9. In the **Direction and Distance** window that just appeared, set the direction to S89-39-09W and the distance to 355 feet, as shown in the following screenshot, and then press the *Enter* key once you have typed in the required distance:

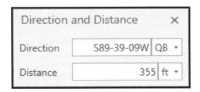

A new line segment should appear that follows the centerline of **Oak Place** and that ends at the intersection of **Pine Drive**.

10. Press your *F2* key to finish the sketch for the new road centerline you have drawn.

    You have just drawn a new street centerline using a new method. You created this new line so that it was a set distance in length and went in a specific south-westerly direction. While that information was not apparent on the plat that you added to the map, it is typical to find that type of information on a plat or engineering design document.

    Creating new features based on specific measurements allows you to create data that is much more accurate than just tracing it from a scanned document or aerial photograph.

11. On the **Edit** tab, click on the **Save** button in the **Manage Edits** group. This will save the new street centerline you just created back to its data source.

    Remember that in ArcGIS Pro, the layers in your map reference back to a data source such as a geodatabase feature class or shapefile. The map itself or project does not store the data. So, as you are creating new features, what you are seeing on your screen is just a sketch of the feature that resides in your computer's **Random Access Memory (RAM)**.

    It does not become part of your GIS data until you save the edits. So make sure to save often, especially if you have not enabled the autosave option, because if, for some reason, your system or ArcGIS Pro crashes, all unsaved edits will be lost.

12. Now you will draw your next segment by once again selecting the **Street_Centerlines** template and then clicking on the endpoint for the segment you just completed.

13. Move your mouse pointer along the road centerline shown on the plat and right-click. This time, select **Distance** from the menu.

14. In the **Distance** window, enter a distance of `485.5 ft` as shown in the following screenshot. This will lock the new segment you are drawing at the distance you entered, but you can still rotate freely:

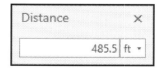

15. Now rotate the new segment you are drawing so that it overlays the centerline shown in the plat. Once you get it aligned successfully, single-click to set the rotation for the segment.

16. At this point, you may need to pan your map over to continue drawing the centerline. If you do, press and hold the center wheel on your mouse. Then, pan your map so you can see **Oak Place** past the short cul-de-sac.

17. To draw the curve, you will use a new tool, the **Arc Segment** tool. Look toward the bottom of the ArcGIS Pro interface for this tool on the toolbar that appeared when you started drawing the new street centerline segment, as shown in the following screenshot:

18. This tool allows you to trace three points to define the arc in the centerline. Single-click just once past the **O** in **Oak** where the curve begins (**Start of Arc**). Then, click near the estimated middle of the curve (**Middle of Arc**) to define the center of the arc. Lastly, click near the estimated end of the curve (**End of Arc**) where the road straightens out once more to define the end of the arc. You can see this in the following screenshot:

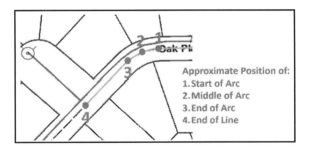

You have just drawn a curve that is embedded in the centerline for the road. This provides a truer representation of the location and geometry of the roads than digitizing a series of small straight segments would have. You still need to finish this segment.

19. Click on the **Line** tool located on the small toolbar where you found the **Arc Segment** tool. This will allow you to continue drawing the segment for this portion of **Oak Place**.

20. The segment should automatically start from the end of the arc you just drew. Move your mouse pointer to the estimated intersection of **Oak Place** and the small unnamed road that runs north-west and double-click to end the sketch (this endpoint is illustrated in the previous screenshot for *step 18* as location 4).

21. Edit the attributes for this segment the same way you did the first.

22. Save your edits.

23. Using the skills you have just acquired, continue drawing the remainder of the street centerlines as shown on the plat. Once completed, your map should look very similar to the following, that is, if you turn off the **Forrest Park Subdivision** plat:

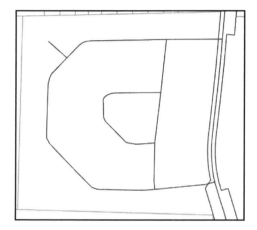

Now to add the rights-of-way for the roads. You could do this the same way you drew the roads. However, since the rights-of-way are based on the road centerlines, it is often easier to use them as a framework to construct your centerlines.

Step 7 – Creating the street rights-of-way

You will use a couple of methods to create the rights-of-way. We will start by using the **Buffer editing** tool. Then, you will use the **Trace** tool.

First, you will create the right-of-way for Oak Place. This road has a 50 foot right-of-way, meaning the right-of-way goes 25 feet from either side of the centerline. This makes it a perfect candidate to use the **Buffer editing** tool.

ArcGIS Pro, like the older **ArcMap** application, contains multiple tools named **Buffer**. There is one editing tool and several geoprocessing tools in the older ArcMap application. There are two primary differences between the editing tool and the geoprocessing tools.

The first is that the editing tool will create new features only in existing layers already on the map, whereas the geoprocessing tools will create completely new layers/feature classes. The second primary difference is that the geoprocessing buffer tools only create polygon features, whereas the editing tool will create either polygons or lines depending on the target layer.

We will use the following steps to create the right-of-way for Oak Place:

1. You will start by ensuring that the **Street Centerlines** and **RW** layers are selectable. You will also ensure that the **RW** layer is editable. In the **Contents** pane, click on the **List by Selection** button. It is the one with blue and white filled polygons.

2. Make the **Street Centerlines** and **RW** layers the only selectable layers in your map. Do this by clicking on the *check mark* located to the left of the other layers so the mark is removed. You do not need to worry about the **Forrest Park Subdivision** plat or the **Imagery** basemap.

3. Next, click on the **List by Editing** button in the **Contents** pane. Ensure that the **RW** layer is the only editable layer by right-clicking on the **RW** layer and selecting **Make this the only editable layer**, as illustrated in the following screenshot:

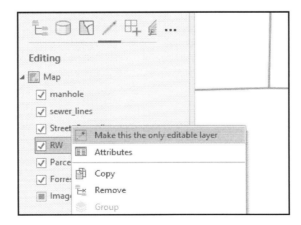

4. Click back on the **List by Selection** button in the **Contents** pane. This will allow you to see which layers you have features selected in.

It is recommended when you are editing that you stay on **List by Selection** in the **Contents** pane so that you can make sure you know what layers you are selecting features in. Watching what you have selected will prevent you from accidentally editing or deleting features you do not intend to.

5. If required, activate the **Edit** tab in the ribbon. Then, click on the **Select** tool in the **Selection** group.

6. Select the first segment of **Oak Place** that you created in the north-east side of the **Forrest Park subdivision**.

7. Next, hold down your *Shift* key and select the remaining segments of **Oak Place**, as shown in the following screenshot:

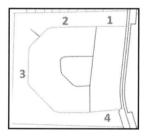

8. In the **Edit** tab, click on the small arrow with the horizontal line above it at the end of the **Tools** group so that you can access all the tools in this group, shown as follows:

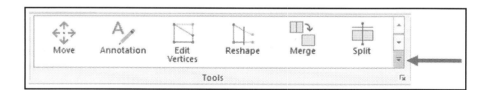

9. Scroll down to the **Construct** tool group and select the **Buffer** tool. The **Modify Features** pane will open with the **Buffer** tool you selected.

10. In the **Buffer** tool, you should see four street centerline segments selected. Confirm that this is the case.

11. Under **Template**, select and verify that **RW** is set as the target template.

This should be automatically selected if the **RW** layer is set as the only editable layer. If you failed to make that setting earlier, you will need to use the drop-down arrow to pick the **RW** layer from the list.

12. Under **Values** in the **Buffer** tool, set the **Buffer Distance** to 25 ft and **Rings** to 1. Also, ensure that **Dissolve** is enabled. This is indicated by a checkmark in the box.
13. Under **Area**, ensure that the **Both** option is selected and that **End** is set to **Square**.
14. At the bottom of the **Buffer** tool, you should see an option to **Show Preview**. Check this box so that you can see the results of the tool before you actually run it.
15. Confirm that your tool looks like the following screenshot and that you are happy with the preview. If this is the case, click the **Buffer** button to run the tool:

You have just created the rights-of-way for **Oak Place**. You are not done, however. You need to do a bit of cleanup where **Oak Place** intersects the major highway outside the subdivision.

16. Using the **Explore** tool on the **Map** tab, zoom into the north-western intersection of **Oak Place** and the highway.

17. Click on the **Snapping** dropdown and enable **Intersection snapping**. Now that you are zoomed in and can see better, you should notice that the new right-of-way you created is overlapping the exiting highway right-of-way. This needs to be cleaned up. Using the intersecting snapping option will help as you will soon see.

18. If required, use the **Select** tool on the **Edit** tab in the **Selection** group to select the new right-of-way you just created. Then, hold your *Shift* key down and select the western right-of-way for the highway that **Oak Place** intersects. You should have the rights-of-way for **Oak Place** and the highway selected, as illustrated in the following screenshot:

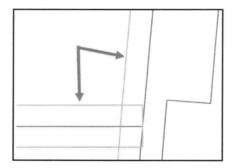

19. Click on the **Modify** button on the **Edit** tab in the **Features** group. This will open the **Modify Features** pane.

20. Scroll down the **Modify Features** pane until you see the **Divide** group. Select the **Planarize** tool. This tool will split line features that are in the same layer that overlap into individual segments at each intersection. It will also delete any duplicate line segments.

21. When the tool opens, you should see the two right-of-way lines you have selected listed at the top. You will accept the default cluster value. Verify that your **Planarize** tool looks like the following screenshot. If it does, click on the **Planarize** button located at the bottom of the pane:

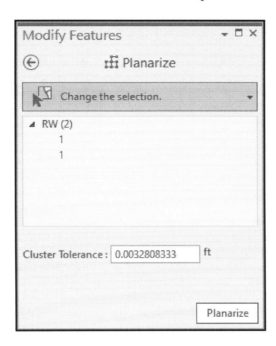

When the tool completes a successful run, you should notice that the number of features selected goes from 2 to 10. That is because this tool has split the rights-of-way for **Oak Place** and the **Highway** into multiple segments based on where they cross or intersect one another. This will make it easier to remove the parts that are not required. That is what you will do next.

22. Close the **Modify Features** pane.
23. On the **Edit** tab, click on the **Clear** button located in the **Selection** group to deselect all the selected features. You are about to delete the features that are not required, so you want to ensure that you do not have features you wish to keep selected.

24. Use the **Select** tool to select the parts of the right-of-way you created that extend into the right-of-way for the **Highway**, as shown in the following screenshot:

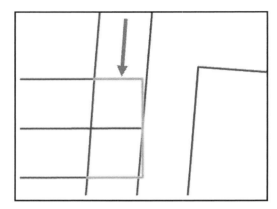

25. Once you confirm that you have the correct features selected, click on the **Delete** button located on the **Edit** tab in the **Features** group. This will remove the selected features, cleaning up the right-of-way for **Oak Place** so that it does not extend into the **Highway** right-of-way.

26. Next, select the segment of the Highway right-of-way, which runs between the north and south right-of-way of **Oak Place**, as shown in the following screenshot:

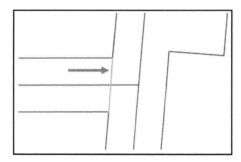

27. Once you have verified that you have the proper segment selected, click on the **Delete** button once again to remove the selected feature.

28. Save your edits.

    You have successfully cleaned up the northern intersection. Now you need to clean up the southern intersection of **Oak Place** and the **Highway**.

29. Using the **Explore** tool on the **Map** tab, zoom to where the southern right-of-way of **Oak Place** intersects the highway, as shown in the following screenshot:

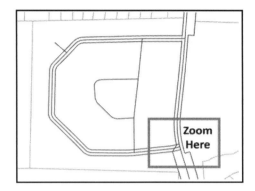

    Luckily, the **Planarize** tool you used earlier already split the right-of-way lines into the necessary individual segments. So all you need to do to clean up this intersection is to delete the unwanted features.

30. Select the portion of the right-of-way you created for **Oak Place** that extends into the highway right-of-way and press the *Delete* key on your keyboard. This will remove the features you do not need.

31. Now, select the portion of the highway right-of-way that runs between the north and south part of the Oak Place right-of-way and press your *Delete* key again.

32. Save your edits.

    You have now created and cleaned up the rights-of-way for Oak Place. However, there are still several other roads in the new subdivision you are adding to your GIS. You will continue to add those streets using the same methods you just learned.

33. Use the methods you just used to create the rights-of-way lines for **Oak Place** to create the new rights-of-way lines for **Pine Drive** and **Popular Circle**. They are the two streets that are located in the center of the subdivision. As illustrated in the following screenshot, the buffer distance will once again be 25 feet:

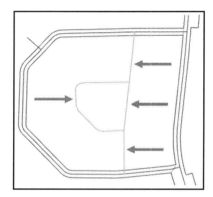

34. Once you have created the new rights-of-way lines for **Pine Drive** and **Popular Circle**, use the **Planarize** tool to split where the rights-of-way lines intersect so that you can clean up those locations.

35. Delete the overlapping portions of the rights-of-way lines as you did for **Oak Place** so that they look like the following screenshot:

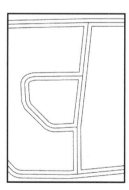

36. Save your edits.

You are almost done creating the rights-of-way for the new subdivision. There is one more small dead-end road that remains. It is located on the north-west side of the new subdivision.

37. Click on the **Clear** button located on the **Edit** tab in the **Selection** group.

38. On the **Map** tab, click on the **Bookmark** button in the **Navigate** group. Select the **Dead End Road bookmark** to zoom you to the location.

39. Click on the **Edit** tab in the ribbon and then choose the **Select** tool. Select the centerline of the short dead-end road, as illustrated in the following screenshot:

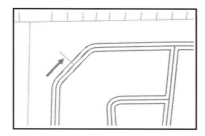

40. Use the **Buffer** tool once again on the **Edit** tab in the **Tools** group. Set the **Template** to **RW**, the **buffer distance** to **50** feet, and the **End** to **round**. Then click **Buffer**.

41. Using the **Planarize and Delete method** you have already learned, clean up the right-of-way lines for the intersection of the dead-end road with Oak place.

42. Save your edits.

You have now seen how to add new features to layers within ArcGIS Pro. If you are not continuing to the next exercise, close ArcGIS Pro and save your project when asked.

Exercise 8B – Splitting polygons

Now that you have created the road for the new subdivision, you need to split those out from the original parent parcel since the right-of-way areas have been deeded or transferred to the city of Trippville for maintenance. You also need to begin splitting out the individual new lots that make up the new subdivision as well.

Step 1 – Splitting out the rights-of-way

In this step, you will use the **Split** tool to cut the right-of-way area out of the original parent parcel that is being subdivided:

1. If required, start **ArcGIS Pro** and open the **Creating new features** project. If you recently completed *Exercise 8A*, it should be in your list of recently opened projects.

2. On the **Map** tab, click on the **Bookmark** button and select the **New Subdivision 1 bookmark** to zoom out so you see the entire new subdivision area.

3. In the **Contents** pane, turn off the **Street Centerlines** layer. You may need to click back on the **List by Draw Order** button at the top to do this.

4. In the **Contents** pane, click on the **List by Selection** button at the top. Then, set the **RW** layer as the only selectable layer by ensuring that it is the only one with a checkmark beside it.

5. In the **Contents** pane, click on the **List by Editing button** at the top. Then, right-click on the **Parcels** layer and select **Make this the only editable layer** from the menu that appears.

6. Activate the **Edit** tab and click on the **Modify** button in the **Features** group to open the **Modify Features** pane.

7. Scroll down to the **Divide** group and select the **Split** tool.

8. Near the top of the tool, you should see two tabs, the **Interactive** and **By Feature** tabs. Select the **By Feature** tab in the **Split** tool. When you do, two more tabs should appear in the tool, the **Input Features**, and **Target Features** tabs.

When you use the **Split** tool with the **By Feature** option, **Input Features** are the features you wish to use in order to split the feature or features in the **Target Features**. **Target Features** are the features that you intend to split or divide.

9. In **Input Features**, select the **Select one or more points, lines or polygons** option at the top. Then, create a selection box by clicking in the north-west corner of the subdivision and dragging a box to the south-east corner, as illustrated in the following screenshot:

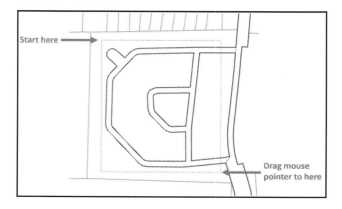

All of the street right-of-ways you created in the previous exercise should now be selected.

10. Now, click on the **Target Features** tab in the **Split** tool. Then, click on the **Select all intersecting features** option at the bottom. This will automatically select all editable features that the selected right-of-way lines cross or touch. Since you have set **Parcels** to be the only editable layer, this will only select the parcel polygon that the selected right-of-way lines are within.

11. You should now have one parcel polygon selected, as illustrated in the following screenshot. If your map and tool match the image, click on the **Split** button in the lower-right corner of the tool:

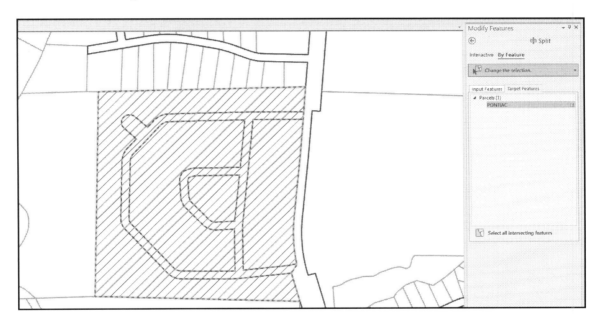

12. Once the **Split** tool completes, click on the **List by Selection** button at the top of the **Contents** pane. Confirm that you have five parcel polygons selected. If you do, you have successfully split the right-of-way areas from the original parent parcel.

13. Clear your selection using the **Clear** button on the **Edit** tab and right-click on the **Parcels** layer in the **Contents** pane. Select **Make this the only selectable layer** from the menu that appears.

14. On the **Edit** tab, click on the **Select** tool in the **Selection** group.

15. Click somewhere inside the right-of-way polygon you just created on the **Parcels** layer when you used the **Split** tool.

16. The city of Trippville does not maintain the right-of-way areas within its **Parcels** layer, so you need to delete the right-of-way area you just selected. Verify that you have the right-of-way polygon selected in the **Parcels** layer and click on the **Delete** button on the **Edit** tab or press your *Delete* key.

17. In the **Contents** pane, select the **List by Draw Order** button and turn off the **RW** layer. You should now see new boundaries for the parcel polygon that has been split by the right-of-way lines you created.

18. Clear any selected features and save your edits.

You have now successfully split the original parent parcel using the right-of-way lines you created in a previous exercise. Now you need to start splitting out the individual lots.

Step 2 – Splitting out individual lot polygons

In this step, you will start splitting out individual lots based on the **Forrest Park Subdivision** you referenced in an earlier exercise:

1. In the **Contents** pane, turn on the `Forrest Park Subdivision.jpg` plat layer.

2. Using the **Explore** tool on the **Map** tab, zoom in to the north-west corner near the intersection of **Oak Place** and **GA HWY 50**.

3. In the **Contents** pane, verify that the **Parcels** layer is set to be the only editable and selectable layer by looking at the **List by Editable** and **List by Selection** buttons.

4. On the **Edit** tab, click on the small arrow below the **Snapping** button. Ensure that **End Point**, **Edge**, and **Vertex snapping** are enabled.

5. Click on the **Modify** button on the **Edit** tab to open the **Modify Features** pane. Then, scroll down to the **Divide** group and select the **Split** tool.

6. Click on the **Select** tool on the **Edit** tab. Then, click in the parcel polygon to the north of **Oak Place**, as illustrated in the following screenshot (remember that the individual black lot lines are coming from the **Forrest Park subdivision** plat):

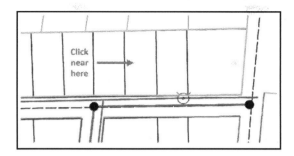

7. In the **Split** tool, in the **Modify Features** pane, ensure that the **Split** icon is highlighted and that you have one parcel selected.

8. Move your mouse pointer to the north-west corner of the first new lot closest to the highway and when you see it, snap to a vertex at the location, as shown in the following screenshot. Click to start the line you are drawing in order to split the selected parcel polygon.

Then, trace the line shown in the **Forrest Park Subdivision** plat with your mouse pointer until you snap to the edge of the northern right-of-way of **Oak Place**, as shown in the following screenshot, and double-click:

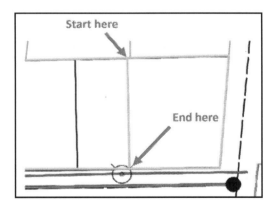

You have just split your first lot for this subdivision by tracing the boundary from the georeferenced plat provided. This is a very common workflow and method for performing this type of work.

9. Using this same method, continue splitting out a few more parcels based on the **Forrest Park Subdivision** plat. How many you split is up to you when you feel comfortable with the process.

10. Save your edits when you are done.

11. Close ArcGIS Pro and save your project when asked.

You have now created new polygon features by splitting them from existing features using a couple of methods. You have now learned to successfully edit data in ArcGIS Pro, along with the **Edit** tab and creating new features.

Summary

The world is not a stagnant place, so neither should your GIS be. It must be able to keep up with the changes that are happening all around us. In this chapter, you have learned that ArcGIS Pro has many powerful tools that allow you to keep your GIS current based on those changing needs and features.

You also learned how to add new features and make changes to existing features using various editing tools within ArcGIS Pro. With these new skills that you have acquired, you will be able to ensure that your GIS spatial data stays up to date.

In the next chapter, you will explore methods for updating the tabular data associated with features as well as how to make changes to the database schema and how to import data into your GIS database.

Further reading

If you would like to learn more about the concepts discussed in this chapter, you might want to check out the following resources:

- *ArcGIS Pro 2.x Cookbook*: *Chapters* 4 and 5
- Editing data with the ArcGIS Pro playlist on eGIS Associates YouTube Channel: https://www.youtube.com/user/eGISAssociates

Learning about Editing Tabular Data

9

In the previous chapter, you learned how to edit spatial data using ArcGIS Pro. But the spatial data is only one half of the **Geographical Information System (GIS)** data. The other half is the attribute or tabular data that is connected to the spatial data. Being able to keep the attributes updated is just as important as maintaining the spatial data.

As you have seen in previous chapters, the attribute table, which is part of a feature class and layer, is used in many ways. You can use it to configure the symbology used to display a layer in a map. Attribute values are used to help define feature templates used to create new features. You can query values in the attribute to select features for analysis or editing. These are just a few ways you can make use of the data stored in the attribute table for a layer. So, it is just as important to ensure it stays as up to date as the spatial features that it is connected to.

Through this chapter, you will be able to edit and maintain the attribute data for the features in your GIS.

This chapter covers the following topics:

- Editing your schema
- Populating field values in a database

Upon completing this chapter, you will have gained a much better understanding of database tables in GIS and how to maintain them. You will have learned various tools and methods that you can use to keep the attributes associated with your spatial features current (that is, they match the current conditions) and accurate.

Technical requirements

Before starting the exercises in this chapter, you will need to complete all the exercises in `Chapter 8`, *Editing Spatial Data*. The exercises in this chapter build on the ones from that chapter.

Like the other chapters in this book, you will need to have **ArcGIS Pro 2.6** or newer installed. A basic license should be sufficient to complete the exercises contained in this chapter. You might find it helpful to have multiple monitors, though it is not required.

Editing your schema

As the needs of your organization grow and change it is important for your GIS to keep up. This means you will need to make changes to the database schema.

What does the word schema mean? Simply put, it means the structure of a database. So schema is not just a GIS term but it is also a term used for other databases as well. In the case of a GIS database, schema refers to things such as what feature classes are stored in the database, what attribute fields are linked to those feature classes, what domains are included in the database, whether any tables or feature classes are related, and more.

ArcGIS Pro allows you to make some changes to your GIS data schema. It will allow you to add new feature classes, add fields, and create domains. It does have some limitations currently such as you cannot create a topology or geometric network. Hopefully, as ArcGIS Pro continues to mature those limitations will disappear.

In this section, you will learn how to make changes to the schema of your GIS database. You will start with how to add a new field to a table. Then you will see how to import data such as a shapefile into your GIS database to create a new feature class.

Adding a field

Sometimes changing your schema is as simple as adding a new field to an attribute table. A field is a column within a database table. The actual act of adding a field within ArcGIS Pro is not overly complicated, especially when compared to editing the spatial data. However, it does require some thought.

When adding a new field, you need to think through the properties that will be associated with that field, such as field name and field type, which we will cover in the next few sections.

Field name

In a database table, each field must have a unique name. That name cannot include spaces or special characters, though underscores are allowed. The allowed length of the field name will depend on the type of database. *Is it a* **dBase**, **Access**, *or* **SQL Server** *table?* Each of these has its own limitations.

As a rule of thumb, I have learned that keeping my field names limited to 7 to 8 characters works best. This will prevent field names from getting shortened if you export the data to a different format that does not support the name length of your native database.

This often happens when your GIS data is stored as a geodatabase that supports long field names, but you export to a shapefile that does not. Shapefiles store attributes in a **dBase** format that does not support long field names. Being an older database type, dBase only supports field names of 7 to 8 characters. So, a field that is named as `parcel_indentification_number` in your geodatabase may get renamed to `parcel_in` when exported to a shapefile.

Alias

An alias is a more descriptive name for a field. An alias can contain special characters such as spaces and it doesn't have the length restrictions associated with the field name. Aliases allow users to better understand the purpose of a field. By default, the alias is what is displayed when a table is opened in ArcGIS Pro.

Field types

When you add a field to a database, you must decide what type of data will be stored in that field. This is the field type.

There are several field types depending on the type of database that you are working with. Here is a list of some of the most common field types you can use in ArcGIS Pro:

Name	Description	Comments
Text or **String**	This stores alphanumeric data. A field can be up to 255 characters long. The default length in ArcGIS Pro is 50 characters.	It does not provide the best database performance compared to other field types. Make sure to set the size as small as possible to conserve storage space.

Integer (**Long** and **Short**)	This stores whole numbers, meaning no decimal places. The difference between long and short integer varies somewhat depending on the database, but generally short integers can store values between -33,000 to 33,000. Long will store values between approximately -2.1 billion and 2.1 billion.	It provides the best performance of all field types. This makes them the optimum type to use if overall database performance is a concern.
Float or **Single**	These store decimal values out to approximately 6 to 8 decimal places depending on the database.	They provide median database performance.
Double	This stores decimal values with 15 or more decimal places depending on the database.	Its performance is similar to float.
Date	This stores date and time. The format depends on the database.	
Binary Large Object (**BLOB**)	This is the BLOB field. It is used to store data that does not fit one of the other field types; not all databases support blobs.	It provides the worst performance of any field type. It can cause issues if exported to a database that does not support this type.
Raster	This stores images or pictures directly in the database. It is a specialized BLOB field.	It has the same issues as a BLOB.
Global Unique Identifier (**GUID**)	The GUID provides a unique identifying value to all records and tables within the database that have this field type.	GUID fields are required if you plan to allow mobile or offline editing or use database replication.

Now that you know what a schema is and how to add a field, it is time for you to add a field to a table.

Exercise 9A – Adding a field and populating values

The Public Works Director has asked you to determine how long each road segment is in miles for a project he is working on. While you do have the road's centerline data, it is not attributed with lengths in miles. So, you will need to add a new field to store the length in miles and then calculate that value for each segment.

We will be adding the field now. In these steps, you will open your project and then add the new field that will store the length of each road segment in miles:

1. Open **ArcGIS Pro** and the Ex9A project located in
   C:\Student\IntroArcPro\Chapter9.
2. In the **Contents** pane, select the **Street Centerlines** layer. The **Feature Layer** group tab should appear in the ribbon.
3. Click on the **Data** tab within the **Feature Layer** group tab.
4. In the **Design** group on the **Data** tab, select the **Fields** button.

   A new tab should open in the main view area of the interface where the map was before. This new view shows the current attribute fields and their properties for the **Street_Centerline** layer.

   Question: *What attribute fields are associated with the **Street_Centerline** feature class and what field types are they?*

5. At the bottom of the existing fields, you should see a row that says **Click here to add a field**; click on that.
6. Name the field Len_Mi.
7. Then click on the **Alias** cell and give the new field an alias of Length in Miles.
8. Then click on the **Data Type** cell and set it to **Float**. You are using the float data type because the Director is looking for length in miles only to two decimal places.

9. Leave all the other settings the same and the table should now look like this:

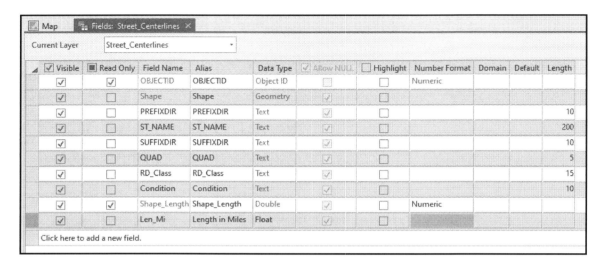

10. Once you have verified that your new field has been added correctly, click on the **Save** button located on the **Fields** tab in the ribbon.

If the **Save** button is grayed out, that most likely means you have data edits that have not been saved. You cannot make changes to the database schema if there are any pending data edits that have not been saved.

11. Close the **Fields** view.
12. Save your project and close ArcGIS Pro.

You have just added a new field to the **Street_Centerlines** feature class that you can use to store the length of each road segment in miles. Next, you will learn how to import data from other sources into your GIS database.

Importing a new feature class

Adding a field is just one change that you can make to the schema of your GIS database. You can also add entirely new feature classes by creating a new one from scratch or importing it from another data source.

It is not uncommon to have data stored in other formats and locations that would be beneficial in your GIS database. Moving all those different data sources into a single GIS database makes them easier to use, find, and manage. ArcGIS Pro contains tools for importing, exporting, and converting data. This allows you to build a comprehensive GIS database that can be integrated with other solutions.

So let's move on to the next exercise, which is about importing a shapefile.

Exercise 9B – Importing a shapefile

A local consultant was hired to locate all the water meters within the City of Trippville. They provided the Public Works Director with a shapefile containing the water meters that they located and attributes collected.

You now need to import this shapefile into the city's geodatabase, so it is stored in the same location as the other feature classes that make up the city's water system.

Step 1 – Opening the project and adding a layer

In this step, you will open the project that you have been working with throughout this chapter. Then you will add the shapefile that was provided to the Director by the consultant, which contains the water meter data:

1. Open **ArcGIS Pro** and the `Ex9A` project that you used in the previous exercise.
2. On the **Map** tab in the ribbon, click on the **Add Data** button.
3. Click on **Folders** located under **Project** in the left pane of the **Add Data** window.
4. Double-click on `Chapter9` folder in the right pane of the **Add Data** window.
5. Select `Water_Valves.shp` and then click the **OK** button.

You have now added the data collected by the consultant to your map. This data is stored as an Esri shapefile. You need to add this collected data to the city's geodatabase as a new feature class. You do that by exporting the shapefile that you just added as a layer to your map to the city's geodatabase.

Step 2 – Exporting to a geodatabase

Now you will export the shapefile to a feature class in the city of Trippville's geodatabase. You will store the newly imported feature class in the **Water** feature dataset along with the other water system-related feature classes:

1. Right-click on the **Water_Valves** layer that you just added to your map.
2. In the displayed context menu, go down to **Data** and select **Export Features**, as shown in the following screenshot:

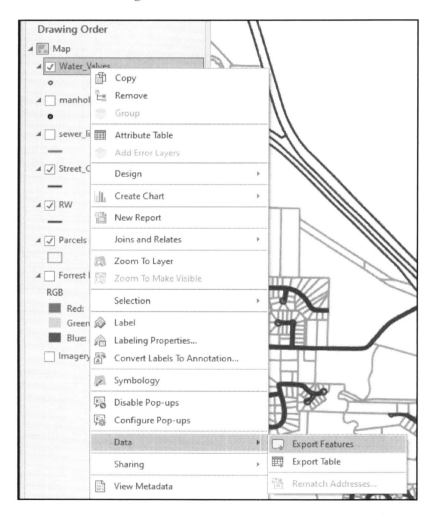

3. This will open the **Export Features** tool within its own floating window. The **Input Features** value should automatically be populated with the **Water_Valves** layer because that was the one you right-clicked on. Now click on the browse button located to the right of the **Output Location**.

4. Click on the **Databases** folder located under the **Project** in the left pane of the **Output Location** window.

5. Double-click on the **Trippville_GIS** geodatabase that is listed in the right panel of the **Output Location** window.

6. Then click on the **Water feature** dataset and click on the **OK** button to set the **Output Location**. This is where the new feature class that you are about to create will be stored.

7. In the cell below the **Output Feature Class**, type Water_Valves.

8. Verify that your **Export Features** tool looks like the following screenshot, then click the **OK** button at the bottom of the window:

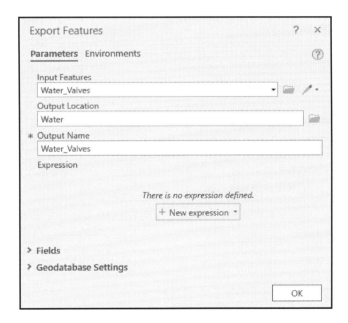

When the tool completes its run, you should see a second **Water_Valves** layer added to your map. This new layer is now using a new feature class that was created in your geodatabase as its source. You will now verify that.

9. Click on the **List by Source** button located at the top of the **Contents** pane.

10. Verify that you see a **Water_Valves** layer listed under the `Trippville_GIS.gdb` workspace and one in the `Chapter9` folder.

11. Right-click on the **Water_Valves** layer in the `Chapter9` folder and click **Remove**. This removes the layer that was based on the original shapefile from the map so that only the one that references the city's primary geodatabase remains.

12. Save your project and close ArcGIS Pro.

You have just converted a shapefile to a geodatabase feature class and verified that the conversion was successful. Importing the data that was in the shapefile into your geodatabase created a new feature class, which is also a change to the schema.

As mentioned at the beginning of the chapter, it is important to be able to make adjustments to your GIS database schema to reflect changing requirements and conditions. You now know how to add new fields to your database so that you can collect new information as it is needed. You have also learned how to import data from outside sources into your GIS to create new layers of information.

Now that you have an understanding of fields, we will move onto the next section about populating the field values in the database.

Populating field values in a database

So far in this chapter, you have learned how to make changes to the schema of your GIS database by adding fields and importing other files. *But how do you populate the new fields that you create or just make changes to the attributes associated with existing features?*

In the section, we will look at several ways to do just that. We will start with ways to edit individual values for existing features. We will explore the way to perform mass edits to populate a table with values.

Understanding methods to edit or add single values

As you make changes to your spatial data you also need to get into the habit of updating the attributes associated with those features. These are stored in the attribute table for the layer. As mentioned at the beginning of this chapter, attributes are used for many operations within ArcGIS Pro including to control symbology and select features via queries. So, it is critical that the attributes for your features be as correct and up to date as your spatial data.

There are several ways that you can edit or update attribute values within ArcGIS Pro. In this section, we will focus on two of the most common methods, the Attributes window and directly in the table view.

Attributes window

The Attributes window is traditionally opened from the **Edit** tab in the ribbon. In this window, you can make changes to the attribute values for individually selected features. You simply click in the cell located to the right of the field name and type in a new value as shown in the following screenshot:

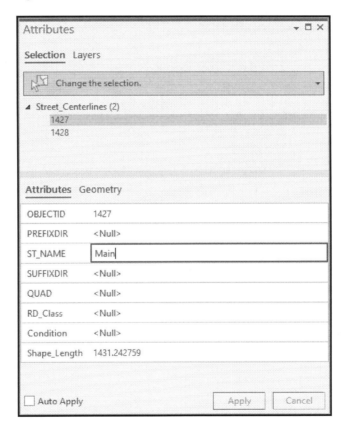

This window consists of two tabs:

- **Selection** tab: The **Selection** tab includes three sections. They are Selection tool, a list of selected features, and list of attribute fields of geometry value, as illustrated in the following screenshot:

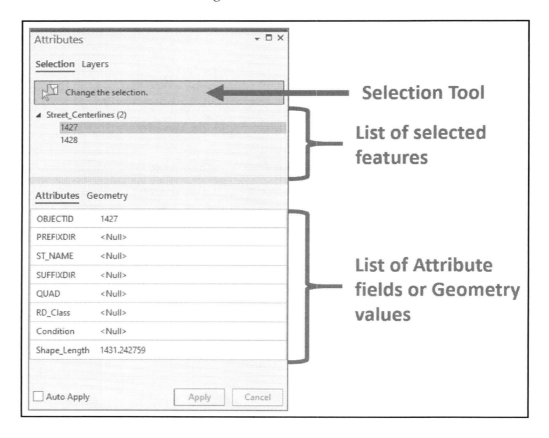

- **Layers** tab: The **Layers** tab in the **Attributes** window allows you to select a specific layer to review and then cycle through all the features within those layers, as shown in the following screenshot:

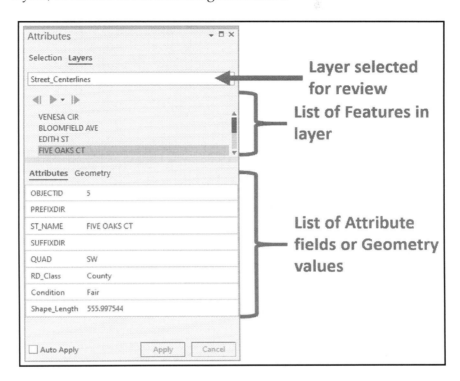

Each of these tabs allows you to edit the attribute values for the selected feature. You will get a chance to use the Attributes window to edit values in *Exercise 9C*. Before you do that though, let's look at the other method for editing attribute values directly in the attribute table.

Editing directly in the attribute table

You can also edit attribute values directly in the attribute table. This can be more efficient because you often will already have the attribute table for a layer already open for other purposes.

Editing in the attribute table can be as simple as clicking in a cell within the table and typing in a new value. This is very much like editing the data contained in an **Excel** spreadsheet, as you can see in the following screenshot:

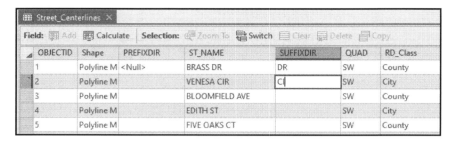

As easy as this is, it also points out a danger that users of the older **ArcMap** software did not need to worry about. In the older ArcMap application, you were required to start an edit session before you could edit any data.

In ArcGIS Pro, this is no longer required. You can edit any data that you have permissions to, at any time. This includes the attribute values in the attribute table for a layer. So, while ArcGIS Pro makes it easier to edit data it also makes it easier to create bad information. It is important to always keep this in mind when working in ArcGIS Pro.

We will move onto the next exercise about editing attributes.

Exercise 9C – Editing attributes

In this exercise, you will update the attributes for the street centerlines that you created in *Exercise 8A* in `Chapter 8`, *Learning to Edit Spatial Data*. You will use the Attributes window to make these changes.

Step 1 – Opening the project and zooming to the correct location

In this step, you will open the project that you will be working in and zoom to the location of the street centerlines that you added to the `Trippville_GIS` geodatabase in *Exercise 8A* of `Chapter 8`, *Learning to Edit Spatial Data*:

1. Open **ArcGIS Pro** and the `Ex9A` project that you had used in *Exercise 9A* and *Exercise 9B*.

2. On the **Map** tab in the ribbon, click on the **Bookmarks** button and select **New Subdivision 1** from the list that appears. This should zoom your map back to a familiar location from *Exercise 8A* in Chapter 8, *Learning to Edit Spatial Data*.

3. On the **Contents** pane, click on the **List by Editing** button. Then right-click on the **Street_Centerlines** layer and select **Make this the only editable layer** from the menu that appears, as shown in the following screenshot:

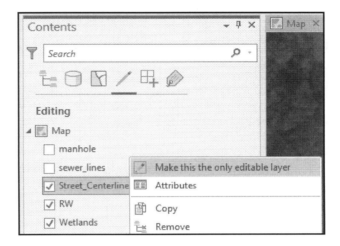

4. Next, click on the **List by Selection** button in the **Contents** pane. Right-click on the **Street_Centerlines** layer again and select **Make this the only selectable layer** from the menu that appears.

You have now opened the correct project and zoomed to the area where you will be editing data. Then you set the Street_Centerlines layer to be the only editable and selectable layer. This will help ensure that you only edit data in the layer you intend to in the next step. In the following step, you will enter the names for each street centerline segment you created in *Exercise 8A* in Chapter 8, *Learning to Edit Spatial Data*.

Step 2 – Adding Street_Centerline attribute values

In this step, you will update the names for each street centerline segment that you had created back in *Exercise 8A* in Chapter 8, *Learning to Edit Spatial Data*, using the Attributes window:

1. Click on the **Edit** tab in the ribbon.
2. Next, click on the **Select** tool located in the **Selection** group on the **Edit** tab.

3. Click on the northeastern-most street centerline segment, as shown in the following screenshot:

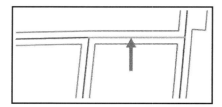

4. Click on the **Attributes** button in the **Selection** group on the **Edit** tab. This will open the **Attributes** window.

5. In the **Attributes** window, verify that you have one **Street_Centerlines** feature selected by looking at the area of the window that shows the list of selected features.

6. Click in the cell to the right of **ST_NAME** and type OAK PL. Press your *Enter* key when done. Your **Attributes** window should look like the example provided in the following screenshot:

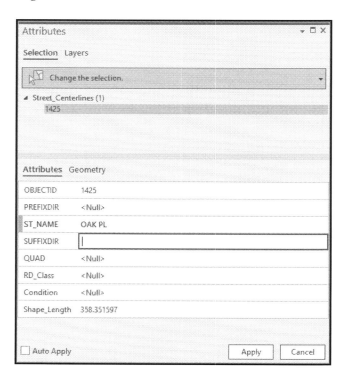

7. Now click on the cell to the right of **RD_Class** and type `City` because the new street centerlines that you entered are city-maintained roads.

8. Lastly, click on the cell to the right of **Condition**. Then type `Good` and press your *Enter* key when done. These are new roads so they should be in good condition.

9. Press the **Apply** key to apply the changes to the attributes table.

10. On the **Edit** tab, click on the **Save** button to save your edits back to the database.

The **Apply** button only applies the changes to the copy of the data stored in your computer's local memory. Remember the layers in a map within ArcGIS Pro all point back to a data source. This data is cached or copied into your computer's **Random Access Memory (RAM)** or local drive. When you save the edits, that is when the changes that you make are actually pushed back to the original data source for all to see.

11. Using that same process, update the **ST_NAME** field for the remaining segments that make up Oak Place, which forms the outer circle for the subdivision, as shown in the following screenshot:

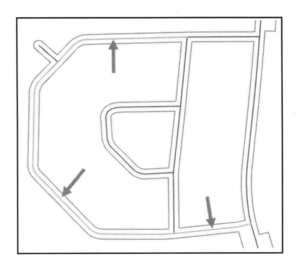

12. Once you are done updating the remaining segments, make sure to save your edits and your project.

13. Close ArcGIS Pro.

You have just updated the attributes for several of the street centerline segments that you created in the previous exercise. As a rule of thumb, it is best to update the attributes at the same time when you are editing the spatial data. This keeps both components of your GIS data accurate and current.

Next, we will explore tools that allow you to edit the attributes for multiple features at a time.

Mass-populating table values by using tools

Often when you add a new field to a table, or when a large number of features need to have similar values altered, it is more effective to make those changes or updates in one mass edit. ArcGIS Pro supports several tools and methods to do just that. We will review some of the most common tools now.

Calculate Field tool

The **Calculate Field** tool is a geoprocessing tool that will mass-populate values into the designated field within a table using an expression. This expression can be as simple as copying values from another field, or as complex as performing a series of mathematical equations and logical functions. These expressions can be written in either **Python** or **Arcade**. You will learn a little more about these two languages in Chapters 12, *Automating Processes with ModelBuilder and Python*, and Chapter 14, *Using Arcade Expressions for Labeling and Symbology*, respectively.

This is a geoprocessing tool even though it opens within its own window instead of within the **Geoprocessing** pane. This means, if you have records in the table selected, it will only populate values into the selected records. If you do not have any records selected, this tool will populate values in the field for all records in the table overwriting any existing information.

Calculate Geometry tool

The **Calculate Geometry** geoprocessing tool calculates values into the desired field based on spatial values. You can use this tool to calculate things such as area, perimeter, central coordinates, number of vertices, and more. The exact spatial characteristics that you can calculate will be dependent on the geometry type of the features in question. For example, you cannot use the Calculate Geometry tool to calculate the area for point features because a point does not have an area.

This tool can also be used to convert units, for example, if you have polygon that was created in imperial units, but you need to know its area in square kilometers. Then you can use the Calculate Geometry tool to convert from imperial units to metric units without you knowing the exact conversation factor.

Now it is time for you to see these tools in action in a hands-on exercise.

Exercise 9D – Using tools to mass-populate field values

In this exercise, you will get to use the Calculate Field and Calculate Geometry tools for multiple features at one time. You will start by using the Field Calculator tool to populate the **Len_Mi** field that you created in *Exercise 9A*. Then you will use the Calculate Geometry tool to calculate the area for Wetlands polygons in acres.

Step 1 – Populating the field using the Field Calculator tool

In this step, you will populate the length of each road segment in miles into the field you created in *Exercise 9A*. You could do this manually for each segment using some of the edit skills that you have already learned. That would be very time-consuming. There is a much more efficient way.

One of the fields that you identified as being associated with the street centerlines was **Shape_Length**. So, now you already have values showing the length of each road segment. It is in feet, though to populate your new field with the correct values in miles you will need to convert feet into miles. As you have previously learned in this section, ArcGIS Pro includes a tool called the Field Calculator, which will allow you to populate a field with values based on an expression for all features in the feature class. We will follow the next steps to do so:

1. Open **ArcGIS Pro** and the Ex9A project that you have used in the previous exercises in this chapter.
2. If needed, activate the Map view in ArcGIS Pro by clicking on the tab at the top of the view area.
3. In the **Contents** pane, ensure the **Street_Centerlines** layer is editable by going to the **List by Editable** button.
4. Right-click on the **Street_Centerlines** layer in the **Content** pane and select **Attribute Table** to open the **Table** window at the bottom of the interface.

5. Right-click on the new field that you created. It should be shown using the alias that you specified when you created the new field – **Length in Miles**. Also, note that the field is **Null**. Null means it is empty. It has no values stored.

6. Select **Calculate Field**, this will open the **Geoprocessing** tool within its own floating window.

7. Within the **Fields** box, double-click on **Shape_Length**. This will insert the name of the field with the correct syntax into the expression box located below the **Fields** and **Helpers** as illustrated in the following screenshot:

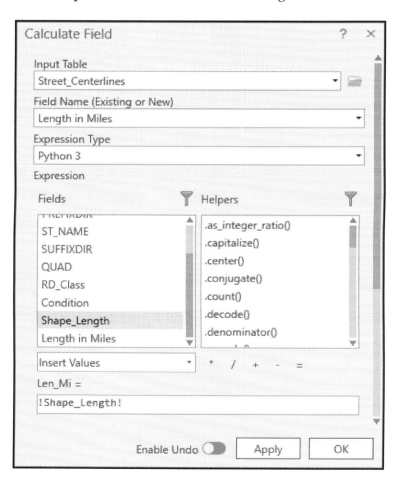

8. Click on the / symbol located below the **Helpers** box to add that to the expression. This symbol will divide the value stored in the **Shape_Length** field for each record by a value that you will specify next.

9. In the expression box, type 5280 after the / symbol. This is the number of feet in a mile. Your expression should look like this:

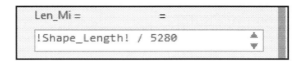

10. Once you verify your expression, click the OK button located at the bottom of the **Calculate Field** window.

11. When the **Calculate Field** is complete, you should now see the field that you created and filled with values now. If you scroll through the table, you will see that it calculated the lengths in miles for all the records in the table. The **Calculate Field** tool is a very powerful and efficient way to populate a field.

12. Close the attribute table for the **Street_Centerlines** layer and save your project.

Next, you will use the Calculate Geometry tool to populate a field with the acreage for the polygons in the Wetlands layer.

Step 2 – Using the Calculate Geometry tool

As you were working on determining the length of the roads in miles, the Public Works Director came by and asked if you could calculate the area of the Wetlands in acres. You will do this using the Calculate Geometry tool and following these steps:

1. In the **Contents** pane, select the **Wetlands** layer.

2. Click on the **Data** tab in the ribbon and then select the **Attribute Table** button in the **Table** group. This will open the attribute table for the Wetlands layer.

3. Review the table that you just opened to see what fields exist within the table. Next, right-click on the **ACREAGE** field in the table and select **Calculate Geometry** from the menu that appears as illustrated in the following screenshot:

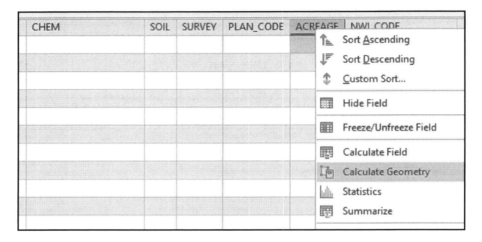

4. In the Calculate Geometry tool window that just opened, verify the **Input Features** parameter is set to **Wetlands**.
5. Under the **Target Field**, verify the first line is set to **ACREAGE**.
6. Under the **Property** column next to **ACREAGE**, select **Area** using the drop-down arrow, as shown in the following screenshot:

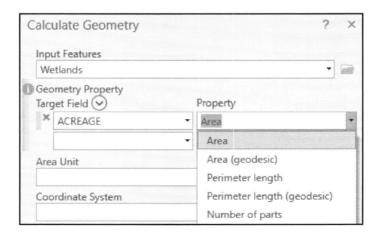

7. A new line should now appear in the **Calculate Geometry** tool window named **Area Unit**. Set this to **Acres** using the drop-down arrow.

8. Set the **Coordinate System** parameter to the Current Map (Map) using the drop-down arrow. This will set the coordinate system to **NAD_1983_StatePlane_Georgia_West_FIPS_1002_Feet**, which is the coordinate system assigned to the currently active map.

9. Verify that your **Calculate Geometry** tool looks like the following and then click **OK**:

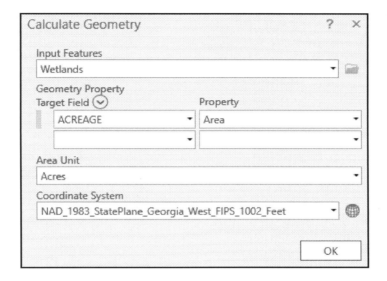

10. Review the **ACREAGE** field to see the values that it now contains.

11. Save your project and close ArcGIS Pro.

You have just used the Calculate Geometry tool to populate a field with the total area for the polygons in that layer. Further, this tool converted the area units from square feet into acres without you needing to know the conversion factor as you did in the previous exercise.

This section has taught you how to populate values into tables within your GIS database. You learned how to enter single values to ensure any new features that you add or change also keep their attributes current. You also learned how to use the **Calculate Field** and **Calculate Geometry** tools to populate the values for multiple records within a table at the same time.

Summary

As you have learned there will always be a need to create and update data. In a GIS, this includes both spatial and tabular information. In the previous chapter, you learned how to edit spatial data including points, lines, and polygons. In this chapter, you learned how to update and create tabular information.

The first thing that we discussed was how to make changes to your database schema. The schema is the structure of your database. This includes what feature classes are included in your GIS database, what fields are in the attribute tables for those feature classes, and a lot more. You now have the skills to add new fields to your attribute tables and can import data from other sources into your GIS database.

You also learned how to update the attribute values for the features displayed in your maps. You now know how to do that individually or en masse using the Calculate Field and Calculate Geometry tools.

So, between this chapter and the previous one, you have gained the basic skills required to keep your GIS database updated and accurate. In the next chapter, you will learn how to analyze data using ArcGIS Pro.

Further reading

If you would like to learn more about the concepts discussed in this chapter, you might want to check out the following resources:

- *ArcGIS Pro 2.x Cookbook*: *Chapter 4* and *Chapter 5*
- Editing data with ArcGIS Pro playlist on eGIS Associates YouTube Channel: https://www.youtube.com/user/eGISAssociates

10
Performing Analysis with Geoprocessing Tools

So far, you have learned that ArcGIS Pro has some powerful tools for visualizing and maintaining GIS data. *But what about analyzing that information? Can it help you identify the landowners you need to contact along a road that will be repaired or get a count of customers within a given area?* ArcGIS Pro has the tools to help you answer these types of questions and a whole lot more.

Answering these types of questions is done by using geoprocessing tools within ArcGIS Pro. *What is Geoprocessing?* Simply put, it is the manipulation of data used inside ArcGIS. Geoprocessing tools can analyze data, convert data from one format into another, add an attribute field to a table, or project data from one coordinate system to another. The sky is the limit regarding what you can do with geoprocessing tools.

In addition to the tools included in ArcGIS Pro, you can purchase extensions that add more capability to the software. The geoprocessing framework also provides avenues for you to create your own custom tools using **ModelBuilder**, **Python**, and other programming languages. You will learn more about ModelBuilder and Python in later chapters.

In this chapter, you will learn how to use some of the most commonly used geoprocessing analysis tools to perform simple **Geographical Information System** (**GIS**) analysis of spatial and tabular data. In addition, you will learn how you can determine which tools will be available to you based on the licensing level and extensions that are assigned to you. As you work through this chapter, you will learn about the following topics:

- Determining which tools to use
- Understanding the analysis process
- Using other common geoprocessing tools for analysis

One thing to keep in mind as you begin to use geoprocessing tools is that most of them create new data. This means that even if you choose the wrong tool or use a bad setting in the tool, in most cases, your original data is protected. This provides a level of protection and helps to put your mind at ease knowing the chances of damaging your data by doing the wrong thing are greatly decreased.

Technical requirements

You must have at least **ArcGIS Pro 2.6** or later in order to complete the exercises in this chapter. A Basic, Standard, or Advanced license level will work.

Determining which tools to use

There are two things that determine which geoprocessing tools will be available to you in ArcGIS Pro. The first is your licensing level. The second is what extensions you might have. Let's take a look at these two items and their impact on the geoprocessing tools that will be available for use.

In this section, you will learn how the licensing level that you have impacts the geoprocessing tools that are available to you. You will also learn about some of the extensions for ArcGIS Pro and how they add more analysis capabilities.

Understanding licensing levels

If you remember from `Chapter 1`, *Introducing ArcGIS Pro*, ArcGIS Pro has three different licensing levels:

- **Basic**
- **Standard**
- **Advanced**

The license level you have will directly impact the geoprocessing tools you will have access to.

The Basic level is the most limiting license level with the least amount of geoprocessing tools. With this level, you will be able to access simple analysis tools such as **Buffer**, **Union**, and **Intersect**. You will not be able to use tools that allow you to find the closest feature in another layer or that erase overlapping areas between two or more layers.

The Standard level includes a few more geoprocessing tools in addition to all the ones available at the Basic level. Many of these are focused on data management and maintenance. For example, the Standard level includes geoprocessing tools for creating relationship classes within a geodatabase. It also includes tools for managing an **Enterprise** or **Workgroup geodatabase**. Finally, it includes tools for creating and managing topologies that allow you to validate or check your spatial data for errors based on the rules you apply.

The Advanced license level has the greatest amount of geoprocessing tools. It includes all the tools found in the Basic and Standard licenses, in addition to more analysis tools. The Advanced license will allow you to locate the nearest feature to another feature or calculate the distances between points. It also has tools that allow you to erase areas of overlap between two or more layers, plus many more analysis tools.

The following table shows you a comparison of the number of geoprocessing tools found in the Basic and Advanced licensing levels of ArcGIS Pro 2.6. The Standard license level will fall somewhere between the Basic and Advanced licensing levels:

Parameters	Basic	Advanced
Analysis	19	29
Cartography	11	41
Conversion	36	42
Data Management	210	346
Editing	0	17
Geocoding	11	11
Linear Referencing	7	7
Multi-dimension	11	12
Server	16	16
Space-time pattern mining	9	9
Spatial Statistics	33	33
Total	363	563

Each licensing level has other limitations besides just which geoprocessing tools are available. You should check Esri's ArcGIS for **Desktop Functionality Matrix** to see a complete listing of the differences between the licensing levels. ArcGIS Pro will be slightly different as not all the functionality found in ArcGIS for Desktop has been ported into ArcGIS Pro. You can view the functionality matrix by going to `https://www.esri.com/content/dam/esrisites/en-us/media/brochures/arcgis-enterprise-functionality-matrix.pdf`.

The license level is not the only thing that impacts which tools you can use to perform analysis within ArcGIS Pro. Esri has also created several extensions that provide additional analysis tools.

In the next section, we will briefly discuss the extensions that Esri has currently available for ArcGIS Pro so that you have some idea about what they are and if they might be useful to you.

Learning about extensions for ArcGIS Pro

Esri also has several extensions for ArcGIS Pro that you can purchase. Extensions are add-ons for the core ArcGIS Pro product. They provide extended functionality to all licensing levels. Each extension has a focused area of increased functionality, which includes additional geoprocessing tools.

There are currently 19 different extensions that have been developed for ArcGIS Pro. The current ArcGIS Pro extensions, as of version 2.6, include the following:

- **Spatial Analyst**
- **3D Analyst**
- **Network Analyst**
- **Geostatistical Analyst**
- **Data Reviewer**
- **Data Interoperability**
- **Image Analyst**
- **Locate XT**
- **Location Referencing**
- **Production Mapping**
- **Publisher**
- **Workflow Manager**
- **Maritime Charting**

- **Defense Mapping**
- **Aviation Airports**
- **Aviation Charts**
- **Bathymetry**
- **Business Analyst**
- **StreetMap Premium**

The name of each extension helps to identify its purpose. For example, the 3D Analyst extension includes tools you can use to create and analyze data in a 3D environment. The Network Analyst extension allows you to perform analysis across a linear network such as a road network to calculate service areas or determine the shortest travel paths or calculate estimated drive times between two or more points.

To use the previously listed extensions, not only do you need to purchase them, but a license must also be assigned to the user in ArcGIS Online or Portal for ArcGIS. We will take a quick look at the first three extensions – Spatial Analyst, 3D Analyst, and Network Analyst, which are the most commonly used, in the upcoming sections.

Spatial Analyst

The Spatial Analyst extension is used to perform spatial analysis using raster-based data. Things you can do with the Spatial Analyst extension include the following:

- Perform terrain analysis with a **Digital Elevation Model (DEM)**
- Calculate slopes
- Determine viewsheds
- Perform hydrological analysis
- Classify images and much more

The Spatial Analyst extension includes over 170 geoprocessing tools that can be found in a toolbox with the same name as the extension:

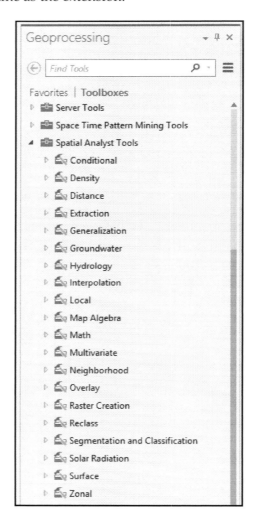

From the preceding screenshot, you can see that these geoprocessing tools are organized into 21 different toolsets within the toolbox.

3D Analyst

The 3D Analyst extension allows you to work with and analyze 3D data within ArcGIS Pro. It has many tools in common with Spatial Analyst. The major difference is that 3D Analyst is designed to work with 3D vector data as opposed to raster data. It does have some ability to create and analyze raster data, but that is not its strong suit. It is not uncommon to use the 3D Analyst and Spatial Analyst extensions together. For example, you might take 3D vector data such as elevation contours and use 3D Analyst to create a DEM for additional analysis with the Spatial Analyst extension.

3D Analyst allows you to work with many 3D datasets, including **Triangulated Irregular Networks (TIN)**, **Light Detection And Ranging Laser (LiDAR LAS)** datasets, and many of the other standard data formats that were discussed in Chapter 8, *Editing Spatial and Tabular Data*. If your data does not have an elevation or height associated with it, 3D Analyst can drape your 2D data over a surface and then use that surface to calculate an elevation for your features in relation to the draped surface.

The 3D Analyst extension includes just over 100 geoprocessing tools grouped into 11 toolsets:

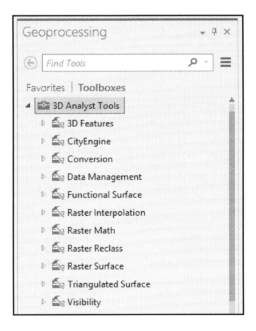

As you saw in Chapter 4, *Creating 3D Scenes*, ArcGIS Pro does support visualizing 3D data as part of its core functionality. So, you might be wondering why you would need the 3D Analyst extension. While visualizing 3D data is part of what ArcGIS Pro allows you to do out of the box with any license level, it does not allow you to perform analysis in 3D. You must have the 3D Analyst extension if you need to determine things such as slope or lines of sight or generate a **Digital Elevation Model (DEM)** in ArcGIS Pro.

Network Analyst

The Network Analyst extension has tools for creating and analyzing network datasets. A network dataset is a collection of linear features that are connected by nodes that allow for bi-directional flow. This means you can move in either direction along the lines within the network. Network datasets are normally associated with transportation-related networks such as roads, railroads, sidewalks, or bike paths. These are typically not used for utilities as those are normally single-direction flow networks.

With Network Analyst, you can calculate the best routes for vehicles, determine service areas based on drive time requirements, find nearest features within the network, and more. So, you might use this extension to help site a new fire station based on the drive time coverage of existing fire stations.

The Network Analyst extension for ArcGIS Pro currently includes 20 geoprocessing tools organized into three toolsets:

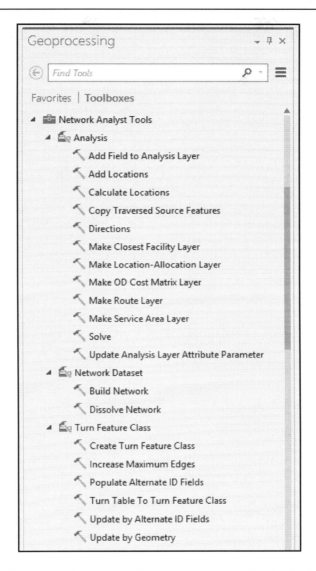

As you can see from the preceding screenshot, the names of the tools should help you understand their purpose and provide a bit more insight into what the **Network Analyst** extension will allow you to do. For example, the **Make Service Area Layer** tool will calculate a service area based on a location, along with a **Network Dataset**. The **Build Network** tool creates the network dataset that you use as the foundation for the other analysis the extension performs.

Now that you have an understanding of license levels and extensions, the following exercise will show you how to determine which license level and extensions have been assigned to you for ArcGIS Pro so that you can determine what capabilities you have.

Exercise 10A – Determining your license level and extensions

As you have just learned, the license level of ArcGIS Pro and the extensions that you have been assigned will impact what you can do in ArcGIS Pro. So, it is important to know what license level and extensions you have to work with.

In this short exercise, you will determine what license level you have and what extensions (if any) have been assigned from within ArcGIS Pro. If you happen to be the administrator for your organization, you can also log into ArcGIS Online or Portal for ArcGIS to determine what licenses have been assigned to each user. However, not everyone has administrative rights, so it is important to know how you can determine this from ArcGIS Pro.

Step 1 – Opening ArcGIS Pro

The first step is to open ArcGIS Pro and then determine what license level is available to you:

1. Open ArcGIS Pro, as you have done in past exercises.
2. Click on **About ArcGIS Pro**, which is located in the lower-left corner of the **Open a recent project** starting window.

   Question: *What version of ArcGIS Pro are you using?*

The **About ArcGIS Pro** window shows you which version of ArcGIS Pro you are using. It also allows you to check whether there are any software updates for ArcGIS Pro.

Step 2 – Determining the license level and extension

Now, you will see what license level you have been assigned and whether any extensions have also been assigned to you:

1. Click on **Licensing** in the left-hand side pane.
2. Review what licenses are available to you. This section will tell you which license level is available, while the middle section will tell you what extensions have been assigned to you.

> Questions: *Which license level of ArcGIS Pro do you have? What extensions (if any) can you use?*

3. Close ArcGIS Pro once you have answered the preceding questions.

Now that you know what version of the software you are running, the license level you have been assigned, and if you have any extensions assigned to you, you should have a much better idea of what capabilities are available to you as you work with ArcGIS Pro. With that knowledge of what you have to work with, it is now time to take a look at the analysis process within ArcGIS Pro.

Understanding the analysis process

GIS analysis normally starts with a question. This question can be a simple one such as what the total length of roads within the city is. They can also be very complex, such as *I need to know the best place to locate my new business within the city so that it has water and sewer services, as well as whether it is near major roads and in a location that will get business customers during the day and families in the evening.*

These questions get you started on the analysis process. This process is normally not linear. You will find that once you answer the initial question, it leads to other questions that start the process all over again. So, the general analysis process looks like this:

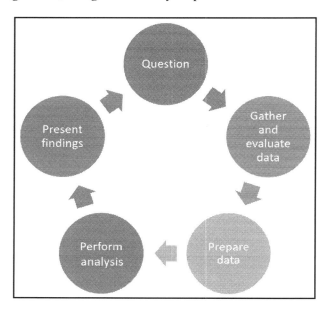

The initial question should cause you to ask questions as well. The question period establishes the specifications of what needs to be answered and what data you will need to answer the question.

Once you know exactly what question you are trying to answer, you need to start gathering the data you will need to perform the analysis. As you gather the data, you need to evaluate it. *Does it contain all the information you need? Is it in the format you need? Are the units the correct ones to answer the questions?* These are all examples of things you need to consider as you gather the data that you will use for your analysis.

Next, you will need to prepare your data for analysis. This may include simplifying it by clipping it to a specific area, projecting it to a different coordinate system, converting data formats, merging layers, generalizing information, or updating it.

Once you have prepared your data, you are then ready to begin your analysis. This can often require the use of multiple geoprocessing tools, along with other tools such as selecting features based on attributes or locations.

After you have completed your analysis, you will need to present your findings. You can do that by creating a map and layout, as you have already learned. You can also create charts and graphs to display your results.

Preparing data for analysis

As you gather and evaluate data for analysis, it is not unusual for the data to need some preparation work to get it into a state that you can use for your analysis. For example, you may download data from **ArcGIS Online** that is in a different coordinate system than the primary one you use for your data. So, you would need to project the downloaded data to the coordinate system that you will use for the rest of your data.

Common data preparation tasks include simplifying data, standardizing units, merging layers, and updating the data. Some of the most widely used geoprocessing tools to perform these tasks are as follows:

- **Clip**
- **Dissolve**
- **Project**
- **Append**
- **Merge**

These tools are available at all licensing levels. We will learn about each of the aforementioned tools in the following sections.

Clip geoprocessing tool

The Clip tool is used to extract data based on the boundary of other data. For example, if you wanted to determine which portions of streets were located in the city limits, you could use the clip tool to cut out the parts of the streets that are inside the city limits to their own layer. The Clip tool acts like a *cookie-cutter*.

This tool can be found in the **Analysis** toolbox and the **Extract** toolset. It can be used to clip points, lines, or polygons. However, the clipping layer must be a polygon. Here is an example of the Clip tool in action:

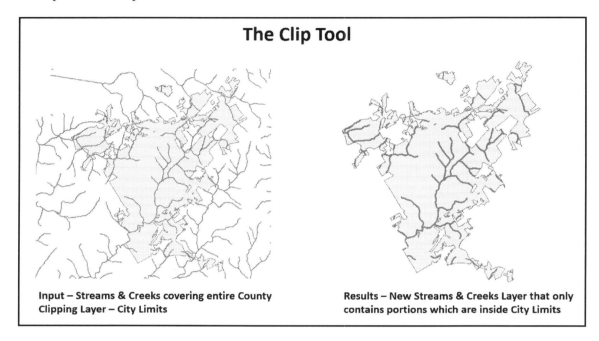

The Clip Tool

Input – Streams & Creeks covering entire County
Clipping Layer – City Limits

Results – New Streams & Creeks Layer that only contains portions which are inside City Limits

From the previous screenshot, you can see that we are trying to isolate the portions of the creeks and streams that are located inside the city limits. The creek and stream layer contains the location of all of them in the entire county. Here, we have clipped them using the city limits layer, which is a polygon. The result is a new layer that contains only those portions of the streams and creeks that are located inside the city limits.

Dissolve tool

The Dissolve tool is used to simplify or generalize a data layer based on a common attribute value. So, for example, if you had a parcel layer that showed each parcel and each parcel was coded with its designated zoning classification and you wanted to know the total amount of area for each zoning classification within the city, the Dissolve tool can be used to create individual polygons for each zoning classification.

The Dissolve tool can be found in the **Data Management Tools** toolbox and the **Generalization** toolset. It works on points, lines, and polygons. Here is an illustration of the example that was described earlier:

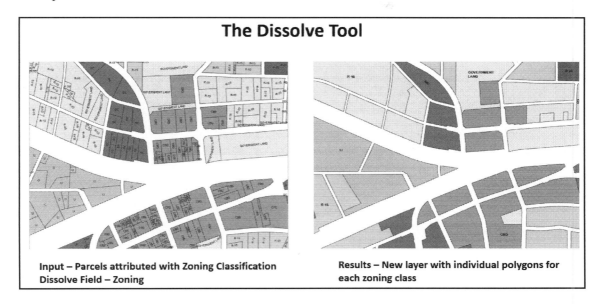

The Dissolve Tool

Input – Parcels attributed with Zoning Classification
Dissolve Field – Zoning

Results – New layer with individual polygons for each zoning class

As shown in the previous screenshot, the initial parcel layer contained many individual polygons that would have made determining the total area for each zoning classification difficult. Once you use the Dissolve tool, a new layer is created so that each zoning class has a single polygon. From there, it becomes much simpler to determine the total area for each zoning class.

Project tool

The Project tool is used to move a spatial layer from one coordinate system to another. It is important to know that when projecting data between coordinate systems, the actual coordinate values for your features must change. The Project tool will take your existing data and translate it into the new coordinate system using the proper math and translations to create a new layer that is in the designated coordinate system.

The Project tool is located in the **Data Management Tools** toolbox and the **Projections and Transformations** toolset. Certain tools and functions work best with different types of coordinate systems. There are two basic types of coordinate systems – **Geographic** and **Projected**. If you are trying to measure distances or areas, then a projected coordinate system works best.

Even though ArcGIS Pro will project data on the fly so that even the data that's in different coordinate systems will be displayed together, it is a recommended best practice that you place all the data that you are analyzing into the same common coordinate system. This avoids errors being caused by issues with different units and transformations.

This tool should not be confused with the **Define Projection** tool, which is located in the same place. The Define Projection tool will assign a coordinate system to a feature class that is undefined. It does not actually project data to a new coordinate system. This is a common mistake for new ArcGIS users.

Merge tool

The Merge tool will take data from two or more layers, or tables, and combine them into a new single output. This is useful if you get the same type of data from multiple sources or locations. For example, let's say you are working with a regional emergency response group and you are trying to develop a regional evacuation plan. You receive road data from multiple jurisdictions. You can use the Merge tool to combine them all into a single layer.

The Merge tool can be found in the **Data Management Tools** toolbox and **General** toolset. The Merge tool can be used to combine points, lines, polygons, and even standalone tables. You can only merge similar features, meaning you can only merge points with points, lines with lines, and polygons with polygons.

Here is another example of when you might want to use the Merge tool. You are responsible for inventorying all the fire hydrants within the city. So, you go out over the course of several days collecting the location of these fire hydrants. This results in a layer that shows all the locations you've collected daily. You wish to combine all the collected locations into a single layer:

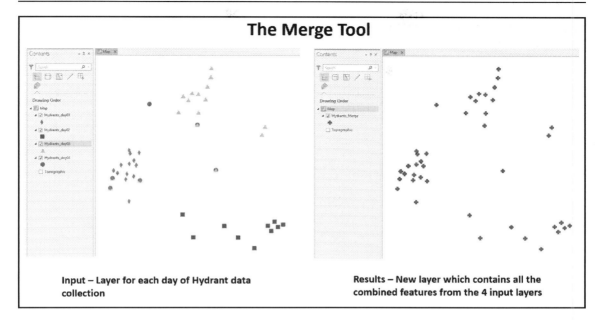

The Merge Tool

Input – Layer for each day of Hydrant data collection

Results – New layer which contains all the combined features from the 4 input layers

From the previous screenshot, you can see that the Merge tool creates a new layer that includes all the features and attributes that were originally in the four separate layers. So, now, you have a single layer to manage, update, and analyze.

Append tool

The Append tool is very similar to the Merge tool. It also combines data from multiple layers or tables into one. The big difference between these two tools is that Append is one of the few geoprocessing tools that changes the input data. It will add features or records to the target input.

You might use the Append tool if you have an existing layer of information and you just need to add newly acquired data to it. For example, continuing with the previous hydrant example, after merging the hydrants from the first four days, you collected some data. Now, you go out and collect more hydrant locations. You wish to add those newly collected hydrants to the merged layer to create.

The Append tool would work in this case. It would continue to add the newly collected location to the existing data layer. It would not keep creating new layers that you would need to manage. This is illustrated in the following screenshot:

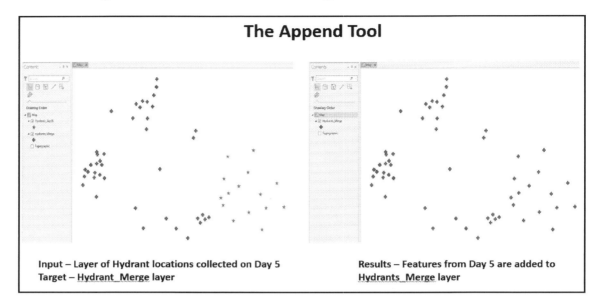

The Append Tool

Input – Layer of Hydrant locations collected on Day 5
Target – Hydrant_Merge layer

Results – Features from Day 5 are added to Hydrants_Merge layer

As shown in the previous screenshot, the hydrants that were in the layer showing the fifth day of the collection have been added to the **Hydrant_Merge** layer in the results on the right. This illustrates how the Append tool adds data from the input layer to the target layer.

Now that you know about some of the most commonly used geoprocessing tools that are used to prepare data for analysis, it is time for you to get some hands-on experience using them. In the next exercise, you will put what you have learned about the Clip and Dissolve tools into action.

Exercise 10B – Using the Clip and Dissolve tools

The Public Works director is working on a report that he must provide to the City Council to support his budget request. He needs to know the total length of each road within the city of Trippville. He has asked you to provide him with those numbers.

Luckily, you already have the city limit and street data within your geodatabase. However, the street data extends outside the city limits and is broken down into individual road segments. So, you will need to take some time to prepare the data before you can provide him with the numbers that he needs.

Step 1 – Evaluating the data

The director has already provided you with the question and you have verified that you already have the data needed for the project. So, now, you just need to evaluate your data to verify the steps you need to complete the project.

In this step, you will open ArcGIS Pro and review the street and city limit data. You will make sure you have the information you need:

1. Start **ArcGIS Pro** and open the Ex10B.aprx file located in C:\Student\IntroArcPro\Chapter10\Ex10B.

2. Once the project opens, you should see a map with two layers, namely **City_Limit** and **Street_Centerlines**. Notice that the streets extend outside the city limits.

Question: *What geoprocessing tool that you have read about in this chapter do you think should be used to create a layer that only contains the streets inside the city limits?*

3. Right-click on the **Street_Centerlines** layer and select **Attribute Table**.

4. The director wants the total length of each road in the city. Review the table for the **Street_Centerlines** layer to see whether there is a field that identifies what road each segment belongs to.

Question: *Which field identifies what road each segment belongs to?*

5. Close the table and save your project.

You have now evaluated your data to determine its suitability to provide the information requested by the director. You know you will have to extract portions of the street centerlines that are located inside the city limits and that you have an identification field you can use to dissolve the street segments by to easily calculate their length.

Step 2 – Clipping the streets

In this step, you will clip the street centerlines, thus creating a new layer that only contains the portions of the streets that are located inside the city limits:

1. Select the **Analysis** tab in the ribbon.
2. From the **Tools** group, which is located in the center of the **Analysis** tab, select **Clip**. This should open the **Geoprocessing** pane on the right-hand side of the interface.

> If you do not see the **Clip** tool, you can use the small arrows located on the right-hand side of the **Tools** group to reveal more tools.

3. Click on the small drop-down arrow located to the right of the cell for **Input Features** and select the **Street_Centerlines** layer.
4. For the **Clip Features**, select **City_Limit** using the same process.
5. Make sure your **Output Feature Class** field is set to `C:\Student\IntroArcPro\Chapter10\Ex10B\Ex10B.gdb\Street_Centerlines_Clip`.
6. Leave the **XY Tolerance** field blank. Your **Geoprocessing** pane should look like this:

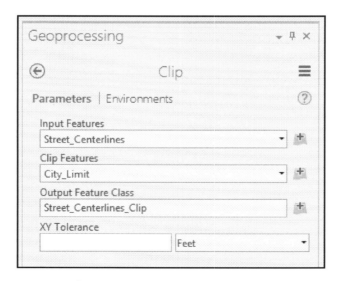

7. Once you have verified that you have everything set correctly, click the **Run** button, which is located at the bottom of the **Geoprocessing** pane.

If you are ever unsure what a tool will do or what the various parameters refer to, locate the small blue question mark surrounded by a circle on the upper right-hand side of the **Geoprocessing** pane and click on it.

This will open the help documentation for the tool. This will provide you with a detailed description of what the tool does, intended use cases, and descriptions of all the parameters. It will also include some sample Python scripting code you can use if you are creating a script that contains the tool you are reviewing. You will learn more about Python in Chapter 12, *Automating Processes with ModelBuilder and Python*.

When the **Clip** tool is complete, a new layer will be added to your map named **Street_Centerlines_Clip**.

8. Turn off or remove the **Streets_Centerlines** layer so that you can see the results of the Clip tool in a better way.
9. Right-click on the new layer you just created and select **Attribute Table**.
10. Right-click on the **ST_NAME** field and choose **Sort Ascending**. This will sort the records based on the name of each road.

Question: *After sorting the records in the table, what do you notice about the number of segments for each road?*

So, now, you can see how the Clip tool created a new layer that only contains those portions of the road that are located inside the city limits. Your original layer remains untouched. You are almost ready to provide the director with the information that he needs. However, you still need to simplify the data so that you can calculate the total length of each road more easily.

Let's move on to the next step regarding simplifying the data.

Step 3 – Simplifying the data and calculating the total length

In this step, you will use the Dissolve tool to simplify the clipped road's centerline layer that you created in the previous step. This will create another new layer in your map:

1. Click on the **Analysis** tab in the ribbon.
2. Click on the **Toolboxes** button in the **Geoprocessing** group tab. This will reactivate or open the **Geoprocessing** pane once again.
3. At the top of the **Geoprocessing** pane, select **Toolboxes**, which is located to the right of **Favorites**. This will display a list of all the toolboxes included in ArcGIS Pro, in addition to any extensions you have access to.
4. Expand the **Data Management Tools** toolbox.
5. Expand the **Generalization** toolset, which is located in the **Data Management Tools** toolbox.
6. Double-click on the **Dissolve** tool.
7. Set the **Input Features** field to **Street_Centerlines_Clip** using the same process that you used for the Clip tool.
8. Set the **Output Feature Class** field to
   `C:\Student\IntroArcPro\Chapter10\Ex10B\Ex10B.gdb\Street_Centerl ines_Dissolve_Name`.
9. Set the dissolve field to **ST_NAME**. The Dissolve tool should now look like this:

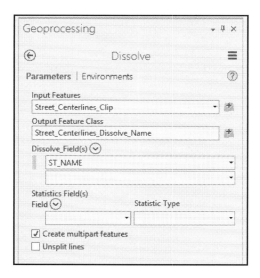

10. Once you have verified that the Dissolve tool is properly configured, click the **Run** button.

11. A new layer is, once again, added to your map. Right-click on this layer and select **Attribute Table**.

12. Right-click on the **ST_NAME** field and select **Sort Ascending**.

13. Scroll through the list of records. Pay attention to the number of records associated with each road name.

Question: *How many records are there with the same road name?*

Now, the information is ready to give to the director. With the dissolve complete, you have a list of each road and its associated total length in the **Shape_Length** field.

In this step, you used the Dissolve tool to simplify the data so that you could easily provide the director with the values that he has requested. The results of the Dissolve tool have summarized the total length of each road within the city by name. Next, we will move on to the last step that's required to meet the request from the director: exporting the data to an Excel spreadsheet.

Step 4 – Exporting a table to Excel

The director appreciates your efforts. However, he does not have ArcGIS Pro. So, he has asked if you can export your results to an Excel spreadsheet. This will allow him to easily incorporate your results in his report.

In this step, you will export the results of your efforts to an **Excel** spreadsheet using tools that can be found in the **Conversion** toolbox:

1. Return to the **Toolboxes** list in the **Geoprocessing** pane by clicking on the small arrow surrounded by a circle in the upper left-hand corner of the pane.

2. Expand the **Conversion Tools** toolbox and then expand the **Excel** toolset.

3. Select the **Table to Excel** script tool. This particular tool is actually a **Python Script**. The scroll icon located next to the tool name identifies it as such.

4. Set **Input Table** to `Street_Centerlines_Dissolve_Name`.

5. Set the output to
   `C:\Student\IntroArcPro\Chapter10\Ex10B\Street_Lengths_by_Name.x ls`.

6. Verify that your **Geoprocessing** pane looks as follows and click the **Run** button:

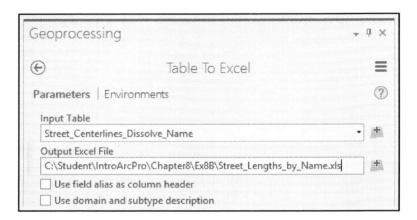

When the **Table to Excel** tool is complete, it does not add the resulting Excel spreadsheet to your map. If you wish to view your results, start **Microsoft Excel** and open the spreadsheet that you just created. It should look very similar to the table you viewed in ArcGIS Pro.

7. Close the **Geoprocessing** pane and save your project.
8. Close ArcGIS Pro.

Congratulations! You have just completed your first analysis project using ArcGIS Pro. Next, we will look at some other tools that are commonly used to perform analysis.

Using other common geoprocessing analysis tools

With over 300 geoprocessing tools available, you have only just begun to scratch the surface of the types of analysis that you can perform with ArcGIS Pro. ArcGIS Pro includes tools that allow you to perform spatial analysis of your data as well. This can be broken down into several toolsets including **Overlay**, **Proximity**, and **Statistics** within the Analysis toolbox. We will learn about each of these in the upcoming sections.

Overlay analysis

Overlay analysis compares two or more layers and locating areas where they overlap one another. Depending on which tool you use, you can determine the areas where they overlap, erase the areas where they overlap, or combine the total areas of all the inputs.

The Overlay toolset includes the following tools:

Tool name	Minimum licensing level	Short description
Erase	Advanced	It clips out areas of overlap from input features.
Identity	Advanced	It calculates areas of overlap and no overlap.
Intersect	Basic	It returns only the area of overlap.
Union	Basic	It combines a total area of input polygons.
Update	Advanced	It replaces the area of overlap with new features.
Spatial Join	Basic	It joins attributes from one feature to another based on a spatial relationship.
Symmetrical Difference	Advanced	It identifies areas where features do not overlap.

ArcGIS Pro introduces a new **Pairwise** toolset, which also performs overlay analysis. The tools in this toolset are designed to be used with extremely large datasets. They will provide similar results to those created with the standard Overlay tools.

Now, we will take a closer look at the two overlay analysis tools that are available at all licensing levels, namely **Union** and **Intersect**.

Union

The Union tool takes the input of multiple polygon layers and combines all the information into a single feature class that contains all the data from the input layers (typically two or more). It is important to remember that this tool only works with polygons. It can't be used with points or lines. If you need to perform this type of analysis on points or lines, you will need to use the **Identify** tool.

You might want to use the Union tool if you wish to determine how much of each parcel was in a floodplain area and how much of each parcel was not in a floodplain area, as shown in the following screenshot:

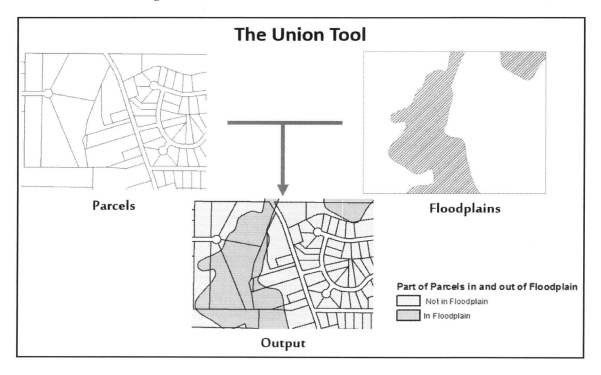

As you can see, the result is a new layer or feature class that contains the attributes from each part of the floodplain that overlaps part of each parcel and the parts of those two layers that do not overlap. Again, your original inputs are still intact.

Intersect

The Intersect tool takes multiple input layers and returns a new layer that shows where the inputs overlap. The resulting layer attribute table will contain the combined attributes of all the inputs. This tool works with all feature types; that is, points, lines, and polygons. If you input multiple feature types, you get to choose what your resulting output type will be.

You might use the Intersect tool if you are working on an emergency evacuation plan for your community. For example, you might need to determine which roads might be blocked due to flooding, so you need to know which segments are in the floodplain. You can use the Intersect tool to overlay the **Street Centerlines** with the floodplains to locate where and how much of each road is in the greatest danger of flooding, as shown in the following screenshot:

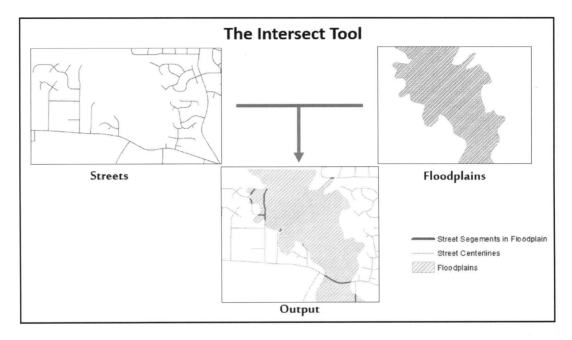

The resulting output of the Intersect tool in this scenario is a new layer that just contains portions of the streets that are located inside the floodplain area. As with other tools, your original input layers have not been changed in any way.

Let's move on to the next toolset – Proximity.

Proximity analysis

Proximity analysis compares, calculates, or shows distances between features in two or more layers. Proximity tools will generate distance buffers, locate nearest features, or calculate distances between features.

The tools included in the Proximity toolset are as follows:

Tool name	Minimum license level	Short description
Buffer	Basic	It creates polygons around existing features at a set distance.
Multiple Ring Buffer	Basic	It can create multiple buffer polygons at various distances.
Create Thiessen Polygons	Advanced	It creates polygons around points showing areas of influence.
Near	Advanced	It identifies how far the nearest feature is between the input and closest feature layers.
Generate Near Table	Advanced	It creates a new standalone table that shows distances between the features in two layers.
Polygon Neighbors	Advanced	It identifies what polygons are next to the source polygon, and also calculates other associated information.

Next, we will take a quick look at the **Buffer** and **Multiple Ring Buffer** tools mentioned in the preceding table.

Buffer tool

The Buffer tool is one of the most frequently used tools in ArcGIS. It creates a new polygon layer around the input layer based on a specified distance. The buffer distance can be a single value or can be based on an attribute field in the attribute table of the features being buffered. You can choose to buffer any feature type. You can buffer points, lines, or polygons.

However, the output will always be a polygon, as shown in the following screenshot:

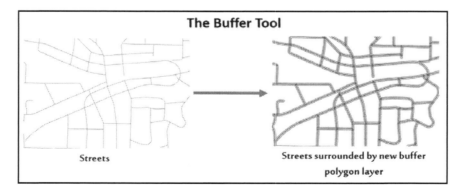

The Buffer Tool

Streets

Streets surrounded by new buffer polygon layer

Buffers are extremely useful. They can be used to help determine whether features in one layer are within the distance of another layer. They can also help us create features for other purposes, such as creating the rights-of-way for roads or railroads, as shown in the preceding screenshot.

In this illustration, you can see that a new polygon layer has been created around the existing street centerlines, all at a uniform distance. This new layer represents the rights-of-way for those roads. Also, each new polygon inherits the attribute values of the street that was buffered. This means that the new polygons are attributed to the road name and any other attributes that were linked to the street segments.

One of the options you have when using the Buffer tool is to dissolve the overlapping buffers. If you choose to dissolve overlapping buffers, then any buffers that overlap will be merged into a single polygon. This reduces the number of features that are in the resulting layer. Also, if you choose to dissolve overlapping buffers, the new polygons will not contain the attribute information that was associated with the features that you buffered.

The following screenshot shows the difference between a buffer that has been dissolved and one that hasn't:

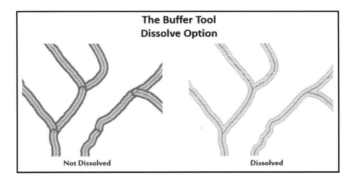

As you can see, the **Not Dissolved** example on the left contains many more polygons than the **Dissolved** one on the right. The example on the left has many overlapping buffers, so if they are dissolved, they become one.

Multiple Ring Buffer tool

The Multiple Ring Buffer tool is a Python script that runs the Buffer tool multiple times to create concentric buffer rings around the buffered features, as shown in the following screenshot:

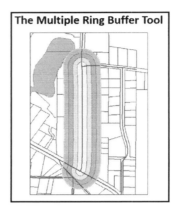

Like the standard Buffer tool, the Multiple Ring Buffer tool works with points, lines, and polygons, but only outputs a new polygon layer. You also have the option to dissolve the overlapping buffers.

Now that you have had an opportunity to learn about some of the most commonly used analysis geoprocessing tools, let's give you a chance to put them into action.

Exercise 10C – Performing analysis

Remember back in Chapter 4, *Creating 3D Scenes, when the Community and Economic Development director asked you to prepare several maps that showed the location of commercial properties that were between 1 and 3 acres?* After his meeting with the business owners, he needs some more assistance with this project.

He needs you to locate commercial properties that are within 150 feet of existing city sewer lines and that have at least 1 acre that is not in a floodplain.

Step 1 – Locating commercial properties near sewer lines

The first step of your analysis will be to locate all the commercial properties that are between 1 and 3 acres in size and that are within 150 feet of an existing sewer line. Luckily, you identified the commercial properties that meet the size requirements in Chapter 4, *Creating 3D Scenes,* so that part is done. So, now, you just need to determine which of them are within 150 feet of the sewer lines.

In this step, you will create a 150-foot buffer around the sewer lines in the city. Then, you will perform a spatial selection to select all the commercial properties between 1 and 3 acres that are touched by or intersect with the buffer you create:

1. Start **ArcGIS Pro.**
2. Open the Ex10C.aprx project, which is located at C:\Student\IntroArcPro\Chapter10.

   When the project opens, you should see a map that looks very familiar to the one you created in Chapter 4, *Creating 3D Scenes.* This map already contains all the basic layers you need to perform your analysis. You can see the commercial properties between 1 and 3 acres, the sewer lines, and the floodplains. Now, you will need to create the 150-foot buffer around the sewer lines.

3. Select the **Analysis** tab in the ribbon.
4. Select the **Buffer** tool to open the **Geoprocessing** pane and **Buffer** tool parameters.
5. Using the skills you learned in the previous exercise, set the **Input Feature** class to **Sewer Lines**.
6. Set your **Output Feature Class** to C:\Student\IntroArcPro\Chapter10\Ex10B\Ex10B.gdb\sewer_lines_Buffer.
7. Set the **Distance** field to 150 and the units to **Feet**.
8. Leave the **Side Type**, **End Type**, and **Method** fields with the default settings.
9. Set the **Dissolve Type** field to **Dissolve all output features into a single feature**. Since you do not need to know which sewer line is near which parcel, this allows ArcGIS Pro to dissolve the resulting buffer, thus making future analysis easier.

10. Verify that your **Geoprocessing** pane looks as follows and click **Run**:

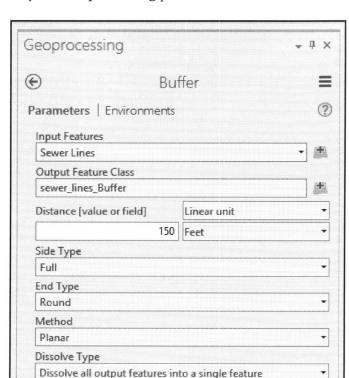

Once you've finished using the Buffer tool, a new layer will be added to your map. This new layer will show the areas that are within 150 feet of the sewer lines. You will now use that new layer to select the commercial properties.

11. Click on the **Map** tab in the ribbon.
12. Select the **Select by Location** button in the **Selection** group on the **Map** tab.
13. The **Select by Location** tool window will open. Set **Input Feature Layer** to **Commercial Properties 1 to 3 AC**.
14. Set the **Relationship** field to **Intersect**. This will select all the commercial properties between 1 and 3 acres that are overlaid by the sewer lines buffer layer.
15. Set the **Selecting Features** field to **sewer_lines_Buffer**.

16. Leave all the other parameters with their default settings.
17. Verify the **Select by Location** tool window looks as follows and click **OK**:

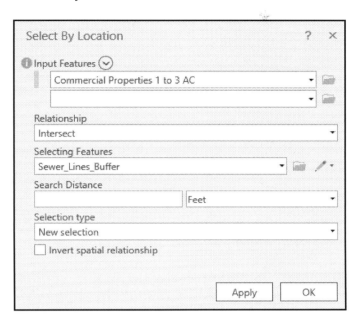

When the **Select By Layer Location** process completes, you should have approximately 18 commercial properties selected. All of these are overlapping or being touched by the sewer line buffer that you created. This means they are all within 150 feet of an existing sewer line. You will now export those selected parcels to their own layer.

Step 2 – Exporting selected parcels

Now that you have identified which commercial properties are within 150 feet of a sewer line, you will export those to a new feature class so that you can use them for further analysis later. This will ensure you don't mistakenly change or corrupt the existing layer by accident:

1. Select **Commercial Properties 1 to 3 AC** in the **Contents** pane.
2. Select the **Data** tab in the **Feature Layer** group.
3. Click on the **Export Features** button located in the **Data** tab to open the **Export Features** tool window.

4. The **Input Features** field should automatically be set to **Commercial Properties 1 to 3 AC**. If not, set it to that layer.

5. Set the **Output Feature Class** field to
`C:\Student\IntroArcPro\Chapter10\Ex10\Ex10B.gdb\CommercialProp_near_sewer`.

6. Verify that your **Export Features** window looks as follows and click **OK**:

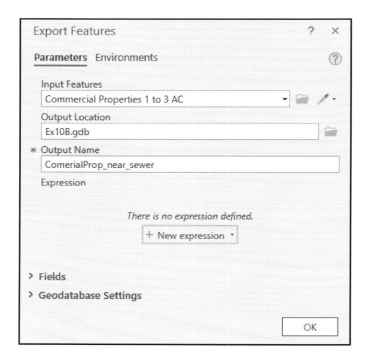

When the process for the **Copy Features** tool completes, a new layer will be added to your map that contains only the commercial parcels that you had selected. If you have features selected in a map or table, most geoprocessing tools will automatically only use those selected records within that tool.

7. Open the attribute table for the **CommercialProp_near_sewer** layer that was just added to your map.

8. Verify the table contains the same number of records that you selected previously. There should be approximately 18.

9. Clear your selection by clicking on the **Clear** button in the **Selection** group on the **Map** tab.

10. Close the table.

11. Turn off **Sewer Lines, Sanitary Sewer Manholes, sewer_line_Buffer,** and **Commercial Properties 1 to 3 AC** layers. You do not need to see those for the rest of your analysis. They might cause confusion.

12. Save your project.

You have just successfully exported the features you had selected to a new feature class, leaving the original data intact. You will use the new feature class you just created in the next step to perform an analysis to determine how much of the commercial properties are located inside the floodplains.

Step 3 – Determining how much of each commercial property is in the floodplain

Now that you have selected the commercial properties that are the required size and that are near the city's sewer system, it is time to calculate how much area of each of those parcels is within the floodplain. To do that, you will use the Union geoprocessing tool to union the new layer that you just created with the floodplains.

This will create a new layer that will split each commercial property into the part that is in the floodplain and the part that isn't:

1. Using the skills that you have already learned, open the attribute tables for both the **CommercialProp_near_sewer** and **Floodplains** layers. Take a moment to review what fields are located in each table and some of the values that they contain. This will help you understand the results produced by the Union tool.

2. Close the tables.

3. Click on the **Analysis** tab in the ribbon.

4. Select the **Union** tool from the **Tools** group. The **Geoprocessing** pane will now display the parameters associated with the **Union** tool.

5. Set your input feature classes to **Commercial Properties 1 to 3 AC** and **Floodplains**.

6. Set your **Output Feature Class** to
   `C:\Student\IntroArcPro\Chapter10\Ex10B\Ex10B.gdb\Commercial_Flo odplain_Union`.

7. Once you've verified that your **Geoprocessing** pane looks as follows, click **Run**:

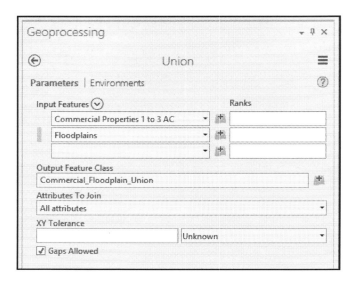

When the process for the **Union** tool completes, it will add a new layer to your map that includes features that are the results of combining the two input layers. Your map should look similar to the following (remember, your colors might be different):

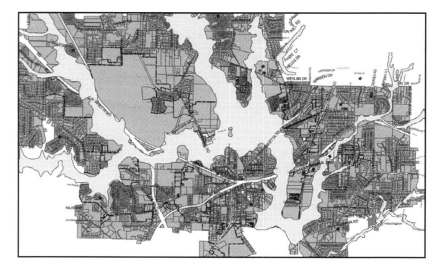

As you can see, the green layer on the map is the result of the Union tool.

8. Open the attribute table for the layer that you just created and that was added to your map.

9. Select **Sort Descending** on the **SFHA** field. All those polygons that are attributed to **IN** are inside the floodplain. All those that are blank, or **NULL**, are outside.

10. You need to update the **ACRE_CALC** field to reflect the new acreage for **Commercial_Floodplain_Union**. Right-click on the **ACRE_CALC** field and select the **Calculate Field** option.

 If the **Calculate Field** option is grayed out, make sure the layer is editable in the **Contents** pane on **List by Editable**. If a layer is not editable, you cannot run the **Calculate Field** or **Calculate Geometry** tools.

11. Set the **Expression Type** field to **Arcade** using the drop-down arrow.

12. In the **Expression** cell located below the **Fields** column where it says **ACRE_CALC =**, type `$feature.Shape_Area / 43560`. This will convert the **Shape_Area** field values that are in square feet into acres. It should look something like this when you are done entering this value:

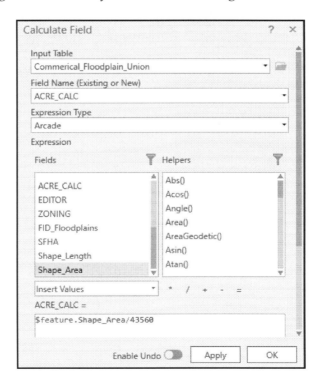

13. Click **OK** once you have verified your expression.
14. Close the table and save your project.

With that, you have used the Union tool to determine how much of each commercial property is within a floodplain and how much is not in the floodplain. Then, you used the Field Calculator tool to calculate the total area of each in acres so that you will be able to complete the next step. In the next step, you will build a query that will select all the commercial properties that are not within a floodplain and are greater than or equal to 1 acre in size.

Step 4 – Selecting commercial parcels that are not in the floodplain

The one problem with using the Union tool in this process is that the resulting layer also includes parts of the floodplain polygons that did not overlap the commercial parcels. This means you need to either simplify that layer by removing those polygons that are in the floodplains or account for them in your query. If you had an Advanced license, you could have used the Identity tool, which would have resulted in you avoiding this step.

In this step, you will select the commercial properties that have at least 1 acre or more not in a floodplain:

1. Click on the **Map** tab in the ribbon.
2. Click on the **Select by Attributes** button to open the tool window.
3. Verify that **Input Rows** is set to **Commercial_Floodplain_Union**. If not, set it accordingly.
4. The **Selection type** field should be set to **New selection**.
5. Click on the **New Expression** button.
6. After the word **Where**, set the field to **Zoning** and the following operator to `is not equal to`. For the value, select the blank option at the top of the list and click **Add**. This will eliminate the polygons that just represent floodplain areas that do not overlap the commercial properties.

7. Click the **Add Clause** button located below the clause you just created.
8. Set the query field to **ACRE_CALC** and the following operator to is Greater Than or Equal to. Type in 1.00 for the value and click **Add**. This selects all the commercial parcels that are of the right size.
9. Click the **Add Clause** button one more time.
10. Set the query field to **SFHA** and the operator to is not equal to. Then, set the value to **IN** and click **Add**. This removes any areas that are inside the floodplain from your final selection.
11. Click the green checkmark to validate your query. Your Geoprocessing pane should look similar to this:

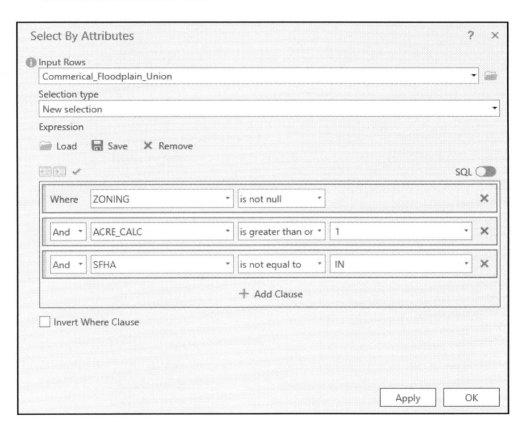

12. Click OK once you've verified everything is set properly. When it is complete, you should have 21 commercial properties selected. These should all be larger than 1 acre in size and outside the floodplain.

13. Using the skills you learned about in the previous step, export your selection to a new layer. Set the symbology for the new layer to something that stands out.

14. Turn off the **Commercial_Floodplain_Union** layer so that your new layer stands out even more.

15. Save your project.

With that, you have just identified the parcels within the city that meet the director's requirements. You used various analysis and selection tools to answer his question. As you can see, it is not unusual to use multiple tools and methods to get the required answers to what may seem to be a simple question. Believe it or not, once you get familiar and comfortable with these tools, the process you just completed can be done in less than 10 minutes. It just takes practice.

Next, you will learn how to access the history of all the geoprocessing tools you use in ArcGIS Pro.

Step 5 – Reviewing your geoprocessing history

The analysis process you just completed involved many steps. *If this was not an exercise with notes to refer to, how would you know all the steps and tools you used to complete the analysis?* Luckily, ArcGIS Pro keeps a record of the geoprocessing tools you use, the parameters you included in those tools, and the results or any errors that were encountered. This provides you with a record of the work you did to arrive at your results.

In this step, you will learn how to access this historical record of your geoprocessing activities:

1. Click on the **Analysis** tab in the ribbon.

2. Click on the **History** button, which is located in the **Geoprocessing** group on the **Analysis** tab. This will open the **History** pane.

3. Take a moment to review the records you can see in the **History** pane. You should see all the geoprocessing tools you have used in this chapter listed, as well as any others you might have used in previous chapters or while doing your daily activities.

4. Right-click on the **Clip** tool in the **History** pane and select the **View Details** option from the menu. This will look as follows:

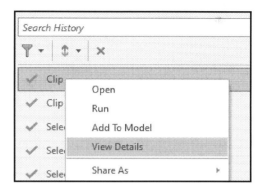

5. A new window should open in ArcGIS Pro displaying the history of this instance of the Clip tool when you ran it. Take a moment to review the information contained in this window.

This information window is useful when a tool fails to run successfully. It will provide you with a list of errors and a warning that might explain what caused the tool to fail.

6. After you are done reviewing the history of the **Clip** tool, close the window.
7. Right-click on the **Clip** tool again to display the menu. Review the options it contains.
8. Save your project and close ArcGIS Pro.

Now, you know how to access the history of all the geoprocessing tools you use within ArcGIS Pro. This allows you to see the tools you used to complete an analysis, determine what might have caused a tool to fail, and more. You can also rerun the tool from the History pane using the exact same setting that was used at the time shown in the pane. This can help save you time by not having to reenter all the parameters again to run a tool. As you can see, the History pane can be a powerful ally when you need to perform analysis.

Summary

In this chapter, you learned that ArcGIS Pro can be used to conduct spatial analysis to help answer a wealth of questions and concerns. It can also help you see patterns and solutions. You now have the skills to use powerful geoprocessing tools that can be used with various types of data to get the answers you need to everyday problems.

In this chapter, you also learned what geoprocessing is and some of the tools that are available in ArcGIS Pro. You then learned how your licensing level and extensions can impact specific tools that are available to you when you need to perform analysis or manage GIS data.

This chapter also exposed you to some of the most commonly used analysis and data preparation tools. You conducted two separate analysis projects using those tools. With the skills and hands-on experience that you have acquired, you can integrate these tools with other tools that you have already been exposed to in order to find answers.

With that, you have learned many skills, including creating projects, maps, scenes, and layouts using ArcGIS Pro, as well as how to edit and analyze data. You have also seen that there is often more than one way to perform the same task.

In the next chapter, you will explore Tasks, which can allow you to standardize workflows to help train new users, document proper workflows, and ensure everyone is using the same methods to complete common processes.

Section 3: Sharing Data and Automating processes

3

Geographic Information System (GIS) is no longer limited to just producing paper maps. We can now share them with the world via the web, digital files, and more.

In this section, you will learn methods for sharing your data and maps with others. You will also be introduced to methods for automating some of your processes using ModelBuilder and Python.

We will cover the following chapters in this section:

- Chapter 11, *Creating and Using Tasks*
- Chapter 12, *Automating Processes with ModelBuilder and Python*
- Chapter 13, *Sharing Your Work with Others*
- Chapter 14, *Using Arcade Expressions for Labeling and Symbology*

11
Creating and Using Tasks

As you have now experienced firsthand, ArcGIS Pro contains a wealth of tools and methods for editing data, creating maps, and performing analysis. In many cases, there are two or three different ways to do the same thing. Also, many geoprocessing tools are very similar, such as **Union**, **Intersect**, and **Identity**. Though these are similar, each is designed to be used in specific circumstances.

All these different tools and methods make ArcGIS Pro a very powerful application. However, it can also make it confusing for the new users and allow experienced users to perform functions very differently. This can result in inaccurate or just wrong results. Things would be much simpler if you could develop standard workflows that everyone could use with step-by-step instructions required to complete specific tasks.

With ArcGIS Pro, you can do just that. They are called **tasks**. Tasks provide step-by-step workflows that can be saved along with your project. There is no limit to the number of tasks you can save with your project. You can save and share them to a network folder, ArcGIS Online, Portal for ArcGIS, and more.

In this chapter, you will learn how to create and use tasks within ArcGIS Pro. This will include the following topics:

- What a task is and considerations to take into account before creating one
- How to create a task
- How to use a task

Once you've completed the chapter, you will better understand what a task is, how to create one, and more importantly, how to use them to standardize common workflows in your organization.

Technical requirements

To complete the exercises in this chapter, you will need **ArcGIS Pro 2.6** or higher installed. Any license level will be acceptable.

Understanding what a task is

Simply put, a task is a series of preconfigured steps required to complete a specific process. Tasks can be very simple, containing only three or four steps, or they can be very complex, containing group tasks within a task and each group can contain multiple steps. It is entirely up to you depending on the purpose of the task and the skill level of those that will be using the task. Tasks allow you to be as detailed as you believe you need to be for your user audience.

This section will help you learn about the components of a task. We will also get some hands-on experience with an exercise on running a task.

Tasks are stored as a **task item** within an ArcGIS Pro project. You access your tasks from the **Catalog** pane. When you open a specific task, it will appear in a new pane called the **Tasks** pane.

Components of a task

Each task that you create in ArcGIS Pro will consist of several components. They are as follows:

- **Task item**: The first is the **task item**, which is stored in the project. It is basically a folder for storing related tasks within your project. You will access **Task Items** from the **Catalog pane**, as shown in the following screenshot:

- **Task group**: The second component is the **task group**. The task group is a subfolder within the task item for grouping related tasks by function or purpose. The following screenshot shows you an example of a task group:

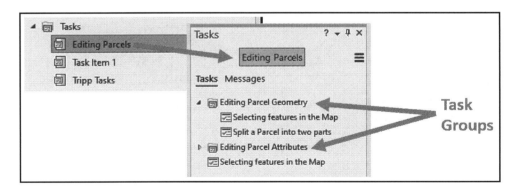

As you can see from the preceding screenshot, you can create task groups inside other task groups, just as you can create folders inside other folders in **Microsoft Windows**. This allows you to create an organizational structure for storing your tasks so that they are easier to find and manage.

- **Task**: The third component is the **task** itself. This is a collection of steps needed to complete a given process such as splitting a parcel, adding a new water line, or geocoding a new address. Tasks can be stored inside a task group or a standalone task, as shown in the following screenshot:

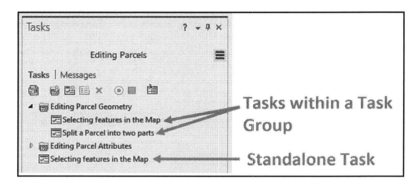

- **Step**: The last component is a **step**. A task will generally contain multiple steps. Steps refer to actions, buttons, geoprocessing tools, models, or scripts accessible in ArcGIS Pro. A common step would be to use the **Explore** tool to zoom to the location of a feature. Another example of a step would be selecting a given feature once the user has zoomed to the right area:

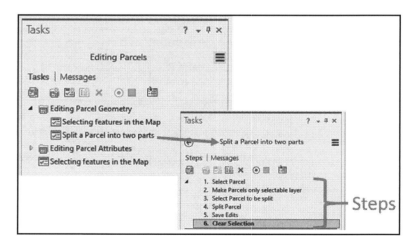

Each step is going to have several parameters that you can set for that step. You will provide general information regarding each step such as a name, instructions for users to follow, and how the step will be run, as shown in the following screenshot:

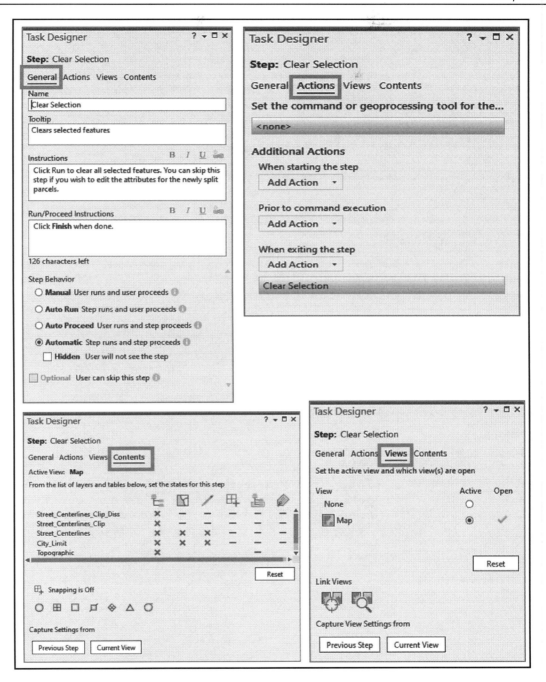

You can reference specific geoprocessing tools or commands within a **Step** under **Actions**. In the preceding illustration, this step references clearing the selection of the **Select by Rectangle** command. You have options to control which map and view the step should use. Lastly, you can control the contents within that view via the step. You can decide which layers will be visible, selectable, or editable.

You can have steps that simply provides instructions for the user and that run automatically. You can hide steps from users if desired. You will learn more about the steps and how to create them later in this chapter.

We will now move on to the next section about running a task.

Running a task

Tasks are run from the **Tasks** pane. The steps are presented to the user as they complete each one and move on to the next step. To get a task to open in the **Tasks** pane, you must first open the task item that contains the desired task you wish to run.

Once you open the task item from the **Catalog** pane, the **Tasks** pane will open and you will be able to select which task stored in the selected task item that you wish to run. You may need to expand a task group in order to find the specific task you are looking for. When you find the specific task you wish to run, simply double-click on it within the **Tasks** pane to run it.

Now let's give you a chance to experience what it is like to run a task with a hands-on exercise.

Exercise 11A – Running a simple task

In this exercise, you will run a simple task that steps you through the process of selecting a feature in the map. This will allow you to get first-hand experience of how to access and run a task in ArcGIS Pro.

Step 1 – Starting ArcGIS Pro and opening a project

You first need to open a project containing stored tasks. In this step, you will start ArcGIS Pro and open a project that has several tasks:

1. Start ArcGIS Pro.
2. Open the `Ex11.aprx` file located in `C:\Student\IntroArcPro\Chapter11`.

   When your project opens, you should see a single two-dimensional map that contains layers representing the city limits, streets, and parcels for the city of Trippville.

3. In the **Catalog** pane, expand the **Tasks** folder so you can see the task items saved in this project.

Question: *What task items do you see included in this project?*

We will now move on to the next step.

Step 2 – Opening and running a task

In this step, you will open a task item and then run a task that steps you through the process of selecting a feature in the map:

1. Double-click on the **Selecting Features** task item in the **Catalog** pane.
2. The **Catalog** pane should open on the left side of the ArcGIS Pro interface. Take note of the tasks included in this task item.

Question: *How many tasks are included in the task item have you opened and what are they?*

3. Double-click on the **Selecting Features** in the **Map** task to open it.

4. Follow the instructions provided within the task's steps. When asked to zoom to an area on the map, you may zoom to any location for this exercise. Make sure to read and follow all the instructions:

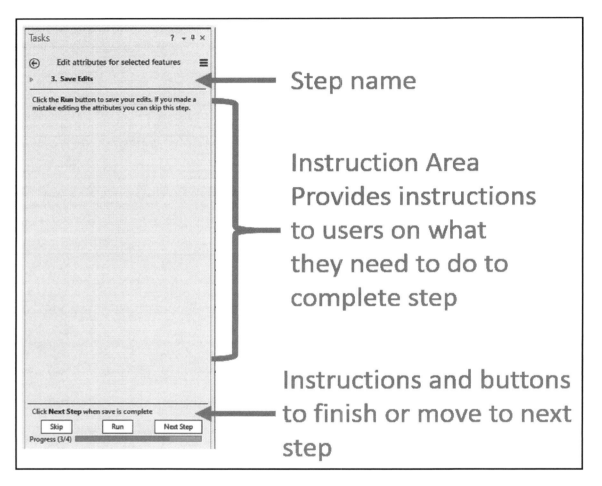

5. When you are done running the task, clear your selection.

 Question: *How many steps did this task have?*

6. Close the **Tasks** pane.
7. Close ArcGIS Pro without saving the project.

You have just experienced how a task works from the user's perspective. This was a very simple task. Tasks can be as complex or as simple as you want them to be. Feel free to try some of the other tasks included in this project.

We will now move on to the next section about creating tasks.

Learning how to create tasks

Creating a successful task is not unlike creating a map or a layout and requires thought and planning. Time spent on the frontend of creating a task will alleviate a lot of frustration and headaches later for yourself and for those that use the tasks you create.

This section will take you through exercises about exploring and creating a task. You will also gain an understanding of the things to consider before creating a task.

Just as you did before when creating a layout, you need to answer several questions:

- *What is the purpose or goal of the task?*
- *What is the workflow that supports this purpose?*
- *How will the task be used?*
- *Who is the audience for your task?*

The answers to these questions will impact the design of your tasks. They will help determine the number of steps to include, which steps may need to be run automatically, the level of instruction you need to provide, what tools need to be included in each step, and more.

After answering those questions, you will then be ready to start creating your task. This may require you to start by creating a new task item and then creating tasks or task groups within that item, or you can add new tasks to an existing task item.

As you create new tasks, you will use the **Task Designer** pane. The Task Designer allows you to add or modify steps. Steps are the heart of any task. They provide users with the instructions needed to complete the task. Steps themselves have several parameters that you will need to configure as you create your task. Again, the answers to the aforementioned questions will help guide the creation of each step.

Before you begin creating a task, let's explore an existing task.

Exercise 11B – Exploring a task

In this exercise, you will take a closer look at the task you ran in *Exercise 9A* from Chapter 9, *Learning about Editing Tabular Data*. You will verify whether it contained the number of steps you thought it did, or if there was more than met the eye.

Step 1 – Opening a project

In this step, you will open the same project you used in *Exercise 10A* from Chapter 10, *Performing Analysis with Geoprocessing Tools*. This will allow you to access the task you ran previously:

1. Open ArcGIS Pro and select **Ex11** from the list of previously opened projects.
2. Expand the **Tasks** folder in the **Catalog** pane.
3. Verify you see the **Selecting Features** task item in the **Tasks** folder.

Now that you have opened the correct project and verified that you see the task item you used in the last exercise, you will now learn how to open it for editing in the Task Designer.

Step 2 – Opening a task in the Task Designer

You will now open the task item in Task Designer. This will allow you to see all parameters, tasks, and steps included within the task item:

1. Right-click on the **Selecting Features** task item and select **Edit** in **Designer**. The **Tasks** pane opens in designer mode on the left side of the interface and the **Task Designer** pane opens on the right side of the interface.
2. Review the parameters for the task item in the **Task Designer** pane. Notice that in addition to standard parameters such as name, author, and description, you can also see what version of ArcGIS Pro the task was created with and track the version of the task as you update and modify it.
3. Now you will make a couple of changes to this task item. Change the name of the task item to Selecting Features in ArcGIS Pro by typing it into the cell located under **Name**.
4. Change the **Author's Name** to your own.
5. Change the description to This task item contains various tasks that demonstrate different methods for selecting features within ArcGIS Pro.

6. Lastly, enable **Auto Increment** of the task item version.

There is no *save* button in the Task Designer. Changes are automatically applied when you click on another parameter, task, or pane. This allows you to test the changes quickly. The actual changes are saved permanently when you save the project. If you close a project without saving, any changes you made to the task item and included tasks and steps will be lost.

7. Save your project.

Now that you know how to open a task in the Task Designer so you can see the various components that are included in a given task, you will explore the components inside the task you just opened.

Step 3 – Reviewing a task's steps

Now that you have the task item opened in the Task Designer, you will now explore the steps of a specific task. In this case, it will be the same task you ran in *Exercise 11A*:

1. In the **Tasks** pane, select the **Selecting features in the Map** task.
2. Click on the blue arrow that appears to the right of the task name to access the task's steps:

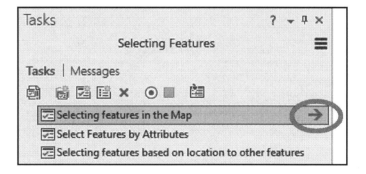

Questions: *How many steps do you see in this task? How does this compare to the number of steps you counted when you ran the task in the last exercise?*

3. Select each step and review the **General**, **Actions**, **Views**, and **Contents** parameters associated with each step. They will be displayed in the Task Designer pane located on the right side of the interface.

Question: *Why do you think the number of steps you counted in Exercise 9A from* Chapter 9, *Learning about Editing Tabular Data, differs from the actual number of steps contained in this task?*

4. Click the back arrow located in the upper-left corner of the **Tasks** pane once you have reviewed each step.
5. Review the other tasks located within this task item and their associated steps.
6. Close the **Tasks** pane when you are done reviewing tasks.
7. Save your project and close ArcGIS Pro.

Now you have a much better idea of how a task is configured and the way steps work. Let's now start looking more closely at the process of creating a task.

Things to consider when creating a task

As mentioned in the previous section, you need to answer those three questions before you begin creating any task. The answers to those questions will guide much of the task design. So how do those three questions impact or guide the design of your task?

Understanding the purpose of the task

Like a map, you are creating a task for a reason. For instance, it could be to show everyone in your organization the proper workflow for splitting a parcel so that everyone does it the same way. It might be to develop a workflow for identifying all parcels located within 300 feet of another parcel that is to be re-zoned so you can create a notification mailing list. Each of these represents a purpose.

Understanding the purpose of the task will help you determine which tools will need to be referenced in your task. The purpose will also help you answer the next question concerning the overall workflow that will be addressed via your task.

Determining the workflow to support the purpose

The task workflow is made up of the steps that will be included in the task. This includes the tools and actions that need to be performed, as well as the order in which those tools and actions need to be performed to achieve the purpose and goal of the task.

Think through your workflow carefully. Write down each step you believe will be required in the task and any tools associated with each step. Once you have the steps written down, you should verify you have taken into account all the needed steps. It is not unusual for experienced users to forget a step because it is something they do automatically without even realizing they do it. This means a task may be incomplete or confusing depending on the audience using the task.

One of the best ways to validate or even develop the initial workflow for a task is to work through the entire process manually within ArcGIS Pro. If you are validating a workflow, make sure to follow it exactly as you have written it down. This will help you to identify any steps you may have missed.

Following your own instructions will be harder than you think. You will want to just do it instinctively, but do not fall into that trap. Make sure you take your time and follow the steps as you have outlined them. Remember, others that may use the task might not have the same skill level as you do. So, missing a tool or step that is intuitive to you may not be to others.

If you work through the process manually to actually develop the steps, then record each step as you do it. Make sure to note the tools associated with that step. Creating a document with screenshots can also be helpful as you do this. That helps ensure you remember all the requirements associated with a given step when you go to create the task.

Using tasks in different ways

There are several reasons you create a task. For instance, you may want to standardize a common workflow within your organization to ensure everyone is doing it the same way; you might want to use it as a training tool for new users; or you may want to establish a best practice for your organization to ensure accuracy and efficiency.

No matter what the purpose of the task is, it impacts the complexity and level of documentation needed for the task. Here are a few examples:

- If you are creating a task that will be used to **train new users**, you will need to make sure you include exact step-by-step instructions with very thorough documentation on exactly what the user needs to do to complete the step. You will want many of the steps to be manually interactive so the user learns the process completely and understands the reasons for each step.
- If you are just trying to **establish a common workflow** within an organization of experienced users, you can often reduce the number of interactive steps and use automatic steps since the users are already familiar with ArcGIS Pro functionality. Also, due to that experience level, you can reduce the level of instructional documentation required for each step.
- Tasks created for training or to **establish best practices** need more time to create as they typically require more effort due to the higher level of complexity of their design and documentation.
- Another consideration that falls under how the task will be used is the **license level** required to perform the steps within a task. Steps often refer to the use of specific geoprocessing tools or ArcGIS Pro commands. As you have learned, some geoprocessing tools are only available with certain licensing levels or extensions.

So as you are developing a task, you need to always consider what skill level, license level, and extensions are required to complete a task. If your task makes use of tools that require a specific license level or extension, you might want to include a step that has the user verify they have the correct license level or extension needed to complete the task.

Determining the audience for a task

Lastly, you need to determine the audience for the task you are creating. You need to know whether your audience is experienced ArcGIS Pro users or new users, or if they have used other GIS software.

The level of experience and skill of your audience will impact your task design. The lower the skill and experience level, the more instruction you will need to provide. You may also need to include steps that would be intuitive to experienced users.

If your audience is a group that is familiar with another GIS software application such as ArcMap, you might need to include references to tools or processes in that application so they can more easily relate ArcGIS Pro functionality to something they are familiar with. This may increase the amount of instruction you create for each step.

Now that you know what you need to consider before creating a task, it is time to learn how to actually create a task.

Creating a task yourself

As you have learned, a task has several components. When creating a new task, you will need to create these components. The first step in creating any task is to have a task item to contain it. This can be an existing or a new task item.

Once you create or identify the existing task item that will contain your task, you then need to decide whether you want the task to be standalone or contained within a task group.

If the task you are creating is not related to other processes or workflows, it is good to leave it as standalone. However, if the task is part of a larger workflow or process, then it is a good idea to store those related tasks within a task group. This makes it easier to find. If you want to store your task within a task group, you would need to create it after you create the task item.

At this point, you are now ready to create your first task. You will use the Task Designer and the answers to those four questions that were listed in the *Learning to create a task* section of this chapter to create a new task.

Creating a task item

There are several ways to create task items. They are as follows:

- If this is the first task item you are adding to your project, go to the **Insert** tab on the ribbon and select the **Task** button in the **Project** group. This will create a new blank task item in your project, as illustrated in the following screenshot:

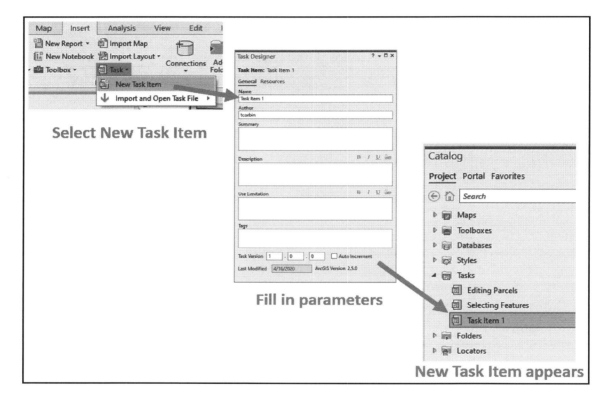

- If you already have task items in your project, then you can add new ones from the **Catalog** pane. You just simply right-click on the **Task** folder and select **New Task Item**, as shown in the following screenshot:

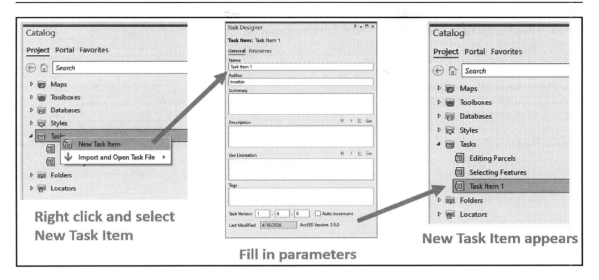

Right click and select New Task Item

Fill in parameters

New Task Item appears

As you have now seen from the preceding screenshot, there is more than one way to create a task item in ArcGIS Pro. It is not unusual in ArcGIS Pro to have more than one way to accomplish something. This provides flexibility and allows you to determine the method that works best for you.

We will now see how to create a task group.

Creating a task group

If you want to store your task within a task group, you will need to create it within the task item. You will do this from the **Tasks** pane while in designer mode.

Simply click on the **New Group** button and fill in the parameters, as illustrated in the following screenshot:

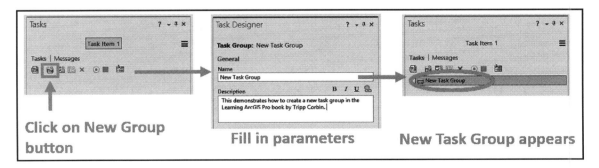

Click on New Group button

Fill in parameters

New Task Group appears

The previous screenshot shows how easy it is to create a new task group. Task groups can help you organize your tasks based on function, usage, or intended audience so that they may be located quickly when needed.

Let's move on to learn how to create a task.

Creating a task

Now you are ready to create the actual task. Remember that you can add tasks to existing task items and task groups. Creating a task is very similar to creating a task group, as shown in the following screenshot:

As you can see from the preceding screenshot, to create a task, click on the **New Task** button in the **Tasks** pane while in designer mode. You can then fill in the associated parameters and the new task is created as illustrated.

Let's now move on to the next section about creating a task.

Exercise 11C – Creating a task

In this exercise, you will create a new task in a project. In the later *Exercise 11D*, you will add steps to this task.

The purpose of the new task is to create a list of parcels located along a road. This will help the city notify those that live and work along the road when it is being repaired. This task will be used as a common workflow for existing and new GIS staff.

Step 1 – Opening a project and creating a task item

In this step, you will open a project and then create the task item that will contain the task you will create in a later step:

1. Start **ArcGIS Pro** and open the **Ex11** project from your list of recently opened projects.
2. Expand the **Tasks** folder in the **Catalog** pane.
3. Right-click on the **Tasks** folder and select **New Task Item**. The **Task** and **Task Designer** panes will open automatically.
4. In the **Task Designer** pane, fill in the parameters of your new task item as follows:
    - In the **Name** field, type Road Repair Tasks.
    - In the **Author** field, type your name.
    - In the **Description** field, type This task item contains tasks associated with road repair projects such as generating notification lists, locating nearby parcels, calculating total lengths, and more.
    - In the **Task version** field, enter 1.0.0.
    - Enable **Auto Increment**.
5. Save your project.

You have just created your first task item. Now you need to add a task to that item.

Step 2 – Creating a new task

You are now ready to create the task. This will ultimately serve as the container for the steps needed to create the list of parcels located along a road that you will create in *Exercise 11D*. You will create a standalone task for this exercise since it is the only task you will create. If this was part of a large set of tasks you were creating, you would have to create task groups to help organize them:

1. In the **Tasks** pane on the left side of the interface, click on the **New Task** button.

2. In the **Task Designer** pane, fill in the parameters for the new task indicated as follows:

  - In the **Name** field, type `Create a list of nearby parcels`.
  - In the **Description** field, add `This task will step you through the process needed to create a list of parcels located along a road segment which will be repaired. The list will allow those that live and work along the road to be notified of the repair and how long it is expected to take.`

3. Close the **Task** designer pane.

   Your **Tasks** pane should now look similar to this:

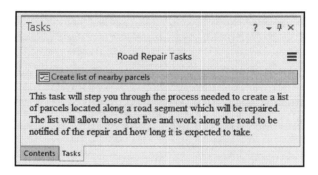

4. Save your project and close the **Tasks** pane.

You have learned about tasks and how to create one for yourself. You also have understood the things to consider while creating a task.

You now have created a task, but it is empty. You still need to add the steps to the task to tell users the process needed to produce the list of parcels located near the road segments that will be repaired. We will do this in the next section.

Adding task steps

Steps are really the meat of your tasks. They provide instructions for completing a process or workflow to the users. Steps can be simple text instructions that tell users how to perform an action. For instance, a step could be as simple as *"use the Explore tool to zoom to the area of interest"*. However, steps can also be very complex. You can include specific tools, layer behavior, and selection controls within a step.

In this section, you will learn about the components of a step, followed by an exercise for adding steps to a task where you will get some hands-on experience.

The complexity of the steps and how many you need will be driven by the answers to those four questions we discussed earlier in this chapter. If you are trying to standardize a specific workflow for experienced users, you may choose to increase the complexity of the step structure to automate it as much as possible. This will increase the efficiency of your team while also ensuring everyone performs the process the same way. If you are designing the task to be a training tool, you may want the steps to be more manual and instructional to allow the user to gain a better understanding of what tools are used and how they work.

So let's take a closer look at the components that make up a step and what purpose they serve. This will provide you with a good understanding so you can build effective steps within your tasks.

Learning about the components of a step

A single step can include several components depending upon its purpose. You can include instructions for the user, determine how the step will run, link it to geoprocessing tools or commands, control view and layer behavior, and manage selections within a single step. Let's look at these components or parameters more closely.

General

The first component of a step is the general information and behavior of the step. This includes the step name, tooltip, instructions, and step run behavior, as shown in the following screenshot:

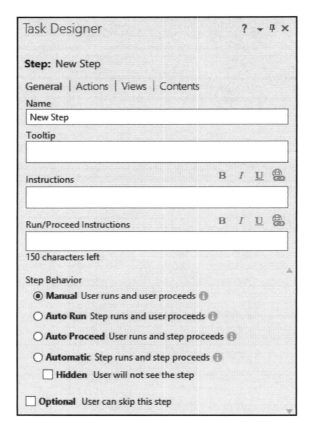

As you can see in the preceding screenshot, there are few fields or parameters in the **General** tab. They are as follows:

- The **Name** of the step is what the user first sees listed in the task. The name should give the user a general idea of what the step is supposed to accomplish, such as *Zoom to area* or *Select parcel to edit*.
- The **Tooltip** is a pop-up window that appears when you move your mouse pointer over the object in question. This should provide more information for the user but still be limited to a short paragraph at most. It will often be very similar to the name.

- **Instructions** are one of the most important parameters of a step. They are where you provide users with instructions on what they need to do during the given step to complete it. These can be as long and detailed as you feel they need to be based on the purpose of the step and the intended audience. They should always be clear and easy to follow. Try to avoid using abbreviations or acronyms if possible since these can cause confusion.
- **Run/Proceed Instructions** tell the user what they need to do once they have completed the instructions to proceed to the next step. For example, click the **Run** button to start the step. Once you have completed the step, click the **Next Step** button to continue.
- Lastly, you will need to determine how the step will run. You have four basic options to choose from, namely, **Manual**, **AutoRun**, **Auto Proceed**, and **Automatic**. The following table helps us understand these four options better:

Step Behavior	Description	Example of Use
Manual	The user must manually click the **Run** button to start the step and the **Next Step** button to proceed.	You want the user to activate the Explore tool and then zoom to a specific area. You are using this as a training tool so you need them to see the Explore tool being activated for use.
Auto Run	This runs the command or geoprocessing tool automatically. The user performs an action with the associated tool and manually clicks the **Next Step** to proceed.	You want the user to select features from the map, so you have linked the Select by Rectangle tool to the step and it runs automatically so the user does not need to activate it. They just select features from the map.
Auto Proceed	The user clicks the **Run** button and runs the step, then it automatically advances to the next step when complete.	You want the user to buffer a feature but the distance will be different depending on circumstances. The user will enter the appropriate buffer distance, then click the **Run** button. When the buffer is complete, it automatically advances to the next step.
Automatic	The step enters step runs without any user interaction. Automatic steps have the option to be hidden.	Your user is working on one map and you need them to change to another. You can include an automatic step that switches the currently active map to a different one before you proceed to the next step.

Now let's move on to the next section about the second component of a step.

Actions

The next component of a step is an **action**. Actions allow you to link an ArcGIS Pro command or geoprocessing tool to the step. An ArcGIS Pro command is any button or tool you see in a ribbon, such as **Add Data** or **Measure**. A geoprocessing tool is any tool available in a toolbox, including custom Python scripts or models you or others may have created. A step is not required to have an action – it can be strictly instructional.

The following screenshot shows you the **Action** tab in the **Task Designer** pane:

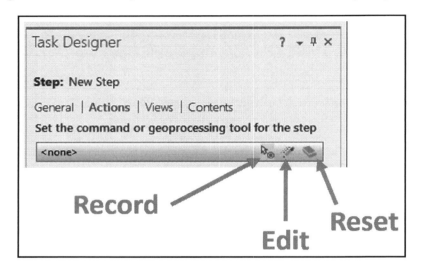

You can add a command or geoprocessing tool to a step in two ways:

- The first is to **edit** the action. This allows you to pick a command or geoprocessing tool from a list. You have the option to search using keywords.
- Another method is to **record**. When you record, you simply find the command or geoprocessing tool you wish to use from the ArcGIS Pro interface and click on it. This is a great option if you have performed the step manually in the past and know exactly which tool you need.

You can also manage selections associated with a step using a feature called **Additional Actions** for when the step starts, prior to running a command, or when exiting the step. Within the step, you can create, modify, save, or clear a new selection, as shown in the following screenshot:

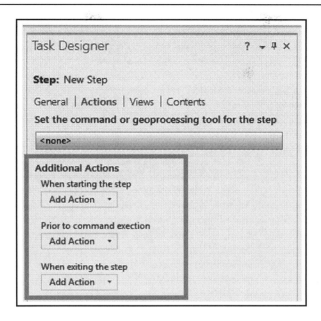

You can save currently selected features to a **selection set**. This selection set can then be used by later steps in the task. You can also save features created or modified by this or previous steps, as shown in the following screenshot:

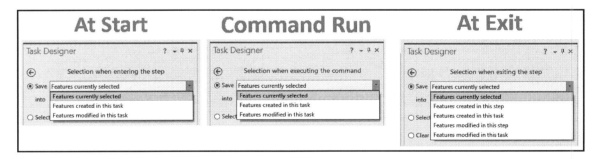

For example, if in a previous step you split a parcel into multiple parcels that remained selected after being split, and you wanted in a later step to edit the attributes for those new parcels, you could save the selection of those split parcels to a selection named Split Parcels that could then easily be recalled in a later step.

You can also clear the selection or create a custom query to select features. The custom query is very similar to the **Select by Attribute** tool and the definition queries that you have used in past chapters.

The use of additional actions is also optional. A step may have no actions or additional actions defined, it may just have a command or geoprocessing tool indicated, or it may have just additional actions defined or even a combination of a command or geoprocessing tool with additional actions.

Views

Views allow you to control what maps, scenes, or layouts are open and active within your project as you run the step. You will see all the views contained in the project that you have open. While you can have many views open at any one time, only a single one can be active.

The following screenshot shows you the **Views** tab in the **Task Designer** pane:

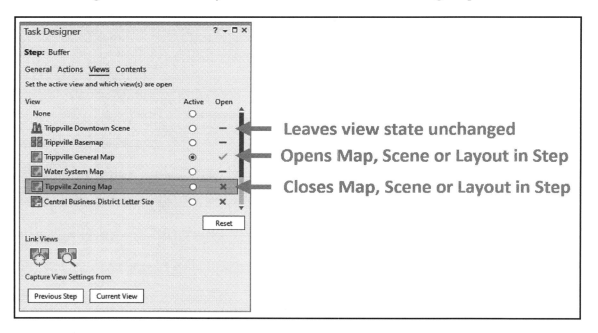

The active view will be the one the step and defined actions are applied to. So if you are creating a step to select a zoning polygon, you might want to make sure the Zoning view is active. If your step has someone adding a north arrow to a layout, you will want the proper layout to be open and active. You may want to close some views to remove possible confusion on the part of the user, as well as to reduce the number of computer resources that might be used.

As you can see in the preceding screenshot, you can set these parameters manually for the step, capture them from the previous step, or base them on your project's current settings as you create the step.

Contents

Just as you can control which views are open and active, you can also control the layers within your **Active View**. Within the step, you can control a layer's visibility, whether it is selectable or not, editable or not, snappable or not, whether it is a selected layer, and the label visibility.

The following screenshot shows you the **Contents** tab in the **Task Designer** pane:

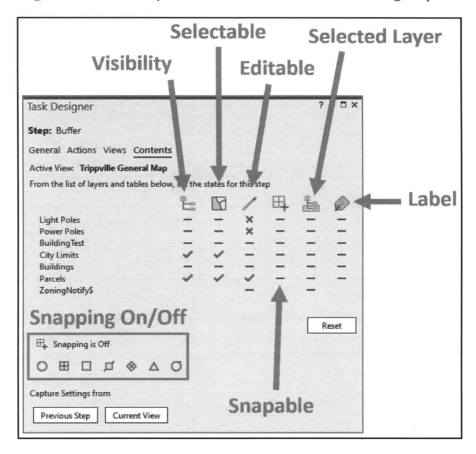

The level of layer control is very powerful. It ensures that your data is protected and only works with the layers you need to in any given step. For example, if you are editing a parcel within a step, you would want to make sure the **Parcel** layer is set as the only editable layer. This will ensure the user doesn't accidentally edit the **City Limits** or **Buildings** layers by accident, as an example.

Now that you have a much greater understanding of how steps are configured and work within a task, you are now ready to begin adding steps to the task you created in the previous exercise.

Exercise 11D – Adding steps to a task

In this exercise, you will add steps to the task you previously created to walk users through the process of generating a list of parcels near a selected road segment that is to be repaired so the land owners can be notified.

Step 1 – Opening the task in the Task Designer

In this step, you will open the task you created in the Task Designer so you can begin creating your steps:

1. Start ArcGIS Pro and open **Ex11** using the skills that you have already learned in previous exercises.
2. Expand the **Task** folder in the **Catalog** pane.
3. Double-click on the **Road Repair Tasks** item that you created in the last exercise. This will open the **Tasks** pane.
4. Right-click on **Create list of nearby parcels task** and select **Edit in Designer**. The **Task Designer** pane should open on the right side of the interface and the **Tasks** pane should enter the designer mode.

You are now ready to add tasks. If this was not a classroom exercise, you would begin referencing your notes from the answers to those four questions from the *Learning to create a Task* section that you need to consider before creating a task. You would pay particularly close attention to the workflow that you outlined for the second question of the four.

For the sake of the exercise, this has already been done and you will just need to follow the exercise instructions.

Step 2 – Adding a step to zoom

In this step, you will add a step that will instruct the user to zoom to the location of the road in question. You will have them use the Explore tool to zoom to the location:

1. Click on the **New Step** button in the **Tasks** pane. The new step is automatically listed in the **Tasks** pane and the parameters for the step are displayed in the **Task Designer** pane.
2. Set the **General** parameters as follows:
    - In the Name field, add `Zoom to the street using the Explore tool.`
    - In the **Tooltip** field, add `Zoom to the street to be repaired.`
    - In the **Instructions** field, type `Using the Explore tool located on the Map tab, zoom to the location of the street segment which will be under repair in the map. If you are already zoomed to the correct area, you may skip this step.`
    - In the **Run/Proceed Instructions** field, type `Once you have successfully zoomed to the location of the street, click Next Step to proceed.`

I personally like to present the name of any tools or buttons I name in the instructions in a bold font. This helps the user spot them as important. So, in the preceding **Instructions** and **Run/Proceed Instructions** fields, I would have made *Explore* and *Next Step* in bold.

3. In **Step Behavior**, set this as an **Auto Run** step. You will be connecting the Explore tool as an action to this step. By making it an Auto Run step, the step will automatically enable the Explore tool without the user having to. All the user will need to do is begin zooming to the proper area within the map.
4. Lastly for the **General** settings, set this as an optional step that allows the user to skip the step if they already are zoomed into the proper location for the street which will be repaired when they start the task.

You have configured the **General** parameters for this step. You now will link it to an action. The action will be the **Explore** tool.

5. Click on **Actions** at the top of the **Task Designer** pane.

6. Move your mouse pointer to where it says **<none>**. Three icons should appear to the right. Click on the **Edit** icon.

7. Click on the drop-down arrow located to the right of **<none>** in the **Command/Geoprocessing** pane.

8. Select **Command** from the drop-down list.

9. Click on the **Browser** button that appears to the right of the selected **Command**.

10. In the search area of the pop-up window, type `Explore` and select **Explore (Open current explore tool)** and click **OK**:

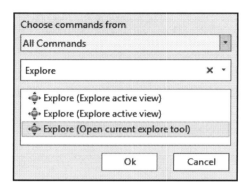

11. Click the **Done** button located at the bottom of the **Task Designer** pane.

You do not need to configure additional actions or change the settings for views or contents in this step since you are just having the user zoom to a location. So, you are done creating this step. Remember, there is no save task or step button. They are saved when you save the project.

12. Save your project.

Congratulations, you have created your first step. But you are not done yet. You have several more steps that need to be created to complete this workflow.

Step 3 – Selecting the road segment

Now you need to add a step that instructs the user to select the road segment that will be repaired. You will use the **Select by Rectangle** tool and instruct the user to select the road from the map:

1. Click the **New Step** button in the **Tasks** pane to create another new step.

2. Complete the **General** parameters as follows:
   - In the **Name** field, add `Select Road Segment`.
   - In the **Tooltip** field, add `Select the road segment which will be repaired`.
   - In the **Instruction** field, add `Click the Run button to start this step. Then, using the Select by Rectangle tool, select the road segment from the map that is scheduled to be repaired. If you have already selected the road segment, you may skip this step.`
   - In the **Run/Proceed Instructions** field, add `Once you have selected the road segment scheduled for repair, click the Next Step button.`
   - Select **Manual** in the **Step Behavior** field.
   - Enable **Optional** to allow the user to skip this step if they have already selected a road segment.
3. Click on the **Actions** option at the top of the **Task Designer** pane.
4. Move your mouse pointer to the area the says **<none>** and click on the record icon.
5. Click on the **Select** tool located in the **Map** tab. Notice this tool is automatically added as the action.

   Since you will have the user select a feature on a specific layer in this step, you want to limit the selectable layers available when they run this step. As you learned earlier, you can do this through the **Contents** settings in a step.

6. Click on **Contents** located at the top of the **Task Designer** pane.
7. When this task is run, you want to make sure the **Streets** layer is visible and selectable. Click on the – located next to **Streets** under the **Visibility** column until it becomes a green checkmark. Do the same for the **Select** column.
8. To ensure no other layers are accidentally selected, you want to set the remaining layers to be non-selectable by clicking on the – in the **Select** column until they all have a red **X** by them.

Your **Task Designer** pane should look like this when you are done:

```
Task Designer                              ?  ▼  ⊣  ✕

Step: Select Road Segment

General | Actions | Views | Contents
Active View:  General

From the list of layers below, set the states for this step

Layer                    ⊟       ▣      ╱     ⊞     ⊟
City Limits              —       ✕      —     —     —
Streets                  ✓       ✓      —     —     —
Parcels                  —       ✕      —     —     —
Topographic              —                          —
```

9. Save your project.

You have now provided users with the instructions they need to zoom to the location of the road scheduled for repair and how to select it. Now you need to tell them how to select the surrounding parcels.

Step 4 – Selecting nearby parcels

In this step, you will create a step that tells users how to select the parcels near the road segment they selected in the last step. You will be using the **Select by Location** command to do this:

1. Click on the **New Step** button once again to create the new step.
2. Set the **General** parameters as follows:
   - In the **Name** field, add `Select nearby parcels`.
   - In the **Tooltip** field, add `Select parcels that are near the road segment you selected in the previous step.`
   - In the **Instructions** field, add `Using the Select by Location tool, you will select parcels that are located within a distance of 100 feet from the selected road segment.`
3. Ensure this tool is configured as follows:
   - Set the **Input Feature Layer** field to **Parcels**.
   - Set the **Relationship** field to **Within a Distance**.

- Set the **Selecting Features** field to **Streets**.
- Set the **Search Distance** field to `100` feet.
- Set the **Selection Type** field to **New selection**.

4. Once you have verified if the setting is correct, click the **Run** button and make sure of the following:

    - In the **Run/Proceed Instructions** field, add `Click Next Step to proceed`.
    - Select **Manual** under the **Step Behavior** option.

5. Click **Actions** and using the **Record** option, set the command to **Select by Location** located in the **Map** tab.

6. The **Geoprocessing** pane will open automatically. Since you are running this step manually, you can close it and return to the **Task Designer** pane.

7. Click on **Contents**, set it so the **Streets** and **Parcels** layers will be visible, and the **Parcels** layer will be the only selectable layer.

8. Save your project.

Now that the nearby parcels are selected, you have one last step to go. You will instruct users on how to export the selected parcels to an **Excel** spreadsheet.

Step 5 – Exporting the selection to an Excel spreadsheet

In this step, you will create a new step that instructs users to export the selected parcels to an **Excel** spreadsheet:

1. Click on the **New Step** button in the **Tasks** pane.
2. Set the **General** parameters as follows:

    - In the **Name** field, add `Export to Excel`.
    - In the **Tooltip** field, add `Exports selected parcels to an excel spreadsheet`.
    - For the **Instructions** field, complete the parameters for the **Table to Excel** geoprocessing tool indicated as follows:

        - In the **Input Table** field, type `Parcels`.
        - In the **Ouput Table** field, type `C:\Student\IntroArcPro\Chapter11\Parcels _TableToExcel.xls`. Click **Run** once you have verified your settings.

- In the **Run/Proceed Instructions** field, click **Finish** to complete the task.
- In the **Step Behavior** options, select the run **Manual** option.

3. Click **Actions** and click on the **Edit** icon.
4. Set the **Type of Command** to **Geoprocessing Tool**.
5. Click the browse button next to the selected **Geoprocessing Tool**.
6. In the **Find tools** cell, type `Excel`.
7. Select the **Table to Excel** Python script and click **OK**.
8. Ensure **Embed** is enabled and set the parameters as described in your instructions. The **Task Designer** pane should look like the following:

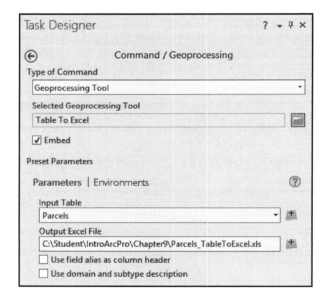

9. Once you have verified your settings, click **Done**.
10. There is no need to change the views or contents settings, so close the **Task Designer** and save your project.

Your task is now complete. You have added all the steps required to select the parcels near a road segment that is scheduled for repair, and then export them to an **Excel** spreadsheet. Now you need to test it.

Step 6 – Running your task

Now that your task is complete, you will run it to see how well it works. This will verify that the task contains all the steps needed to complete the desired process and to verify your instructions are clear and the steps flow as expected:

1. Using the skills you have learned, locate and run the task you just created. Follow the instructions in each step closely. Check that they make sense and you end up with the expected results.
2. Make any adjustments to the task and its steps that you believe are needed.
3. Save your project and close ArcGIS Pro.

Assuming everything ran as expected, you have just created your first complete task. You developed a workflow that others will be able to follow to accomplish a specific process using your step-by-step instructions.

Challenge

Using the skills you have learned in this chapter, select a previous exercise from this book, or a common process from your office and develop a task for it. You can also develop a task to replicate that workflow.

Summary

In this chapter, you have learned how tasks can be used to standardize processes, train new users, and establish best practices within your organization. You have also gained an understanding of all the components that make up a task and the considerations you need to take into account when creating your own tasks.

Finally, you have the skills needed to create your own tasks in ArcGIS Pro. You worked through the process of creating a new task from the beginning, ultimately creating a task that exports the selected data to an Excel spreadsheet. This included creating the task item, task, and task steps.

In the next chapter, you will begin to explore ways you can automate a multi-step process using ModelBuilder and Python. These allow you to create models or scripts that can string a series of tools and workflows together into a single tool that can save you time and effort, especially with processes you perform on a regular basis.

12
Automating Processes with ModelBuilder and Python

As you have now learned, performing analysis or editing a feature requires many steps. The more you use ArcGIS Pro, the more you will find yourself doing the same process again and again. You may also realize that some of the processes that you do repeatedly really require very little interaction on your part beyond selecting a feature and then telling ArcGIS Pro where to save the outputs.

Wouldn't it be beneficial if you could automate processes that you perform repeatedly? You can create the proverbial **Easy** button where you simply click on a single tool, fill in a few parameters, and the tool goes off, providing you with the results after it is done executing. This would certainly make your job easier.

In this chapter, with ArcGIS Pro, you will learn how to create **Easy** buttons or tools using **ModelBuilder** and **Python scripts**. This will provide you with the skills to create automated processes that can run multiple tools together in sequence or at the same time to complete an operation. ModelBuilder uses a visual interface to create automation models without the need to be a programmer.

Python is the primary scripting language for the ArcGIS platform. With it, you can create very powerful scripts that can be used within ArcGIS Pro, but also that can also integrate processes across all components of ArcGIS, including **Enterprise**, **Online**, **Extensions**, **Portal**, and more. However, creating Python scripts does require writing code.

In this chapter, you will learn the following topics:

- Differentiating between tasks, geoprocessing models, and Python scripts
- Creating geoprocessing models
- Running a geoprocessing model
- Making a model interactive
- Learning about Python

Technical requirements

As with other chapters in this book, you will need to have **ArcGIS Pro 2.5** or later. Any license level of ArcGIS Pro will work for the exercises in this chapter.

Differentiating between tasks, geoprocessing models, and Python scripts

You learned about tasks in the last chapter and have read the introduction for this chapter; now you may be wondering what the difference is between a task, geoprocessing model, and Python script. That is a great question.

You will find the answer to this question in this section, but to understand it, you must first understand what each of these things is. You already know what a task is, so we will now focus on gaining a better understanding of what models and Python scripts are. Once you understand that, you can then understand the differences between the three.

Learning about geoprocessing models

A **geoprocessing model** is a custom tool created within the ModelBuilder window, which contains multiple geoprocessing tools along with their various parameters (including inputs, outputs, options, and other values) that work together as part of an integrated process that will run as if it was a single tool. The following diagram shows a sample of a very simple model:

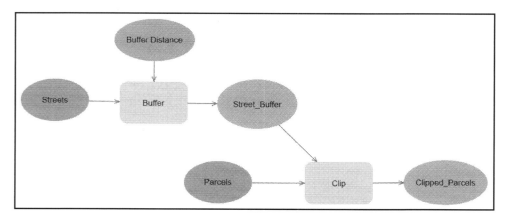

From the preceding diagram, you can see that it contains two geoprocessing tools that you learned about in `Chapter 10`, *Performing Analysis with Geoprocessing Tools*, the **Buffer** and **Clip** tools. In the model, the **Buffer** tool creates buffer polygons around the input, **Streets**.

The resulting buffer polygons are then used to clip out the features in **Parcels**, which is the **Clip** features input that is located inside the buffer polygons. Since both geoprocessing tools reside inside the model, the user only has to run the model instead of having to run each tool individually. The model automatically runs the tools based on the parameters specified within it. You will learn more about the components of a model and how to create one later in this chapter.

Geoprocessing models can include geoprocessing tools, Python scripts, iterators, model-only tools, and other models. This allows them to be as simple or complex as you need them to be to accomplish the process that you have designed them to complete. The ModelBuilder window allows users to create geoprocessing models in a visual environment. No coding is required to build a model.

Esri actually refers to ModelBuilder as a visual programming language.

Geoprocessing models can be created using **ArcGIS Desktop** (**ArcMap** or **ArcCatalog**) or ArcGIS Pro. However, models created in one software do not always run successfully in the other. The simpler a model is, the more likely it will be cross-application compatible. Another downside to a geoprocessing model is that it can only be run from ArcGIS Pro or ArcGIS Desktop. You cannot schedule them to run automatically at a specific date and time. At least not by themselves.

Let's now learn about Python scripts.

Understanding Python scripts

A **Python script** is also a custom tool that can run multiple geoprocessing tools along with their various parameters as part of an integrated process. However, unlike a model that does not require you to write programming code, Python scripts do. You must know the Python scripting language in order to create Python scripts. The following code is a small snippet of a Python script created for ArcGIS:

```
#-------------------------------------------------------------
# Name:       Union Tool Sample Script
# Purpose:    Runs the Union Geoprocessing tool from ArcGIS
```

```
# Author:      Esri & Tripp Corbin
#
# Created:     09/15/2015
# Updated:     05/08/2020 by Tripp Corbin, GISP
#
# Usage: Union two feature classes
#-------------------------------------------------------------
# Import the system modules
import arcpy

# Sets the current workspace to avoid having to specify the full path
# to the feature classes each time
arcpy.env.workspace =
"C:\\student\\IntroArcPro\\Databases\\Trippville_GIS.gdb"

#Runs Union Geoprocessing tool on 2 Feature classes
arcpy.Union_analysis (["Parcels", "Floodplains"],
"Parcels_Floodplain_Union", "NO_FID", 0.0003)
```

The preceding code starts with several comment lines that provide a general description of the purpose of the script and who created it. The next line after the commented description is an `import` command that loads the `arcpy` model so that the script can access ArcGIS functionality. This is followed by some more descriptive comments, and then a variable is defined to set the workspace where data used in the script will be accessed or saved to. Lastly, the script runs the `Union` tool, which you learned about in `Chapter 10`, *Performing Analysis with Geoprocessing Tools*.

Python scripts have several advantages over a geoprocessing model:

- First, Python is not limited to ArcGIS. Python can actually be used to create scripts for many other applications, such as **Excel**, **SharePoint**, **AutoCAD**, **Photoshop**, **SQL Server**, and more. This means that you can use a Python script to run tools across multiple platforms to create a truly integrated process.
- Second, Python scripts can be run from outside of ArcGIS. This means you can schedule them to run at specific times and days using your operating system's scheduler application. If your script does include ArcGIS geoprocessing tools, the script will require access to an ArcGIS license to run successfully, but ArcGIS does not need to be open and active at the time when the script is scheduled to run.
- Third, Python can be used to create completely custom geoprocessing tools. It is not limited to just the geoprocessing tools that you will find in ArcGIS Pro toolboxes.

Now let's see the difference between tasks, geoprocessing tools, and Python scripts.

What is the difference between the three?

Now that you have a much better understanding of what tasks, geoprocessing models, and Python scripts are, you will be able to properly understand the differences between them. Each can serve a purpose in standardizing and automating common workflows and processes.

The following table will provide a clearer understanding of the differences between the three:

Parameters	Task	Geoprocessing model	Python script
Run a single geoprocessing tool automatically	Yes, it can run a single tool automatically as part of a step.	Yes	Yes
Allow users to provide input to tools before running	Yes	Yes	Yes
Run multiple geoprocessing tasks automatically and in sequence	No	Yes	Yes
Be included in a task	No	Yes	Yes
Be included in a geoprocessing model	No	Yes	Yes
Provides a documented workflow	Yes	Yes	No
Run from outside (externally) of ArcGIS Pro	No	No	Yes
Integrate with other applications	No	No	Yes
Be scheduled to run at specific times and days	No	No	Yes
Requires knowledge of programming language	No	No	Yes

So, as you can now see from the preceding table, there is a good bit of difference between tasks, geoprocessing models, and Python scripts. Tasks are for defining workflows that include several steps. A task might include the use of a geoprocessing model or a Python script, but a geoprocessing model or a Python script cannot reference a task.

Now that you have an understanding of the differences between tasks, geoprocessing models, and Python scripts, we will start exploring how to create a geoprocessing model.

Creating geoprocessing models

As mentioned earlier, geoprocessing models are custom tools that you create from within ModelBuilder. ModelBuilder provides the graphical interface for building models as well as allowing you to access additional model-only tools, iterators, environmental settings, and model properties.

Models are created for several reasons. The first and most common reason is to automate repeated processes performed in ArcGIS Pro. If you have an analysis, a conversion, or another process that you perform on a regular basis, then a model can be used to automate it.

Secondly, you can use a model to think through and create a flow chart process within ArcGIS Pro. This can help you ensure that you have considered all the tools and data that you will need to complete a process. Once completed, the model then provides the tool for completing that process as well as the visual and textual documentation that explains how the process was performed.

You can share models with those in your organization so that they can use it to perform the process. This can reduce your workload and allow you to concentrate on other tasks that require higher knowledge and skill levels. Because a model runs the geoprocessing tools contained within it automatically, you can create a model that is easy for other less **Geographic Information System** (**GIS**)-savvy members of your organization to run by themselves without needing a full understanding of ArcGIS Pro. This also helps standardize our methodologies, ensuring that everything is done in a consistent and approved manner.

All of this helps to save us time and money through increased efficiency, which is ultimately the main power of ModelBuilder. Like tasks, models consist of multiple components and have their own terminology associated with them. We will learn about this in the next section.

Understanding model components and terminology

Before you can create a model, you need to understand the pieces and parts that form them. Models include a series of connected processes. Each process includes a tool that can be a geoprocessing tool, another model, or a Python script. Each tool has variables that serve as inputs or outputs.

The following diagram shows you two connected processes:

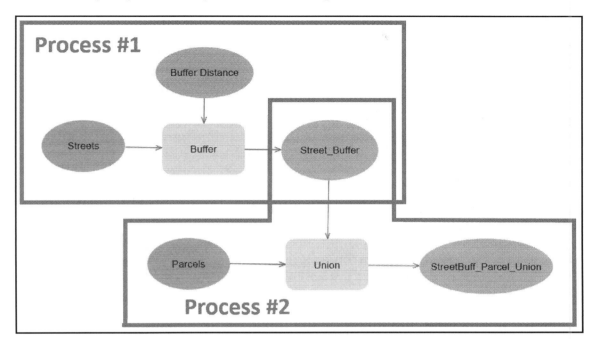

As you can see in the preceding diagram, the model contains two processes built around the **Buffer** and **Union** tools. Each of these tools has a number of variables feeding into it. Variables are identified by the blue and green ovals. Notice that the two processes are sharing a variable – **Street_Buffer**. This variable is an output of the **Buffer** tool and also an input for the **Union** tool.

There are three basic types of variables that are included in a model. They are as follows:

- **Data variables**: These variables are existing data that is used as an input to a tool, script, or model. These can be layers in a map, standalone tables, text files, feature classes, shapefiles, and more.
- **Value variables**: These variables are additional information that a tool may use to run. In the case of the **Buffer** tool, the distance used to create the buffer is considered a value variable as are the options to dissolve, end type, and the other parameters found that appear when you run the **Buffer** tool normally in the **Geoprocessing** pane.
- **Derived variables**: These variables are the outputs of a process. Again, this can be a new layer, feature class, table, raster, or more depending on the tool used in the process.

The following diagram shows you an example of the three types of basic variables in a model:

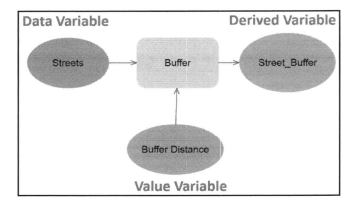

Since ModelBuilder is a visual programming language, as you can see from the preceding diagram, you can distinguish the types of variables based on their colors. While you can adjust these settings by default, **Data Variable** is a darker blue. **Value Variable** is a lighter blue and **Derived Variable** is green.

Next, we will learn how to save a model that you have created.

Saving a model

If you wish to save a model that you created so that you can use it again or share it with others, you must save it in a custom toolbox that you will create. Models cannot be saved in a system toolbox that is automatically included with ArcGIS Pro when it is installed.

When you create a new project, ArcGIS Pro automatically creates a custom toolbox for that project. It is stored in the `Project` folder as a `.tbx` file. This provides you with an easy to use place to store your models. This toolbox is also automatically linked to your project and accessible in the **Catalog** pane, as follows:

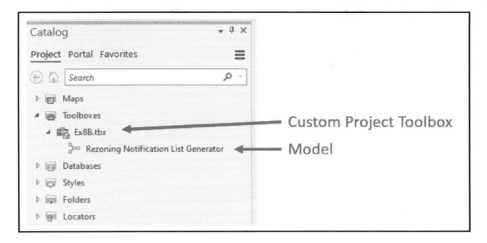

Custom Project Toolbox

Model

You can also create custom toolboxes within a geodatabase so that along with it, your models and Python scripts are stored as well with your GIS data, as illustrated in the following screenshot (this is a good option if the models or tools that you save to the toolbox will be used in multiple ArcGIS Pro projects):

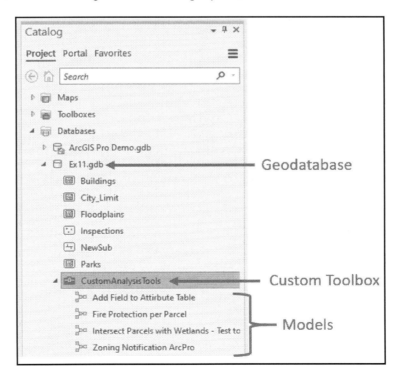

Geodatabase

Custom Toolbox

Models

You can also create other custom .tbx files besides the one that is automatically created with a new project. Using a custom .tbx file is perfect if the tool and models you save to it will not only be used with multiple projects but also across multiple databases or in the case of consultants and multiple clients. The following screenshot shows you an example of a custom toolbox file located in a folder:

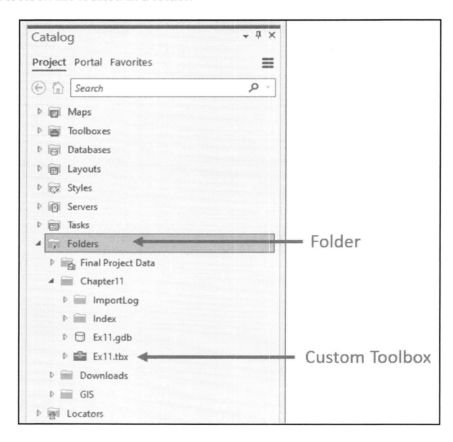

Using custom .tbx files to store models also makes it easier to share them with others since they are smaller than a geodatabase, which also includes all the GIS data. The .tbx files can easily be emailed, uploaded to **File Transfer Protocol** (**FTP**) sites, or placed in your ArcGIS Online account.

Now that you have a good general understanding of what a model is, its components, and how to save one, it is time to put that knowledge to use.

Exercise 12A – Creating a model

A new ordinance was just passed to protect the streams in the Trippville area. It requires all new building or improvement projects to take place at least 150 feet from the centerline of all creeks or streams. This will hopefully protect the banks from erosion and reduce polluted runoff from reaching them.

The community and economic development director has asked you to calculate the total area of each parcel that is inside the non-disturb area and how much of each parcel is out. Since you will need to update this analysis anytime a new subdivision or commercial development is added, for this, you have decided to create a model that you can run every time you need to perform these calculations.

In this exercise, you will create a simple model that will calculate how much of each parcel is inside and outside a non-disturb buffer area around the streams. This model will include a couple of geoprocessing tools and their associated variables.

Step 1 – Opening the project and the ModelBuilder window

The first step is to open the project and then the ModelBuilder window so that you can begin creating the model:

1. Start **ArcGIS Pro** and open the `Ex12.aprx` project found in `C:\Student\IntroArcPro\Chapter12`.
2. When the project opens, expand the `Toolboxes` folder in the **Catalog** pane.
3. Right-click on the **Ex12** toolbox that you see on your screen.

4. Select the **New** | **Model** option, as illustrated in the following screenshot:

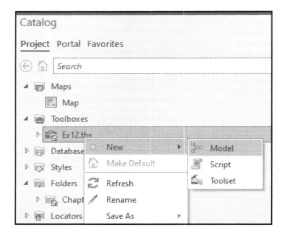

ModelBuilder should now be open and the **ModelBuilder** tab should have appeared in the ribbon. The **ModelBuilder** window and tab are used together to create or edit models. As you can see in the following screenshot, the **ModelBuilder** tab contains tools for saving the model, navigating in the **ModelBuilder** window, and adding content to the model:

You will now begin using these tools to create your model.

Step 2 – Adding model components

In this step, you will begin adding tools and variables to your model. You will explore some of the different methods that can be used here. You will start by adding the process that will generate the non-disturb buffers around the streams:

1. Click on the **Tools** button on the **Insert** group on the **ModelBuilder** tab in the ribbon. This opens the **Geoprocessing** pane on the right side of the interface.
2. Click on the **Toolboxes** tab at the top of the pane to expose the various toolboxes within ArcGIS Pro. These toolboxes will be your system toolboxes.

3. Expand the **Analysis Tools** toolbox and then the **Proximity** toolset.

4. Drag and drop the **Buffer** tool from the toolbox into the **ModelBuilder** window so that it looks like this:

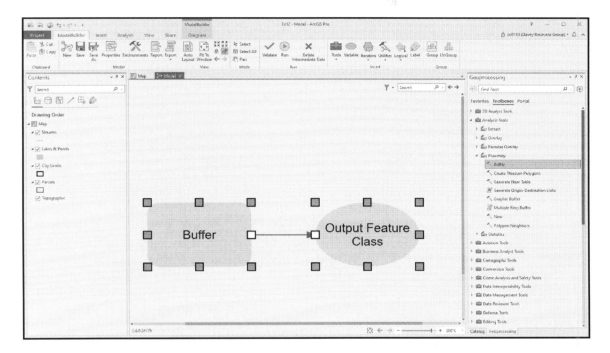

You have just added your first process to a model. Model processes will exist in one of three states: **not ready to run**, **ready to run**, and **have been run**. The process that you just added is in the **not ready to run** state.

ArcGIS Pro indicates that visually by displaying the tools and variables in gray. A process will be in the **not ready to run** state until all required variables have been defined. In the case of the **Buffer** tool, you have not yet defined the three variables required: **input feature class**, **buffer distance**, and **output feature class**. You will now do that.

5. The input feature class for the **Buffer** tool used in the model will be the **Streams** layer in your map. So, you will now add that layer as a variable to the model. Select the **Streams** layer in the **Contents** pane and drag it into the **ModelBuilder** window. It will be added as a blue oval, as shown in the following screenshot:

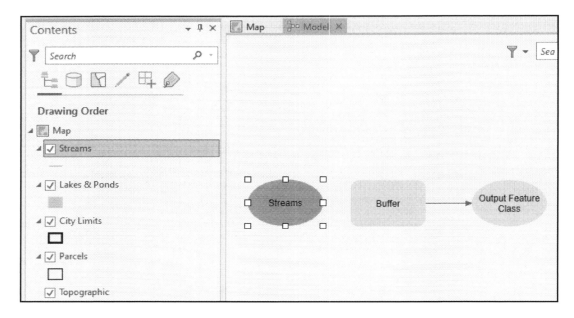

6. Click somewhere within the blank space in **ModelBuilder** to deselect the **Streams** variable.

7. You now need to connect the **Streams** variable that you just added to the **Buffer** tool. Click on the **Streams** variable and with your left mouse button still depressed, move your mouse pointer until it is over the **Buffer** tool. Then, release your mouse button.

8. A small pop-up menu should appear; select **Input Features**. You have just defined the input feature class for the **Buffer** tool.

9. Now double-click on the **Buffer** tool in the **ModelBuilder** window. This will open the **Tools** dialog window in ModelBuilder so that you can define additional variables.

10. The output should automatically be set to **Streams_Buffer**, which is being saved to `C:\Student\IntroArcPro\Chapter12\Ex12.gdb\`. Verify whether this is true by hovering your mouse over the output feature class name. This will be fine for this exercise so that you will leave it as is without changing it.

11. In the **Distance [value or field]**, type `150`, and verify that the units are **Feet**.

12. Since the director has not indicated that retaining any of the stream attributes in the new buffer layer is important for the calculations, you will have the resulting buffers dissolve. Click on the drop-down arrow under **Dissolve Type** and select **Dissolve all output features into a single feature**:

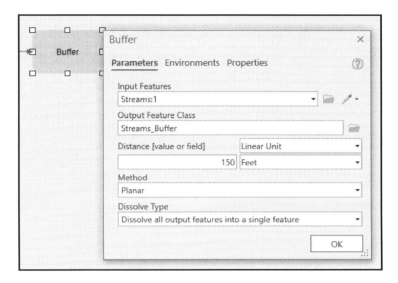

The **Buffer** tool window should now look similar to the preceding screenshot. Depending on what you may have done previously, the name of the input feature may be slightly different.

13. Click **OK** once you have verified your settings.

14. Click on the **Auto Layout** button on the **ModelBuilder** tab.

Your model should now include a single completed process that is in the **ready to run** state. You can tell it is ready to run because the tool and all lined variables are now displayed with a colored fill that is not gray, as shown in the following screenshot:

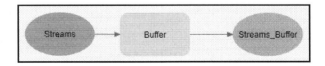

Now let's save your model to ensure your hard work is not lost in case something happens.

15. Click on the **Properties** button in the **Model** group on the **ModelBuilder** tab.
16. Fill in the following details in the respective properties:
    - Type `ParcelsStreamProtectionBuffer` in **Name** field.
    - Type `Parcels Stream Protection Buffer Analysis` in the **Label** field.
    - Leave all other properties with default settings.
17. Verify that your **Tool Properties** window looks like the following screenshot and then click **OK**:

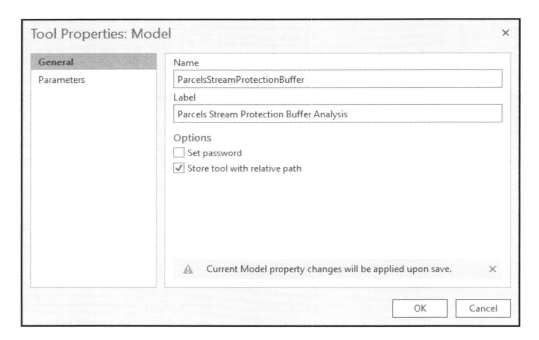

18. Click the **Save** button located in the **Model** group on the **ModelBuilder** tab to save the model. If you still have the **Catalog** pane open, you should see the name of the model change from model to the label that you entered previously.

The name for a model cannot contain spaces or other special characters with the exception of underscores. The label can be much more descriptive and does not have the same restrictions.

The process that you just created in the model will generate the buffer areas around the streams. Now you need to add another process that will calculate how much of each parcel is inside and outside that buffer area.

You will use the **Union** tool to union the parcels with the newly created stream buffer. This will create a new feature class that will split each parcel where it is overlapped by the stream buffer, thus allowing you to determine how much is inside and outside the buffer.

Step 3 – Adding another process

In this step, you will add another process to your model. This process will include the **Union** tool. You will then link this new process to the one that you created in the previous step:

1. Click on the **Tools** button in the **ModelBuilder** tab again to open the **Geoprocessing** pane.
2. Expand the **Overlay** toolset in the **Analysis** toolbox.
3. Add the **Union** tool to your model by right-clicking on the tool and selecting **Add to model**.
4. If required, using your scroll wheel, zoom out in the **ModelBuilder** window until you have room to see both the **Union** tool and the **Buffer** tool.
5. With the **Union** tool and the **Output Feature Class** variable selected, use your mouse to move them so that they are located below the **Buffer** tool, as shown in the following screenshot:

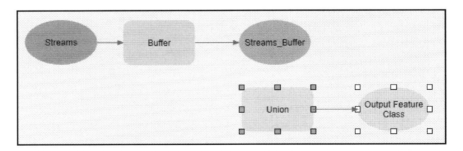

You have now added the **Union** tool to the model. Now you need to link it to the output from the **Buffer** tool and define the rest of its required variables.

6. Double-click on the **Union** tool to open the tool window.
7. In the **Union** tool window, click on the small arrow next to **Input Features**, and then select **Parcels** from the list that displays.

8. Repeat this same process to select **Streams_Buffer** located under **Model Variables**.

9. Set the output to `C:\Student\IntroArcPro\Chapter12\Ex12.gdb\Parcels_StreamBuff_Union`.

10. Verify that your **Union** tool settings match the following screenshot and click **OK**:

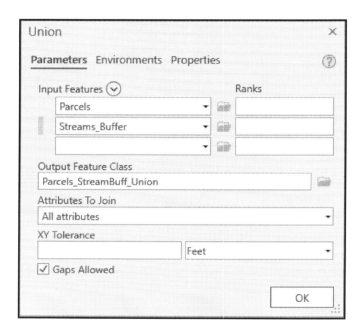

Your entire model should now be in the **ready to run** state and look similar to this:

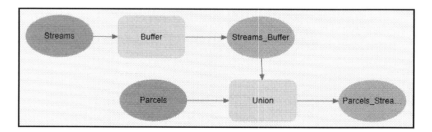

As compared to the preceding diagram, your layout may be different. That is acceptable as long as the proper connections are made, and the processes are in the **ready to run** state.

11. Save your model and your project.
12. You may close ArcGIS Pro or leave it open if you plan to continue.

You have learned how to create a model and have understood its components. After creating a model, of course, you will want to run it. There are many ways to run a model. So, we will look at how to run a model in the next section.

Running a model

You can run the entire model and the processes in the **ready to run** state or just a single process in the model. In this section, you will explore the different ways you can run a model you create in ModelBuilder.

If you wish to run the entire model, the easiest way to do that is simply double-click on it, from the toolbox it is stored in. This will run all processes in the model that are in the **ready to run** or **have been run** state. If you have allowed the users to provide values for some of the variables within the model, they will be prompted to enter those before the model is run.

Otherwise, if you did not allow for user input, the model will just indicate that there are no parameters in the geoprocessing window and all you need to do is click the **Run** button. You will learn how to make a model interactive a little later in this chapter.

You can also choose to run the model or processes in the model from the **ModelBuilder** window. Clicking on the **Run** button in the **ModelBuilder** tab will run all ready to run processes within the model. It will not run processes that are in the **have been run** or **not ready to run** state. This allows you to build and test a model as you go without being required to run the entire model.

Now that you know a little more about how to run a model, you will get to put that knowledge into practice.

Exercise 12B – Running a model

In this exercise, you will first run your model from within ModelBuilder. Then, you will get to run it directly from the toolbox so that you can see what your users will experience when they run the model.

Step 1 – Running the model from ModelBuilder

In this step, you will run the model that you created in *Exercise 12A* in `Chapter 12`, *Automating Processes with ModelBuilder and Python*, from within ModelBuilder. You will also explore how to run individual processes so that you can test your model as you create it:

1. If you closed ArcGIS Pro after the last exercise, start ArcGIS Pro and open the `Ex12.aprx` project.
2. Expand the **Toolboxes** folder in the **Catalog** pane and then expand the **Ex12** toolbox.
3. Right-click on the model that you created in *Exercise 12A* and select **Edit** from the displayed context menu. This will open the **ModelBuilder** window.

   If you created your model successfully in the last exercise and saved it, all processes should be in the **ready to run** state. This is indicated by all tools and variables having a solid color fill applied. If any are filled with gray or empty, then you need to go back to *Exercise 12A* in `Chapter 12`, *Automating Processes with ModelBuilder and Python*, and work back through the exercise.

4. Right-click on the **Buffer** tool in ModelBuilder. Select **Run** to run the **Buffer** tool with the connected variables that you defined in the model. A small window will pop up inside ModelBuilder that displays the progress of the **Buffer** tool and will let you know when it completes. When the tool is finished, notice what happens to the graphics for the **Buffer** tool and its associated variables, as shown in the following screenshot:

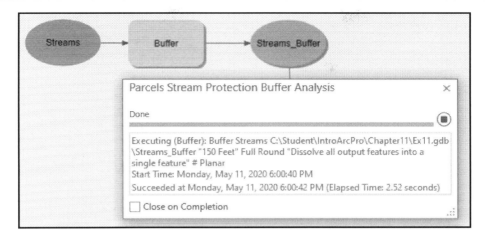

The **Buffer** tool process is now in the **has been run** state. This means you have successfully run that process in the model.

 Question: *How have the graphics for the **Buffer** tool and its associated variables changed?*

As you are beginning to learn, the state of a process will impact how it runs. Now that this process is in the **has been run** state, it will not run again if you click the **Run** button in the ribbon. The **Run** button will only run those processes that are in the **ready to run** state. Let's verify that, though.

5. Close the pop-up window that appeared when you ran the **Buffer** tool by clicking on the **x** located in the upper right corner.
6. Click the **Run** button in the **Run** group on the **ModelBuilder** tab. Watch what happens to the model as it is run.

 Question: *Did the model try to re-run the **Buffer** tool? What tool or tools did the model run when you clicked on the **Run** button and why?*

We will now move on to the next step about how to reset the run state.

Step 2 – Resetting the run state

In this step, you will learn how to reset the run state of all the processes in the model that are in the **have been run** state back to the **ready to run** state:

1. Click on the **Validate** button in the Run group on the **ModelBuilder** tab in the ribbon as illustrated in the following screenshot:

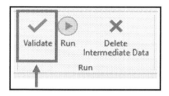

 Question: *What happens to all the processes in the model that were in the* **have been run** *state?*

2. Click the **Run** button on the ribbon and watch how your model runs this time. All the processes will run this time because all of them are in the **ready to run** state.

   Now you will actually verify that your model ran and created the feature classes that it was supposed to in the project database.

3. Expand the **Databases** folder in the **Catalog** pane and then expand the **Ex12** geodatabase.

   If you do not see anything in the geodatabase, then you may need to right-click on it and select **Refresh**. That should allow it to display the new feature classes that your model has created.

 Question: *What do you see in this database?*

4. Right-click on each feature class that you see in the **Ex12** geodatabase and select **Delete** until the database is empty. If you are asked whether you are sure that you want to permanently delete these items, select **Yes**. Deleting these feature classes will allow you to verify the model runs properly when you run it directly from the toolbox in the next step.

5. Close the **ModelBuilder** window. If asked to save the model, do so.

We will now move onto the next step about how to run the model from a toolbox.

Step 3 – Running the model from a toolbox

In this step, you will now run the model directly from the toolbox. This will be how most users will access and run models that you create. Running the model using this method will allow you to have the same experience that your users will have when they run the model:

1. Make sure the **Map** view is active by clicking on the **Map** tab at the top of the view area.
2. In the **Catalog** pane, expand the **Toolboxes** | **Ex12** toolbox.
3. Double-click on the **Parcels Streams Protection Buffer Analysis** model you created, as shown in the following screenshot:

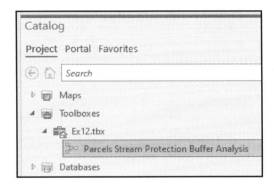

4. When you double-click on your model, it should open in the **Geoprocessing** pane. It will state that there are no parameters. This is expected because you have not defined any variables as parameters that will accept user input. Click the **Run** button at the bottom of the **Geoprocessing** pane.
5. When the model is finished, return to the **Catalog** pane.
6. Go to **Databases** | **Ex12** geodatabase again.

Question: *What feature class is now in the Ex12 geodatabase and how does that compare to when you ran the model from inside ModelBuilder?*

When you ran the model from inside ModelBuilder, it produced two different feature classes within the **Ex12** geodatabase. However, when you ran it from the toolbox, it only produced one. *Why is that?*

The answer is the feature class that was created by the **Buffer** tool in the model is considered **intermediate data**. Intermediate data is any feature class or table that is created within a model that is then used by other tools and is not a final result of a series of linked processes.

When you run a model from a toolbox, it will automatically clean up after itself. This means it automatically deletes the intermediate data that is created as the model runs. The only data it leaves is the final results of any processes in the model, which is not intermediate data. The end result is that you have the data that you need without also being left with a lot of partial datasets or layers that can clutter your database.

7. Save your project and close ArcGIS Pro.

You have now learned how to run your model using various methods depending on where you are within the application. While creating or editing your model, you now know how to run individual processes that are included in the model. You also learned how to run your model from ModelBuilder and from a toolbox.

Now that you have created and run your first model, you can now run this model anytime you need to update the calculations for the areas of each parcel in and outside a floodplain.

We will learn how to make our model more interactive for the user in the next section.

Making a model interactive

So, you have created your first model. It is a very efficient tool that will help you quickly update information. However, *what happens if the buffer distance changes or the director wants to look at different layers such as land use or just the commercial properties?* In this section, you will explore different ways you can allow users to provide input for specified parameters included within your model.

Right now, the model you created is hardcoded to a specific set of variables. If something changes, you will be forced to edit the model before it can be used. *Wouldn't it be more effective to allow others to specify different values for the variables in the model when they run it?* You can allow that. It simply requires you to designate a variable as a parameter within the model. This allows the user to provide a value before they run the model.

To designate a variable as a parameter so that a user can specify a value when it is run, you simply right-click on the variable in **ModelBuilder** and select **Parameter**. When you do that, a small capital **P** will appear next to the variable indicating that it is now a model parameter, as illustrated in the following diagram:

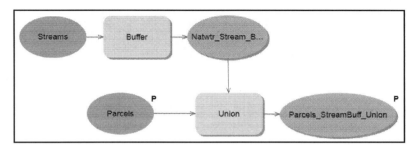

In the preceding diagram, you can see that the **Parcels** and **Parcels_ StreamBuff_Union** variables are both marked as parameters. This will allow the user to select the values that they wish to use for those variables. This means they will be able to union the stream buffers with another layer besides just the parcels layer and control where the results are saved to and the name they are given.

Making a model interactive can greatly increase its functionality. It will allow the model to be used in different scenarios and with different datasets. The downside is that the more interactive you make a model, the greater the chance of introducing operator error. Users may select the wrong input layer for a tool or forget where they set the final results to be saved. This can result in more problems than the model was designed to solve. So, it is always a balancing act between flexibility and hard coding to eliminate error sources.

Now let's give you an opportunity to make your model interactive.

Exercise 12C – Allowing users to provide inputs to run models

The director was impressed with the model that you created. It allowed them to easily calculate the area of each parcel that was in and out of the stream protection area. The council is considering changing the buffer distance for the non-disturb area and the director wants to look at the impact of several different distances. So, they will need to be able to run the model in a way that allows them to specify different buffer distances and save the overall results with different names so that they can review the results of the different distances.

In this exercise, you will make the previous model you created interactive to those users and provide their own values to variables within the model. You will allow users to specify the buffer distance that they want to use and the final output of the model.

Step 1 – Marking variables as parameters

In this step, you will learn how to designate variables as parameters within a model. You will make the buffer distance and the output of the **Union** tool parameters within your model:

1. Open **ArcGIS Pro** and the Ex12.aprx project.
2. Expand the **Toolboxes** folder in the **Catalog** pane.
3. Expand the **Ex12** toolbox and right-click on the **Parcels** stream. Right-click on the **Protection Buffer Analysis** model you created in the previous exercise. Select **Edit** to open it in **ModelBuilder**.
4. Right-click on the **Output Variable** for the **Union** tool and select **Parameter**. A small **P** should appear beside the variable, as shown in the following screenshot:

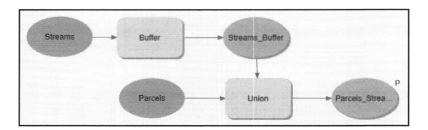

5. Then, save your model.

By making the output of the **Union** tool a model parameter, users will now be able to choose where they will save the final output of the model and what it will be named. This is one of the two requirements that the director asked for. Now you need to allow users to specify a buffer distance.

The buffer distance is currently hardcoded into the model. You need to make it a parameter as you did the output of the **Union** tool. However, the buffer variable is hidden. So, first, you will need to make it visible within the model and then designate it as a parameter.

Step 2 – Exposing hidden variables

In this step, you will expose the distance variable for the **Buffer** tool so that you can make it a parameter:

1. Right-click on the **Buffer** tool in ModelBuilder.
2. Select the **Create Variable | From Parameter** option. This will display a list of all the hidden variables associated with the **Buffer** tool.
3. Select **Distance [value or field]**, as shown in the next screenshot:

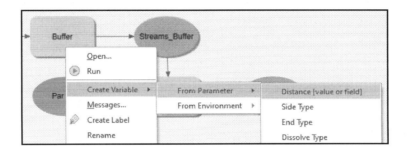

The **Distance** variable should now be visible in your model. Now that it is visible you will be able to designate it as a parameter.

4. Move your mouse pointer so that it is over the **Distance** variable that you just added to our model. When your pointer changes to two crossed arrows, indicating that it is now in move mode, drag the **Distance** variable so it is above the **Buffer** tool, as shown in the following screenshot:

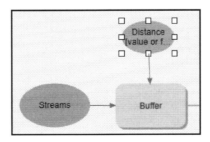

5. Right-click on the **Distance** variable and select **Parameter**. The small capital **P** should now appear next to the **Distance** variable, indicating it is now a model parameter.
6. Save your model.

Your model should now look very similar to this:

The model shown in the preceding screenshot should now meet the requirements that the director asked for. They will now be able to use different distances from the streams and see the impact that it will have on the parcels. The director can save the result to a different name and location each time they run the model.

The last step is to verify your work. You need to test run the model to see whether it allows users to specify a distance and the output values.

Step 3 – Running the model

In this step, you will run the model from the toolbox to make sure it will allow the director to input a distance and specify where the output will be saved. Since you have not changed the overall logic or functionality of the model, there is no need to test the processes inside the model again:

1. Close the **ModelBuilder** view.
2. If needed, expand the **Toolboxes** folder and the **Ex12** toolbox in the **Catalog** pane.
3. Double-click on the model that you created to open it in the **Geoprocessing** pane.

   Notice that this time when you open the model in the **Geoprocessing** pane, it looks different. Instead of saying no parameters, it is asking for user input. The user can provide values for the two variables that you designated as parameters.

4. Change the value for the **Parcels_Stream_Union** variable to
   `C:\Student\IntroArcPro\Chapter12\Ex12.gdb\`***%Your Name%_Results***
   (that is, `Tripp_Results`).

5. Change the **Distance** value to any value that you wish that is not 150 feet. You can even change the units if you desire.
6. After you are done changing the values of the variables, click the **Run** button at the bottom of the **Geoprocessing** pane.
7. Once the model has finished running, close the **Geoprocessing** pane.
8. In the **Catalog** pane, verify that the resulting output feature class is in `Ex12.gdb`.
9. Save your project and close ArcGIS Pro.

You have now created your first interactive model. This model provides more flexibility for the user, allowing them to investigate different scenarios. Next, you will be introduced to Python, which is the primary scripting language for the ArcGIS platform. You can use Python scripts to automate processes and then schedule them to run at specific times. Python scripts can also be used to help integrate ArcGIS with other applications. This makes the Python scripting language a powerful tool for increasing the effectiveness of your GIS.

Learning about Python

Python is the primary scripting language for the ArcGIS platform. It has replaced others, such as **Visual Basic (VB)**. **ArcGIS Pro 2.5** is currently compatible with **Python 3.6.9**, which is automatically installed when you install ArcGIS Pro.

Python has been fully integrated with the ArcGIS Geoprocessing **Application Programming Interface (API)** via the `ArcPy` module. This means you can use the geoprocessing tools from within ArcGIS Pro within your scripts, allowing you to automate and schedule tasks.

Unlike ModelBuilder, Python is not limited to just the ArcGIS platform. It is used to create scripts that access functions in other applications, the operating system, and the computer. This gives you the ability to create scripts that extend and integrate ArcGIS Pro's functionality across platforms and applications. As a result, Python is a very versatile tool in the GIS developer's arsenal.

Python scripts can be stored within ArcGIS Toolboxes or in standalone folders as `.py` files. Unlike other programming languages such as **C++** or VB, creating Python scripts doesn't require special application development software. You can use simple text editors such as **Notepad** or **WordPad**. There are several free **Integrated Development Environment (IDE)** applications for Python, such as **PythonWin** or **IDLE**. IDE applications provide a better development environment over text editors because they include automatic coding hints and debugging tools. When you install ArcGIS, it automatically installs Python and IDLE.

ArcGIS Pro also includes a Python window that can be used to write Python scripts, run tools using Python, and load Python scripts to view code. New Python developers often find the Python window helpful because of its integrated interface and its autosuggest function, which helps guide proper syntax.

Let's look at some Python basics first.

Understanding Python basics

Since this is your first introduction to Python, it is a good time to introduce some fundamentals and best practices. These will serve you well as you begin to write your own scripts.

Commenting and documenting your scripts

When you begin creating a Python script, it is considered a best practice to include documentation within the code that will help other developers understand what is happening within the code and the purpose-specific parts of the script. This can also prove helpful for yourself if you have to come back to a script that you wrote some time ago and need to make changes.

This in-code documentation is traditionally accomplished using commenting. Think of commenting code as a form of metadata stored within the code itself. It provides users and other programmers with the *who, what, where, when,* and *why* data. They may need this data to successfully use, integrate, or edit a script that you create. Different programming languages use different methods to comment code. Python uses the **pound sign** (#) to identify comment lines within its code, as illustrated in the following screenshot:

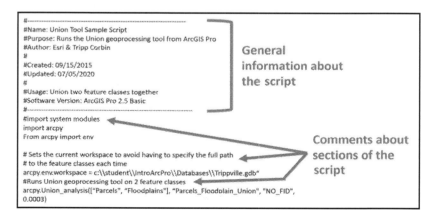

As you can see in the preceding screenshot, anytime Python encounters a line that starts with a #, it ignores that line and moves to the next. It will keep ignoring lines until it encounters one that does not have a # at the beginning.

Traditionally, the first group of lines in a Python script is used to provide basic information about the script, such as its purpose, who created it, when was it created, what ArcGIS version it was created for, and so on. Providing this basic information is considered an industry best practice.

Now let's learn about the variables that we use in Python.

Learning about variables

Like a model, a Python script can contain variables. When you define a variable in Python, you give it a name and a value. Also similar to a model, the value assigned to a variable can be hardcoded, can reference the result of another process, or can be a function of `ArcPy` or another module.

For example, you could define a variable that would be used as an input for the **Buffer** tool as follows:

```
In_buf_fc = "streams"
```

This variable would then be used by the **Buffer** tool in a Python script as follows:

```
Buffer_analysis (In_buf_fc, "C:\\GIS\\Trippville.gdb\\Streams_Buffer",
    "125 Feet", "FULL", "ROUND")
```

You can see from the preceding sample code, the use of the defined variable has been highlighted. In an actual script, you would not *embolden* the variable. That was just done in this example to help you see the use of the variable more easily.

Another particularly important thing to keep in mind when writing scripts is that Python is case sensitive. This means a variable named `Mapsize` is not the same as one named `mapsize`. To Python, those are two different and distinct objects. This is one of the most common causes of problems when writing and running Python scripts.

Python also has other restrictions when defining a variable within a script:

- Variable names must start with a letter. They cannot start with a number.
- Variable names cannot include spaces or other special characters. The one exception is an underscore (_).
- Variable names cannot include reserved keywords such as the following:
  - Class
  - If
  - For
  - While
  - Return

Now let's move on to learning about data paths used in Python.

Understanding data paths

Often when you define a variable, access data, or save the results of a tool, you need to reference a specific file or data path. In a traditional **Windows** environment, this typically requires you to define the path using backslashes. For example, you have been accessing the data and exercises for this book by going to `C:\Student\IntroArcPro`. This is an example of a path.

Unfortunately, you cannot use this common method of defining a path within a Python script. Backslashes are reserved characters within Python that are used to indicate an escape or line continuation. So, when specifying a data path, you must use a different method. Python supports three methods for defining a path:

- Double backslashes: `C:\\Student\\IntroArcPro`
- Single forward slash: `C:/Student/IntroArcPro`
- Single backslash with an `r` in front of it: `r"C:\Student\IntroArcPro"`

You can use either of the preceding methods when creating your own scripts. While it is acceptable to use any of these within a single script, it is recommended that you try to use the same method throughout the entire script. This will help you locate possible errors and fix them more quickly.

Let's learn about the `ArcPy` module in the next section.

Learning about the ArcPy module

The `ArcPy` module is a Python site package that allows Python access to ArcGIS functionality. The level of functionality is limited to the ArcGIS Pro license level and extensions available to the user running the script.

Through the `ArcPy` module, Python can not only be used to perform geoprocessing tasks using tools in ArcGIS Pro system toolboxes or other custom tools, but it can also execute other functions, such as listing available datasets within a given location or describing an existing dataset. It can also create objects, such as points, lines, polygons, extents, and more.

The `ArcPy` module contains several sub-modules. These sub-modules are specific purpose libraries containing functions and classes. These sub-modules include the following:

- Data access module (`arcpy.da`)
- Mapping module (`arcpy.mp`)
- Spatial Analyst module (`arcpy.sa`)
- Network Analyst module (`arcpy.na`)

The Spatial Analyst and Network Analyst modules require access to ArcGIS extensions of the same name.

The `ArcPy` module must be loaded into a script in order for Python to access ArcGIS Pro functionality. This is typically done at the very beginning of a new script using the following syntax:

```
import arcpy
```

This one line allows Python to access ArcGIS Pro tools and functions. Additional modules can also be loaded using that same line, such as the operating system (`os`) or system (`sys`) modules.

Now that you have a very basic understanding of the `ArcPy` module, *how do you know the proper syntax for using geoprocessing tools in a Python script?* In the next section, you will find out how to locate the proper syntax for the various geoprocessing tools included in ArcGIS Pro.

Locating Python syntax for a geoprocessing tool

Finding the Python code needed to execute a specific geoprocessing tool is as easy as opening the help information for the tool. Esri has included sample Python code for all the geoprocessing tools in ArcGIS Pro and its extensions.

This includes the proper syntax to use within a script along with a description of the variables that can be used with the tool. Help for a specific tool can be accessed in the **Geoprocessing** pane when the tool is opened by clicking on the small blue question mark located on the upper right side of the pane, as shown in the following screenshot:

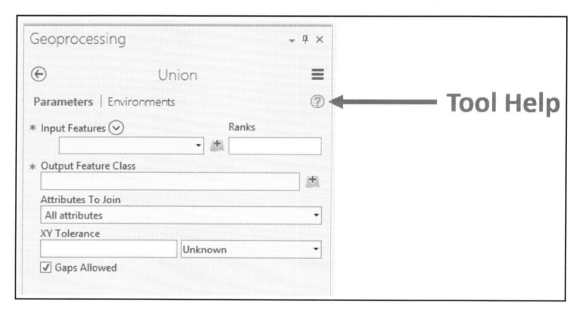

The **Syntax** page in the help information will show you the proper format for the code along with a description of the possible variables that may be included. The following screenshot shows an example of the syntax for the **Union** tool from the Esri help:

Syntax

`Union_analysis (in_features, out_feature_class, {join_attributes}, {cluster_tolerance}, {gaps})`

Parameter	Explanation	Data Type
in_features [[in_features, {Rank}],...]	A list of the input feature classes or layers. When the distance between features is less than the cluster tolerance, the features with the lower rank will snap to the feature with the higher rank. The highest rank is one. All of the input features must be polygons.	Value Table
out_feature_class	The feature class that will contain the results.	Feature Class
join_attributes (Optional)	Determines which attributes from the input features will be transferred to the output feature class. ▪ ALL —All the attributes from the input features will be transferred to the output feature class. This is the default. ▪ NO_FID —All the attributes except the FID from the input features will be transferred to the output feature class. ▪ ONLY_FID —Only the FID field from the input features will be transferred to the output feature class.	String
cluster_tolerance (Optional)	The minimum distance separating all feature coordinates (nodes and vertices) as well as the distance a coordinate can move in X or Y (or both).	Linear unit
gaps (Optional)	Gaps are areas in the output feature class that are completely enclosed by other polygons. This is not invalid, but it may be desirable to identify these for analysis. To find the gaps in the output, set this option to NO_GAPS, and a feature will be created in these areas. To select these features, query the output feature class based on all the input feature's FID values being equal to -1. ▪ GAPS —No feature will be created for areas in the output that are completely enclosed by polygons. This is the default. ▪ NO_GAPS —A feature will be created for the areas in the output that are completely enclosed by polygons. This feature will have blank attributes and its FID values will be -1.	Boolean

Help for all tools in ArcGIS Pro can be accessed from the ArcGIS Pro help online via the Tool Reference. The address to access it is `http://pro.arcgis.com/en/pro-app/tool-reference/main/arcgis-pro-tool-reference.htm`.

The help will also include code sample snippets that help put the syntax into context with a larger process. It is often possible to copy the sample code from the help and then paste it into your script; then, you can easily adjust the copied code to meet your needs, as shown in the following screenshot:

Union Example 2 (Stand-alone Script)

The following stand-alone script shows two ways to apply the Union function in scripting.

```
# unions.py
# Purpose: union 3 feature classes

# Import the system modules
import arcpy
from arcpy import env

# Set the current workspace
# (to avoid having to specify the full path to the feature classes each time)
env.workspace = "c:/data/data.gdb"


# Union 3 feature classes but only carry the FID attributes to the output
inFeatures = ["well_buff50", "stream_buff200", "waterbody_buff500"]
outFeatures = "water_buffers"
clusterTol = 0.0003
arcpy.Union_analysis (inFeatures, outFeatures, "ONLY_FID", clusterTol)

# Union 3 other feature classes, but specify some ranks for each
# since parcels has better spatial accuracy
inFeatures = [["counties", 2],["parcels", 1],["state", 2]]
outFeatures = "state_landinfo"
arcpy.Union_analysis (inFeatures, outFeatures)
```

The preceding screenshot is an example of a sample code snippet for the **Union** tool that is found in the help. As you can see, it provides an understandable example of the code in a real-world context. This provides a much better understanding of how the tool can be used within a custom script you might create. Notice the comments included within the code sample and how they help to provide a better understanding of the purpose of the various parts of the code.

If you would like to explore the relationship between ArcGIS and Python in more detail, you might find this link helpful and informative: `https://pro.arcgis.com/en/pro-app/arcpy/get-started/installing-python-for-arcgis-pro.htm`

Now it is time for you to try your hand at writing a simple Python script.

Exercise 12D – Creating a Python script

The city of Trippville operates a GIS web application that allows citizens and elected officials to access parcel data. This GIS web application combines data from the city with other data layers from ArcGIS Online and **Google Maps**. As a result, the parcels must be projected from the local state plane coordinate system to the **WGS 84 Web Mercator (Auxiliary Sphere) system**. This is the common coordinate system used by **Esri**, **Google**, and **Bing** for GIS web applications and data.

You can also update the **Acres** field as new parcels that are added or combined before the new data is added to the web application. You can use the **Calculate Field** tool to accomplish this with an expression that converts the **Shape_Length** field, which is in feet, to acres.

In the past, you have manually performed these operations. However, you will be going on vacation and the director wants the parcel data to still be updated regularly while you are gone. They can copy the data to the web application but do not know how to perform the other operations. So, they want you to create an automated routine that can perform these operations automatically on a regular schedule.

Since the director wants this routine to run on an automated schedule, you will need to write a Python script. A model will not work in this case. In this exercise, you will write a basic Python script that will calculate the acreage of each parcel, update the **Acres** field, and then project the data from the state plane coordinate system that is currently in the WGS 84 Web Mercator (Auxiliary Sphere).

Step 1 – Opening IDLE

In this step, you will open the IDLE application so that you can begin creating your script:

1. Click on your **Start** button. This is normally located in the lower-left corner of your screen in your taskbar. In **Windows 8.1** or **Windows 10,** it appears as just four white squares.

2. In Windows 8.1 or 10, click the small downward-pointing arrow to access all installed programs or apps.

3. Navigate to the **ArcGIS program** group in the list of all programs. In **Windows XP** or **Windows 7**, you may need to expand the group to see the programs inside.

4. Locate the IDLE (Python GUI) application and click on it to launch the program.

   You have now opened the Python IDLE application. You will write your script within this application. It will open with the shell window.

   The shell window displays messages and errors generated by a script when it is run from IDLE. You do not actually write scripts within this window. You will need to open a new code window to begin writing the script.

5. Click the **File** | **New File** option. This will open the code window that you will use to write your script. You should now be able to see something like this:

6. Click **Options** in the top menu and select **Configure IDLE**. You can do this in either of the IDLE windows.

7. Click on the **General** tab and set **Default Source Encoding** to **UTF-8** as shown in the following screenshot:

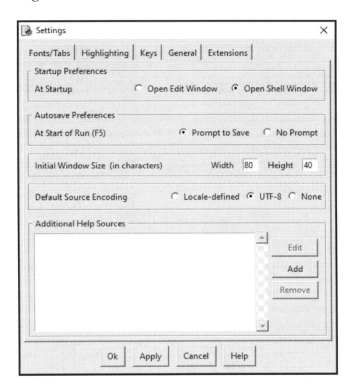

8. Click **Apply** and **Ok**.

Now that you have configured your IDLE options, it is time to start writing a script.

Step 2 – Writing the script

Now you will begin writing the script that you need to accomplish the tasks you performed manually before. To start, you will insert some basic information concerning your script in accordance with best practices. Then, you will import the ArcPy module, and lastly, you will write the code for the script:

1. First, you will save your empty script, so that it has a name. In the **Untitled** window, click on the **File | Save** option.

2. In the **Save As** window, navigate to `C:\Student\IntroArcPro\Chapter12`, name your file `AcresWebProject.py`, and click **Save**.

You have just saved your empty script. You should see the new name and path shown at the top of the code window.

3. Now you will add the general information at the beginning of the script as comments. Remember that # identifies a comment within Python code. Type the following example code into the IDLE code window (the `Purpose` part should all be typed on a single line; if you split it on to multiple lines, you will need to place # at the start of each line):

```
#*************************************************
#Script Title: AcresWebProject.py
#Script Author: Your Name
#Script Created on: Today's date
#Last Updated on: Today's date
#Last Updated by: Your Name
#Purpose: This script calculates the parcels area in acres and
updates the acres field. It then projects the parcels to the WGS 84
Web Mercator coordinate system so it can be used within the City's
web application.
#Software: ArcGIS Pro 2.5 (or the version you are running)
#*************************************************
```

4. Now you need to add the code line that imports the `ArcPy` module so that the script can access the ArcGIS Pro tools. Add the following code to your script in the code window:

```
#Imports the ArcPy module for ArcGIS
import arcpy
```

5. Save your script by clicking **File** and then **Save**. If you get a warning, just click **OK**.

Now you will define some variables within your script that specify the location of the parcels data and where to save the results of the **Project** tool.

6. Type the following code after the `import` statement in the code window:

```
#Specifies the input variables for the script tools
#If the data is moved or in a different database then these paths
will need to be updated
Parcels = "C:\\Student\\IntroArcPro\\Databases
    \\Trippville_GIS.gdb\\Base\\Parcels"
```

```
Parcels_Web = "C:\\Student\\IntroArcPro\\Chapter12\\Ex12.gdb
    \\Parcels_Web"
```

The preceding code you have just added to your Python script starts with two lines of comments which explain what the next lines do. As you have learned, comment lines are indicated with the # symbol. The next two lines define two variables.

The first is Parcels. This variable points to the location of the Parcels feature class, that is stored in the **Base** feature dataset within the **Trippville_GIS** geodatabase. The second variable you have defined in this code is Parcels_Web. It references the Parcels_Web feature class in the **Ex12** geodatabase.

7. Save your script.

    Now you need to begin adding the code for the tools that you will need to run in the script. You will use the ArcGIS Pro help to get the proper syntax for the **Calculate Field** and **Project** tools. Then, modify it so that it works properly in your script.

8. Open ArcGIS Pro and Ex12.aprx.
9. Click on the **Analysis** tab and the **Tools** button to open the **Geoprocessing** pane.
10. In the **Geoprocessing** pane, click on **Toolboxes** located near the top of the pane.
11. Expand the **Data Management Tools** toolbox and the **Fields** toolset.
12. Select the **Calculate Field** tool.
13. Click on the **Help** button. It is the blue question mark in the upper right corner.
14. You have opened the online tool reference for this tool; click on **Syntax**.
15. Highlight and copy the syntax for the tool. It should read as follows:

    ```
    CalculateField_management (in_table, field, expression,
        {expression_type}, {code_block})
    ```

16. Active the IDLE code window and paste the copied syntax onto a line below the variables that you defined earlier.
17. Add a comment above the code that you just pasted into the script that says calculates the area in acres for each parcel and updates the acres field.

18. Now edit the code sample syntax that you just pasted into the script as follows:

```
arcpy.CalculateField_management (Parcels, "Acres", "!Shape_Area! /
    43560", "PYTHON_9.3", "")
```

19. You have now defined the `CalculateField` tool within a Python script, so it includes all the variables it needs to run; save your script.

20. Now you need to add the **Project** tool to the script and define its syntax properly. Using the same process that you used for the **Calculate Field** tool, open the help for the **Project** tool and copy the syntax into your script. The **Project** tool is located in the same toolbox but is in the **Projections and Transformations** toolset.

21. Add an appropriate comment to the script that is above the code for the project tool, which will let others know its purpose similar to the comment that you added for the **Calculate Field** tool.

22. Modify the **Project** tool code as follows (to make things easier you can copy the syntax from the `Project Tool Sample.txt` file in the `Chapter12` folder):

```
arcpy.Project_management(Parcels, Parcels_Web,
"PROJCS['WGS_1984_Web_Mercator_Auxiliary_Sphere',
GEOGCS['GCS_WGS_1984',DATUM['D_WGS_1984',SPHEROID['WGS_1984',637813
7.0,298.257223563]],PRIMEM['Greenwich',0.0],UNIT['Degree',0.0174532
925199433]],PROJECTION['Mercator_Auxiliary_Sphere'],PARAMETER['Fals
e_Easting',0.0],PARAMETER['False_Northing',0.0],PARAMETER['Central_
Meridian',0.0],PARAMETER['Standard_Parallel_1',0.0],PARAMETER['Auxi
liary_Sphere_Type',0.0],UNIT['Meter',1.0]]",
"WGS_1984_(ITRF00)_To_NAD_1983",
"PROJCS['NAD_1983_StatePlane_Georgia_West_FIPS_1002_Feet',GEOGCS['G
CS_North_American_1983',DATUM['D_North_American_1983',SPHEROID['GRS
_1980',6378137.0,298.257222101]],PRIMEM['Greenwich',0.0],UNIT['Degr
ee',0.0174532925199433]],PROJECTION['Transverse_Mercator'],PARAMETE
R['False_Easting',2296583.333333333],PARAMETER['False_Northing',0.0
],PARAMETER['Central_Meridian',-84.16666666666667],PARAMETER['Scale
_Factor',0.9999],PARAMETER['Latitude_Of_Origin',30.0],UNIT['Foot_US
',0.3048006096012192]]")
```

The preceding code seems extremely complicated, and to some extent it is. It contains all the parameters required to define two coordinate systems. The first is the coordinate system for the `Parcels` feature class. The second is the coordinate system used by the output feature class, `Parcels_Web`.

23. Save your script.

Your script should look like this on your screen:

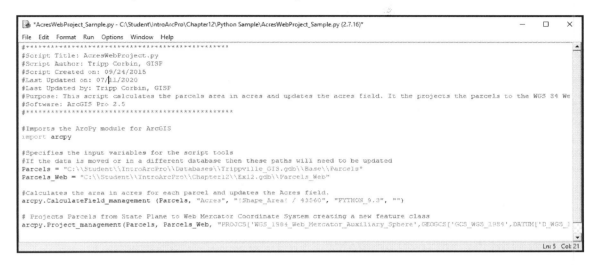

24. Once you have verified your script and saved it, close IDLE.

We'll now move on to the next step.

Step 3 – Adding the script to ArcGIS Pro and running it

Now that you have created a Python script, you need to add it to ArcGIS Pro and test it. In this step, you will add the script you just created to a toolbox in your project and then run it:

1. If necessary, start ArcGIS Pro and open `Ex12.aprx`.
2. In the **Catalog** pane, expand the **Toolboxes** folder.
3. Right-click on the **Ex12** toolbox and select **New>Script** from the menu.
4. Fill out the information for the new script as follows:
   - Type `CalcAcresProject` in the **Name** field.
   - Type `Calculate Parcel Acres and Project to Web Mercator` in the **Label** field.

5. Click on the **Browse** button located next to the **Script File** cell, then navigate to
   C:\Student\IntroArcPro\Chapter12, and select the AcresWebProject.py
   script that you just created. Your window should now look like this:

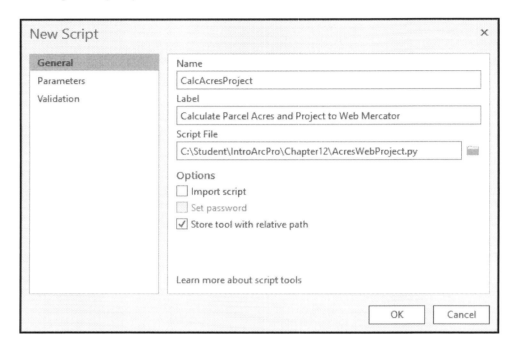

6. Click **OK** once you have verified everything is set correctly.

   The script will appear in the **Ex12** toolbox. This means you can now run it in
   ArcGIS Pro. You must add all Python scripts that you create to a toolbox before
   they are able to be used in ArcGIS Pro. For those with experience with ArcGIS for
   Desktop, it should be noted that ArcGIS Pro does not support Python add-ins yet.
   That functionality should be added to a future version.

   Now you will need to run the script to test and make sure it works as expected.

7. Double-click on the Python script that you just added to the toolbox. This will
   open it in the **Geoprocessing** pane. Since you hardcoded all the variables into the
   script, it has no parameters that the user needs to define.

8. Click the **Run** button at the bottom of the **Geoprocessing** pane.
9. Once the script has completed running, return to the **Catalog** pane.
10. Expand the **Databases** folder and expand Ex12.gdb. If the script ran successfully, you should see a new feature class named Parcels_Web. You may need to right-click on the **Ex12** geodatabase and refresh in order to see the new feature class that was created.

    If you do see the new feature class, congratulations! You have just created and run your first Python script. If your script did not run successfully, you may wish to compare it to the sample included in the Python Sample folder located in C:\Student\IntroArcPro\Chapter12\.

11. Save your project and close ArcGIS Pro along with IDLE, if it is still open.

You have just created your first Python script, which projects data from one coordinate system to another. Since this is a Python script, you could use the scheduling functionality found in your operating system to schedule this script to run at a specified frequency automatically so you do not have to worry about it. This can reduce your overall workload and ensure that required functions run on a regular schedule.

Summary

In this chapter, you learned that ArcGIS Pro contains two methods for automating and streamlining tasks; that is, you can create a model or a Python script. Which one will work best will largely depend on your skills and how they will be used. You have gained the skills to create and run your own model.

We learned that models are created in ModelBuilder, which provides a graphical interface for creating tools that will automate a series of processes required to accomplish an analysis or other workflow. Each model will contain a series of processes. Each process will include a tool that can be a geoprocessing tool, script, or another model, along with their associated variables. As you create a model, you can choose to make it interactive by designating variables as parameters. The biggest limitation of models is that they can only be run from inside of ArcGIS Pro. This means they cannot be scheduled to run automatically.

Python scripts can be used to automate processes that can then be scheduled to run at specified times and dates. Unlike the case with models, creating Python scripts does require knowledge of the Python language and the ability to write code.

In addition to the ability of Python scripts to be run on a schedule, they can also be used to access functionality from other applications other than ArcGIS Pro. Through this chapter, you have gained the skills to create scripts that can integrate the functionality of several different applications into a single automated script.

In the next chapter, you will learn how you can share the various maps and data you create in ArcGIS Pro with others on your computer network and those that are not on your network. You will also learn ways to share your GIS content with others that do not have GIS software.

Further reading

If you would like to learn more about creating Python scripts for ArcGIS, you might want to get *Programming ArcGIS with Python Cookbook* by Eric Pimpler.

Sharing Your Work with Others 13

As you have learned throughout this book, ArcGIS Pro has powerful tools for creating amazing 2D and 3D maps, and for performing a wealth of spatial analysis tasks. All this functionality means little if you cannot get the results into the hands of those that need it.

The need to access **Geographic Information System (GIS)** information is also being fueled by the growing use of geospatial and mobile technologies by the masses. Almost everyone nowadays has a smartphone or tablet and has used some sort of mapping application such as **Google Maps**, **Waze**, **Bing Maps**, or the local county tax parcel application. All of this means that people are becoming much more geospatially and technology savvy. They expect to be able to access and use the data and analysis that you provide.

ArcGIS Pro provides several methods and tools for sharing your GIS content with others. Which of the available tools or methods will work best depends on the following several factors:

- First, *what is it that you are trying to share? Is it data, an entire map, or a tool?*
- Second, *what software and skills do your audience possess?*
- Third, *what do you want to allow them to do with the shared content – print, edit, query, or download it?*
- Forth, *how will they connect to your GIS information?*

The topics that we will cover in this chapter include the following:

- Sharing content with those on your network
- Sharing content with those not on your network
- How to export to other GIS data formats
- How to export to non-GIS data formats
- How to publish content to the web via ArcGIS Online

Throughout this chapter, you will learn about various methods for sharing data. You will be able to use these various methods to share your GIS data with others, whether or not they have GIS software.

Technical requirements

In addition to an ArcGIS Pro license, you will also need an **ArcGIS Online** user login that has publisher or administrator permissions to complete all the exercises in this chapter.

Sharing content with those on your network

Sharing GIS content with those that are on your computer network is relatively easy. The biggest consideration will be to is whether they have access to GIS software or not. In this section, we will see how to share information with those that are on your computer network whether they have GIS software or not.

Sharing your GIS data is easier if they also have ArcGIS Pro, **ArcGIS Desktop**, or some other GIS application. As long as they have the ability to access the data files, many of these applications have the ability to open the same types of data. This should allow them to add that data into their application.

If there are people on your network who do not have GIS software, it gets a bit more complicated, because while they might be able to access the data, they will not have the required software. In this situation, you will need to export your GIS content to a more common non-GIS format such as a .pdf file. Luckily, ArcGIS Pro also supports that ability.

Regardless of whether they have GIS software or not, they will need permissions and access to the databases, files, and folders where you store your GIS content. If they do not have the proper permissions, they will not be able to make use of the data or files that you create.

Sharing data if users have ArcGIS Pro

If other users on your network have ArcGIS Pro, they will be able to open the projects that you create as long as they have access and permissions to the project and data sources used in the project. You can also share layers, maps, tasks, and layout files to standardize your content. We will look at all these files in the few upcoming sections.

Understanding the layer file

A layer file in ArcGIS Pro has a `.lyrx` file extension. They store all the property settings associated with a layer in a map such as a source, symbology, field visibility, labeling, definition queries, and more. Layer files allow you to standardize these settings so the layer will appear the same across multiple maps and projects.

Using a layer file to add a new layer uses the same process as adding a layer using a feature class. However, instead of choosing a **geodatabase**, **shapefile**, **Computer-Aided Design** (**CAD**) file, or **raster**, you select the layer file instead. When you do that, your layer will be added to your map with all the properties preconfigured, so you don't need to go back and set all the layer properties manually. This can save you valuable time.

 Layer files created in **ArcMap** may also be used in ArcGIS Pro in the same way those created in ArcGIS Pro can. However, layer files created in ArcGIS Pro cannot be used in the older ArcMap application.

Creating a layer file is relatively easy. You simply select the layer in the **Content** pane. Then you activate the **Share** tab and choose **Layer File**. From there, you fill out the required information and click **Save**. It is that easy.

Why don't you give it a try?

Exercise 13A – Creating a layer file and using it

Now, this is your opportunity to put the knowledge that you have gained into action via a hands-on exercise. In this exercise, you will create a layer file and then use it to add a new layer to a map within a project using ArcGIS Pro.

Step 1 – Creating the layer file

In this step, you will create the layer file for the Trippville Zoning layer. It appears that several people have been using the Zoning layer in several maps but have been doing so with their own personal settings. This is causing confusion, so the Community Development Director wants you to develop a standard based on the Official Zoning Map for the city:

1. Start **ArcGIS Pro** and open the `Ex13.aprx` project file located in `C:\Student\IntroArcPro\Chapter13`.

2. Examine the map, paying close attention to the Zoning layer. Note what settings such as symbology and labeling have been applied to the layer.

Questions: *What type of symbology is being applied to the Zoning layer? Is the layer labeled?*

3. Select the Zoning layer in the **Contents** pane and then click on the **Share** tab in the ribbon.
4. Click on the **Layer File** button in the **Save As** group. This will open the **Save Layer(s) As LYRX File** window.
5. Navigate to C:\Student\IntroArcPro\Chapter13 using the tree on the left side of the window.
6. Name the new .lyrx file as Trippville Official Zoning and click **Save**.

You have just created a layer file for the Zoning layer as it appears in the Official Zoning Map in the Ex13 project. This will allow you to easily add this layer to other maps found in this project or others so that it will maintain all its existing layer properties such as symbology, labeling, definition queries, scale ranges, and more.

Step 2 – Using the layer file to add a layer to a map

In this step, you will test the layer file that you created to ensure it works as expected. You will use it to add a new layer to a new blank map in your project:

1. In the **Catalog** pane, expand the Folders folder. Then expand the Chapter13 folder so that you can see its contents.
2. Right-click on the Trippville Official Zoning.lyrx file and click the **Add to New** option, then select **Map**, as shown in the following screenshot:

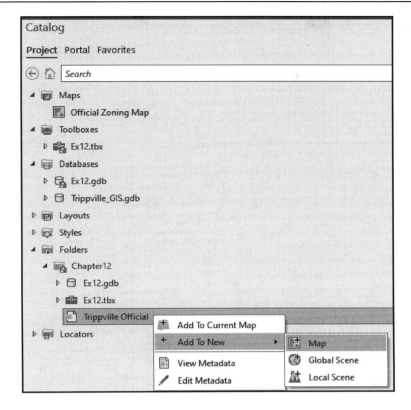

A new map has just been added to your project and it should contain the Zoning layer, automatically symbolized and labeled the same way as it was in the Official Zoning Map. This was because you added the layer using a layer file instead of going directly to the feature class in the geodatabase, as you have done in past exercises.

3. Save your project and close ArcGIS Pro.

As you have now experienced, a layer file can allow you to quickly add layers to a map that are already configured, which can save you and others in your organizations a great deal of time. Layer files can also be used to standardize how specific layers are displayed in various maps throughout your organization.

Let's now move on to the next section about map files.

Learning about map files

Map files are similar to a layer file except they save the settings for an entire map. This includes all the layers shown in the **Contents** pane when that map is active and the settings for each of those layers. Map files can be created for either a two- or three-dimensional scene from an ArcGIS Pro project. Map files have a .mapx file extension.

For those who have used ArcGIS Desktop (**ArcMap** and **ArcCatalog**), it is important to remember that a map or scene in ArcGIS Pro is just one component of a project. Unlike a map document in ArcMap, which is often called a map, maps in ArcGIS Pro are a single item and do not include things such as layouts and other maps (these are called data frames in ArcMap).

Map files allow you to share maps that you create in ArcGIS Pro so others can include them in their projects or you can use others' in yours. This can save a lot of time because the map will not need to be created from scratch. It can simply be imported into the project and then adjusted to meet the current requirements.

Adding a new map to your project from a map file is not difficult. Simply click on the **Insert** tab in the ArcGIS Pro ribbon, then select **Import Map**. From there, you simply navigate to the location of the map file and import it.

Creating a map file follows the same basic process as creating a layer file. You go to the **Share** tab in the ribbon. Instead of selecting **Layer File**, you select **Map File**.

For those of you who have been using ArcGIS Desktop, remember that a map in ArcGIS Pro is not exactly the same as a map document. In an ArcGIS Pro project, you may have several maps along with separate layouts. When you create a map file in ArcGIS Pro, it will only contain the active map that was selected when you created the map file. This will not include any layouts that may include the map.

Map file challenge

Using the skills that you have learned for creating a layer file in the previous sections, create a map file based on the Official Zoning Map in the Ex13 project. Then open a new project and try to import the map file to create a new map within that project.

Next, we will look at layout files.

Understanding layout files

Layout files allow you to share layouts you create so that they can be used as templates by yourself and others. Layout files will include all the elements you see in the layout including maps, legends, borders, north arrows, scale bars, titles, logos, disclaimers, and more.

If the data referenced in the maps included in the layout is not accessible or in a different location, you will need to resend your data sources. Layout files, such as layer and map files, do not store any GIS data.

The process to create and import layout files is very similar to the process used for map files. Again, it starts on the **Share** tab in the ribbon, then the **Layout File** button in the **Save As** group.

Layout file challenge

Try exporting the layout included in the `Ex12` project to a layer file. Then open a new blank project or one of the previous projects that you have worked with and import the layout file into the project.

Here's a hint: try using the **New Layout** tool on the **Insert** tab in the ribbon. Notice what happens when you import the layout file.

Through this section, you have learned the various ways by which you can share your GIS content with others on your network who have GIS software such as ArcGIS Pro. This included creating layer files, map files, opening existing projects, and more. This allows others throughout your organization to open and use the content you have created.

We will now discuss the scenario where the users do not have ArcGIS Pro for sharing data on the network.

Sharing data if users don't have ArcGIS Pro

If you want to share your GIS content with those users who don't have ArcGIS Pro, your options are much more limited. Depending on the software and abilities of your potential users, you can export your content to other GIS formats, non-GIS formats, or try publishing to **ArcGIS Online**, **Portal for ArcGIS**, or **ArcGIS Server** as a web map or layer.

Exporting to other GIS formats

ArcGIS Pro will allow you to export your data to many different GIS formats such as **shapefiles**, **Keyhole Mark-up Language (KML/KMZ)**, or CAD files (.dwg, .dxf, or .dgn). Some of these allow you to export multiple layers into a single file, while others only support single layers.

Shapefiles are a very common GIS data format that originated with Esri. A shapefile (.shp) only stores a single layer or feature class. So, if you wish to use this format, you may need to export multiple layers, each to its own shapefile.

Most GIS-enabled applications such as **QGIS**, **Grass**, **MapWindow**, and **Map3D** are able to read and display shapefiles. Some even have the ability to edit. In addition, most **Global Positioning System/Global Navigation Satellite System (GPS/GNSS)** software applications and collectors are also able to import and export shapefiles. As a result, shapefiles have become the de facto data sharing format for many.

The KML format is also popular. It is the format used by **Google Earth**, which is a free application. Exporting to KML would allow you to view your data in relation to the data you see on Google's maps, as illustrated in the following screenshot:

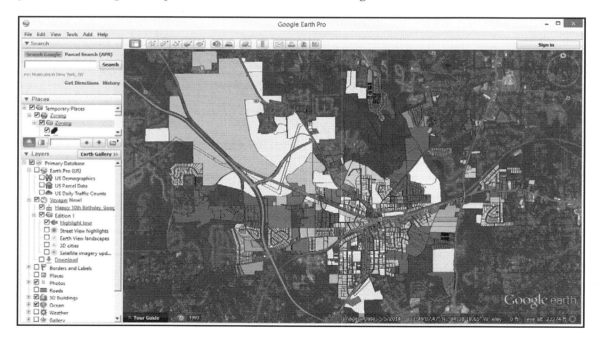

You will find the tools to export to these other GIS formats in the **Conversion Tools** toolbox and their individual toolsets. Each format has its own toolset, as shown in the following screenshot:

As you can see from the preceding screenshot, ArcGIS Pro is able to convert a wide range of data formats. In the following exercise, you will learn how to export data from the city of Trippville's geodatabase to a shapefile so that it can be used in another GIS software application.

Exercise 13B – Exporting data to a shapefile

The Planning Director is working with a consultant who is using **QGIS**. They need to be able to open and make edits to the city zoning data to look at different options for possible future developments.

Shapefiles can easily be used in QGIS, certainly more so than the geodatabase file that the city uses to store its GIS data. So, you will export the existing zoning data to a shapefile.

Step 1 – Opening the project and verifying the data

Of course, before you can export the data, you need to open the project. In this step, you will open the appropriate project containing the data you need to export:

1. Open ArcGIS Pro and the Ex13 project, if you closed it earlier.
2. Select the **Official Zoning Map** tab at the top of the view area to make it the active map.
3. Select the **Analysis** tab from the ribbon and click on the **Tools** button in the **Geoprocessing** group to open the **Geoprocessing** pane.
4. In the **Geoprocessing** pane, click on the **Toolboxes** tab at the top of the pane just below the **Find Tools** search box.
5. Expand the **Conversion Tools** toolbox by clicking on the small arrow located to the left. Then click on the **To Shapefile** toolset.
6. After that, select the **Feature Class To Shapefile** tool.
7. To set the **Input Features**, click on the small drop-down arrow located to the left of the cell, and select the **Zoning** layer.

Note that when you add the Zoning layer as an input, another input cell appears in the tool. The **Feature Class To Shapefile** tool allows you to convert multiple layers or feature classes to individual shapes at one time. Each input will become a unique shapefile with the same name as the input layer or feature class.

8. Set the **Output Folder** to `C:\Student\IntroArcPro\Chapter13\`.

Your **Feature Class To Shapefile** tool should look like the following screenshot:

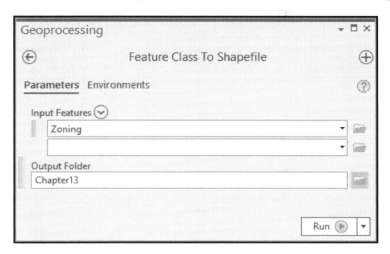

9. Once you have verified that the **Feature Class To Shapefile** tool is properly configured, click the **Run** button located at the bottom of the **Geoprocessing** pane.

This tool will produce a new shapefile. This new shapefile will contain all the same data that was included in the original Zoning layer, which is based on a geodatabase feature class. As mentioned earlier, shapefiles are often used to share data between software packages because just about any GIS application can read and edit them.

Now you will verify that the tool successfully created the new shapefile by adding it as a layer to a new map.

Step 2 – Creating a new map and adding the shapefile as a layer

In this step, you will add the new shapefile that you just created to a map to verify that it was successfully created:

1. In the ribbon, click on the **Insert** tab to activate it.
2. Next, click on the **New Map** button located in the **Project** group on the **Insert** tab. This will add a new blank map to your project.

3. In the **Catalog** pane, expand the `Folders` folder, then double-click on the `Chapter13` folder to see its contents.

4. You should see the `Zoning.shp` file that you created in the `Chapter13` folder. Right-click on it and select **Add to Current Map**.

Your map should now look similar to the following screenshot. Remember that your colors may be different because ArcGIS Pro assigns random colors to newly added layers. Your map may also contain a basemap depending on your organization's settings:

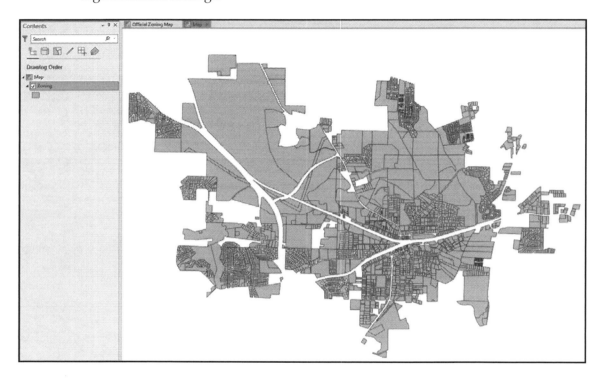

You may be wondering why the new shapefile layer that you just added does not have the same symbology as the Zoning layer that you exported from the Official Zoning Map. Remember that the actual source for a layer, be it a shapefile, geodatabase feature class, or something else, does not store the way we visualize that layer. Those settings are stored in the map, a layer file, or a layer package.

5. Save your project.

We now move on to the main step in this exercise.

Step 3 – Applying symbology using a layer file

In this step, you will use a layer file to apply the symbology that you saw in the Official Zoning Map to the shapefile-based layer that you just added to your new map. This will help you verify that all the important attribute information was included in the exported shapefile:

1. Select the **Zoning** layer in the **Contents** pane so that the **Feature Layer group** tabs appear in the ribbon.
2. Next, click on the **Appearance** tab in the ribbon.
3. Click on the **Import** button located in the **Drawing** group on the **Appearance** tab in the ribbon. This will open the **Import Symbology** tool in a floating window.
4. Verify that the **Input Layer** is set to **Zoning**.
5. To set the **Symbology Layer**, click on the browse button located at the end of the cell. It looks like a file folder.
6. In the **Symbology Layer** window that opens, click on **Folders**, located beneath **Project** in the left panel of the window.
7. In the right panel of the window, double-click on the `Chapter13` folder.
8. Select the `Trippville Official Zoning.lyrx` file and click **OK**.
9. Notice that once you click **OK**, the values for type, the source field, and the target field are automatically assigned. Verify that your **Apply Symbology From Layer** tool window looks like the following screenshot:

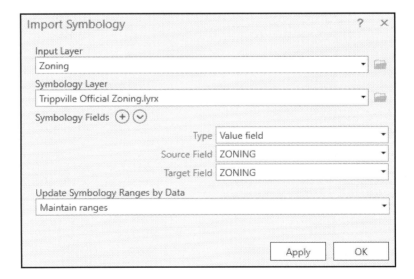

You will see that the values for the **Source** and **Target** fields were automatically assigned because the fields in both the source and target were the same field type and had the same name. This tool allows you to manually assign these values using the drop-down arrows at the end of the fields.

10. After you have verified the settings for the tool, click the **OK** button to apply the new symbology from the layer file.

Your map should now look similar to the following screenshot:

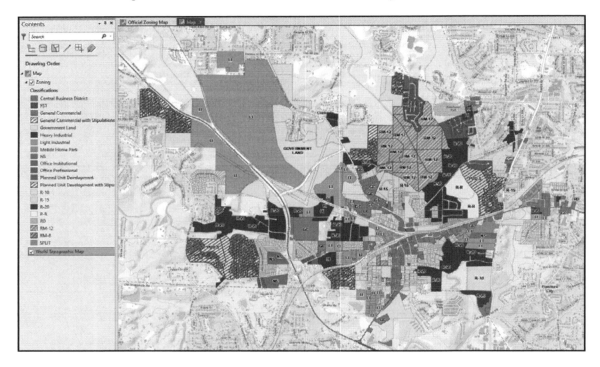

11. Save your project and close ArcGIS Pro.

You now know how to export a layer to a shapefile so that you can share it with others. You have also learned how you can apply symbology to a layer using a layer file.

The next step of sharing this data with someone else could be done by emailing it or uploading it to an online resource such as **Google Drive** or **ArcGIS Online**. We will learn how to upload to ArcGIS Online later in this chapter. When you do try to share the shapefile with someone else, remember that a shapefile actually consists of multiple files. You will need to make sure that you send all of those, and not just the .shp file that you see in ArcGIS Pro. We will learn about this in the next section.

Exporting data to non-GIS formats

ArcGIS Pro supports exporting maps, layouts, and tables to other non-GIS formats. This includes several raster and vector formats. This can allow others who don't have ArcGIS Pro to view what you have created. Many of the non-GIS formats that you can export to with ArcGIS Pro can also be inserted into other non-GIS applications as well, such as **Word** and **PowerPoint**. This will allow you to incorporate GIS information into reports and presentations.

Exporting maps and layouts

With ArcGIS Pro, you can export maps and layouts in various types of vector graphic or raster formats. This includes the following:

- **Bitmap image files** (.bmp) can be exported as **raster** format files.
- **Enhanced MetaFiles** (.emf) can be exported as **Vector Graphics**.
- **Encapsulated PostScript** (.eps) files can be exported as **Vector Graphics**.
- **Graphics Interchange Format** (.gif) files can be exported as **raster** format files.
- **Joint Photographic Experts Group** (.jpeg) files can be exported as **raster** format files.
- **Portable Document Format** (.pdf) files can be exported as **Vector Graphics**.
- **Portable Network Graphic** (.png) files can be exported as **raster** format files.
- **Scalable Vector Graphics** (.svg) files can be exported as **Vector Graphics**.
- A .svgz file, which is a .svg file compressed with **gzip compression**, can be exported as **Vector Graphics**.
- **Truevision Graphics Adapter** (.tga) files can be exported as **raster** format files.
- **Tagged Image File Format** (.tiff) files can be exported as **raster** format files.

Many of these formats can then be easily opened in other applications such as web browsers (such as **Chrome, Internet Explorer**, or **Firefox**), free applications (such as **Adobe Acrobat Reader** and **Microsoft Paint**), or other GIS applications.

Most of the raster formats can also be embedded or inserted into documents, spreadsheets, and presentations. This allows them to be included in reports, studies, letters, exhibits, and more.

The **Portable Document Format** (**PDF**) format actually supports some ability to create an interactive file. When you export to .pdf, you have the option to include layers and/or attributes if you desire, as illustrated in the following screenshot:

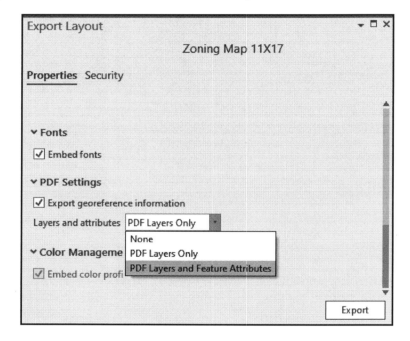

As you can see from the preceding screenshot, this option is under the **PDF Settings**. PDFs also allow you to secure the file so that it requires a password to open it.

Next, we will learn about exporting tables in your GIS to other formats.

Exporting tables

If you just need to export the attributes found in the **Attribute** table for a layer, you can export the information to various formats as well. This can be accomplished in two ways:

1. The first is from the **Table** pane. Click on the options button (the three horizontal lines) in the upper-right corner, and select the **Export** table option, as shown in the following screenshot:

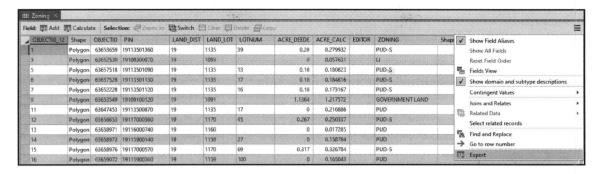

2. The second way is to go straight to the **Copy Rows** geoprocessing tool, located in the **Data Management Tools** toolbox and the **Tables** toolset. Both methods end up producing the same result.

Both of the previously stated methods will allow you to export an entire table or a set of selected records to another table. You have the option of exporting to the following formats and types:

- **A geodatabase standalone table**
- **dBase** (`.dbf`)
- **Comma-delimited text files** (`.csv`)
- **Tab-delimited text files** (`.txt`)
- **Info**

 Info is a database type that goes back to the 1970s. It was the forerunner to databases such as **dBase**. Esri purchased it for use as the primary database for their old product called **ArcInfo**.

ArcGIS Pro also allows you to export a table to a spreadsheet. You will need to use the **Table to Excel Python geoprocessing script** found in the **Conversion Tools** toolbox and the **Excel** toolset. This will allow you to export an entire table or a set of selected records to an Excel spreadsheet for others to use.

In the next section, we will explore methods that you can use to share data with others who are not on your computer network.

Sharing content with those not on your network

Sharing content with those not on your network is a bit more challenging. As you have learned, maps and layouts don't actually store the GIS data that they reference. Instead, they point to the original source. The source can be a database stored within the project folder structure or it might be located someplace else entirely. It is even possible for a project, map, and layout to include multiple layers, all of which reference data from completely different sources.

This is why it is difficult to share your work with those who are not able to connect to the same resources you are using. You can't just send them a map or layer file because neither of those includes the underlying data. You could possibly zip the project folders together into a single file that you could email or put on a **File Transfer Protocol** (**FTP**) site for download, but that only works if all the data that you use within a project is stored in the project structure.

If only you could create a file that packaged all the data that you referenced in a project, map, or layer. Luckily, with ArcGIS Pro, you can do just that. It has tools that allow you to package the project, map, or layer together with its referenced data so that you can then share it with those not on your network.

Packages are also a great way to archive data. A package creates a snapshot of the data in the state that it was in when you created the package. This provides you with a backup of the data at that point, which you can reference later as needed. This also means packages are disconnected from your live data. So if you make changes to that data, you will need to recreate the package if you want it to include the changes.

In this section, you will explore the various packages that you can create and learn how to create them. You will start with the smallest type of package, the **layer package**, and work your way up to the largest, being the **project package**.

Learning about the layer package

A **layer package** is very similar to a layer file. It too stores all the property settings for a layer so that when it is added to a map those settings are automatically applied. In addition to saving those settings, a layer package also includes the data referenced by the layer. This means a layer package can be shared with someone who does not have access to your data. They can then add the layer package to a map and see the layer with your settings and the data in the state it was when it was packaged.

Because layer packages only include a single layer, they tend to be much smaller than other packages. This makes them more ideal for emailing to others.

Creating a layer package is similar to creating a layer file. You can select the layer in the map that you wish to package. Then select the **Share** tab in the ribbon. Next, you select the **Layer** button in the **Package** group. This will launch the packaging wizard.

We now move on to the next section, which includes an exercise for creating a layer package.

Exercise 13C – Creating a layer package

The Community Development Director has engaged the services of a consulting firm to help with the preparation of the city's long-range comprehensive plan. The consulting firm needs a complete copy of the city's Zoning layer, so the director has asked if you can create a file that he can send to the consultant that contains all the standard city zoning symbology and data.

In this exercise, you will create a layer package of the Zoning layer. Then you will test it to make sure it works.

Step 1 – Creating the layer package

In this step, you will create the Zoning layer package. You will work through the package wizard and you will provide all the data and input it needs to successfully create the package:

1. Start ArcGIS Pro and open the Ex13.aprx project that you have been using in the other exercises in this chapter.
2. Select the **Official Zoning Map** tab at the top of the view area to activate the map.
3. Select the **Zoning** layer in the **Contents** pane.
4. Next, select the **Share** tab in the ribbon.
5. Click on the **Layer** button located in the **Package** group on the **Sharing** tab in the ribbon.
6. Select the **Save package to a file** option at the top of the **Package Layer** pane. Notice you can automatically upload a layer package to ArcGIS Online to share with those in or outside your organization.

7. Click the **Browse** button at the end of the cell to provide a **Name** and **Location** for the layer package file.

8. Using the tree on the left side, navigate to `C:\Student\IntroArcPro\My Projects`, name the package `Trippville_Zoning`, and then click **Save**.

9. Type the following in the **Summary** and **Tags** fields:
   - Type `Showing the zoning classifications of parcels in the City of Trippville` into the **Summary** field.
   - Add `Zoning`, `Trippville`, and `Parcels` tags into the **Tags** field.

The **Package Layers** pane should now look like this:

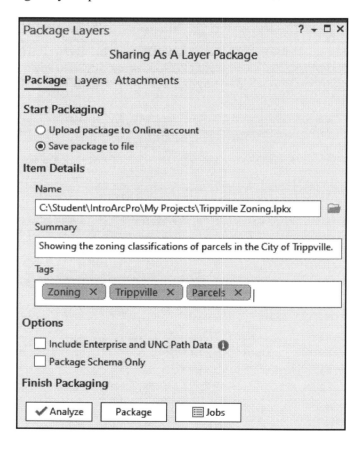

10. Click the **Analyze** button to see whether there will be any problems while creating the package.

    The analysis of the layer will either show no errors or possibly a single error. If you get a single error, it is because the layer description is missing. Since this is an error and not just a message, it must be fixed before you can proceed with creating the package.

    If you get the error, proceed with the following steps. If you do not get any error, skip to *step 15*.

11. Right-click on the error and select **Change Layer Description** from the presented context menu. This will open the **Layer Properties** window for the Zoning layer.

12. Type `Zoning Layer for the City of Trippville` into the **Layer Properties** window. Feel free to update any of the other missing values as well.

13. When you are done updating the **Layer Properties**, click **OK**. The error should now have a green checkmark in place of the red and white error icon.

14. Click the **Analyze** button once again to ensure there are no issues that would cause the package creation to fail.

15. If no errors are returned, click the **Package** button.

16. When the package is successfully created, close the **Package Layers** pane.

Next, you need to verify that the package has indeed been created successfully.

Step 2 – Testing the package

In this step, you will create a new map in your project and add the layer package that you created to it:

1. In the **Catalog** pane, right-click on the `Maps` folder and select **New Map** from the presented context menu. A new map should appear in your project.

2. Click on the **Map** tab in the ribbon.

3. Click on the **Add Data** button in the **Layer** group.

4. In the **Add Data** window, navigate to the `C:\Student\IntroArcPro\My Projects` folder. Once there, you should see the `Trippville_Zoning.lpkx` file that you just created.

5. Click on the `Trippville Zoning.lpkx` file and then the **OK** button to add the layer to your map.

The Zoning layer should now be visible on your new map. You will now verify the source of the Zoning layer.

6. Click on the **List by Data Source** button on the top of the **Contents** pane.
7. If needed, resize the **Contents** pane so that you can see the entire path to the Zoning layer's data source.

 Questions: *What is the path to the Zoning layer's data source? Is this different to the data source used by the Zoning layer that you used to create the layer package?*

8. Save your project and close ArcGIS Pro.

Congratulations! You just created and tested your first package. You now have the skills and knowledge to share your layer data and settings with others. Next, you will investigate map packages.

Understanding map packages

Just as a layer package bundles the data for a layer together with its property settings, a **map package** bundles all the data associated with the layers contained in a map plus the property settings for those layers. So, a map package bundles everything that you see in a map together into a single file with a .mapx extension.

Map packages provide an easy way to share an entire map with others who may not be able to connect to your data sources. One thing to consider though is size. Because a map package will contain all the layers and their referenced data within a single file, it is possible for them to get very large.

I have personally created one for a client that was over 20 GB in size. The reason for it being so large was that the client had pictures stored in the database of the features. In addition, the map included local aerial photography. So when the map package was created it included the layers, the layer properties, the attached pictures of the features, and the aerial photos that were used in the map.

Of course, that is not the norm and actually represents a worst-case scenario for size when creating a map package. However, it does illustrate just how large map packages can be. When creating a map package, it is best to first remove any unneeded layers from the map to keep the map package size to a minimum. Turning off layers' visibility will not cut it. Non-visible layers will still be included in the map package, so they must be physically removed from the map.

Creating a map package follows the same basic process as creating a layer package. You activate the two- or three-dimensional map that you wish to package and then proceed to the **Share** tab. You then click the **Map package** tool and work through the wizard.

Map package challenge

You now have the skills to create a layer package, plus the information needed to create a map package for the Official Zoning Map contained in the Ex13.aprx project. Now, save the new map package to the same location where you saved the layer package created in *Exercise 13C – Creating a layer package*. Then, compare the size of the layer package to the size of the map package that you created.

Learning about project packages

Project packages tend to be the biggest type of package that you can create. Project packages bundle everything that you include in a project into a single file. This includes maps, layers, data, toolboxes, tasks, attachments, geoprocessing history, and connections. Project packages will have a .ppkx file extension.

Because a project package literally includes everything that is part of a project, they tend to be large, certainly much larger than either a map or layer package. This means they are not typically well suited for sharing via email. However, it is possible to publish them to an FTP site for download, save to an external device, or even publish to ArcGIS Online. If you publish to ArcGIS Online, you will be charged credits for storing the package. The number of credits you are charged will depend on the size of the package. This is also true for layer and map packages that you may also publish to ArcGIS Online.

Project packages are a great way to archive a project once it is complete or as specific milestones are reached. They are snapshots of the project at the time the given package was created. Since it is all stored in a single file, they are much easier to manage and maintain backups for.

Again, project packages are created using the same basic method as map or layer packages. You will be required to provide certain information, including a summary, description, and tags, before the package will be created successfully.

Once created, a package can be successfully imported into ArcGIS Pro as a complete project including the maps, layers, layouts, connections, and so on that were included when the package was created. However, similar to map and layer packages, the newly imported project package will point to a **copy** of the original data sources and not the original data sources themselves.

Project package challenge

Using the skills and knowledge that you have gained up to now, try creating a project package for one of the projects that you have used as you worked through this book. Once created, compare the size of the project package to the size of the map and layer packages that you created.

You have now learned several ways through which you can share your GIS content with those inside and outside your network, as well as with those with or without GIS software. This ability to share data with others increases the value of your GIS by making it available to a larger audience. Next, you will learn how to take sharing your GIS with others to the next level using ArcGIS Online.

Publishing to ArcGIS Online

One of ArcGIS Pro's big strengths is its integration with ArcGIS Online and Portal for ArcGIS. This allows you to easily publish data and maps to the web that can then be accessed by others even if they do not have GIS software installed.

ArcGIS Online is Esri's cloud-based **Software-as-a-Service** (**SaaS**) solution. This allows you and others both in and outside your organization to access data, maps, and applications via the internet. This makes it much easier to share your GIS with others because they can access the content you share with them via a normal web browser.

In this section, you will learn how you can publish a map that you create in ArcGIS Pro to ArcGIS Online so that it can be accessed by others through the web browser.

Exercise 13D – Publishing a map to ArcGIS Online

The Planning Director wants to make the city of Trippville's Zoning Map accessible to others, even if they do not have ArcGIS Pro software. She wants those that access the map to have the ability to turn layers on and off, query data, view attribute tables, and even print the map. Because of the level of functionality the director desires and that users will need to be able to access the map even if they do not have GIS software, you will need to publish this as a web map to ArcGIS Online.

In this exercise, you will optimize the Official Zoning Map so it performs well when viewed through the internet. Then, you will publish the map to ArcGIS Online. Lastly, you will share the map so others can access it.

Step 1 – Optimizing your map

In this step, you will optimize the Official Zoning Map to ensure it will perform well when others view it in the browser over the internet:

1. Start ArcGIS Pro and open the EX13.aprx project that you have been working on in this chapter.
2. Click on the **Official Zoning Map** tab in the view area to make it the active map being used.
3. Right-click on the **Zoning** layer. Then select **Zoom to Layer** from the menu that appears.
4. Next, select the **Official Zoning Map** from the top of the **Contents** pane. Then right-click and select **Properties**, as illustrated in the following screenshot:

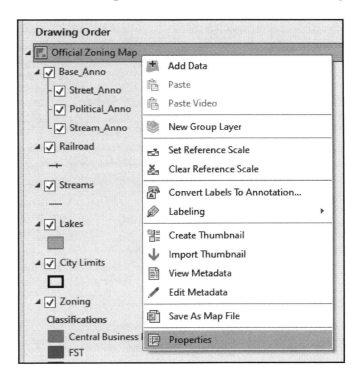

5. In the **Properties** window, click on the **Extent** option located in the left panel of the **Map Properties** window.

6. Click on **Use a custom extent** located at the top of the right panel in the window.

7. Below where it says **Get extent from**, select **Current visible extent**. This will set how far the map will zoom out when someone presses the **Zoom Full Extent** button in ArcGIS Pro or the **Home** button in a web application.

8. Next, click on the **Metadata** option in the left panel of the **Properties** window. Then enter the following values:
   - Type Public Zoning Map for the City of Trippville for the **Title** field.
   - In the **Tags** field, add Zoning, planning, codes, and map.
   - In the **Summary** field, it should display the **Zoning Classification** for parcels within the City of Trippville.
   - In the **Description** field, type This map was created by the city of Trippville GIS and Planning Departments. It displays the zoning classification for each parcel in the City as defined by the city's zoning ordinance.
   - For the **Credits** field, type City of Trippville GIS and Planning Departments.
   - In the **Use Limitations** field, type This map is for general reference only. It is not to be considered the full legal map of record. It is recommended that any data contained herein be verified by calling the City Planning Department.

9. Verify that your **Map Properties** window looks like the following and click the **OK** button when you are done:

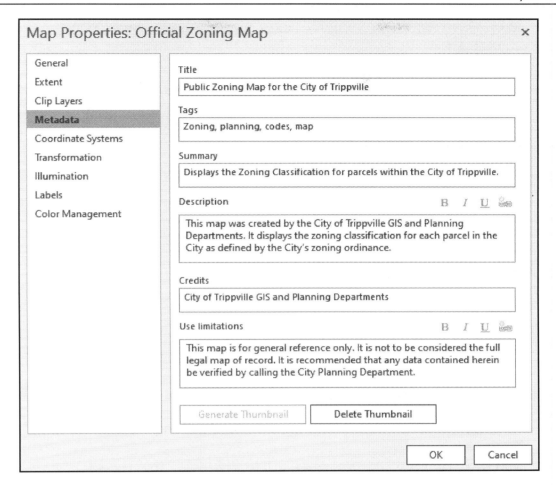

You have just completed the first step to optimize your map before you publish it to ArcGIS Online. You have set the extents so that when users zoom to the full extent in ArcGIS Pro or use the **Home** button found in most web applications, they do not end up zooming out to the entire planet.

Instead, they will zoom out to the scale that allows them to see the entire Zoning layer. Then, you configured the metadata for the map. This is used by search engines and tools to locate items. Fully configuring the map's metadata is often required before ArcGIS Pro will allow you to publish to ArcGIS Online or Portal.

Next, you will work on optimizing your layers. You will start by applying scale ranges to your layers. This will control when they become visible based on the zoom scale of the map.

10. Right-click on the **Base_Anno** layer and select **Properties** from the context menu that appears.

11. Select the **General** option in the left panel of the window. Under where it says **Out beyond**, select **1:10,000** using the drop-down arrow. This will make it so that this layer will not become visible until someone zooms in to the scale that you selected or closer. Click **OK** to apply the setting and close the **Properties** window.

Annotation and labels do not perform well even in the desktop environment, let alone when viewing maps via the browser, so it is considered a best practice to limit the use of these as much as possible. The use of scale ranges is a good start.

12. Select the **Zoning** layer in the **Contents** pane, then click on the **Labeling** tab in the ribbon.

13. Set the **Out Beyond** value to **1:10,000** using the drop-down arrow. This will limit the appearance of the labels for the Zoning layer so they will not show up in the map until someone zooms to that scale or closer.

14. Select the **Appearance** tab in the ribbon while ensuring the Zoning layer is still selected.

15. In the **Visibility Range** group, set the **Out Beyond** value to **1:50,000** using the drop-down arrow.

16. Do the same thing for the remaining layers, then save your project.

One of the best things you can do to optimize a map for publishing to the web is to limit how much data can be drawn at any given time. The scale ranges that you just set are a very effective method for doing that. You can also use things such as definition queries and selection layers as well.

Step 2 – Publishing a map to ArcGIS Online

Now that you have taken steps to optimize your map so that it will perform better when published to ArcGIS Online, it is now time to actually publish it.

This step will require you to have an ArcGIS Online user account that has publishing rights to your organization's ArcGIS Online portal. Publishing this map will also use some of your organization's ArcGIS Online credits if you leave it stored in ArcGIS Online for an extended period:

1. Click on the **Share** tab in the ribbon.
2. Click on the **Web Map** button located in the **Share As** group on the **Share** tab. This will open the **Share As Web Map** window.
3. Notice that the **Name**, **Summary**, and **Tags** fields are already filled in. Those came from the metadata that you created for the map.
4. Set the **Select a Configuration** field to **Copy All Data: Exploratory**. You are using this setting because the Planning Director specifically mentioned that users need to be able to perform queries on the map. The other options are not optimized to allow this or allow too much functionality such as editing data, which is not desired for this map.
5. If you have a folder in your ArcGIS Online account and you want to upload this map too, you can select it using the drop-down arrow for the folder selected. Otherwise, this will just default to the root for your ArcGIS Online user account.
6. Set the **Share with** option to **Everyone**, as illustrated in the following screenshot, because the Planning Director wants everyone including the general public to have access to view this map:

7. Next, click on the **Analyze** button to verify your map is ready to publish.

When the analysis of your map is complete, it should return a couple of errors and several warnings. The errors must be fixed before you can publish it to ArcGIS Online. The warnings should be examined but do not have to be fixed to be published. You will now fix the errors.

8. Under the **Official Zoning Map**, you should see one error that says **00230 Service Layer has a different projection than the maps projection**. This means the basemap and the other layers are using a different coordinate system. Right-click on this error and select **Update map** to use basemap's coordinate system.

It is possible that you might see a different error if your map does not have a basemap assigned. If that is the case, go to the **Map** tab, click on the **Basemap** button, and select the **Topographic** basemap from the options shown.

9. Click on the **Analyze** button again. The other error should disappear now as well. Adjusting the coordinate system fixes both errors.

10. Now take a moment to read the remaining warnings. You will not attempt to fix these issues in this exercise because they will not greatly impact the quality or functionality of the map. However, if this was a map for your organization, then you may want to fix them prior to publishing.

11. Now that you have fixed the errors and reviewed the warnings, it is time to publish this map to ArcGIS Online. Remember that once you publish this to ArcGIS Online, it will be hosted in your organization's account and will use some credits each month for as long as it remains there.

    The number of credits used should be very small, but you do need to bear this in mind before you proceed. If you are ready to publish, click the **Share** button located at the bottom of the **Share as Web Map** window.

Once you click **Share**, ArcGIS Pro will start to package the map and upload it to ArcGIS Online. This may take some time depending on the capabilities of your computer and the speed of your internet connection.

We will now move to the next step.

Step 3 – Viewing the new map in ArcGIS Online

In this step, you will view the map that you just published using ArcGIS Online's **Web Map Viewer**:

1. At the bottom of the **Share As Web Map** window, you should see an indicator showing that the process of publishing the map was successful. Below that, you should see a link that says **Manage the web map** – click on that link.

2. Your default web browser should open, showing the properties of the new web map that you just published. Click on the **Open in Map View** button located at the top right of the page. This will open ArcGIS Online's Web Map Viewer application.

3. If for some reason the **Share As Web Map** window or ArcGIS Pro was closed after the tool completed successfully, you can still get to your map. Just follow these steps:

    1. Open your favorite web browser, such as **Chrome**, **Internet Explorer**, **Edge**, **Firefox**, or any other.

    2. Go to www.arcgis.com.

    3. Click on the **Sign In** button located either in the middle of the page or the upper-right corner.

    4. Enter your login information for ArcGIS Online.

    5. Click on the **Content** tab at the very top of the page, then make sure **My Content** is selected.

    6. Locate the Official Zoning Map from the list of content that you have created. If this is your first time, it will be the only one listed.

    7. Lastly, click on the **Open in Map Viewer** button.

4. You should now see the zoning map that you published from ArcGIS Pro. It is now available for others to see. Take a moment to review the new web map you just created.

5. Click the **Share** button located at the top of the map. This will open the **Share** window. Here, you will see a link that you can send to others via email or social media so they too can access the map.

6. Click **Done** and close your browser when you are finished exploring the map.

7. Go back to ArcGIS Pro and save your project, then close the application.

Congratulations! You just published a map from your desktop to the web using the integration between ArcGIS Pro and ArcGIS Online. Now anyone with internet access will be able to access your map. This will allow them to see the zoning values for parcels within the city of Trippville. You can use this same process to share data and maps that you create for your organization with others, expanding the reach of your GIS.

Summary

In this chapter, you have learned many different methods that can be used to share your GIS content with others. You have seen how you can use project, map, and layer files to share and standardize content for those on your computer network who have access to the same data sources as you do.

You have also learned how you can export your content so that others without ArcGIS Pro can access and use your data. This chapter has provided you with the skills for exporting your GIS data to non-GIS formats so those without GIS software can use information from your GIS in documents, reports, presentations, and spreadsheets.

Lastly, you have also learned how to share data with others not on your network by using packages. Packages are not limited to just data sharing, but can also be used to archive or back up important data at specific states of existence so they can be recalled if needed.

In the next chapter, you will learn about **Arcade**, Esri's new expression language. You can use Arcade to create complex labels and to control symbology such that it will be compatible across the ArcGIS platform.

Further reading

If you would like to learn more about sharing your GIS content, you may want to consider the following:

- *ArcGIS Pro 2.x Cookbook*, by Tripp Corbin, published by Packt (*Chapter 12* and *Chapter 13*)

14
Using Arcade Expressions for Labeling and Symbology

Previously, in `Chapter 12`, *Automating Processes with ModelBuilder and Python*, you learned about two programming languages that can be used to automate processes within **ArcGIS Pro**—**ModelBuilder** and **Python**. As you learned, ModelBuilder is considered a graphic or visual programming language, while Python is a syntax-driven scripting language. With the release of **ArcGIS Pro 2.0** and **ArcGIS Enterprise 10.7**, Esri has introduced a new language called **Arcade**. Arcade is a new lightweight expression language that has many uses within the ArcGIS Platform as you will learn throughout this chapter.

This chapter will introduce you to the basic uses and syntax for Arcade. After completing this chapter, you will be able to create expressions that can generate text labels or control symbology.

In this chapter, you will learn about the following topics:

- Learning about Arcade
- Understanding labeling expressions
- Understanding symbology expressions

Technical requirements

As with previous chapters of this book, you will need **ArcGIS Pro 2.6** or later to complete the exercises included in this chapter.

Learning about Arcade

As mentioned previously, Arcade is a lightweight expression language for ArcGIS. It is compatible with ArcGIS Pro, ArcGIS Enterprise, and ArcGIS Online. This means the expressions that you create in one application will successfully render the same way in the others. Because it is lightweight, meaning it does not require as much processing power to execute, it performs faster than other languages, making it perfect for web maps, as well as for working with large datasets.

Each new release of ArcGIS includes increased use and capability of Arcade throughout the platform, including ArcGIS Pro. Initially, Arcade was used to create labeling expressions and control symbology, as you will learn in this chapter. It has since been expanded so that it can also be used to create fields on the fly that appear in information pop-up windows, establish attribute rules within your GIS database, create expressions in various geoprocessing tools, and more.

It should be noted, for those who have used the older applications that ArcGIS Pro is now replacing, that Arcade is not compatible with **ArcMap** or **ArcCatalog**, nor does it appear that Esri has any intention of making Arcade compatible with these older applications.

You may ask yourself *what is the difference between Arcade and other languages such as Python?* That is a very good question. The primary difference is that as an expression language, Arcade cannot be run externally from one of its parent applications, such as ArcGIS Pro. Languages such as Python don't have this same limitation. You can run a Python script from outside of ArcGIS using **Windows Scheduler**, the **command line**, and more. One thing that Arcade has in common with other languages is that it has its own syntax. So, let's explore some of Arcade's general syntax, which is used to create expressions, in this section.

Understanding Arcade syntax

The syntax for Arcade has many things in common with other languages, such as Python or **Structured Query Language** (**SQL**). The first thing that we should define is its syntax. The syntax is the way that the code must be formatted in order for the expression, script, or application to run successfully. Now, you will examine specific examples of the syntax used in Arcade.

Understanding the text string syntax

When creating an expression using Arcade, if you want something to be treated as text, you must enclose it in single quotes, as in the following Arcade expression:

```
'Owners Name is '+$feature['Parcels.Owner_Name']
```

Please note that the preceding code can't include an *apostrophe* for the term `Owners`, as it may be misinterpreted by the compiler as a single quote.

This will create text labels on a map that looks as in the following diagram:

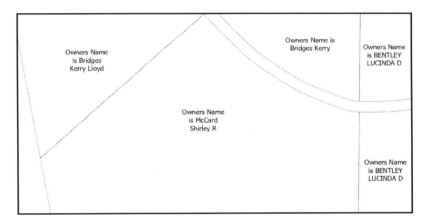

As you can see in the preceding screenshot, the expression creates text labels that appear on the map for each parcel. The phrase **Owners Name is** appears from the part of the expression that is enclosed in single quotes to indicate a text string. The actual owner's name, which is displayed in the map, is pulled from the attribute table associated with the `Parcels` layer.

Next, we will explore how to add comments to your expressions.

Inserting comments into expressions

When writing any code, be it with Arcade, Python, or another programming language, it is considered best practice to add comments within your code that explain the function of a section within the code or provide descriptive information about the code, such as who created it, when it was written, the date it was created, and more.

Arcade supports both single-line and multiple-line comments in your Arcade expressions. To add a single-line comment to your code, use //, as in the following code snippet:

```
//The following line labels a parcel with its owner's name.
```

When ArcGIS Pro, ArcGIS Enterprise, or ArcGIS Online processes the Arcade code, it will ignore any line that starts with // as if it does not exist and will automatically proceed to the next line in the Arcade expression.

Often, you will need to add more comments within your code that require multiple lines. To add multiple-line comments in Arcade, you must start the first comment line with /* and end the last line with */, as in the following code:

```
/*
This expression was built using Arcade for ArcGIS Pro 2.5 and ArcGIS
Enterprise 10.8.
It will label each parcel with its Parcel Identification Number and the
Owner Name.
*/
```

Applications will ignore everything between /* and */ and go to the next line of code in the expression.

Comments provide valuable information within your expression so that you and others can understand the purpose of the code used. This can be very helpful if, in the future, you or someone else needs to make updates to the expressions.

Adding text string values and comments are very useful, but what if you need to use data found in a table in your expression to label a feature or apply specific symbology? We will explore the syntax required for that in the next section.

Adding data from a table

As you are creating expressions to generate labels or symbology, you will need to pull data from the layer's attribute table. This is done by using a syntax that starts with $feature, as in the following code:

```
$feature.Land_Value
```

As you can see from the preceding code, $feature is an example of a global variable. This is followed by a period and then the field name that you wish to retrieve the value from.

This would return a label displaying the land value for a feature or generate a symbol for each land value.

In the next section, we will introduce variables in Arcade expressions.

Defining a variable

When writing code for expressions, scripts, or applications, a variable is something that you can assign a value to and then use the variable in place of the value. This makes it easier to type as you write your code because the variable that you create is often shorter than the real value.

For example, you could create a variable called X and then say that it equals Peachtree Industrial Boulevard. So, any time in your code that you need to reference the Peachtree Industrial Boulevard value, you could just type X in the code and the application would know that that meant Peachtree Industrial Boulevard.

In Arcade, to create a variable, you must declare it using a Var statement. The following code is an example of a variable in an Arcade expression:

```
Var owner = "Tripp"
Return owner;
```

The preceding code will return a value of Tripp to the application running the expressions. One other thing that you need to know about Arcade when creating a variable is that it is not case sensitive like other languages, such as Python. So, to Arcade, a variable called owner is the same as Owner or OWNER.

So, you now know about some of the common Arcade syntaxes that are used when creating various types of expressions. It is important to understand the syntax if you are going to successfully create expressions on your own. The syntax forms the foundation for any expression that you wish to create.

Now, it is time to look at specific types of expressions, starting with labeling in the next section.

Understanding labeling expressions

As you learned in Chapter 3, *Creating 2D Maps*, labeling is a method to display text in a map based on attribute values connected to the features being labeled. However, in that chapter, you were only shown how to label each feature using a single attribute field. *What if you wanted to label features with values found in multiple fields?* For example, say you wanted to label each parcel with its parcel identification number and the owner's name. *How would you do that?*

Arcade allows you to create expressions that can do just that and more. You can label based on multiple fields and even split values on to multiple lines. You can even add descriptive text to the label as well. This section will teach you how to create expressions that will allow you to create labels that do all of these.

Now, we will examine how to label features using multiple field values.

Configuring expressions to label with multiple field values

Creating an Arcade expression that labels features with values pulled from more than one field in its attribute table is pretty straightforward, meaning the syntax is not complicated. It could be as simple as using the following code, for example:

```
$feature.Parcel_No+$feature.Acre
```

The preceding code would label each feature in the layer with its parcel number (`Parcel_No`) and its area in acres (`Acre`), as in the following screenshot:

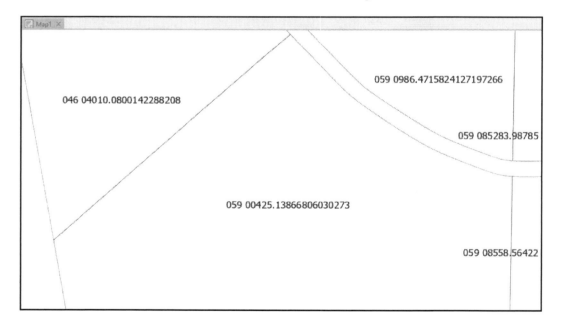

As you can see from the preceding screenshot, while each feature is labeled with both the parcel number and its acreage, it is hard to tell where one stops and the other begins. Adding a space between the two values would certainly help. To add a space between the two values, see the sample code that follows:

```
$feature.Parcel_No+' '+$feature.Acre
```

Here, we added +, followed by a single quotation mark with a space, and then another single quotation mark. This is then followed by another +, before the syntax for the `Acre` field. This results in labels that look like the following:

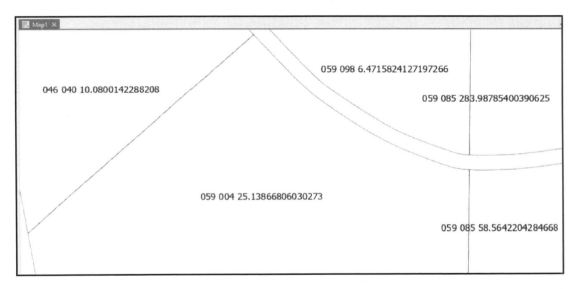

As you can see from the preceding screenshot, the labels are a bit clearer now that a space has been added between the value for the parcel number and the acres. However, it could still be made better. So, next, we will look at a method to split the values on to their own line and add more descriptive text.

Making labels more readable

While it can be extremely useful to label features with values from multiple fields, as you have seen, the label can be confusing or hard to read. Splitting those values on to separate lines and adding some descriptive text that explains what the values represent can make the label much easier to understand.

To split a label into multiple lines, you will need to use the `Textformatting.Newline` command in your expression. If we use the expression that we created in the previous section to split the parcel number and acre values on to separate lines, the new expression would look like this:

```
$feature.Parcel_No+Textformatting.Newline+$feature.Acre
```

This results in labels that look as follows:

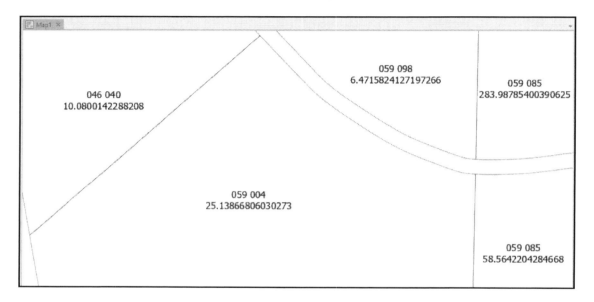

As you can see from the preceding screenshot, the parcel number is displayed on the top line and the acreage is on the bottom line. You know this because you created the expression. However, someone else viewing the map may not understand what the two values are because there is no context or description. *So, how do you add descriptive text to the labels?*

You have already seen an example of that in the *Understanding the text string syntax* section of this chapter. You simply add your desired descriptive text enclosed in single quotes, as in the following code:

```
'Parcel ID Num = '+$feature.Parcel_No+Textformatting.Newline+'Area in Acres
= '+$feature.Acre
```

This will result in labels that look as in the following screenshot:

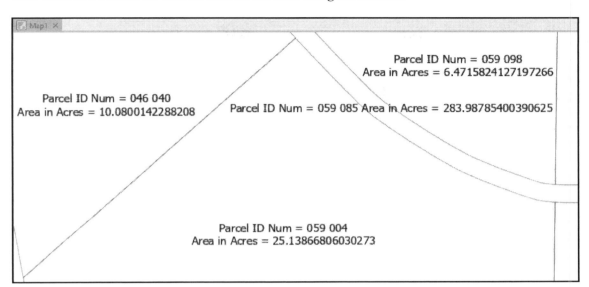

As you can see in the preceding screenshot, these labels are now much easier to read and understand. Now, it is your turn to put the knowledge that you have just learned into practice via a hands-on exercise.

Exercise 14A – Creating an Arcade label expression

The public works director has asked you to create a map that labels each sewer line with its size and the material that the pipe is made of. The attribute data for the city's sewer lines includes this information, but it is split between two fields. So, you will need to create an Arcade expression to accomplish this request.

In this exercise, you will create an Arcade labeling expression that will label each sewer line with both its size and material. You will then work to make the label easier to understand by adding descriptive text.

Step 1 – Opening your project and reviewing the available data

In this step, you will open an existing project that already has a map that contains the sewer line data as a layer. You will then review the data available for the sewer lines to verify which fields you will need to use for the labels that you need to display:

1. Start **ArcGIS Pro** and open the Ex14A.aprx project file, located in C:\Student\IntroArcPro\Chapter14. When the project opens, you should see the sewer system map, which contains the Sewer Lines layer that the public works director wants to be labeled with the size and pipe material.

2. Next, you will examine the attribute table for the sewer lines to verify that the required data exists. Right-click on the **Sewer Lines** layer in the **Contents** pane, then select **Attribute Table** from the menu that appears, as in the following screenshot:

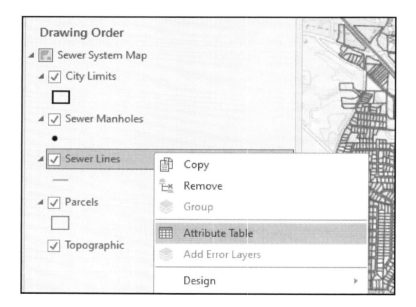

The attribute table for the Sewer Lines layer should open below the map view area. It's now time to review the table.

3. Take a few moments to review the attribute table for the Sewer Lines layer. Notice what fields are included in the table. Locate the two fields that might contain the data requested by the director.

Question: *What are the names of the fields that contain the data that the director wants you to create labels for?*

4. Once you have identified the two fields that contain the data needed to create the labels requested by the director, close the attribute table.

You have now verified that you have the data required to create the requested labels for the sewer lines by reviewing the attribute table for that layer. Now, it is time to start building the labeling expression that will label the sewer line features.

Step 2 – Creating a simple label expression

In this step, you will use the two fields that you identified in the last step to create an Arcade labeling expression. This will result in the sewer line features being labeled with text indicating their size and pipe material:

1. Click on the **Map** tab in the ribbon. Then, click on the **Bookmark** button in the **Navigate** group. Select the **Sewer Labeling Area** bookmark, as in the following screenshot, to zoom the map to a better scale for viewing labels:

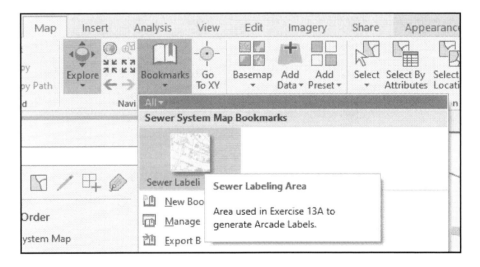

2. Select the **Sewer Lines** layer in the **Contents** pane. The **Feature Layer** group contextual tab should appear in the ribbon.
3. Click on the **Labeling** tab in the **Feature Layer** group contextual tab.
4. Click on the **Label** button in the **Layer** group on the far left-hand side of the **Labeling** tab to turn on labels for the Sewer Line layer.

When you turn on the labels, you should see some text appear just above each feature in the Sewer Line layer. The text that appears is not the value that the director had asked for. You will start building the expression next, which will display the requested values.

5. Click on the **Expression** button to the right of the **Field** cell, as shown in the following screenshot. This will open the **Label Class** pane:

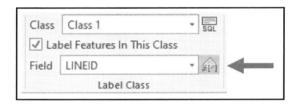

6. In the **Label Class** pane, verify that the **Language** field is set to **Arcade** using the drop-down arrow.
7. In the **Expression** panel of the **Label Class** pane, delete the existing expression by selecting the entire expression with your mouse and pressing the *Delete* key on your keyboard.
8. In the **Fields** panel, locate and double-click on **PIPE SIZE**. That value should appear in the **Expression** panel, as in the following screenshot:

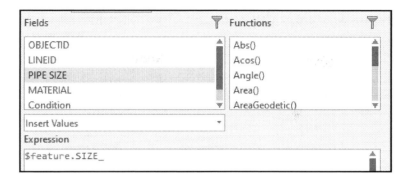

Notice how the $feature syntax is automatically added and the SIZE_ field appears instead of PIPE SIZE. The $feature syntax was automatically added because you double-clicked in the **Fields** panel to add that selection to the expression.

So, ArcGIS Pro knew to add the proper syntax. The reason you see **PIPE SIZE** in the **Fields** panel and **SIZE_** in the **Expression** field is that one is a field alias and the other is the true field name. PIPE SIZE is the field alias. Field names cannot contain spaces. So, we often create alias or alternate names that are more descriptive so that we can better understand what we see in a field. The actual name of the field in the table is SIZE_.

9. Next, type + after $feature.SIZE_ in the expression panel and type ' '. *There is a space between the two single quotation marks.* This will add a space after the pipe size in the displayed label.

10. Type another + character after the last quotation mark and then double-click on **MATERIAL** in the **Fields** panel so that it is added to the expression. Your expression should now look as in the following code:

```
$feature.SIZE_+' '+DomainName($feature, 'MATERIAL')
```

Notice that the syntax for the MATERIAL field is a bit different than what was used for the PIPE SIZE field. That is because the MATERIAL field has been assigned a domain, which is a list of acceptable values that limits the user's ability to place any values other than those on the list into that field. This helps improve data accuracy.

11. Click on the **Apply** button. The text in the map should change so that you can now see that the sewer lines are labeled with their size and material, as shown in the following screenshot:

12. Save your project by clicking on the **Save Project** button on the **Quick Access Toolbar**.

You have created a label expression that meets the minimum requirements requested by the public works director. However, you could improve on it a bit more. For example, the pipe size is just a number; there is nothing to indicate the units associated with that number. It could be inches, centimeters, or something else. So, let's add to your expression to clarify the units for the pipe size.

13. In the **Expression** panel in the **Label Class** pane, click with your mouse just after **$feature.SIZE_** in the expression that you have created. Then, type +'in' so that your expression should now look as follows:

```
$feature.SIZE_+'in'+' '+DomainName($feature, 'MATERIAL')
```

14. Once you have verified that your expression is correct, click the **Apply** button to apply the change to your expression. The labels should update to now include the text after the pipe size number. This indicates the sizes are in inches.

15. Save your project and close ArcGIS Pro.

In this exercise, you learned how to create an Arcade labeling expression that labels features based on values found in two different fields. You also learned how to format that expression to include a text string to indicate the units and add a space between values. Next, you will look at how Arcade expressions can be created so that they can control the symbology for a layer.

Understanding symbology expressions

Now that you understand how Arcade expressions can be used to label features, it is time to look at another use for Arcade. You can also use Arcade expressions to control the symbology for features within a layer.

You can use Arcade expressions to generate symbology categories or ranges based on equations, functions, or data logic. This can provide much greater flexibility with your data and how you can display it. For example, you might have a road that is attributed with the traffic count values. However, you want to symbolize them with a simple low, medium, or high volume for those who may not know about low, medium, or high traffic count numbers. An Arcade expression will allow you to do that.

This section will show you how to create a symbology expression, along with some common operators.

Now that you have a general idea of what a symbology expression can be used for, it is time to create one.

Creating a symbology expression

As mentioned, symbology expressions allow you to create symbology categories or ranges based on a function, equation, or data logic. *So, how do you do that?* Well, one of the common ways is to use if statements.

if statements are used to create conditional logic. That means the statements make use of operators, such as equal to, not equal to, greater than, or less than, to group data. For example, if you wanted to symbolize parcels based on land value by identifying them as having a high, medium, or low value per acre, you might create an expression that looks like this:

```
var value = ($feature['Parcel_Polygon.par_val']
  /$feature['Parcel_Polygon.Acre'])
if (value <= 10000){
    return 'Low Value';}
if (value > 10000 && value <= 50000){
    return 'Medium Value';}
else {
    return 'High Value';}
```

The first line in this expression defines a variable named value. This is the value of the parcel divided by the area of the parcel in acres. This represents the value per acre for each parcel.

The next lines then evaluate whether the result is Low Value, Medium Value, or High Value, which becomes the display category for the parcels. A low value is any number less than or equal to 10,000. A medium value is any number that is greater than 10,000 and less than or equal to 50,000. A high value is any number that does not meet the other two criteria—so, any number greater than 50,000.

You can see the results in the following map screenshot:

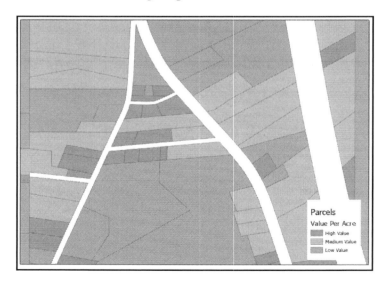

Next, we will look at some of the common operators that you might use in your expressions.

Understanding the common operators

Arcade supports many operators. Operators are logical functions that are included in an expression, such as equal to or not equal to. These operators are typically represented by a symbolic character or multiple symbolic characters. Some of the common operators you will use are as follows:

- **Basic operators**
- **Logical operators**

The basic operators are as follows:

- The + operator: This adds two numbers or concatenates two strings.
- The – operator: This subtracts two numbers.
- The * operator: This multiplies two numbers.
- The / operator: This divides two numbers.
- The ++ operator: This increments a number variable by 1.

The logical operators are as follows:

- The | | operator: This means or.
- The && operator: This means and.
- The == operator: This means equal to.
- The != operator: This means not equal to.
- The < operator: This means less than.
- The <= operator: This means less than or equal to.
- The > operator: This means greater than.
- The >= operator: This means greater than or equal to.

Now, it is your turn to create a symbology expression with a hands-on exercise.

Exercise 14B – Creating a symbology expression

The road superintendent recently completed an inspection of all the roads in the city, giving them a score between 1 and 100. The higher the score, the better condition the road is in. They would now like you to create a map showing the results of their inspections that they can present to the city council. However, instead of displaying the actual score for each road, they would like the roads symbolized as good, fair, or poor based on the score. A score of 1 to 40 would be considered poor. A score of 41 to 70 would be considered fair. A score of 71 or above would be considered good.

In this exercise, you will create a symbology expression that will evaluate the score for each road segment and return whether it is poor, fair, or good.

Step 1 – Evaluating the Street_Centerlines layer

In this step, you will open the project that contains the map showing the street centerline data. You will then open the attribute table for that data and review the information to determine where the inspection scores are located and what values are present:

1. Start **ArcGIS Pro** and open the Ex14B.aprx project file located in C:\Student\IntroArcPro\Chapter14. When the project opens, you should see a map containing two layers—Street_Centerlines and City_limit—and a basemap.

2. Right-click on the **Street_Centerlines** layer in the **Contents** pane and select **Attribute Table** from the menu that appears, as in the following screenshot:

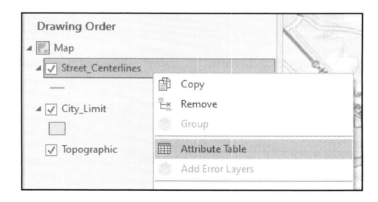

3. Review the available fields in the attribute table for the **Street_Centerlines** layer.

Question: *What field contains the inspection score for each road segment?*

4. Take a moment to scroll down and review the values in the **Inspection Score** field that you just identified.

5. Now, you need to determine what type of field **Inspection Score** is and what its true name is. Right-click on the **Inspection Score** field and select **Fields** from the menu that appears, as in the following screenshot:

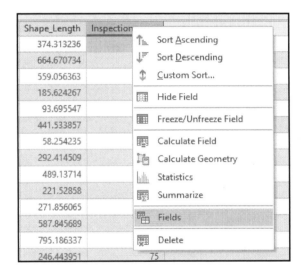

You may ask yourself how we knew that **Inspection Score** was not the true name of the field. Field names in databases have specific limitations. First, they must start with a character and not a number. Second, they cannot contain special characters, such as spaces, &, @, and so on. Note that underscores are allowed.

Depending on the type of database, there may be other restrictions as well. Since the name displayed was **Inspection Score**, which contains a space, we know this is not the true name but is rather an alias.

6. The **Fields** window should now be open. Review the information displayed in the window.

Question: *What is the true field name for the* **Inspection Score** *field? What is the data type for the* **Inspection Score** *field?*

It is important to know these two things. The true name for the field is what you will need to use in the Arcade expression that you will build. The data type will also impact the syntax and what you can do with the values contained in the field.

7. Close the **Fields** window and the `Street_Centerlines` attribute table.

Now that you know which field you will need to use to build your symbology expression and what its data type is, it is time for you to create the expression.

Step 2 – Creating a symbology expression

In this step, you will create an Arcade expression that will generate the symbology requested by the street superintendent. This expression will evaluate the score for each street segment and place it into the desired categories of poor, fair, and good:

1. In the **Catalog** pane, select the **Street_Centerline** layer so that the **Feature Layer** contextual group tab appears, containing the **Appearance**, **Labeling**, and **Data** tabs.

2. Click on the **Appearance** tab in the ribbon. Then, click on the **Symbology** drop-down arrow and select **Unique Values**, as in the following screenshot. This will open the **Symbology** pane:

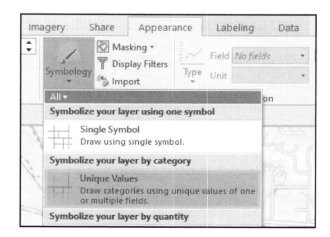

3. Next, click on the **Set an expression** button, located to the far right of the **Field 1** options, as illustrated in the following screenshot. This will open the **Expression Builder** window:

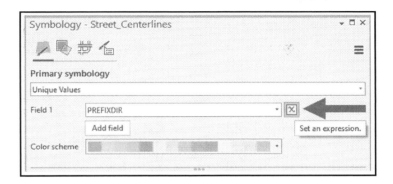

4. In the cell located to the right of **Title**, type `Overall Condition`. This will be the title that appears in the **Contents** pane and the legend.

   Under the title that you just changed, there are two panels—**Fields** and **Functions**. The **Fields** panel contains a list of all the fields present in the attribute table for the `Street_Centerlines` layer. The **Functions** panel contains a list of general math, spatial analysis, and other functions that you can use in your expression. You will use the **Fields** panel later in this exercise.

   Under these two panels is the **Expression** panel. It is here that you will create your expression. This should already contain a simple expression calling on a single field. You will need to delete the current expression and build your own new one next.

5. Use your mouse to select the current expression displayed in the **Expression** panel. Once selected, press the *Delete* key on your keyboard to erase the current expression.

6. Start your new expression by defining a variable that references the inspection score for each segment. In the **Expression** pane, type the following code, and then press *Enter*:

   ```
   Var score = $feature.Insp_score
   ```

   You have now associated the `score` variable with the inspection score found in the database for each street centerline segment. So, when you need to reference that field in your expression code, all you need to do is use `score`.

Next, you will use `If` statements to evaluate the inspection score for the segment so that they can be placed into the desired symbology categories.

7. In the **Expression** panel, add the following code and press *Enter* to move to the next line. This first line will segregate all the street segments that have an inspection score of 40 or less:

```
If (score <=40)
```

8. Next, you will add a line of code to your expression that tells it what to do with any street segments with an inspection score less than or equal to 40. Add the following code after the last line of code that you wrote:

```
{return 'Poor';}
```

Your expression should now look as in the following screenshot:

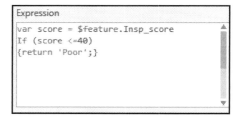

You have created your first `If` statement. You still have more to write, though.

9. In the **Expression** panel, add the following code to your expression:

```
If ((score>=41)&&(score<=70))
    {return 'Fair';}
```

This `If` statement evaluates all the road segments with an inspection score greater than or equal to 41 and less than or equal to 70. Then, it puts them into the `Fair` category. Remember that the `&&` expression is the Arcade syntax for *and* in the expression.

Now, you need to create the code that handles the values that are greater than 70, which will be placed in the `Good` category.

10. In the **Expression** panel, add the following code to your expression for those features that have an inspection score that is greater than 70:

```
else{return'Good';}
```

11. Verify that your expression looks as in the following screenshot, then click **OK** to apply the new expression that you just created:

```
Expression
var score = $feature.Insp_score
If (score <=40)
{return 'Poor';}
If ((score>=41)&&(score<=70))
{return 'Fair';}
else{return'Good';}
```

12. Close the **Symbology** pane so that you can see the map.

Your map should now look similar to the one in the following screenshot. Your colors may be a bit different, but you should now see the three categories that your Arcade expression generated, plus the **<all other values>** category, which appears by default. Also, notice above the symbology categories that the title that you entered has appeared as well, as follows:

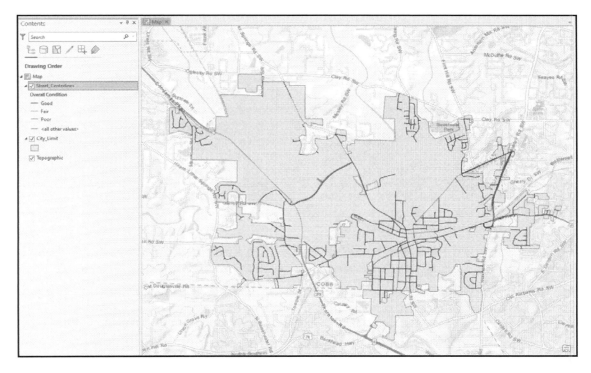

13. Save your project and close ArcGIS Pro.

Congratulations! You have just created your first symbology Arcade expression. This will allow you to create more useful maps based on logical statements and equations. This further increases the flexibility of your geographical information system.

Summary

In this chapter, you have learned how Arcade expression can allow you to create maps that contain more descriptive labels and logical symbology. This further enhances your ability to use your GIS data by allowing you to create even more useful and detailed maps.

As you have seen, Arcade, like Python, has its own syntax. You now have a general understanding of this new syntax and what it requires.

This chapter just touched the surface of what you can do with Arcade in the ArcGIS platform. With each new release of ArcGIS Pro, ArcGIS Enterprise, and ArcGIS Online, Esri is adding more capability to the Arcade expression language.

Further reading

For more information about Arcade syntax and capability, go to `https://developers.arcgis.com/arcade/`.

GIS glossary

Annotation: Annotation is one option in ArcGIS for storing text to place on your maps. With annotation, each piece of text * stores its own position, text string, and display properties. Annotation is managed individually, unlike labels, which are managed as a group. This means a user can change the properties of single annotation features including color, font, size, bold, underline, or italics.

Arcade: This is an expression language that was introduced with **ArcGIS 10.6** and **ArcGIS Pro 2.0**. Arcade can be used to create expressions that control labeling and symbology as well as create new informational fields on the fly in the HTML lookup window. Esri continues to work to expand the capabilities of the Arcade expression language with each new release.

ArcCatalog: An application included with ArcGIS Desktop. It was used to manage GIS data and resources. This is one of the older applications from Esri that ArcGIS Pro is replacing.

ArcGIS: A suite of GIS applications from Esri that includes several integrated components such as ArcGIS Enterprise, ArcGIS Pro, ArcGIS Online, **Collector**, **Survey 123**, and more. It is designed so organizations can implement components as needed to support their operations and workflows. This makes ArcGIS extremely scalable.

ArcGIS Enterprise: Esri's server-based solution to support enterprise operations through the use of web services, web and mobile applications, multiple user databases, and more. It includes several components – Web Server, Datastores, Web Adaptor, and Portal.

ArcGIS Online: An Esri cloud-based GIS solution for sharing data, maps, and applications. It is one component of the ArcGIS solution suite.

ArcGIS Pro: Esri's newest desktop GIS application. First released in 2015, ArcGIS Pro is replacing the older ArcGIS Desktop applications (ArcMap, ArcCatalog, ArcGlobe, and ArcScene) as the primary desktop application within the ArcGIS solution suite. ArcGIS Pro allows users to visualize, edit, analyze, and share GIS data via an intuitive user interface built around a new 64-bit engine.

ArcMap: An application included with ArcGIS Desktop. It was the primary desktop GIS application from Esri from 1999 to 2018 when it was replaced by ArcGIS Pro. ArcMap allowed users to visualize, edit, analyze, and share GIS information.

Attribute: A specific characteristic (variable) of a feature such as a name, date, size, or material, that can be edited, deleted, and have operations performed on it. Normally associated and stored within a database table in a GIS.

CAD (Computer-Aided Design): This is a software that is used by engineers and surveyors. `.dxf`, `.dwg`, and `.dgn` are common CAD formats.

Concatenate: This is used to join two or more items. In GIS, this usually refers to joining the data found in two or more attribute fields together into a single field.

Coverage: This is the native data format for **ArcInfo Workstation 7.x** and earlier. It uses multiple folders and files to store both the spatial (location) and attribute (descriptive) data for geographic features. A single coverage can include multiple feature classes.

Data Frame: This is an organization unit in an **ArcGIS Map Document** (`.mxd`) that is opened with the ArcMap application. It contains layers in the **Table of Contents** that share a related theme or map purpose.

Data View: One of two views in ArcMap. Data view allows you to view data for the purposes of analysis and editing.

Datum: A datum is a component of a coordinate system or spatial reference. In very general terms, it is the point that connects the mathematical model of the earth, called an ellipsoid or spheroid, to the physical earth. There are two basic types of datum, horizontal and vertical. With horizontal datums, there are two types of those as well: earth-centered and local.

Feature: Any item contained in your spatial data (that is, a fire hydrant, a manhole, a parcel, a water line, a building, and so on). They are stored together in a feature class.

Feature class: The general meaning of this term refers to a collection of features that share a common geometry (point, line or polygon), attribute table, and spatial reference (coordinate system, datum, projection). Normally associated with Esri's geodatabase format but can be applied to other formats as well including shapefiles which store a single feature class or CAD and coverages which store multiple feature classes. In a geodatabase, these can be standalone or grouped in a feature dataset.

Feature dataset: This is a collection of feature classes stored together within a geodatabase that shares the same spatial reference; that is, they share a coordinate system, and their features fall within a common geographic area. Feature classes with different geometry types (points, lines, and polygons) may be stored together in a single feature dataset. Feature datasets are required for the use of geodatabase topologies and geometric networks.

Geodatabase: This is the native data format for the ArcGIS platform. There are three basic types – personal, file, and SDE/Enterprise. Geodatabases store geometry, a spatial reference system, attributes, and behavioral rules for data. Various types of geographic datasets can be collected within a geodatabase, including feature classes, attribute tables, raster datasets, network datasets, topologies, address locators, custom toolboxes, and many others. The personal geodatabase is being retired and is not supported in ArcGIS Pro, ArcGIS Enterprise, or ArcGIS Online.

Labels: Labels are one of two primary methods for adding text to a map. They are dynamically placed, meaning the user configures basic properties but the software makes the final decision on the placement and display of the text. Label text strings are based on feature attributes that are found in the database table. Labels may be expanded to include additional text and multiple fields through the use of Arcade expressions.

Layer: Any spatial or tabular data used in a map. Located in the **Table of Contents** in ArcMap or the **Contents** pane in ArcGIS Pro. Layers have properties including **Name**, **Symbology**, **Label Settings**, **Display Settings**, and **Source Location**. Layers do not store data. They point to or reference data stored as a geodatabase, shapefile, CAD file, coverage, or raster format.

Layer file: An external file that stores layer property settings such as symbology, data source, display settings, and label settings so that they may be easily used in other maps and by other users that have a connection to your GIS data. They can be created using ArcMap or ArcGIS Pro. If created with ArcMap, they will have a .lyr file extension. If created with ArcGIS Pro they will have a .lyrx file extension. They are used to standardize layer settings within an organization. Layer files do not actually store data. They point to or reference data that might be stored as a shapefile, geodatabase feature class, CAD file, raster, or something else.

Layer package: An external file that stores both a copy of the data and the layer property settings. They can be created using ArcMap or ArcGIS Pro. If created with ArcMap, they will have a .lpk file extension. If created with ArcGIS Pro, they will have a .lpkx file extension. Layer packages are used to share data with those who do not have access to your GIS database or files. They can also be used as an archive for historically important data or as a backup.

Layout: A worksheet where you design your final map product, comprising the view, charts, tables, legend, map scale, text, and the north arrow, sometimes, they are referred to as a virtual page.

Map: A collection of related layers within an ArcGIS Pro project. They allow you to visualize, edit, and analyze spatial and tabular data.

Map frame: A map that has been added to a layout in ArcGIS Pro. A single layout can contain one or more map frames.

Map package: There are two types of map packages, one created using ArcMap with an .mpk file extension and one created with ArcGIS Pro that has a .mpkx file extension. Map packages created with ArcMap contain everything found in a .mxd file. This includes data frames, layers, and the layout, along with all referenced data. Map packages created with ArcGIS Pro only contain the layers and data included in the single map from a project that the file is based on. They will not include layouts or information from other maps within a project.

NAD 27: This stands for **North American Datum 1927**. It is a local horizontal datum located in Meades Ranch, Kansas, in the United States, which is the approximate center of the continental United States.

NAD 83: This stands for **North American Datum 1983**. It is an earth-centered horizontal datum.

Project: This term has different meanings depending on the context. One is a noun and one is a verb. The first is the files used by ArcGIS Pro. ArcGIS Pro uses project files with a .aprx file extension. A single project can contain multiple maps, data connections, layouts, and so on that are related to a common purpose. The second meaning is related to coordinate systems. *To project data* is the act of moving data from one coordinate system to another and displaying it on a two-dimensional plane.

Project package: Basically, this is a file that contains all the contents in an ArcGIS Pro project, including maps, layouts, and toolboxes, as well as copies of the related data. It is used to share a project with others who don't have access to your GIS data or to archive a project. They use a .ppkx file extension.

Projection: The representation of the earth's curved three-dimensional surface on a 2-dimensional surface (a flat map).

Query: Essentially, this is a question used to select features that have specific attribute values or relationships. Within ArcGIS, there are two basic types of selection queries, **Select by Attribute** and **Select by Location**:

- **Select by Attribute** will select features in a given layer based on some value criteria the user enters, such as Parcel Owner Name = John Smith or Pipe Size.
- **Select by Location**, sometimes referred to as a spatial query, selects features in one or more layers based on their spatial relationships, such as all parcels within the city limits, or all roads within a distance of 100 feet from a hospital.

Raster: This is a simple storage model for spatial data. It stores information using equal-sized cells. Each cell is assigned a number. This number can represent things such as counts, color, elevation, temperature, wind speed, average rainfall, population density, and so on. Rasters are often associated with, but not limited to, aerial photography, **Digital Elevation Models** (**DEM**), land use classification, and vegetation classification.

Scene: This is a three-dimensional map. It allows you to look at features not only from a top-down view, as you do with a traditional map, but also by rotating along the z axis. They can be created natively in ArcGIS Pro without the need for an extension or add-in. If you are working in the older ArcGIS Desktop environment, you will need the 3D Analyst extension, which includes the ArcScene and ArcGlobe applications required to create a scene.

Shapefile: Shapefiles are the native format for Esri's ArcView GIS 3.x application and earlier. This format has become the *de facto* data transfer format for GIS. Many GIS and GPS packages have the ability to read, import, and export shapefiles. A shapefile stores a single feature class (a point, line, or polygon). Viewed as a single file by ArcGIS software, it is actually made up of multiple files (`.shp`, `.shx`, `.dbf`, and others). Shapefiles are one of the two data formats that are editable within ArcGIS.

Spatial query: A query that uses the spatial relationship between features in one or more layers to select data. In ArcGIS, this is accomplished with the **Select by Location** query. This allows users to select features in one or more layers based on their spatial relationships such as all parcels within the city limits, or all roads within a distance of 100 feet from a hospital.

Table: A collection of data stored in rows and columns. The columns are referred to as fields and the rows records. They are typically part of a database. In GIS, each layer will also have a connected table referred to as the attribute table. In an attribute table, each record or row is linked to a feature in the layer.

Topology: The general meaning of topology is a model of how spatial features are related to one another. *Do they connect? Are they next to each other? Do they overlap?* In ArcGIS, a topology is a part of the geodatabase that defines rules on how features in one or more feature classes must relate to one another. A geodatabase topology can only be created within a feature dataset and only the feature classes with that dataset can participate in the topology.

Vector: A simple storage model for spatial data. It stores information using specific coordinates (X, Y, and sometimes Z) that form points, lines, or polygons.

Other Books You May Enjoy

If you enjoyed this book, you may be interested in these other books by Packt:

Mastering Geospatial Development with QGIS 3.x - Third Edition
Shammunul Islam, Simon Miles, Et al

ISBN: 978-1-78899-989-2

- Create and manage a spatial database
- Get to know advanced techniques to style GIS data
- Prepare both vector and raster data for processing
- Add heat maps, live layer effects, and labels to your maps
- Master LAStools and GRASS integration with the Processing Toolbox
- Edit and repair topological data errors
- Automate workflows with batch processing and the QGIS Graphical Modeler
- Integrate Python scripting into your data processing workflows
- Develop your own QGIS plugins

Learning Geospatial Analysis with Python - Third Edition
Joel Lawhead

ISBN: 978-1-78995-927-7

- Automate geospatial analysis workflows using Python
- Code the simplest possible GIS in just 60 lines of Python
- Create thematic maps with Python tools such as PyShp, OGR, and the Python Imaging Library
- Understand the different formats that geospatial data comes in
- Produce elevation contours using Python tools
- Create flood inundation models
- Apply geospatial analysis to real-time data tracking and storm chasing

Leave a review - let other readers know what you think

Please share your thoughts on this book with others by leaving a review on the site that you bought it from. If you purchased the book from Amazon, please leave us an honest review on this book's Amazon page. This is vital so that other potential readers can see and use your unbiased opinion to make purchasing decisions, we can understand what our customers think about our products, and our authors can see your feedback on the title that they have worked with Packt to create. It will only take a few minutes of your time, but is valuable to other potential customers, our authors, and Packt. Thank you!

Index